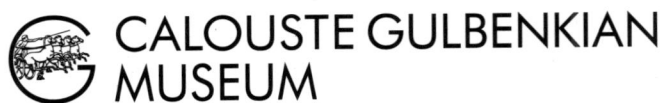

CALOUSTE GULBENKIAN
MUSEUM

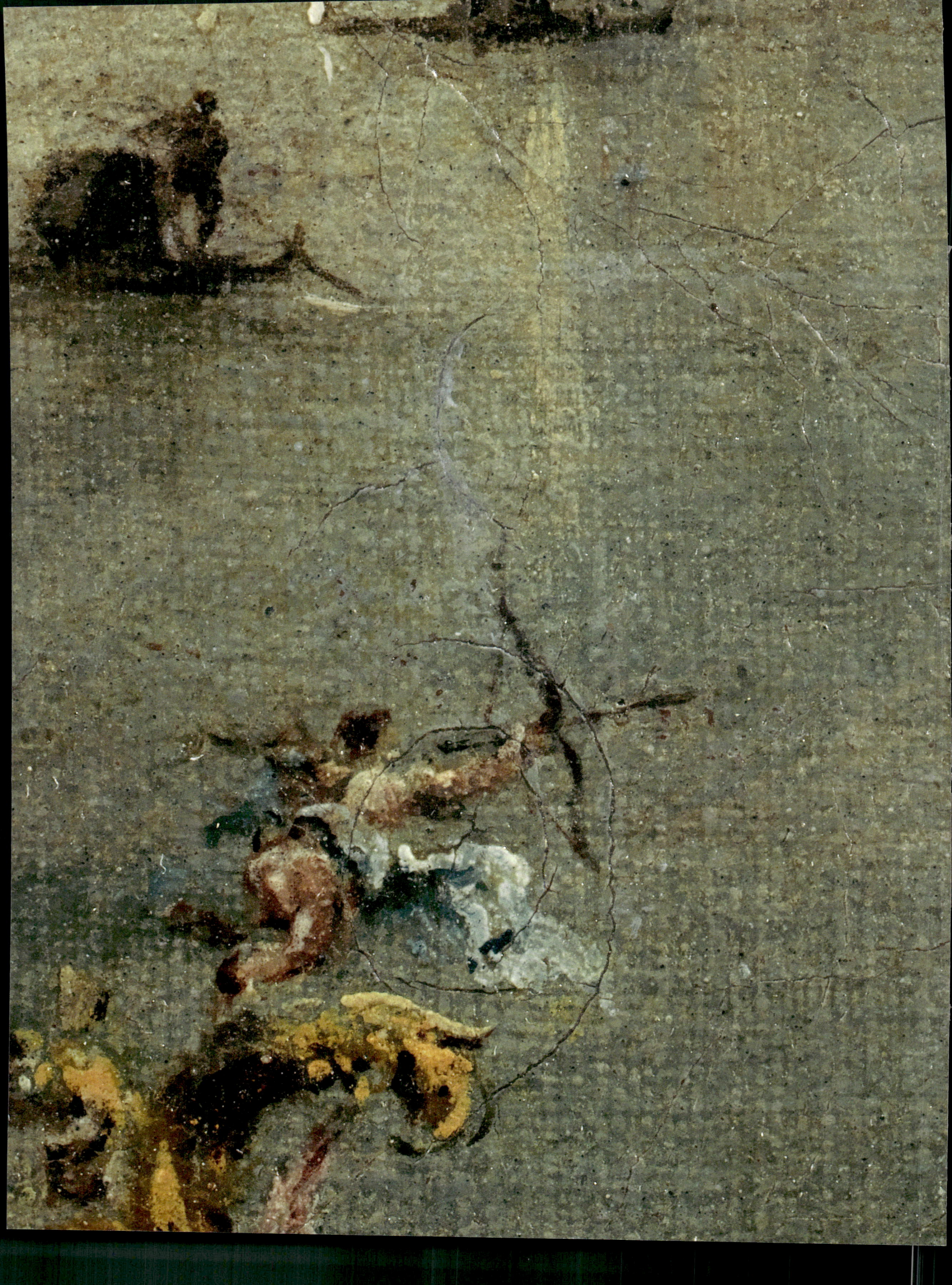

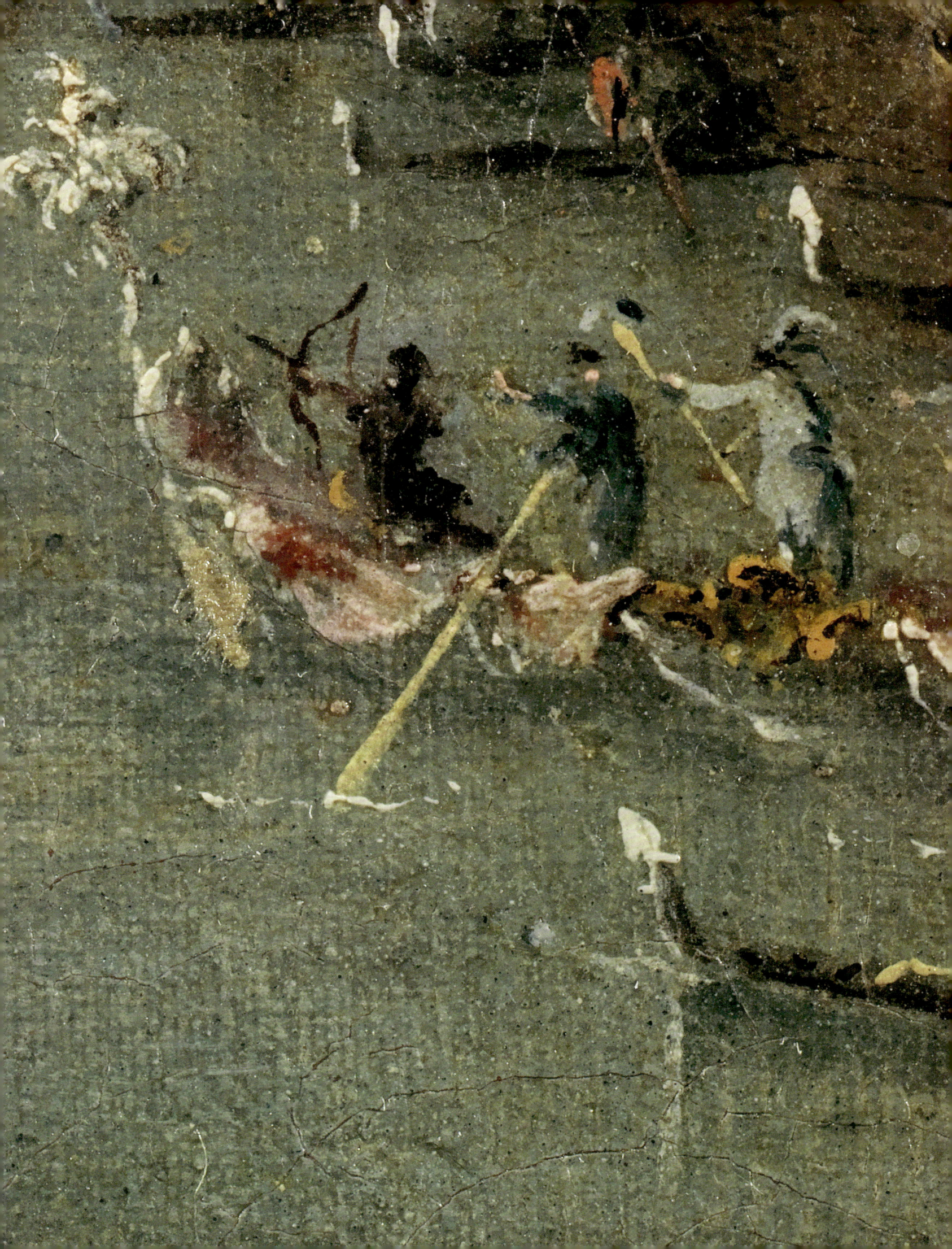

VENICE: THE ETERNAL DESTINATION

Guilherme d'Oliveira Martins,
Trustee of the Calouste Gulbenkian Foundation

Following their successful 2009 collaboration on the exhibition devoted to the French painter Henri Fantin-Latour, the Calouste Gulbenkian Museum and the Museo Nacional Thyssen-Bornemisza are once again bringing together works from their collections, celebrating old affinities that reveal an enduring essence. This new project, which starts in Lisbon and will travel to Madrid in early 2025, takes as its theme Venetian painting from the eighteenth century, of which both institutions possess significant works that are a natural complement to one another.

The invitation 'Veni Etiam' has been repeated countless times over the centuries, urging visitors to take even greater pleasure in their return to Venice. The city's name thus became a call to eternal travel and constant return. Indeed, La Serenissima has always been a point of departure and arrival, a focal point among European states for culture and all forms of art. During the eighteenth century, the city reached its peak as a symbol and expression of the sublime encounter between east and west, as a mark of affluence and cosmopolitanism and as the representation of the great wealth of European culture.

It has been synonymous with opportunity and a mode of representation of a landscape that manifested a supreme convergence between nature and humankind. And while the city was a meeting point for those who had explored the limits of the known world via the Asian routes, such as Marco Polo, it soon became an expression of the most beautiful representations of the *commedia dell'arte* and the balance of architecture and urbanism, through the famous Venetian *vedute*, which merged everyday life with celebrations, major events and the magic of festivals.

The magnitude of the city's creativity was symbolised by the *Bucintoro* the official galley that carried the Doge during the Feast of the Ascension to celebrate the union of city and Sea. In addition to performance and representation, there were dances and melodies, fantastical masks, *pierrots*, colombines and harlequins. But the starring role was always played by the city. And the representations gained greater theatricality, movement and drama. The Venice carnival was thus an important stop on the Grand Tour, the paradigm of a cultured education among European travellers. The city itself was the true work of art. Giambattista Piazzetta concerned himself with transparency and movement. Giambattista Tiepolo and Antonio Canaletto performed magic feats through the metamorphosis of reality. Perspectives, cornucopias, flames and flourishes provided the illusion and the canals were made into mirrors, kaleidoscopes that allowed viewers to get to know every little detail of the Grand Canal.

Venice is a magnificent theatre, the landscape transfigured, the city transformed into life itself in the hands of its greatest painters, through the genius and sensitivity of Marco Ricci, Piazzetta, Canaletto, Tiepolo, Marieschi and Belotto, or Francesco Guardi's insightful observations of its more intimate side, bringing strength to the artistic metropolis, the magical city. A long-time painter of figures, Guardi innovated by extending panoramic views, which became highly successful thanks to the exceptional demand from regular Grand Tour travellers.

Francesco Guardi was the last painter to immortalise La Serenissima as the consummate city of festivity, the symbol of a new era that eternalised the city beyond those times of heroism. Happiness is the feeling that transforms into thought. The famous *capricci* reveal an artistic memory in which the sublime heralds fantastical landscapes and architectures expressing fertility – the ancient ruins already announcing romantic innovation. In Guardi, Calouste Gulbenkian found that ability to prolong those feelings beyond their moment of materialisation, the best works standing out for their beauty and intensity. And the great collector held a special affection for them, particularly *Regatta on the Grand Canal, The Feast of Ascension in the Piazza San Marco, The Departure of the Bucintoro, The Rialto Bridge after the Design by Palladio, The Giudecca Canal with the Church of Saint Martha* and *View of the Molo with the Ducal Palace*.

Calouste Sarkis Gulbenkian was a great admirer of the work of Francesco Guardi and a close reader of the excellent 1904 monograph by George Simonson. The Museum Collection thus possesses 19 of the artist's finest paintings, acquired between 1907 and 1921, comprising what is arguably one of the most important groups of his work in the world. Goethe understood perfectly that the most beautiful painting from the Venetian school was the city itself, ready and waiting for the best artists to turn the ephemerality of the landscape into an illustration of eternity. The light is still the best source material available to us.

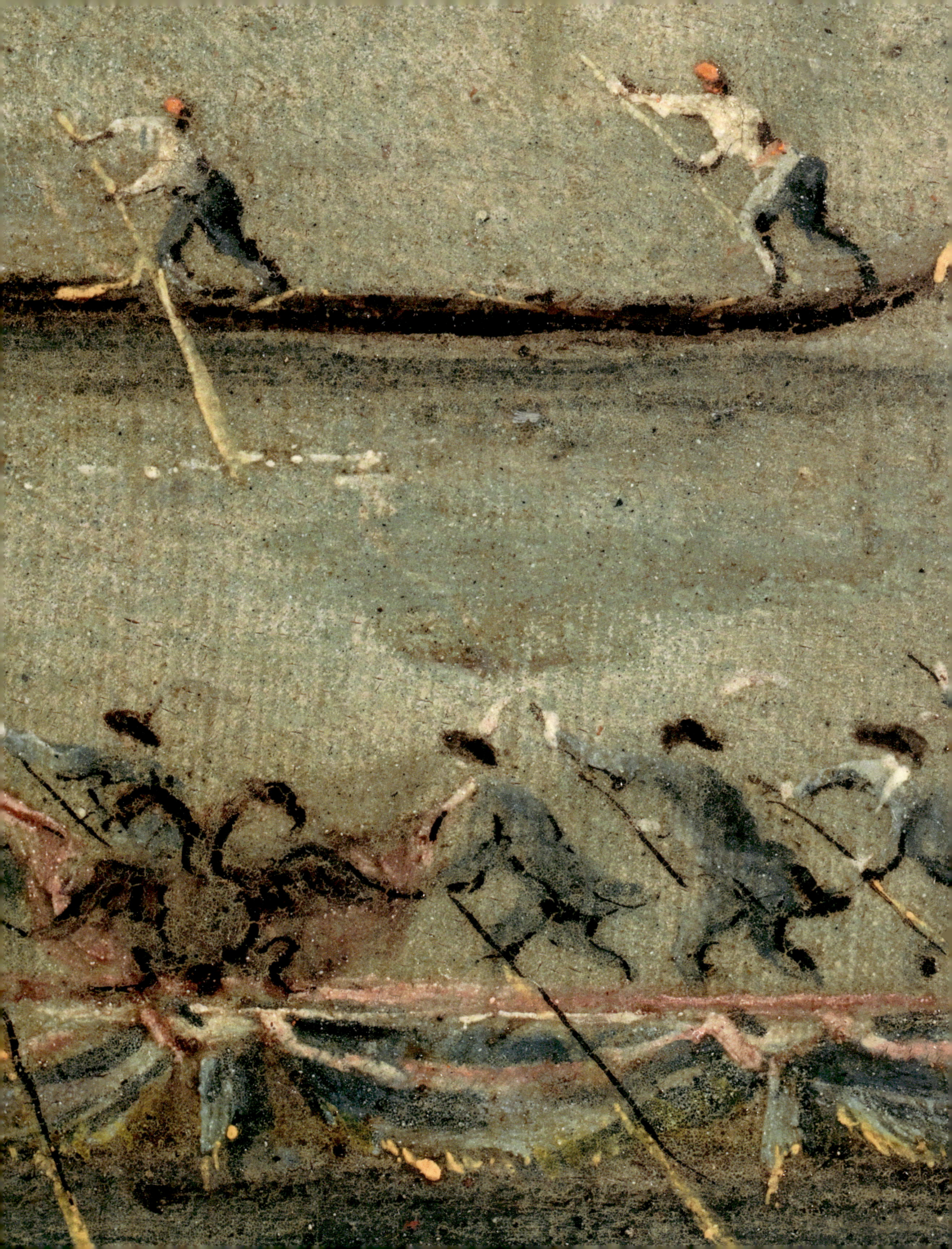

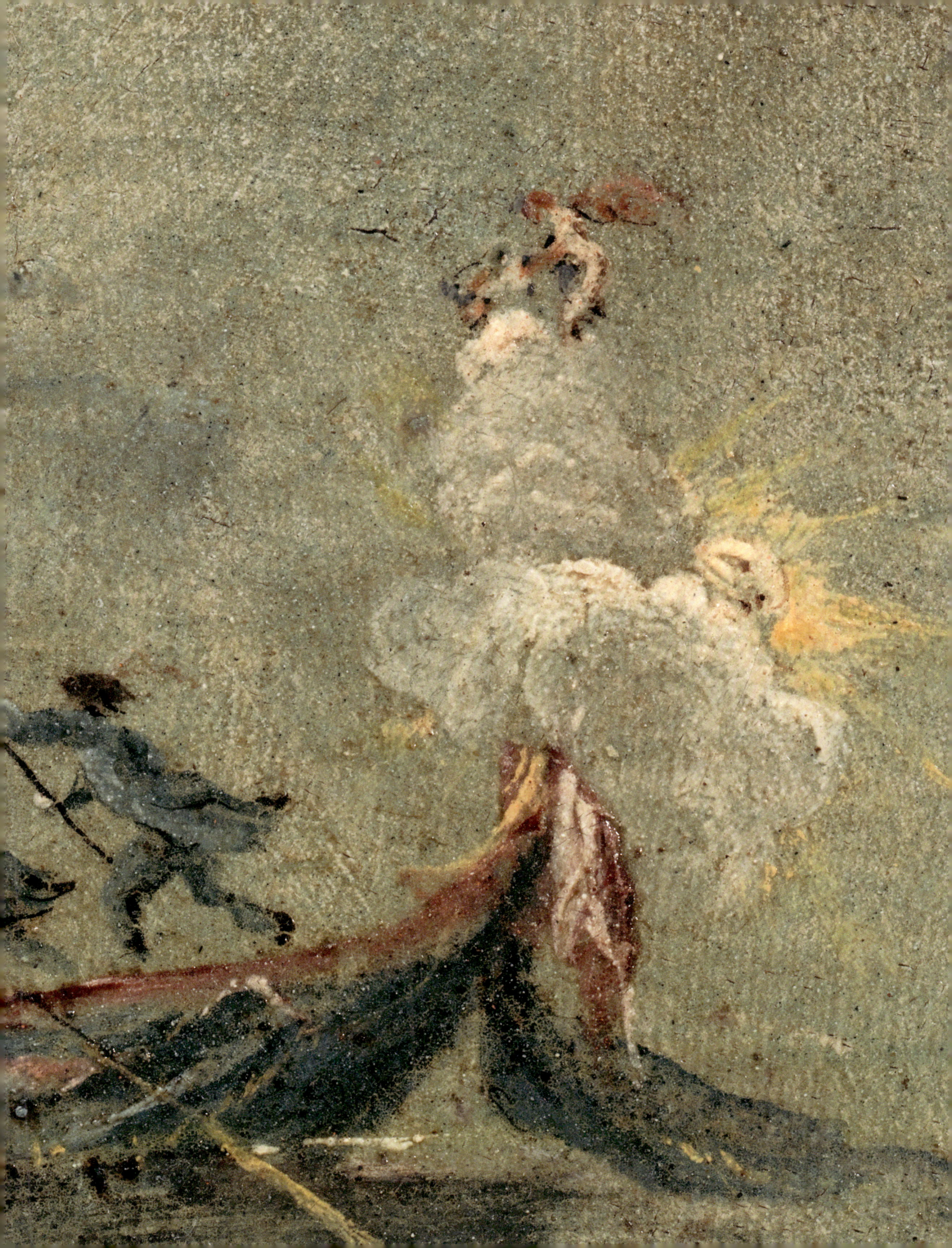

SPLENDOUR AND VENICE OR THE TRIUMPH OF ILLUSION

António Filipe Pimentel,
Director of the Calouste Gulbenkian Museum

Venice – a masterpiece of human creation – has always been a source of fascination for visitors and artists alike. This is reflected in the Gulbenkian Collection, which includes views of the city created in the nineteenth century by various painters, from Corot to John Singer Sargent. But it was at the dawn of the eighteenth century that the city (with its spectacular views and special ambience) truly became the place of a specific artistic production (the renowned *vedute*, or panoramic views) and resulting trade, which would make it the great protagonist of this genre. And it is precisely this context that brought about one of the unquestionable highlights of the collection of Calouste Sarkis Gulbenkian: the nearly 20 paintings the Collector acquired by the great *vedustiste* Francesco Guardi (1712–1792), which not only form the greatest concentration of works by the artist in the world, but also affirm Venice as a favourite theme of his (the continuity of which, in the nineteenth-century painting section, only serves to confirm this premise).

Indeed, the city (for centuries Europe's gateway between east and west) was an endless source of fascination for someone born in the Ottoman Empire, who lived and worked in England and France and who would mirror that same cultural syncretism in his own collection. However, the paintings by Guardi (the only *vedutiste* who seemed to really interest him – and obsessively so) are, in a sense, subordinate in relation to the great masters who dictated the success of the genre (also in commercial terms) – particularly Canaletto and Bellotto – who did not appear to capture his attention in quite the same way. Indeed, Guardi's vibrant painting differs from the compositional clarity of earlier masters, but is essentially *Venetian* in the priority given to colour over drawing, and not without a hint of melancholy (which some have sought to associate with the epilogue of a city immersed in an inexorable process of political and social disintegration), which, with its para-impressionist brush work and not-infrequently radical perspectives, seems to have particularly seduced the Collector.

In truth, the political and administrative disintegration of Venice was a *fait accompli* even before the end of the century, when, in 1797, the impact of the Napoleonic conquest overturned the proud, millennium-old republic of La Serenissima. Prior to this, however, throughout the eighteenth century, the city was able to preserve the illusion of its former grandeur and the splendour of an aristocratic republic, with its Doge and his ceremonial court, the axis around which an intense and equally unique social life was organised, with festivals – from Carnival to the Feast of the Ascension – that drew in the crowds. At the same time, the city, (still) the centre of the most important state on the peninsula, was a focal point for a number of renowned intellectuals and artists, who turned Venice into an obligatory port of call for educated European aristocrats on their Grand Tour.

For that reason, when deprived of the commercial resources that had brought about its former opulence (due to the competition of emerging powers and rival Italian cities), the city found its main source of wealth in that very particular form of tourism. And this gave artists (e.g. painters) a broad field in which to expand. Thanks to them, Venice became the central theme in a lively trade in *vedute*, largely aimed at nurturing the nostalgia of the foreign traveller, who quickly started to prioritise this pictorial genre, now widely admired among consumers and critics alike. Over time, and through the development of the *painting of customs*, there was an attempt to immortalise the *feste* (the city's bountiful celebrations) – and it is here that the two aspects merge in Guardi's work: an intimate and rococo sensibility that also finds a corollary with another genre, which the artist never stopped cultivating: *capricci* (the representation of fantastical architectures), also evoking a literary and pre-romantic sensibility.

At the start of the century, Venice itself thus became a work of art, the focus of the practice of artists who sought to capture, with their morphological outlines, the very spirit of the city. Indeed, pressured by a market eager to send travellers home with souvenirs of those unrepeatable summer holidays, successive generations of artists had to make the city the central theme of their work – a lucrative trade that they also attempted in other locations (as was the case with Canaletto and, in particular, Bellotto). These views of the magnificent city, all the more magnificent at the tip of their paintbrushes, with perspectives that were usually reproduced and using very particular tones and *chiaroscuro* effects, were an illusionist's *pro memoria* trick, making each artist's work a truly singular approach to a common landscape (just as illusionistic as the *feste* that inhabit Guardi's painting).

All of this – and the evocative power of this *Splendour in Venice*, reflected in the 19 paintings by this artist that Gulbenkian meticulously collected (as well as in the Venetian landscapes by painters from later generations scattered throughout the collection) – was what Luísa Sampaio, curator of the Painting Collection and curator of this exhibition, shrewdly perceived and accordingly proposed to the board. The Lisbon museum was not able to tell the story on its own, however, centred as it is on its Founder's affinities: it was necessary to find the missing part to fit perfectly into the envisioned project. The stunning collection of the Museo Nacional Thyssen-Bornemisza, in Madrid (with its magnificent paintings by Canaletto and Bellotto, not to mention Piazzetta, Tiepolo, Marieschi and Pietro Longhi), along with its curator, Mar Borobia – both companions on earlier ventures with the Lisbon museum – met this need wonderfully. We are extremely grateful, therefore, to Luísa Sampaio and Mar Borobia, as well as to the Museo Nacional Thyssen-Bornemisza, particularly its esteemed director, Guillermo Solana, for the generous loan of 14 paintings that allowed this story to be fully illustrated.

Among those who kindly loaned pieces, all of whom are worthy of our heartfelt gratitude, we would like to mention, in particular, Ca' Rezzonico, Museo del Settecento Veneziano, the source of a significant series of 12 prints from works by Canaletto. The museum's director, Alberto Craievich, is also the author of an excellent text in this catalogue, that allows us to delve into the complex history of Venetian *vedute* painters over the eighteenth century. Meanwhile, Mar Borobia sheds light on the presence of eighteenth-century Venetian painting in the Thyssen-Bornemisza Collection and Vera Mariz focuses on Calouste Gulbenkian's particular *admiration* for the work of Francesco Guardi.

This exhibition also presented an opportunity for Susana Campos to carry out important conservation and restoration work on three of Francesco Guardi's most iconic paintings (*The Feast of Ascension in the Piazza San Marco*, *Regatta on the Grand Canal* and *The Lock Gates at Dolo*), which can now be enjoyed in their original splendour. Finally, among the House Team (Museum and Foundation), as ever entirely devoted to the success of this undertaking, we must mention Mariano Piçarra, who, as usual, was in charge of the challenging museography for this exhibition, and Carla Paulino, who coordinated the publication of this catalogue. Thank you all very much!

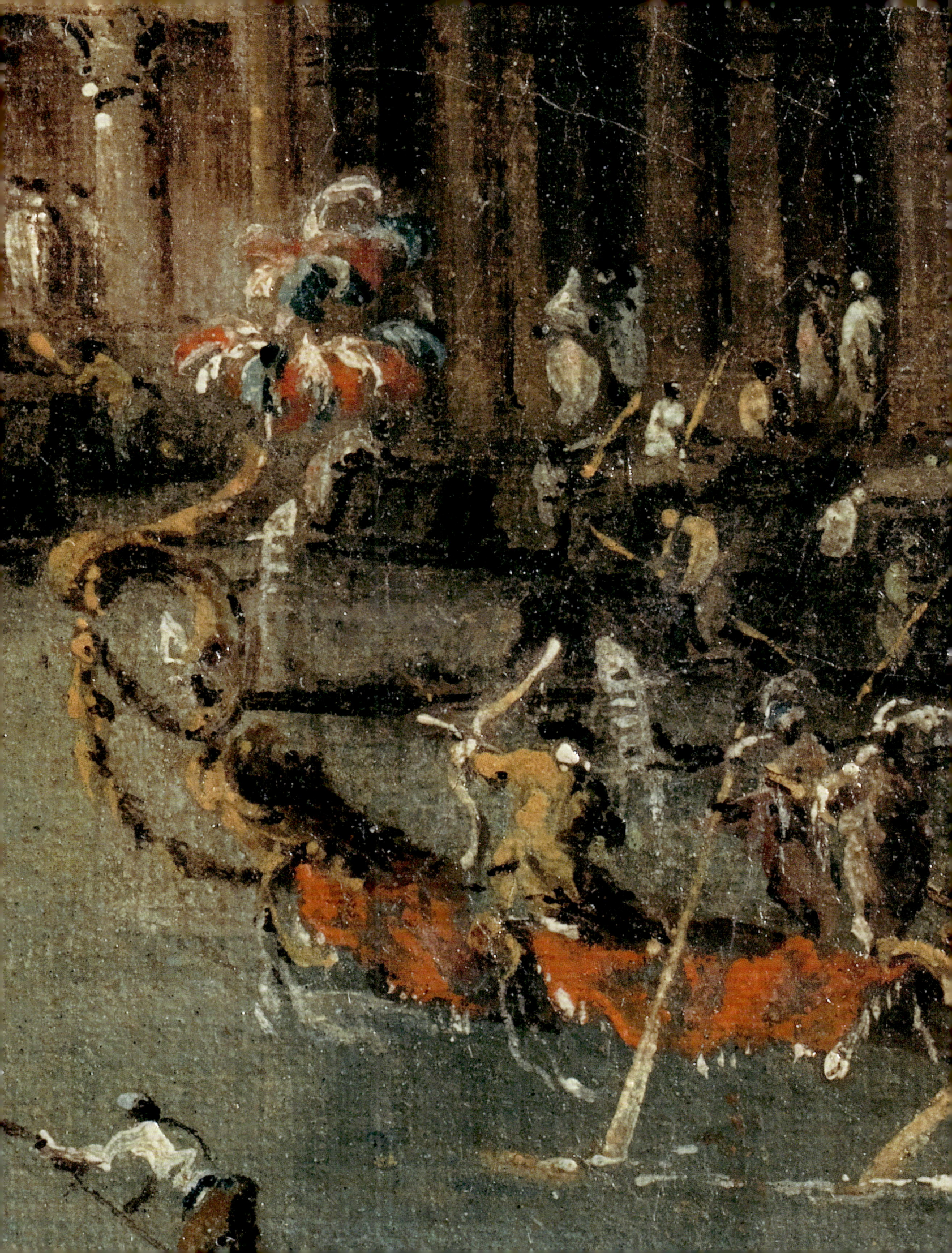

ES

SA

YS

EVOCATION AND REVERIE

The history behind the eighteenth-century Venetian painting collection at the Museo Nacional Thyssen-Bornemisza

Mar Borobia

[1] The paintings referred to in the text that belong to the Museo Nacional Thyssen-Bornemisza include the museum's inventory number so that they can be distinguished from the rest of the works mentioned, which at some point belonged to the creators of the collection or their heirs.

[2] For more information on this topic, see CONTINI, Roberto – *Seventeenth and Eighteenth-Century Italian Painting. The Thyssen-Bornemisza Collection*. London: Philip Wilson Publishers, 2002, pp. VII-XI.

Italian painting is undoubtedly the best represented among the Old Masters in the Museo Nacional Thyssen-Bornemisza,[1] both in terms of continuity and sheer number of works. This interest in the Italian artists was demonstrated when Heinrich Thyssen-Bornemisza (1875–1947) officially presented his collection in Munich in 1930. A firm, continuous line was drawn all the way from the Primitives up to the eighteenth-century Venetian art, though sparser regarding the seventeenth century, with a sole painting by this particular school dating from that period. This line was further consolidated by the acquisitions made by the first baron's son, Hans Heinrich Thyssen-Bornemisza (1921–2002), who increased the number and quality of this group of paintings, especially during the 1970s. Twenty years later, in the 1990s, Baroness Carmen Thyssen-Bornemisza, Hans Heinrich's wife, bolstered the eighteenth-century Venetian presence with a number of views (*vedute*) and other themes.

The foundation laid by Heinrich was built on by his son, who attached special importance to the eighteenth century and its predominant Venetian school. In both cases, artistic interests and personal taste coalesced, and the result was an extraordinary collection of views and history painting, themes that will be the focus of this chapter on the Thyssen-Bornemisza Collection.[2]

BACKDROP: THE 1930s

A first step in evaluating the series of Venetian paintings in the Thyssen-Bornemisza Collection leads us inexorably to its first catalogue, published in 1930. In this publication the collection appeared under its former name, Sammlung Schloss Rohoncz,[3] and its purpose was simply to accompany the large exhibition at the Neue Pinakothek in Munich, the site chosen by its owner, Heinrich Thyssen-Bornemisza, to present his previously little-known collection to the public. The exhibition brought together 428 paintings by European artists from the fourteenth to the eighteenth centuries, including a section on the nineteenth century, with 66 works.[4] From this ambitious collection, 153 paintings were selected for reproduction in the black-and-white catalogue. This first catalogue of the collection included objects from the decorative arts in an appendix featuring sculptures, textiles, furniture and gold and silverware, encompassing a total of 88 pieces, with photographs of 36 of them.[5]

In Munich, the eighteenth-century Venetian school's place in the collection was cemented, since all the Italian works exhibited from that century were by artists linked to the 'City of the Lagoon'. Works by a great number of this school's famous artists adorned the walls of the Neue Pinakothek, including Rosalba Carriera (1673-1757), Jacopo Amigoni (1685-1752), Giambattista Piazzetta (1682-1754), Giambattista Tiepolo (1696-1770), Canaletto (1697-1768), Pietro Longhi (1702-1785), Francesco Guardi (1712-1793) and Bernardo Bellotto (1720-1780), with 14 oil paintings in total,[6] half of which were views of Venice, with black and white reproductions of works by its two great luminaries: Canaletto and Francesco Guardi. The best represented artist was undoubtedly Francesco Guardi, with five oil paintings, but none of the works from this first group has ever graced the galleries of the Museo Nacional Thyssen-Bornemisza in Madrid, except for one: *Study for a Ceiling Painting*, known today as *The Apotheosis of Hercules* [inv. 397 (1930.114)], attributed in this 1930 catalogue to Giambattista Tiepolo and now for some time to his son Giandomenico (1727-1804).

The foreword to the catalogue was written by Friedrich Dörnhöffer, general director of the Bavarian State Painting Collections. In it, Dörnhöffer speaks of the birth of a collection whose future was assured and which had been conceived with a universal scope, given the artistic movements and schools represented, which spanned a broad chronology between the fifteenth and nineteenth centuries. He also gave indications of how the works had been assembled and of the great discretion Heinrich Thyssen-Bornemisza had shown in making his purchases. The baron seems to have begun collecting in the early 1920s, stepping up his acquisitions considerably in the second half of the decade.[7] The documentation was handled by Rudolf Heinemann, a friend of the first baron in art matters, and a close

3 *SAMMLUNG SCHLOSS Rohoncz. Gemälde. Ausstellung Neue Pinakothek*. Munich: F. Bruckmann, 1930.

4 *Ibidem*, pp. 109–25, nos. 362–428. Among the painters represented were famous names such as: Ferdinand Georg Waldmüller (1793–1865), Jean-Baptiste-Camille Corot (1796–1875), Gustave Courbet (1819–1877), Arnold Böcklin (1827–1901), Camille Pissarro (1830–1903) and Pierre-Auguste Renoir (1841–1919), among many others.

5 The Thyssen-Bornemisza Collection is all too often associated with paintings alone, yet this is a grave misconception given that, since its inception, its creators showed a strong commitment to accumulating a significant corpus of sculptures and objets d'art. Their keen interest in this other facet of collecting manifested itself in a series of catalogues, the most notable of which is the one compiled by Adolf Feulner in 1941. See HEINEMANN, Rudolf (ed.) – *Stiftung Sammlung Schloss Rohoncz*. Villa Favorita (Lugano, Castagnola): [S.n.], 1937, vols. 1 and 2; FEULNER, Adolf (ed.) – *Stiftung Sammlung Schloss Rohoncz*. Villa Favorita (Lugano, Castagnola): [S.n.], 1941, vol. 3.

6 By Carriera there was *Portrait of a Young Girl as Ceres*; by Amigoni the portrait *Bust of a Young Woman*; by Piazzetta a pair of paintings depicting religious scenes, *Jesus and The Woman of Samaria* and *Samson and Delilah*; by Giambattista Tiepolo *Study for a Ceiling Painting*; by Canaletto *View of Piazza del Popolo, Rome*; by Longhi *Masked Party in a Courtyard* and a portrait; by Francesco Guardi *View of the Molo, Rural Scene, View of the Lagoon, The Piazzetta, Looking toward San Giorgio Maggiore* and *Piazza San Marco*; by Bellotto *View of Riva degli Schiavoni with the Piazzetta in Venice from the Sea*.

7 *SAMMLUNG SCHLOSS Rohoncz. Gemälde*, pp. VII-XI, note 4. The exhibition took place between 30 June and 10 October 1930. In *Die Thyssens als Kunstsammler* (Paderborn: Ferdinand Schöningh, 2015, pp. 205, 214–15), Johannes Gramlich comments that after the death of Heinrich Thyssen's father, August, in April 1926, he was afforded greater financial autonomy, which enabled him to spend more money on purchasing works of art.

collaboration between them began from that moment on, which would bear fruit in the following publications.

The second catalogue of the collection was published in 1937, although several events took place between the first and second editions. The first was the purchase, in 1932, of a mansion by the lake in Lugano, Switzerland, which was to become Heinrich Thyssen's residence and the collection's home. A private museum was set up there, with several rooms displaying the works and objets d'art. The second was a consequence of the Munich exhibition, which led to criticism of the quality of the works on display, their attributions and the condition of several pieces, which apparently prompted the collection's owner to keep it private once the event was over.[8] However, this decade also saw the prolific purchase of masterpieces that undoubtedly raised the collection's profile and grandeur.[9]

The novelties we find in 1937 regarding eighteenth-century Venetian painting are particularly noteworthy.[10] The first is that the work attributed to Bellotto in 1930, *Piazzetta and Riva degli Schiavoni,* became part of the Canaletto inventory. The paintings in this volume were unchanged except for the portrait by Longhi, but we find four exceptional entries that expand the group to 17, indicating a notable interest in the school. The masterpieces added were: *Capriccio with a River and Bridge* by Bernardo Bellotto (cat. 28), *The Grand Canal with San Simeone Piccolo and Santa Lucia* (cat. 15) and *The Grand Canal with Santa Lucia and Santa Maria di Nazareth* (cat. 16) by Francesco Guardi, and *The Death of Hyacinthus* by Giambattista Tiepolo (fig. 5, p. 52).[11]

The catalogue, which added the name 'Stiftung' [foundation] to the collection, was published in Lugano, with Rudolf Heinemann once again cataloguing the paintings and providing the editing. The novelty is that, in addition to Friedrich Dörnhöffer's introduction from 1930, there is another by Max J. Friedländer, while the book is dedicated to August Thyssen. In his text, Friedländer praised Heinrich Thyssen's efforts to amass a vast collection encompassing the entire history of painting; he also pointed out the opportunities that had presented themselves to Heinrich Thyssen, and which he had taken advantage of, when renowned private collections were dissolved during that decade, affording the opportunity to acquire major works. Another aspect that Friedländer emphasised in this introduction was that the baron had endeavoured to collect numerous examples of the collection's flagship genre, portraiture, for which he had a great passion. Many, though not all, of these portraits now hang in the museum.[12]

The canvas by Bernardo Bellotto (cat. 28) came from a Viennese collection and its last known location before entering the Thyssen Collection was in London, at Thomas Agnew & Sons. It is a youthful work by the artist, Canaletto's nephew, which has been dated to around

8 GRAMLICH, Johannes – *Die Thyssens als Kunstsammler*, pp. 239–54, note 8.
9 The eighteenth-century Italian works aside, we highlight the following in order of purchase between 1933 and 1935: *The Penitent Saint Jerome* by Tiziano [inv. 406 (1933.4)]; *The Annunciation Diptych* by Jan van Eyck [inv. 137 (1933.11.1-2)]; *Family Group in a Landscape* by Frans Hals [inv. (1934.8)]; *Saint Catherine of Alexandria* by Caravaggio [inv. 81 (1934.37)]; *Jesus among the Doctors* by Dürer [inv. 134 (1934.38)]; *Portrait of Henry VIII of England* by Hans Holbein the Younger [inv. 191 (1934.39)]; and *Portrait of Giovanna degli Albizzi Tornabuoni* by Domenico Ghirlandaio [inv. 158 (1935.6)].
10 HEINEMANN, Rudolf (ed.) – *Stiftung Sammlung Schloss Rohoncz*, vol. 1; FEULNER, Adolf (ed.) – *Stiftung Sammlung Schloss Rohoncz*, vol. 3.
11 The titles of the paintings are slightly different from the present ones. Thus Bellotto's work was entitled *View of Brenta* in the 1937 publication, while Guardi's pair were called *View of the Grand Canal with San Geremia and Santa Maria di Nazareth* and *View of the Grand Canal with San Simeone Piccolo and San Geremia.*
12 HEINEMANN, Rudolf (ed.) – *Stiftung Sammlung Schloss Rohoncz*, vol. 1, pp. XIII–XV; FEULNER, Adolf (ed.) – *Stiftung Sammlung Schloss Rohoncz*, vol. 3.

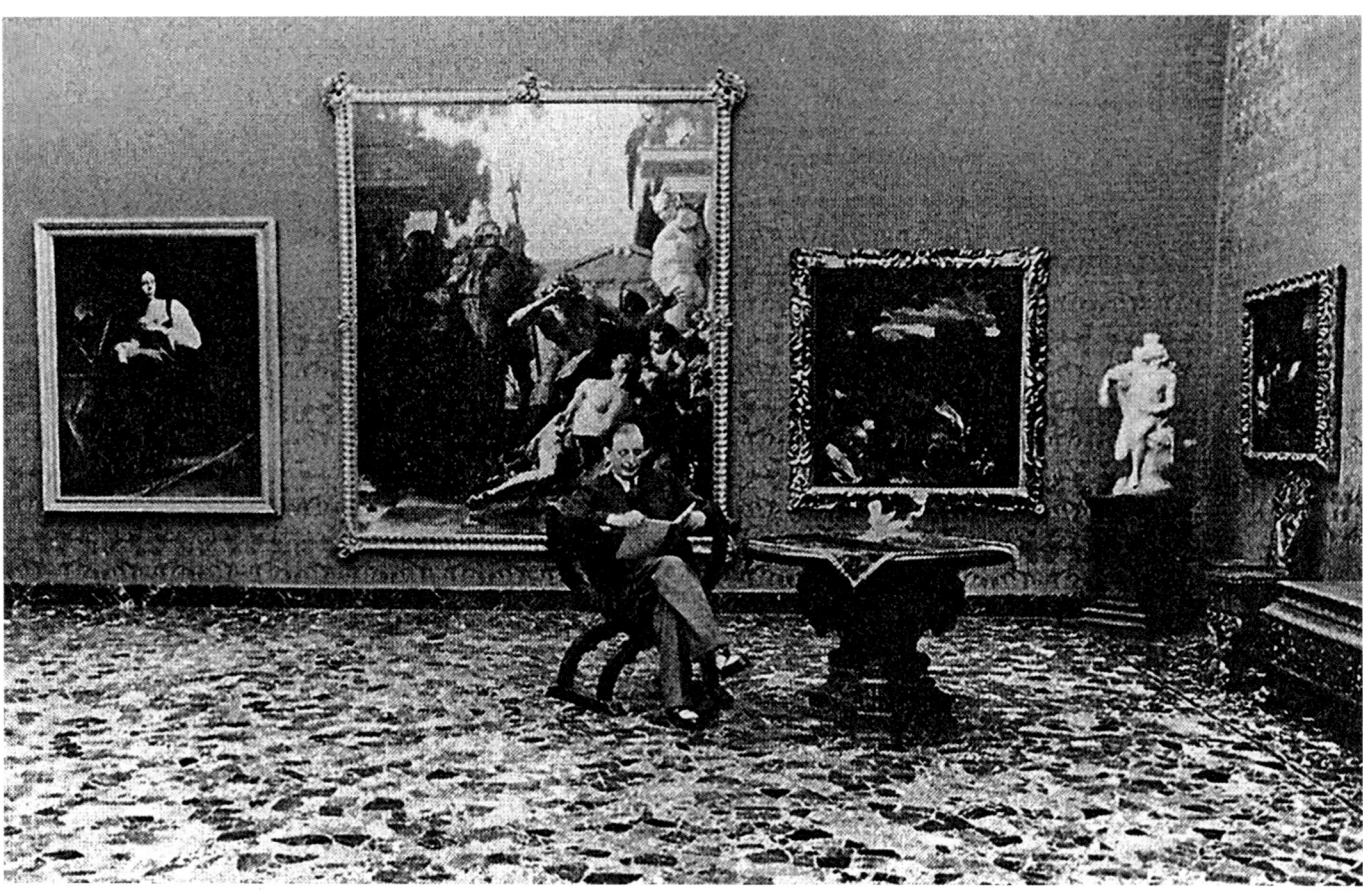

Fig. 1
Heinrich Thyssen-Bornemisza
inside one of the rooms
at Villa Favorita. Archivo
fotográfico del Museo
Nacional Thyssen-Bornemisza.

1745. Its style recalls that of his relative the master, although it reveals features characteristic of Bellotto's style, such as the use of light, which is more contrasting than in Canaletto's paintings.

The two works by Guardi (cats. 15-16), which depict two sections of the Grand Canal, also have a British provenance and belong to the Venetian artist's mature period. The views are organised along broad diagonals that form the banks of the canal, where the buildings stand in a line and a loose brushstroke merges the water and the sky.

Giambattista Tiepolo's large canvas, *The Death of Hyacinthus* illustrates an episode from Ovid's *Metamorphoses* in which the object that caused the youth's death, a disc thrown by Apollo, is transformed into a tennis ball and the setting into a playing court, with a racket appearing in the lower right corner. The dramatic and exaggerated poses of the two protagonists, the procession of silent witnesses who attest to the episode, as well as the cupid and the statue of the god Pan, exude a more than admirable irony that can be seen in other works by Tiepolo. The replacement of the disc by the balls and the racket owes to a translation of Ovid's book by Giovanni Andrea dell'Anguillara, dated 1561. Mention should also be made of a version of the game, known as *Pallacorda*, which was popular during the artist's lifetime.[13] There is a photograph of Heinrich

13 *GIAMBATTISTA TIEPOLO, 1696-1770.* Exhibition catalogue. Ca' Rezzonico, Museo del Settecento Veneziano, Venice; The Metropolitan Museum of Art, New York, 1996–97. New York: The Metropolitan Museum of Art, 1996, no. 23.

14 Both the Bernini sculpture and the rock crystal are now on display at the Museo Nacional Thyssen-Bornemisza following a long-term loan agreement with their owners.

15 SCHWARTZ, Barth Davis – 'Thyssen in all candor. A far-ranging conversation with the world's most powerful collector'. In *Connoisseur*. January 1984, p. 68.

16 THYSSEN-BORNEMISZA, Hans Heinrich – *Yo, el barón Thyssen. Memorias*. Edited by Carmen Thyssen. Prologue by Luis María Ansón. Barcelona: Planeta, 2014, p. 154. As already mentioned, after a few years he recovered *The Death of Hyacinthus* by Tiepolo, which his brother Stephan had inherited.

17 HEINEMANN, Rudolf (ed.) – *Aus dem Besitz der Stiftung Sammlung Schloss Rohoncz: Ausstellung in der Villa Favorita, Castagnola-Lugano*. Villa Favorita (Lugano, Castagnola): [S.n.], 1952.

Thyssen (fig. 1) sitting reading in one of the rooms of his private museum at Villa Favorita, with this painting hanging in the background between Caravaggio's *Saint Catherine of Alexandria* [inv. 81 (1934.37)], *The Parable of the Sower* by Jacopo Bassano [inv. 31 (1934.42)], and Bernini's early sculpture *San Sebastian* (inv. K35 FAM.DEC1614). Above the table next to him is a piece of rock crystal and enamelled gold entitled *Chimera* (inv. DEC.1240), now in the collections of the Thyssen-Bornemisza heirs.[14]

The magazine *Connoisseur* recounts an anecdote about this painting, as told by Hans Heinrich Thyssen-Bornemisza in 1984. In the article, the baron said of *The Death of Hyacinthus*:

'years ago, I didn't like it. It was inherited by my brother Stephan in 1948. Rudolf Heinemann, who was my father's advisor as well as my own, said: "if your brother sells this painting, you must buy it at all costs." So I bought it from my brother [...] and over time, my feelings about it changed. Now I use it as a template. When I'm deciding what to buy, keep or sell, I compare it to this painting. I ask myself: "Do I want to keep this work or the one I've been offered? More often than not, I return the work in question."'[15]

RUPTURE AND RECOVERY: THE 1950s

No catalogue or guide to this body of works was published throughout the 1940s. However, during this period an event did occur that changed the direction of the collection and its contents. On 26 July 1947 Heinrich Thyssen-Bornemisza died and Hans Heinrich was selected from among his four sons to take over the artistic reins. He inherited the noble title, Villa Favorita and a significant portion of the paintings and objets d'art, though not without quarrels with his immediate family. The collection was inevitably divided unevenly among the four heirs according to their interests, with Hans Heinrich receiving the largest number of items. It appears that Hans Heinrich received 363 paintings, his sister Gaby (Gabrielle) 104, his brother Stephan 33 and his sister Margit 31. Consequently, from that moment on the collection was divided and one of Hans Heinrich's objectives was to reunite it.[16]

The first catalogue published after the division of the collection was that of 1952, edited by Heinemann and comprising both old-master and nineteenth-century paintings as well as objets d'art.[17] Following the split, the works by Jacopo Amigoni, Bernardo Bellotto, Rosalba Carriera, three by Francesco Guardi and the one by Tiepolo remained in the baron's

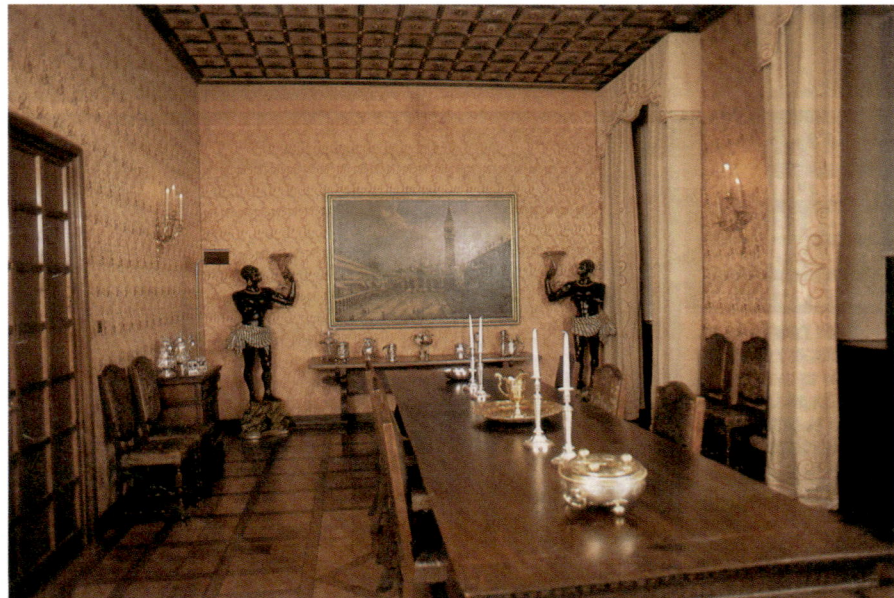

Fig. 2
View of the dining room
at Villa Favorita, with
*The Piazza San Marco
in Venice*, by Canaletto.
Archivo fotográfico del Museo
Nacional Thyssen-Bornemisza.

hands. Canaletto, Longhi and Piazzetta disappeared from the catalogue, and the seven canvases by Guardi recorded in 1937 were reduced to three. However, in 1958 the second baron decided to increase the number of works by the painters already in the collection and to restore other important artists who had disappeared. This declaration of intent is recorded in a short text from 1958, which states: 'my aim is to preserve the collection as my father assembled it and, as far as possible, to complete and expand it.'[18] In addition, alongside the catalogue number in the 1958 publication, letters are included to indicate to the reader which paintings were not in the 1937 catalogue and which were new acquisitions. A total of 464 paintings are listed between the museum galleries and the private rooms at Villa Favorita. In the 1958 publication, Canaletto's name returns with two views of Venice that are two of the artist's masterpieces, *The Piazza San Marco in Venice* (cat. 1) and *The Grand Canal from San Vio, Venice* (cat. 2), alongside a third canvas *The Grand Canal near San Stae*, as well as another work by Giandomenico Tiepolo: *The Expulsion of the Money-changers from the Temple* [inv. 398 (1955.3)]. The presence of both Francesco Guardi with *A Harem Scene* and another of a seraglio[19] and Giambattista Tiepolo with *Christ on the Route to Calvary*, now entitled *Christ on the Way to Golgotha*, was also reinforced. Canaletto's two perspectives, *The Piazza San Marco in Venice* and *The Grand Canal from San Vio, Venice*, were part of a series of four oil paintings from the Liechtenstein Collection. The pair of canvases are among the artist's earliest views of Venice and display the most notable characteristics of his style. The baron said that he acquired these two paintings on a trip to Vaduz and that he showed them to a group of experts at a dinner at Villa Favorita, since they decorated the dining room (fig. 2). The experts' opinion was that the canvases were of good quality but that they were not by Canaletto and therefore unsuitable for the museum.

18 HEINEMANN, Rudolf (ed.) –
Sammlung Schloss Rohoncz. Villa
Favorita (Lugano, Castagnola):
[S.n.], 1958, p. VII.
19 The canvas entitled *Scene in the
Garden of a Seraglio* is now in the
Carmen Thyssen Collection and
is on display in the museum. It is
attributed to Giovanni Antonio
Guardi (1699–1760), as is its pair.

[20] HENDY, Philip – *Some Italian Renaissance Pictures in the Thyssen-Bornemisza Collection*. Villa Favorita (Lugano, Castagnola): [S.n.], 1964.

[21] The anecdote is recounted in detail in the baron's memoirs (see THYSSEN-BORNEMISZA, Hans Heinrich – *Yo, el barón Thyssen...*, pp. 221–22, note 17).

[22] These are *The Grand Canal from Palazzo Balbi towards the Rialto* and *River of Mendicanti*.

[23] Hans Heinrich recounts that when his guests asked him for an explanation of the oil painting, he joked that it represented him removing unwanted people from his house. See the baron's memoirs (see THYSSEN-BORNEMISZA, Hans Heinrich – *Yo, el barón Thyssen...*, p. 223, note 17).

[24] HEINEMANN, Rudolf J. (ed.) – *Collection Chateau de Rohoncz*. Villa Favorita (Lugano, Castagnola): [S.n.], 1964.

[25] 'Addedum to the ilustration volumen 1969 of the Thyssen-Bornemisza Collection, 1971. Villa Favorita-Castagnola-Ticino. Plate 274a.'

Shortly afterwards the National Gallery in London organised an exhibition of the painter's work for which they asked for both paintings, which the baron loaned, as one of the experts who had attended his dinner was the then director of the gallery, Philip Hendy, who a few years later, in 1964, had written a catalogue of several Italian Renaissance works from the baron's collection.[20] At the end of the exhibition the National Gallery attempted to acquire both paintings, much to the baron's surprise.[21] The other pair of canvases from this series of four is currently in the Ca' Rezzonico Museum in Venice.[22] The same source recounting the purchase and exhibition of the Canalettos in London contains another anecdote about the painting by Giandomenico Tiepolo, *The Expulsion of the Money-changers from the Temple*, which apparently hung at the foot of the staircase in Villa Favorita for a time.[23]

EXTRAORDINARY YEARS: THE 1960s AND 1970s

The 1960s began rather timidly as far as old-master paintings were concerned. The first published catalogue dates from 1964,[24] in which we find another Canaletto, *The Bucintoro* (cat. 3), and a new attribution for the work *The Way of Calvary*, now considered to be by Francesco Ricci. As for the rest, the artists and works from the 1958 catalogue remain the same. *The Bucintoro*, of British provenance, was purchased from Agnew's of London. The canvas takes its title from the Doge's galley, which left the Arsenal on special occasions, such as the day when the city commemorated its symbolic betrothal to the Sea. Canaletto painted this great celebration with the barge on other occasions, since it provided the perfect excuse to depict iconic corners of the 'City of Canals' in his paintings.

The 1969 catalogue also includes new features, the most significant of which is the change of the collection's name to Thyssen-Bornemisza.[25] In another development, this publication features four authors, who divide the content by national schools. Johann Conrad Ebbinge-Wubben was responsible for Dutch and Flemish painting, Christian Salm for German painting, Charles Sterling for French artists and Rudolf Heinemann for Italian and Spanish artists. This was the first such specialisation seen in the collection's catalogues, but not the last. In this new edition, Giambattista Piazzetta returns, with an exceptional portrait from his early years of maturity, *Portrait of Giulia Lama* (cat. 31), which displays an outstanding use of *chiaroscuro*. The ambience achieved by the artist, as well as the sensuality of the model, make this portrait one of the Venetian painter's most exceptional works. The second major acquisition from this period is by an artist previously unknown among *vedute* specialists. This is Michele Marieschi (1710-1743) and his *The Grand Canal with Santa Maria della Salute* (cat. 4)[26]. Marieschi chose another of the city's symbolic buildings for his oil painting, the Church of Santa Maria della Salute, which stands between the Abbazia di San Gregorio and the Seminario Patriarcale. The foreground is enlivened by the gondolas and the figures in procession, with a banner depicting the Virgin visible. As for Francesco Guardi, this new edition includes three new miniatures depicting views of the environs of Venice.

In the 1970s, the first guide to the works exhibited in the Villa Favorita galleries was published by Sàndor Berkes and Gertrude Borghero.[27] In its brief introduction Berkes comments that this practical and necessary publication was intended for visitors to the gallery, which had opened its doors to the public by Hans Heinrich Thyssen-Bornemisza. There are fewer paintings by Canaletto and Guardi, but those not included were not on display to visitors, as was the case with the large pair of Canaletto works hanging in the residence's dining room. After some years with no works by Pietro Longhi in the collection, *The Tickle* (cat. 33) is now included, depicting an intimate scene in an affluent Venetian interior, where the figures enjoy themselves in a moment of leisure, engaging with the viewer as they do so. Another artist previously absent from the collection was Giovanni Battista Pittoni (1687-1767), by whom two canvases had now been acquired: *Rest on the Flight into Egypt* [inv. 323 (1976.31)] and *The Sacrifice of Polyxena* [inv. 324 (1977.18)]. Another painting by Giambattista Tiepolo, *The Death of Sophonisba*, was also added in the 1970s (cat. 34). This work, painted with a notably free brushstroke, is one of a group of preparatory sketches made with more ambitious compositions in mind. Of particular note are the texture of the canvases and the use of colour, characteristic of the master, as well as the evocation of Veronese in the setting. The problem with the collection guides as compared to the catalogues is that they do not include all the acquisitions made by Hans Heinrich Thyssen-Bornemisza, but merely the works exhibited in the 20 rooms built by the first baron.[28] This decade of major purchases also saw the addition of two landscapes by Marco Ricci, *Landscape with a Storm* [inv. 227 (1977.15)] and *Winter Landscape* [inv. 338 (1977.57)], as well as *Mary Magdalene Comforted by Angels* by Sebastiano Ricci [inv. 339 (1977.47)], and *The South Façade of Warwick Castle* by Canaletto [inv. 78 (1978.13)].

[26] The painting is recorded in an appendix to the 1969 catalogue, added in 1971 [*NACHTRAG ZUM Abbildungs-Katalog 1969 der Sammlung Thyssen-Bornemisza*. Villa Favorita (Ticino, Castagnola): [S.n.], 1971].

[27] *GEMÄLDE-GALERIE. THYSSEN-BORNEMISZA*. Villa Favorita (Lugano, Castagnola): [S.n.], 1977.

[28] This part of Villa Favorita was built between 1933 and 1937 by the architect Giovanni Geiser. The 20 rooms were open between 1936 and 1939 for friends and guests, and closed thereafter. The museum became public in 1948 under his son Hans Heinrich Thyssen-Bornemisza.

Three guides were published during the 1980s. The first, in 1981, was edited by Gertrude Borghero and included introductory remarks by Simon de Pury, then curator of the collection.[29] De Pury informed visitors to Villa Favorita that not all the works in the collection were on display due to a lack of space. Among the changes was the first black and white reproduction of Rosalba Carriera's *Portrait of a Young Girl as Ceres*. The work attributed to Ricci with the scene of Calvary, *Christ on the Way to Golgotha*, was definitively transferred to the inventory of Giambattista Tiepolo, while the portrait by Giambattista Piazzetta, *Giulia Lama,* was joined by a religious scene from the Old Testament: *The Sacrifice of Isaac* [inv. 318 (1980.75)]. This 1981 guide includes an important addition: a plan of the 20 exhibition rooms built by Heinrich Thyssen-Bornemisza with the corresponding list of contents (fig. 3). In it we can see how room XVII was dedicated exclusively to eighteenth-century Venetian masters, being the only Italian school of sufficient importance to be housed in its own space. However, this was not always the case, as in the March 1955 *Galleria* supplement, in an extensive article devoted to the Villa Favorita art gallery, extolling its important role as a cultural reference point in Ticino, a guide to its contents includes a note that room XVII exhibited eighteenth-century British painting. Moreover, the only record of a Venetian painter is Giambattista Tiepolo and his *The Death of Hyacinthus*, which decorated the staircase (fig. 4).[30]

Little time elapsed between the publication of the last two guides, one dating from 1986 and the other from 1989. In the first, the layout of the rooms remains unchanged, with the same content, that is to say there are no new works. Edited by Gertrude Borghero, it is preceded, as in the previous publication, by a short text by Simon de Pury mentioning the new acquisitions and the baron's preoccupation with improving the standard of the collection, which led him to dispose of paintings considered to be of lesser quality. For the first time, however, it includes a long text by Baron Hans Heinrich in which he gives a brief history of the collection and expresses his predilection for the landscape genre; he also describes his collection as comprising some 1,400 paintings ranging from the twelfth to the twentieth centuries.[31] As the administrative director and curator Irene Martin points out in her introduction, the 1989 edition is a revision of the 1986 edition, incorporating the latest research and improving the organisation of the content with visitors in mind. Four new eighteenth-century Venetian paintings were actually added to the collection in the 1980s but they do not appear in these two guides, which only featured the works on display in the exhibition rooms.[32] These include a pair of Canalettos, *The School of San Marco* (cat. 17) and *Capriccio with Colonnade in the Interior of a Palace* (cat. 18),[33] dating from the painter's last period.

[29] BORGHERO, Gertrude (ed.) – *Thyssen-Bornemisza Collection. Catalogue of the Exhibited Works of Art*. Villa Favorita (Lugano, Castagnola): [S.n.], 1981.

[30] 'TESORI D'ARTE nel Ticino. La Pinacoteca di Villa Favorita a Castagnola'. In *Galleria. Rubrica di cultura e d'arte a cura di V. Gilardoni* (No. 3, March 1955, p. 29). In the second edition of the 1986 guide, published in 1987, the eighteenth-century Venetian masters shared a space with the French masters of the same century.

[31] BORGHERO, Gertrude (ed.) – *Thyssen-Bornemisza Collection*. Milan: Electa, 1986.

[32] WATTEVILLE, Caroline de – *Thyssen-Bornemisza Collection. Guide to the Exhibited Works*. Milan: Electa, 1989.

[33] These two paintings by Canaletto are part of the Carmen Thyssen Collection and are on display in the Museo Nacional Thyssen-Bornemisza.

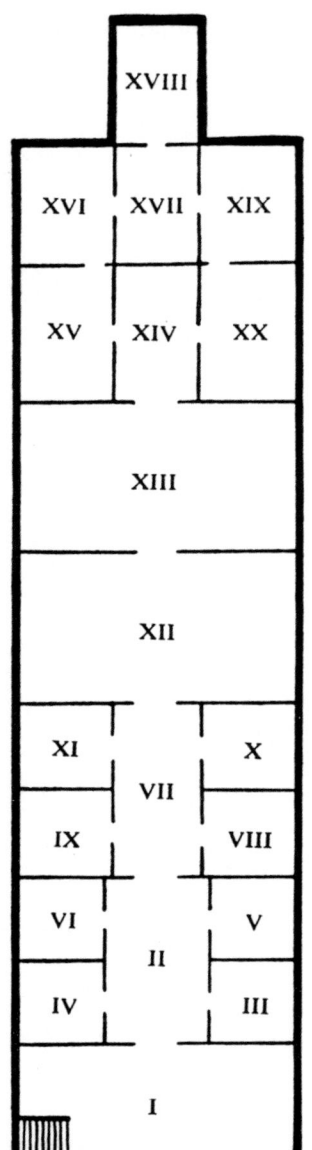

XVIII	French masters of the XVII and XVIII century.
XIX	French and Italian painting of the XVII century. Sculptures by Houdon.
XVII	Venetian masters of the XVIII century.
XVI	Italian High and Late Renaissance.
XX	Spanish painting, XVI to XVIII century.
XV	Italian High Renaissance.
XIV	International Gothic and Early Renaissance.
XIII	Venetian masterpieces of the XVI century. Italian Baroque sculptures and furniture.
XII	Dutch and Flemish masterpieces of the XVII century.
XI	Dutch genre painting, XVII century.
X	Dutch landscape painting, XVII century.
IX	Dutch interior and still-life painting, XVII century.
VIII	Rembrandt and his circle.
VII	Dutch and Flemish painting from Mannerism to Baroque.
VI	Dutch painting, XV century.
V	Flemish masters of the XV century.
IV	Lukas and Hans Cranach and Old German portrait painting around 1550.
III	German Renaissance (Bavaria and Donauschule).
II	Old German panel painting 1450-1520.
I	Italian panel painting, XIII to XIV century. French and Italian sculpture, XIII to XVI century and ivory reliefs.

Fig. 3
Map of the rooms at Villa Favorita in 1981. Archivo fotográfico del Museo Nacional Thyssen-Bornemisza, Madrid.

Fig. 4
View of the staircase of Villa Favorita, with *The Death of Hyacinthus*, by Giambattista Tiepolo. Archivo fotográfico del Museo Nacional Thyssen-Bornemisza.

The other pair comprises two mythological themes by Sebastiano Ricci, *Neptune and Amphitrite* [inv. 340 (1982.33)] and *Bacchus and Ariadne* [inv. 341 (1982.34)].

During the 1990s, the collection of eighteenth-century Italian paintings now on display at the Thyssen Museum in Madrid was enriched by the addition of works from the Baroness Carmen Thyssen collection. Among the paintings acquired during that decade are a Guardi, *View of the Giudecca Canal and the Zattere* (inv. CTB.1995.1), a Canaletto, *Porta Portello, Padua* (cat. 27), and a Piazzetta oil painting, *Portrait of a Young Woman in Profile with a Mask in her Right Hand* (cat. 32), wherein it has been suggested that the sitter could be the artist's wife, Rosa Muziolo, who served as a model for other famous compositions.[34]

[34] These four oil paintings are on display on the ground floor of the museum, in the Carmen Thyssen Collection rooms.

26

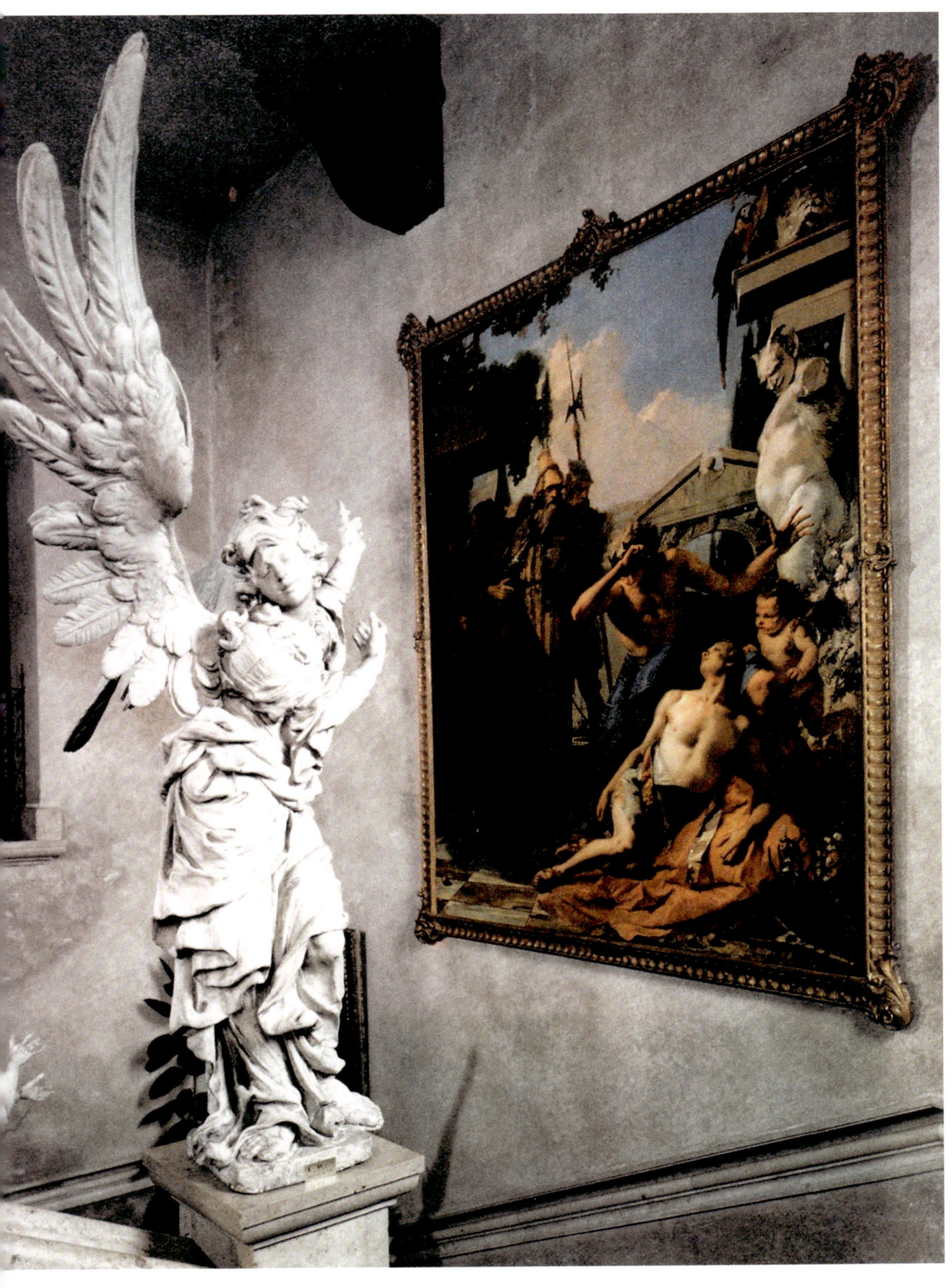

[35] See note 19.

The complete catalogue of Italian paintings from the seventeenth and eighteenth centuries, edited by Roberto Contini, was published in 2002. It brought to fruition the ambitious project to revise attributions, research the provenance of the works in depth and greatly expand the bibliography on the paintings. This process began with Colin Eisler's update on the Flemish Primitives, which was published in 1989. Roberto Contini's catalogue is extremely useful for discovering which works formed part of the collection of eighteenth-century Venetian paintings, as it included the collection as a whole, most of which went on to be exhibited in the Museo Thyssen-Bornemisza's galleries following its inauguration in October 1992. Only nine oil paintings from that publication failed to reach the museum, instead remaining in the possession of the baron's heirs. These include *A Greek Favourite in the Harem* by Giovanni Antonio Guardi, a companion piece to the oil painting in the Carmen Thyssen-Bornemisza Collection;[35] *Portrait of a Lady* by Pietro Longhi; *Bathsheba at Her Bath* by Sebastiano Ricci; *View of the Punta della Dogana in Venice, The 'Piazzetta' of San Marco Looking towards San Giorgio Maggiore*, three small imaginary *vedute* and two *capricci*, also in small format, by Francesco Guardi.

It is clear, therefore, that almost the entire collection of eighteenth-century Venetian painting, including the most important works, passed to the museum in Madrid named after its creators. Baron Hans Heinrich Thyssen-Bornemisza's desire to make his great works of art accessible to everyone was thus fulfilled.

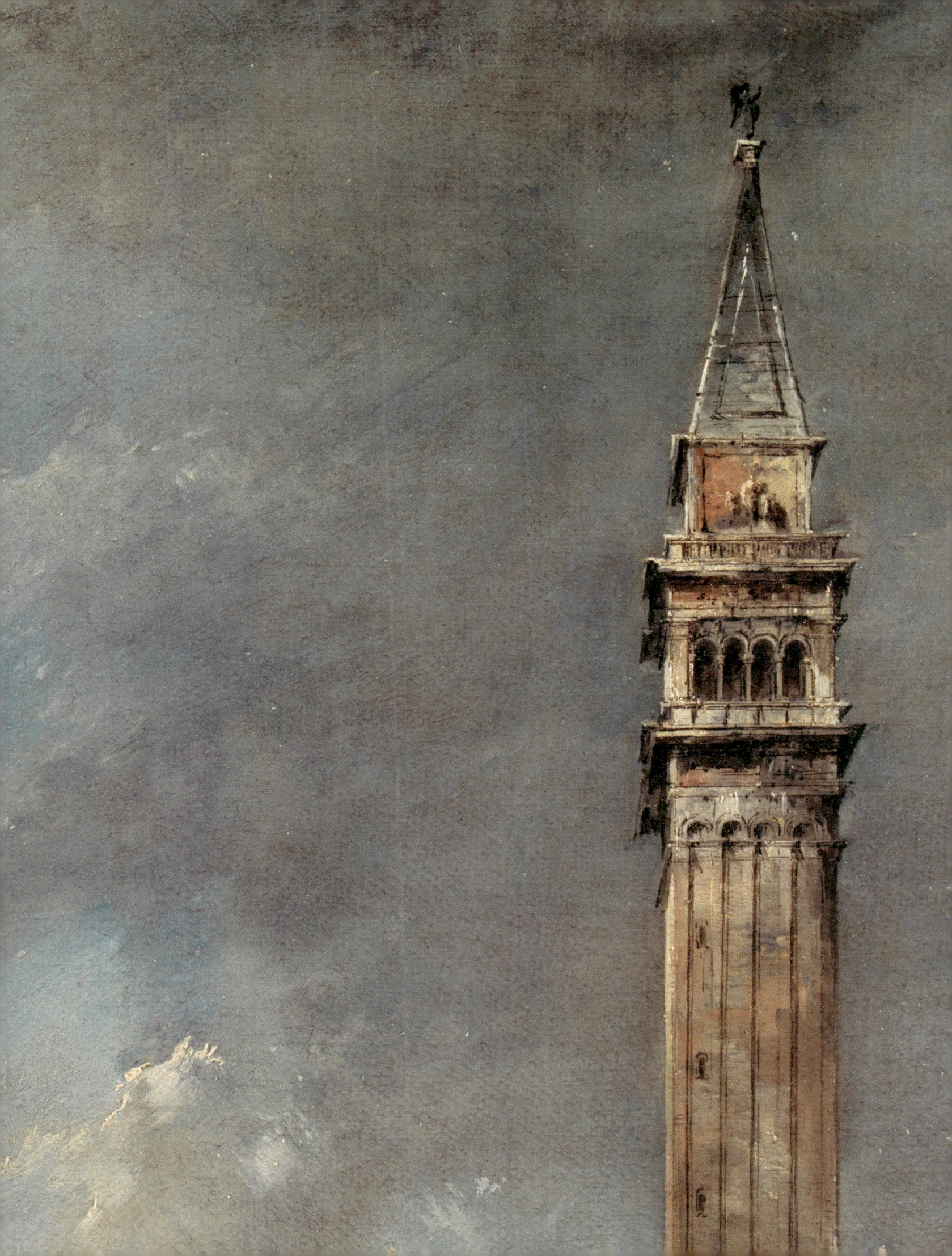

CALOUSTE GULBENKIAN, A 'GREAT ADMIRER' OF FRANCESCO GUARDI

Vera Mariz

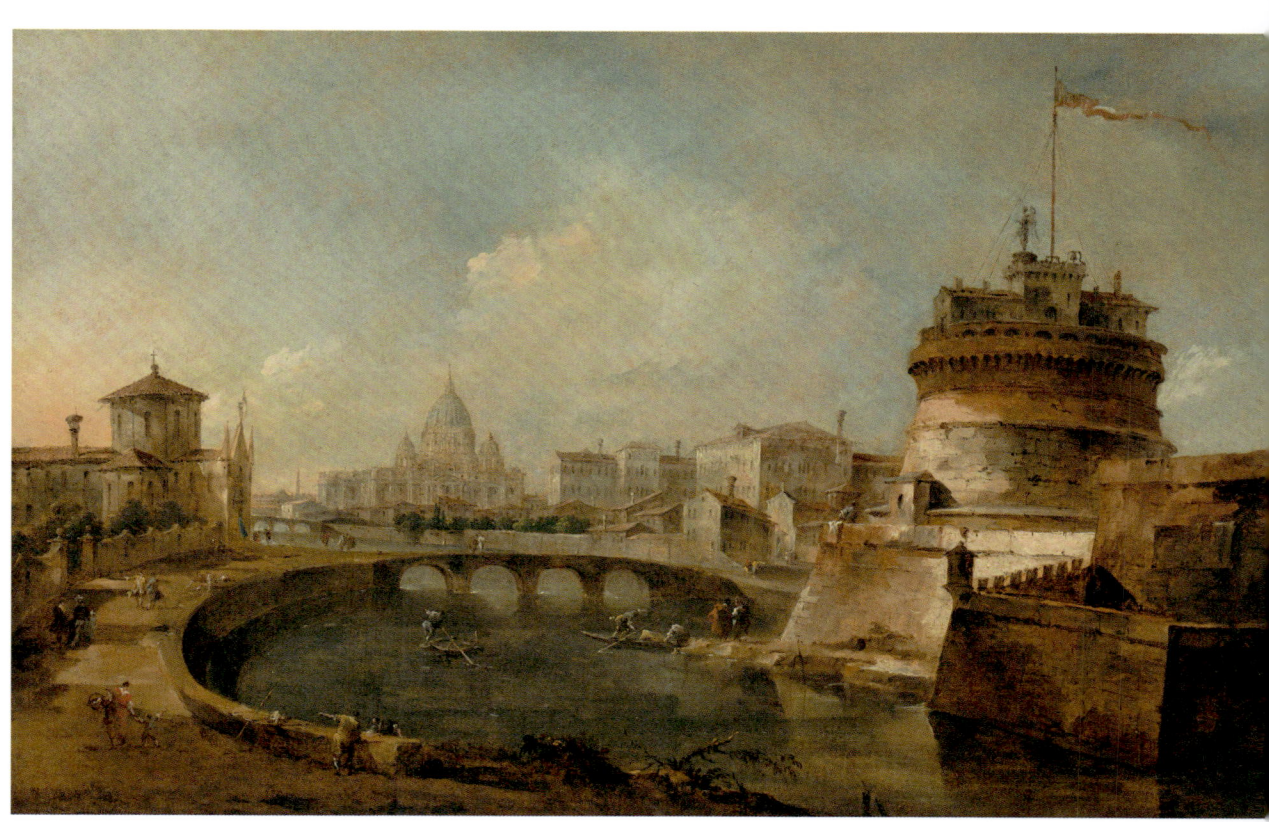

Fig. 1
Francesco Guardi,
*Fanciful View of the Castel
Sant'Angelo*, Rome, returned
by Calouste Gulbenkian
to Agnew's. National Gallery
of Art, 1956.9.2.

[1] Letter from David H. Young to
Calouste Gulbenkian. 22 February
1915; Invoice from Agnew's. 27 June
1914. Gulbenkian Archives,
LDN 00066.
[2] Letters from Calouste Gulbenkian
to Charles Romer Williams. 11 July
1914 and 1 August 1914. Gulbenkian
Archives, LDN 00066. This painting
currently belongs to the National
Gallery of Art (inv. no. 1956.9.2).
[3] Letters from Calouste Gulbenkian
to Agnew's. 10 June 1915. Gulbenkian
Archives, LDN 00066.
[4] CONLIN, Jonathan – '"Renowned
and unknown": Calouste
Gulbenkian as collector of
paintings'. In *Journal of the History
of Collections*. Vol. 30, No. 2,
19 July 2018, pp. 317–37.
[5] Also referred to in the
documentation as 'Island near
Venice'. Invoice from Agnew's.
26 February 1901. Gulbenkian
Archives, MCG 00608.
[6] 'Ledger'. 1898–1903. Gulbenkian
Archives, MCG 01235.

On the morning of 3 August 1914, when Germany declared war on France, Calouste Gulbenkian's secretary David H. Young made his way across Paris with a painting by Francesco Guardi. His destination was the Thomas Agnew's & Son gallery through which, some months earlier, the Collector had acquired this *view of Rome* for five thousand pounds.[1] Although it was a good painting, when compared to other works by the same artist that he already owned, Gulbenkian appeared hesitant. Feeling somewhat underwhelmed, and with growing doubts as to how the work could contribute to his collection, he decided to return it (fig. 1).[2]

This was nothing new and the dealers Gulbenkian turned to most often were, to a certain degree, accustomed to his quirks. Generally, when he changed his mind, the return resulted in a credit to be used in future transactions. In this case, however, Gulbenkian stipulated that if he did not use the sum within six months, he would be reimbursed in cash. Despite initial resistance from Charles Romer Williams, Lockett Agnew's adopted son, Gulbenkian's vast experience as a businessman eventually prevailed.[3] Lockett was furious when he found out about the affair, which would live long in the firm's memory for its peculiarity.[4]

The Calouste Gulbenkian Museum currently possesses 19 paintings by Francesco Guardi, acquired between 1907 and 1921. It is an impressive number, making the collection one of the most significant in the world. However, as the episode described above demonstrates, the collection's history is a complex and dynamic one, involving works that have joined and left the collection, as well as those that were merely studied or coveted by Gulbenkian.

The first recorded purchase of a Guardi painting dates back to 1901: *Venice Seen from the Lagoons*, acquired from Agnew's for 400 pounds, along with a work by William Collins (valued at 67 pounds and 10 guineas).[5] A couple of years later, in 1903, this and other paintings that no longer satisfied the Collector were put up for sale at a Christie's auction.[6] The painting's reserve price was not met and it ended up withdrawn from the auction and sold to Agnew's for less than what Gulbenkian had paid for it. This transaction was not a financially advantageous one, but it demonstrates the Collector's determination to improve the quality of the collection, which at the time was still in its infancy.

A few months later, in December 1903, Gulbenkian bought another painting, *The Church of San Giorgio Maggiore*, at a Christie's auction.[7] However, like the previous one, it did not remain in the collection, which at the time was being assembled at the Collector's home at 38 Hyde Park Gardens in London. The popularity that Guardi enjoyed in England certainly influenced this growing fascination with the painter and indeed, although initially overshadowed by Canaletto, Guardi's recognition as a great painter of Venetian *vedute* gained traction during the nineteenth century. This was partly due to the scattering of important collections, such as those of Dover-Clifden and Cavendish-Bentinck, which brought high-quality works onto the market.[8]

Many of these paintings were listed in the monograph published in 1904 by George A. Simonson, a copy of which was in Gulbenkian's library.[9] It was probably through this book that he learnt about various works in private collections, some of which he would acquire years later. This is the case with paintings from the Drummond, Kann and Crews collections, which accounted for some of the highest prices Gulbenkian paid for Guardi's works.

Among these is *The Grand Canal near the Rialto Bridge* (cat. 11), acquired in 1919 for seven thousand five hundred pounds at the auction of George A. Drummond, a Scottish businessman and banker who settled in Montreal, where he amassed a significant collection.[10] The purchase was brokered by Knoedler, who was also charged with securing a frame.[11] This illustrates the importance Gulbenkian attached to frames, not only for their practical function, but primarily for their aesthetic appeal. This is demonstrated by the replacement, in 1914, of the old frames for *The Feast of Ascension in the Piazza San Marco* (cat. 7) and *View of the Molo with the Ducal Palace* (cat. 9) with two Louis XV style ones.[12]

Among the most expensive transactions was also *Grand Canal at the Rialto Bridge* (cat. 12), purchased in 1907 for five thousand pounds.[13] Like *The Lock Gates at Dolo* (cat. 29), it belonged to the Rodolphe Kann Collection, which was put up for sale by a consortium led by Joseph Duveen, to whom the Collector repeatedly expressed an interest in inspecting and acquiring some of the works.[14] Along with other collectors and enthusiasts, Gulbenkian had the opportunity to see the collection at the Kann residence, at 51 Avenue d'Iéna in Paris, notable for the fact that he returned several times.[15]

These visits provided detailed knowledge not only of the Kann Collection, but also of the building itself, which Gulbenkian would go on to purchase in 1922. The building would also undergo extensive remodelling so that it could function as both a family residence and home to the collection.[16] In 1927, Guardi's 19 paintings, which until then had been scattered around residences in London and Paris, as well as in dealers' warehouses, came together at their new home in Avenue d'Iéna (fig. 2).

7 Invoice from Thomas Gribble. 12 December 1903. Gulbenkian Archives, MCG 00872.
8 'FRANCESCO GUARDI and England'. In *The Burlington Magazine for Connoisseurs*. Vol. 82, No. 478, 1943, pp. 3–5.
9 SIMONSON, George A. – *Francesco Guardi 1712-1793*. London: Methuen & Co, 1904.
10 *THE DRUMMOND Collection of Pictures and Drawings*. London: Christie's, 1919.
11 Letter from Knoedler to Calouste Gulbenkian. 1 July 1919. Gulbenkian Archives, LDN 00145.
12 Invoice from Agnew's. 23 June 1914. Gulbenkian Archives, MCG 00657.
13 Duveen Brothers, Paris Ledger Kann Collection. 1907. Getty Research Institute.
14 Joseph Duveen to Calouste Gulbenkian. 7 August 1907 and illegible date [1907]. Gulbenkian Archives, LDN 00013.
15 Duveen Brothers, Visitors' book, Guest signature book of Rodolphe Kann. 1907. Getty Research Institute.
16 DIAS, João Carvalho (ed.) – *L'Hotel Gulbenkian, 51 Avenue d'Iéna. Memória do Sítio*. Lisbon: Calouste Gulbenkian Foundation, 2011.

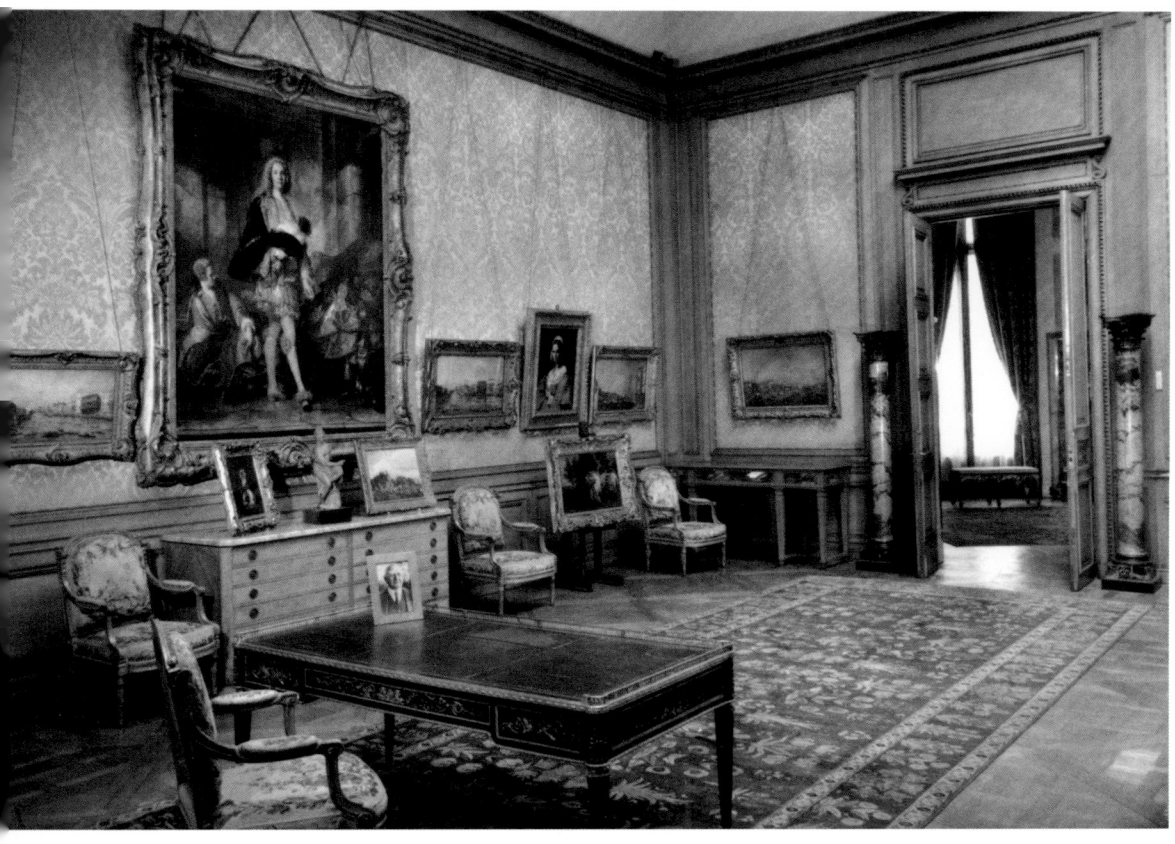

Fig. 2
Painting Gallery at 51
Avenue d'Iéna. Calouste
Gulbenkian Museum.

The fact that Gulbenkian chose eight of these paintings for his Painting Gallery attests to his sincere admiration for the master. In addition to the works from the Drummond and Kann collections, there were four *vedute* from the Earl of Camperdown Collection – *The Feast of Ascension in the Piazza San Marco* (cat. 5), *Regatta on the Grand Canal* (cat. 6), *The Departure of the Bucintoro* (cat. 8) and *The Rialto Bridge after the Design by Palladio* (cat. 13) – and *The Feast of Ascension in the Piazza San Marco* (cat. 7) from the Ashley Collection. The rest were distributed across different rooms, such as the Salon Sycomore, where a group of six works featured, along with paintings by Corot, Daubigny, Boldini, Rousseau, Troyon and Lépine, demonstrating the Collector's penchant for landscape painting. Gulbenkian also kept several works by Guardi in his private quarters, including a small *capriccio* next to his bed.

Although he continued to buy paintings until 1953, his last Guardi purchase was in 1921, with *View of the Island of San Pietro di Castello* (inv. 267). A few years later, through Evelyn Fitzgerald, Gulbenkian had the opportunity to see two works from the Walter Burns and Henry Harris collections. This time, his intention was purely in the 'capacity of a student' and not as a potential buyer, explaining that 'I have a sufficient number of Guardis, but I always like to see other interesting ones.'[17] Indeed, the fact that his purchases ceased in the early 1920s does not indicate a lack of interest; on the contrary, it suggests that the number and quality of the works he already owned had made him more discerning (fig. 3).

17 Letter from Calouste Gulbenkian to Evelyn Fitzgerald. 20 November 1923. Gulbenkian Archives, LDN 01584.

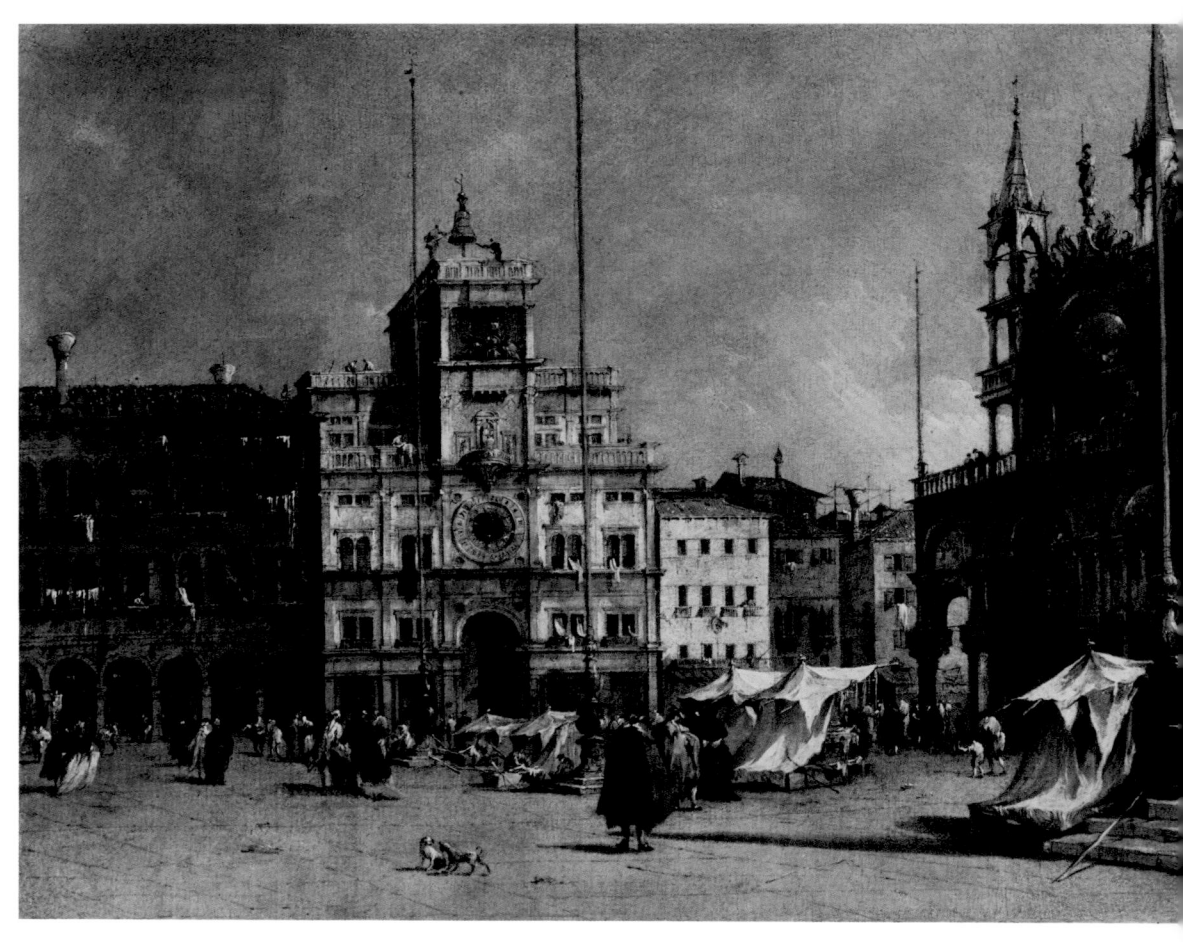

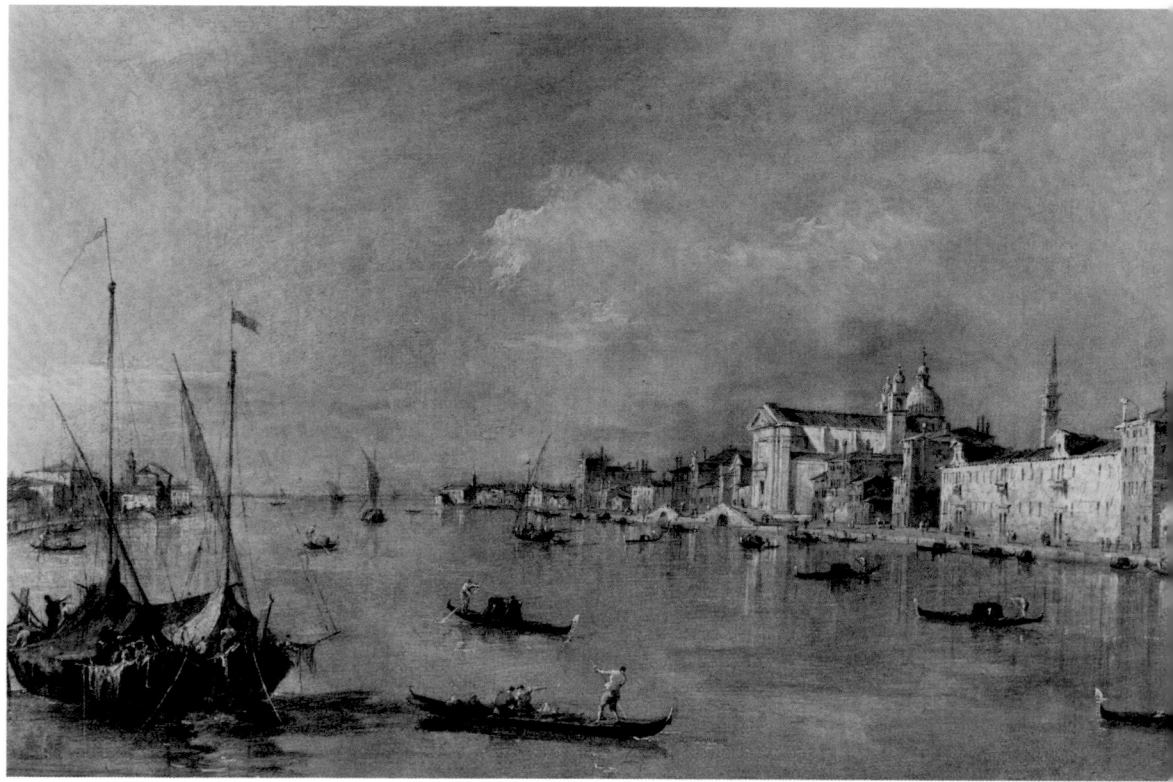

Fig. 3
Francesco Guardi, *Torre dell'Orologio*, from Henri Rothschild's Collection. Gulbenkian Archives, J05-033-084 to J05-033-150.

Fig. 4
Francesco Guardi, *Zattere*, from Henri Rothschild's Collection. Gulbenkian Archives, J05-033-084 to J05-033-150.

[18] See PERDIGÃO, José de Azeredo – *Calouste Gulbenkian Collector*. Lisbon: Calouste Gulbenkian Foundation, 1969.

[19] Letter from Calouste Gulbenkian to Kenneth Clark. 22 April 1943. Gulbenkian Archives, MCG 02896.

[20] Telegram from Kenneth Clark to Calouste Gulbenkian. 22 June 1943. Gulbenkian Archives, MCG 02446.

[21] Telegram from Kenneth Clark to Calouste Gulbenkian. 28 September 1943. Gulbenkian Archives, MCG 02446.

[22] Letter from George Davey to Calouste Gulbenkian. 14 July 1943. Gulbenkian Archives, MCG 02912.

[23] Letter from Calouste Gulbenkian to Kenneth Clark. 4 September 1943. Gulbenkian Archives, MCG 02896.

[24] Letter from Calouste Gulbenkian to George Davey. 15 September 1943. Gulbenkian Archives, MCG 02912.

[25] Letter from Calouste Gulbenkian to Kenneth Clark. 17 July 1943. Gulbenkian Archives, MCG 02446.

[26] Letter from Calouste Gulbenkian to Kenneth Clark. 1 November 1943. Gulbenkian Archives, MCG 02896.

[27] The works now belong to private collections. MORASSI, Antonio – *Guardi I Dipinti*. Venice: Electa, 1993, no. 357 and 624.

[28] Letter from Galleazo Ciano to Calouste Gulbenkian. 1 March 1935. Gulbenkian Archives, MCG 01853.

[29] *PICTURES FROM the Gulbenkian Collection Lent to the National Gallery*. London: Waterloo and Sons, 1937.

After 1921, only two possible acquisitions truly captivated Gulbenkian: a painting of the Torre dell'Orologio and another of the Zattere, which he attempted to purchase in 1943. These works belonged to Baron Henri Rothschild, who lived in Estoril at the time and expressed his intention to sell some of the works.[18] In light of this possibility, Gulbenkian consulted Kenneth Clark, who gave his honest opinion: 'I do not think his Guardi will add anything to what we possess.'[19] After an initial examination, Clark concluded that none of the Guardi paintings were of the same quality as those that Gulbenkian already possessed.[20] Nonetheless, he would ultimately recommend the purchase of the two works, praising their excellent condition and the beauty of their colour.[21] The favourable opinion of Clark and George Davey, who was also consulted about the potential deal, served to heighten the Collector's interest.[22]

Before making an offer, Gulbenkian was able to examine photographs sent to Lisbon. In September 1943, he concluded that the *Torre dell'Orologio* painting was the better of the two paintings, confirming his intention to proceed with the purchase.[23] This decision stemmed not only from confirmation of the quality of the paintings, but also from the fact that they were *vedute* of Venice quite different from the ones he already owned, something that he prized.[24]

However, something the Collector did not anticipate, having already secured the acquisition of other works from the Rothschild Collection, was that the baron would back out of the sale. Describing him as 'a very whimsical person',[25] Gulbenkian attributed this backtrack to the possibility that the baron had been informed about other potential buyers. A patient businessman accustomed to protracted negotiations, Gulbenkian did not give up: 'Baron Henri is no longer [a] seller, for the time being, [...] I should have liked to secure the Orlogio and the Zattere, but we must wait.'[26] Despite his persistence, his efforts were ultimately fruitless, and the deal did not materialise (fig. 4).[27]

Although he greatly valued privacy and discretion, Gulbenkian did agree to several loans for exhibitions. One such case was in 1935, at the exhibition *L'Art Italien*, held at the Petit Palais, Paris. After being approached to loan the *Holy Family and Donors* by Carpaccio, he ended up loaning a much larger number of works considered to best showcase his Italian art collection.[28] In the end, among the paintings selected were seven by Guardi, the one by Carpaccio, and the *Sacra Conversazione* by Cima da Conegliano.

A further loan to the National Gallery, in 1936, confirmed the growing idea that the collection would one day become part of a museum for public enjoyment.[29] Among the 30 paintings sent from Avenue d'Iéna to Trafalgar Square that year were *The Feast of Ascension in the Piazza San Marco* (cat. 5), *Regatta on the Grand Canal*, *The Lock Gates at Dolo* and *View of the Island of San Pietro di Castello*.

These works would remain on display in London until September 1938. At this point, with war imminent, Kenneth Clark, director of the National Gallery, decided to move them to Bangor in Wales.[30] The Munich Agreement eased the tension, however, and just over a month later the works returned.[31] Alas, this peace would not last and, in anticipation of Britain's declaration of war on Germany, the museum was completely emptied, including a container with the loaned Gulbenkian paintings inside.[32] The four Venetian *vedute* were again sent to Bangor and then to the Manod mines, where the underground tunnels offered greater security against bombing.[33]

They would finally return to the National Gallery at the end of 1945. Since many of the galleries had been destroyed, they were placed in a different room.[34] This process was closely monitored by the Collector, who on several occasions expressed his concern that all the works should be exhibited in a single gallery and under suitable conditions: 'You know how devoted I am to my children and I like them to thrive in a proper atmosphere.'[35] For this reason, when the need to carry out work on the building resulted in the Guardi paintings being sent into storage in 1947, Gulbenkian strongly expressed his displeasure to Philip Hendy, Clark's successor.[36] Although the *vedute*, unlike other paintings, returned shortly afterwards, the strain on the relationship with the museum was evident (fig. 5).

Gulbenkian's concern for the future of the collection, and the abandonment of the project to build an annexe to the National Gallery to house all his works of art, led him to negotiate a new loan. Thus, in 1950, after extensive talks, the Guardi paintings and other works went to the National Gallery of Art in Washington, DC.[37] They remained there until 1960, when, after Gulbenkian's death and the creation of the Foundation, they were transferred to the Pombal Palace in Oeiras, before being installed in the Calouste Gulbenkian Museum in 1969.

During all these journeys, or 'peregrinations'[38] as the Collector described them, there was a constant concern for the condition of the works. This can be seen on the occasion of the transatlantic transfer in 1950, when, anticipating the potential risks of the journey, each of the paintings was inspected in turn. This task was entrusted to Martin de Wild, a conservator-restorer who had been looking after the Gulbenkian Collection for over twenty years. De Wild was accompanied by Lord Crawford and Balcarres, trustee of the National Gallery, who praised *The Feast of Ascension in the Piazza San Marco* and *Regatta on the Grand Canal* as 'the best pair of Guardis I know.'[39]

On this occasion, an examination of *Regatta on the Grand Canal* revealed that, although it was in good condition, the varnish had aged, detracting from the nuances of colour and sunlight typical of the skies in Guardi's paintings. As a result, both De Wild and Lord Balcarres agreed that, although not essential, it would be desirable to clean the paintwork

[30] Letter from Kenneth Clark to Calouste Gulbenkian. 28 September 1938. Gulbenkian Archives, MCG 02618.

[31] Letter from Kenneth Clark to Calouste Gulbenkian. 5 October 1938. Gulbenkian Archives, MCG 02618.

[32] Letter from Kenneth Clark to Calouste Gulbenkian. 4 September 1939. Gulbenkian Archives, MCG 02445.

[33] BOSMAN, Suzanne – *The National Gallery in Wartime*. London: National Gallery, 2008.

[34] Letter from Kenneth Clark to Calouste Gulbenkian. 30 November 1945. Gulbenkian Archives, MCG 02449.

[35] Letter from Calouste Gulbenkian to Kenneth Clark. 2 January 1946. Gulbenkian Archives, MCG 02470.

[36] Letter from Calouste Gulbenkian to Philip Hendy. 8 April 1947. Gulbenkian Archives, MCG 02447.

[37] *EUROPEAN PAINTINGS from the Gulbenkian Collection*. Washington: National Gallery of Art, 1959; DIAS, João Carvalho – 'A Coleção Gulbenkian e o "exílio" americano'. In *Coleções de Arte em Portugal e Brasil nos Séculos XIX e XX. Coleções em Exílio*. Edited by Maria João Neto and Marize Malta. Casal de Cambra: Caleidoscópio, 2018, pp. 63–78.

[38] Letter from Calouste Gulbenkian to Philip Hendy. 15 October 1947. Gulbenkian Archives, MCG 02450.

[39] Letter from Lord Crawford to Calouste Gulbenkian. 10 February 1950. Gulbenkian Archives, MCG 02923.

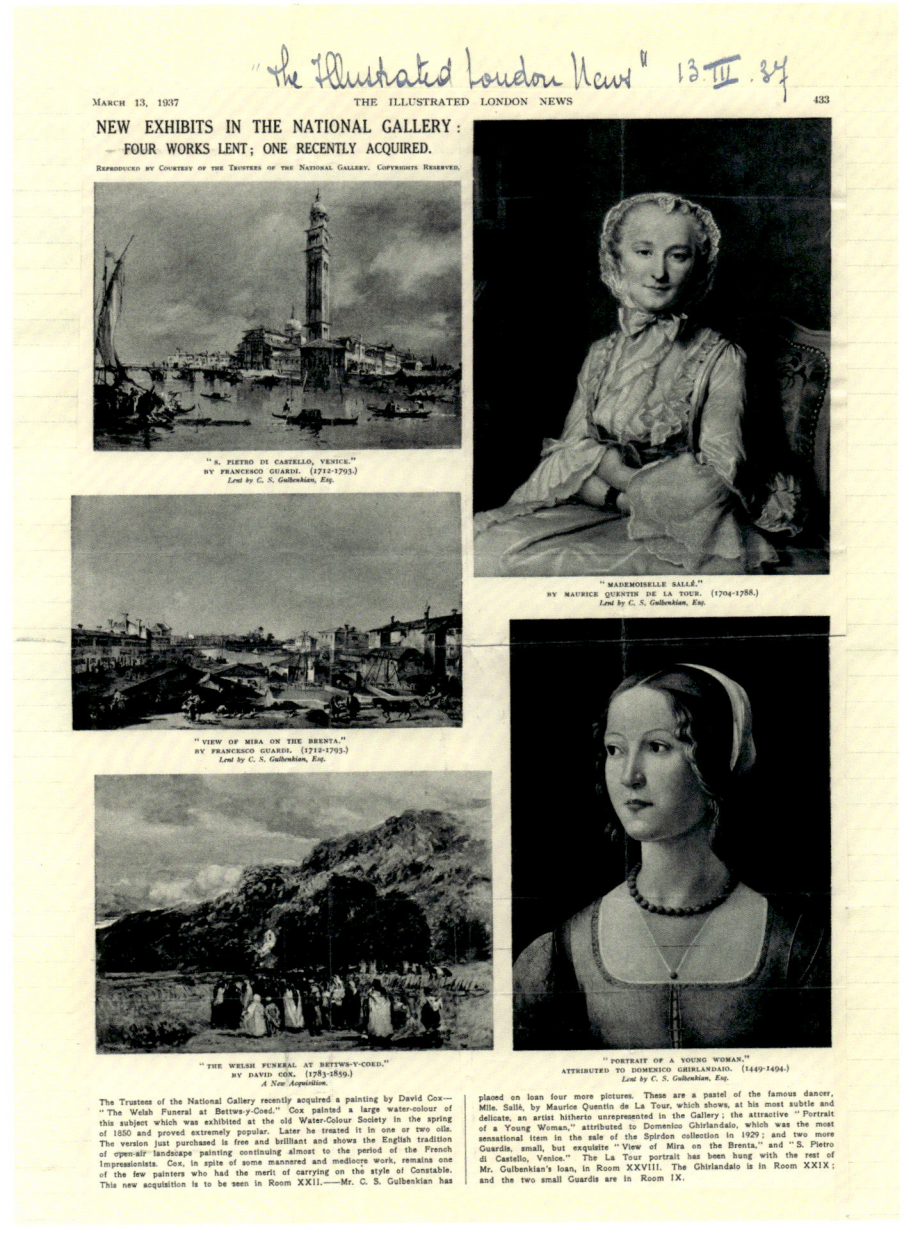

and restore its original lustre and vivacity. This would mean that *The Feast of Ascension in the Piazza San Marco*, usually exhibited as its pair, would undergo the same process in order to maintain a chromatic coherence. Although aware of the possibility that the cleaning process could sometimes trigger other issues, Gulbenkian authorised the work on both canvases. Despite being firmly against any drastic interventions, he also authorised the cleaning of *View of the Island of San Pietro di Castello*: 'In this way, all my pictures will have been "dressed up" and I hope they will hold their own when they get to Washington' (fig. 6).[40]

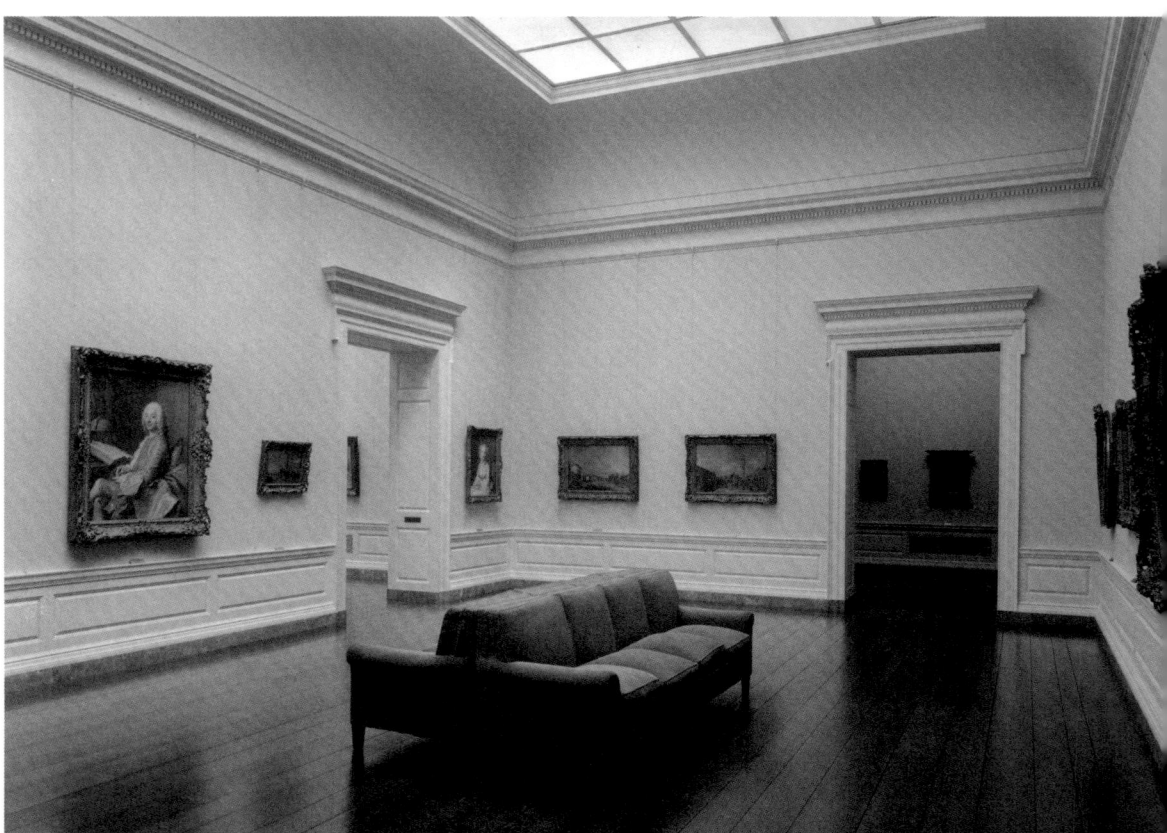

After completing his mission in London, De Wild travelled to Paris to examine the paintings in the Avenue d'Iéna residence, including those by Guardi which, in October 1950, were awaiting cleaning.[41] As Marcelle Chanet, the collection's curator, remarked, this was not a superfluous intervention, given that the works had been subjected to unusual conditions during the war.

In fact, in June 1940, in the face of the German threat, a package containing seven unframed Guardi paintings was sent in a Rolls-Royce to Vichy, where Gulbenkian was also headed.[42] Shortly afterwards, these and other works were returned to Avenue d'Iéna, which enjoyed diplomatic protection, first from the Iranian embassy and then from the Swiss. They remained in the underground levels for six years, only being removed at the end of the war. At that time, all the paintings were brought to the Grand Salon, the largest room in the house and one of those receiving the best natural light and ventilation, returning to their pre-war arrangement only after careful examination. These delicate transfer operations were followed with great apprehension from afar by the Collector in Lisbon.[43]

[41] Letter from Marcelle Chanet to Calouste Gulbenkian. 24 October 1950. Gulbenkian Archives, MCG 01830.

[42] 'Liste des objets retires du 51. Ave. d'Iéna. 1940'. Gulbenkian Archives, MCG 01202.

[43] Letter from Calouste Gulbenkian to Marcelle Chanet. 16 June 1945. Gulbenkian Archives, MCG 01907.

Fig. 6
Regatta on the Grand Canal and *The Feast of Ascension in the Piazza San Marco* at the National Gallery of Art, Washington.

No other painter is as well represented in the Gulbenkian Collection as Francesco Guardi. This fact alone could be enough to prove a particular preference for the vivacity, dynamism and splendour of this artist's works. However, when looking at the way the collection was assembled, the rigour of the acquisitions, the care devoted to the works' protection and conservation, as well as the openness to sharing them with the public, this predilection takes on an altogether different dimension. Ultimately, it adds another layer of meaning to the Collector's words when he said of Guardi: 'I am a great admirer of the Master, and own around twenty of his works.'[44]

[44] Original text: 'Je suis un grand admirateur du Maître, et possède une vingtaine environ de ses oeuvres' (Letter from Calouste Gulbenkian to Antonio Morassi. 7 March 1940. Gulbenkian Archives, MCG 02684).

VENICE IN THE 1700s

Alberto Craievich

Venice was a place of surprising contradictions in the eighteenth century. On the one hand, the city continued to be the most important state on the Italian peninsula and one of the most cosmopolitan centres in the world – a magnet for all foreign travellers – with intellectuals who had a massive influence throughout Europe. On the other hand, the State seemed isolated and stagnant. Venice counteracted its actual political and military weakness with opulent public ceremonies, celebrating a grandeur that was by now in the past.

Built between 1719 and 1729, the Serenissima's last ceremonial barge – the *Bucintoro* – epitomized this dichotomy: a dazzling symbol of the link between the city and the Sea and the focus of ceremonies celebrating Venice's greatness, it was in fact a sham vessel, unable to sail: 'the whole ship is one single ornament. All the wood carving is gilded and serves no purpose except to be a true monstrance showing the people their masters in a splendid pageant.'[1]

In the last century of its history, the Venetian Republic experienced an extraordinarily vigorous period of creativity. Every art form was affected by radical change: from theatre to music, from sculpture to the decorative arts and all the painting genres. Before long, the city became a dominant force in Europe across all the arts, matched only by France. This was the last time that this could be said about Italian art.

In the early decades of the eighteenth century, painting was still dominated by a group of figures whose artistic language was controlled and elegant, with muted colours and balanced compositions, inspired by Bolognese and Roman classicist painting. The presence of Antonio Balestra between 1697 and 1718 signalled a new artistic development; this painter from Verona offered a particularly soft interpretation of the prevailing academic taste, which owed a debt to Correggio's graceful style. Meanwhile, Louis Dorigny – a French painter who had trained with Charles Le Brun – revived the fresco technique in Venice. It was no coincidence that both these artists came to Venice shortly after spending time at the Accademia di San Luca in Rome.

The rapid movement towards a new and radically different artistic form, breaking all links with both the rigour of classicism and the theatricality of the Baroque, was led by an artist who was already mature by this time: Sebastiano Ricci. Halfway through an industrious

[1] GOETHE, Johann Wolfgang von – *Italian Journey 1786–1788*. Translated by W. H. Auden and E. Mayer. San Francisco: North Point Books, 1982, p. 72.

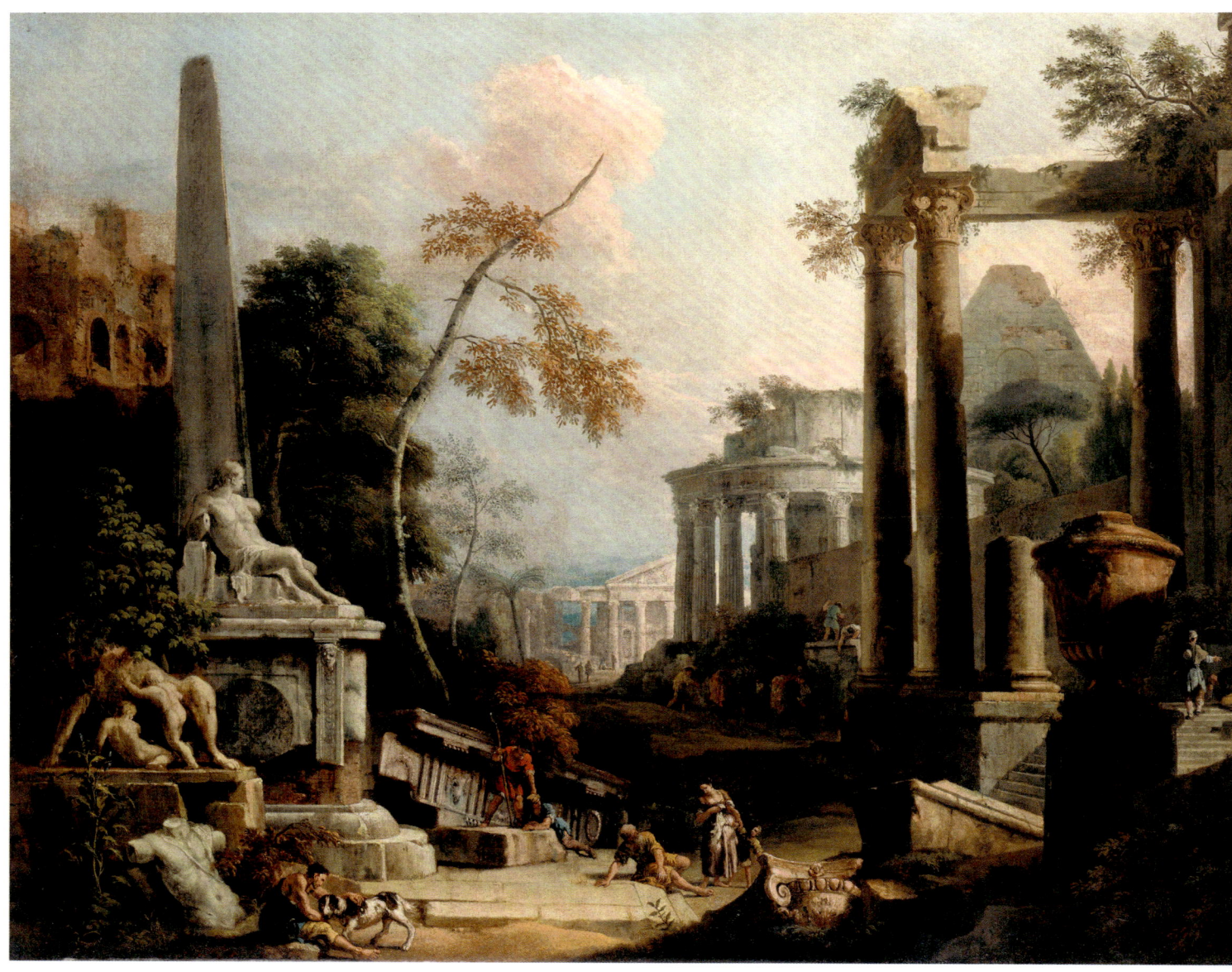

career, he developed a style which incorporated all the typical elements of the future eighteenth-century Venetian School: a painting of the emotions which demanded speed of execution, improvisation and the prioritization of colour over drawing. This change in Ricci's figurative approach resulted from a rethinking of the art of the past, which had matured during his travels abroad. Such travels would become a common factor among many Venetian painters of the time, including Jacopo Amigoni and Antonio Pellegrini, who joined Ricci in the creation of a new and modern style.

According to Anton Maria Zanetti, the works of these artists were 'a sweet dream, an enchantment purely of the senses'[2] to be compared with a vase of fresh flowers or a basket of ripe fruit. This was a seductive form of painting which sought to please the eye, in harmony with the artistic developments in France during the Régence.

Fig. 1
Marco Ricci and Sebastiano Ricci, *Landscape with Classical Ruins and Figures*, c. 1725–30. Oil on canvas, 123.2 × 161.3 cm. The J. Paul Getty Museum, Los Angeles.

2   Original text: 'un dolce sogno, un incanto puramente del senso' (ZANETTI, Anton Maria – *Della pittura veneziana e delle opere pubbliche de' veneziani maestri libri V*. Venice: Giambattista Albrizzi, 1771, p. 396).

Meanwhile, Sebastiano's nephew, Marco Ricci, offered a reinvented version of landscape painting, which in Venice was usually practised by foreign artists. As compared to works of the late seventeenth century, he introduced a new luminous quality, respecting naturalism but restrained in colour. He experimented successfully with new techniques, such as tempera on kidskin, which enabled him to convey the atmospheric quality of any site with a limpid visual effect. It was Marco Ricci who established the foundations of the eighteenth-century *capriccio* (fig. 1) and who, during his time in England, revolutionized eighteenth century genre painting, developing the modern *conversation piece*. Also in the early years of the century, the artist Rosalba Carriera switched from miniatures on ivory to pastel portraits, taking a new approach to portrait painting with the creation of extraordinarily natural images – the antithesis of official portraiture. These were often pictures to contemplate in private, among family and friends, which conveyed no messages of rank or status – affectionate portraits that even now surprise us with their intimate spontaneity.

Between 1694 and 1695, Caspar van Wittel travelled around the north of Italy. It is likely that he visited Venice on this trip, as is indicated by several drawings of city views produced with a camera obscura. In later years, Van Wittel would use these celebrated studies to paint many views of Venice, dated between 1697 and 1717 (fig. 2).

However, another artist was the catalyst for change in this domain. Born in Udine in 1663, Luca Carlevarijs moved to Venice and took up residence on the Fondamenta dei Carmini, where he would live for the rest of his life. His early works were in the field of landscape painting and his first successes came about under the patronage of the aristocratic Zenobio family. The shift in Carlevarijs's career occurred in 1703, when he published *Le Fabriche e Vedute di Venezia disegnate, poste in prospettiva et intagliate da Luca Carlevarijs* a series of 103 engravings (104 in the final edition) in which the most important buildings of the city were arranged according to typological criteria. This marked the birth of the Venetian pictorial genre known as *vedutismo*. The first of his *vedute* (views) that can be securely dated followed shortly afterwards (in 1706) and were made for the merchant Stefano Conti, from Lucca. From these works, he developed a restricted iconographic repertoire, confined to the area around the Basilica of San Marco and the Basin of San Marco, seen from different angles and often produced in series of two or four paintings (fig. 3).

He replicated these views with minor variations for more than twenty years, with the architectural elements reproduced under a limpid, diaphanous light. The most recognizable elements of his art are his small, highly coloured figures, the famous *macchiette*: quickly sketched daubs evoking, in a lively and amusing way, the cosmopolitan crowds assembling on the Molo or in the Piazza.

Fig. 2
Caspar van Wittel (1653–1736),
*View of Venice from the Island
of San Giorgio*, 1697. Oil on
canvas. Museo Nacional del
Prado, Madrid, inv. P00475.

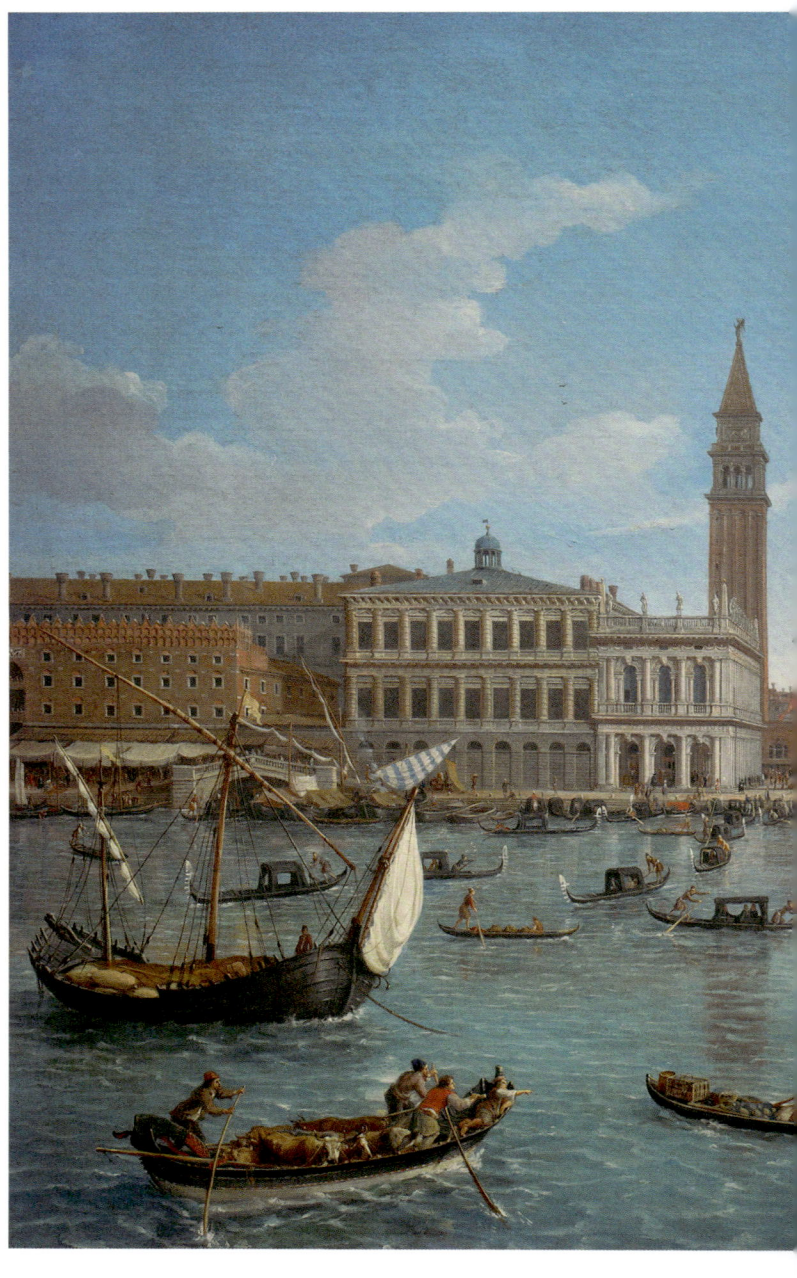

During this time, Carlevarijs developed a specific genre,
the 'commemorative *veduta*', celebrating events that were particularly
symbolic, such as foreign ambassadors making their formal entry into
Venice or the opulent regattas organized during the visits of the most
important European sovereigns. The celebration of these events
was nothing new in Venice: it formed part of a tradition that went
back to the Renaissance.

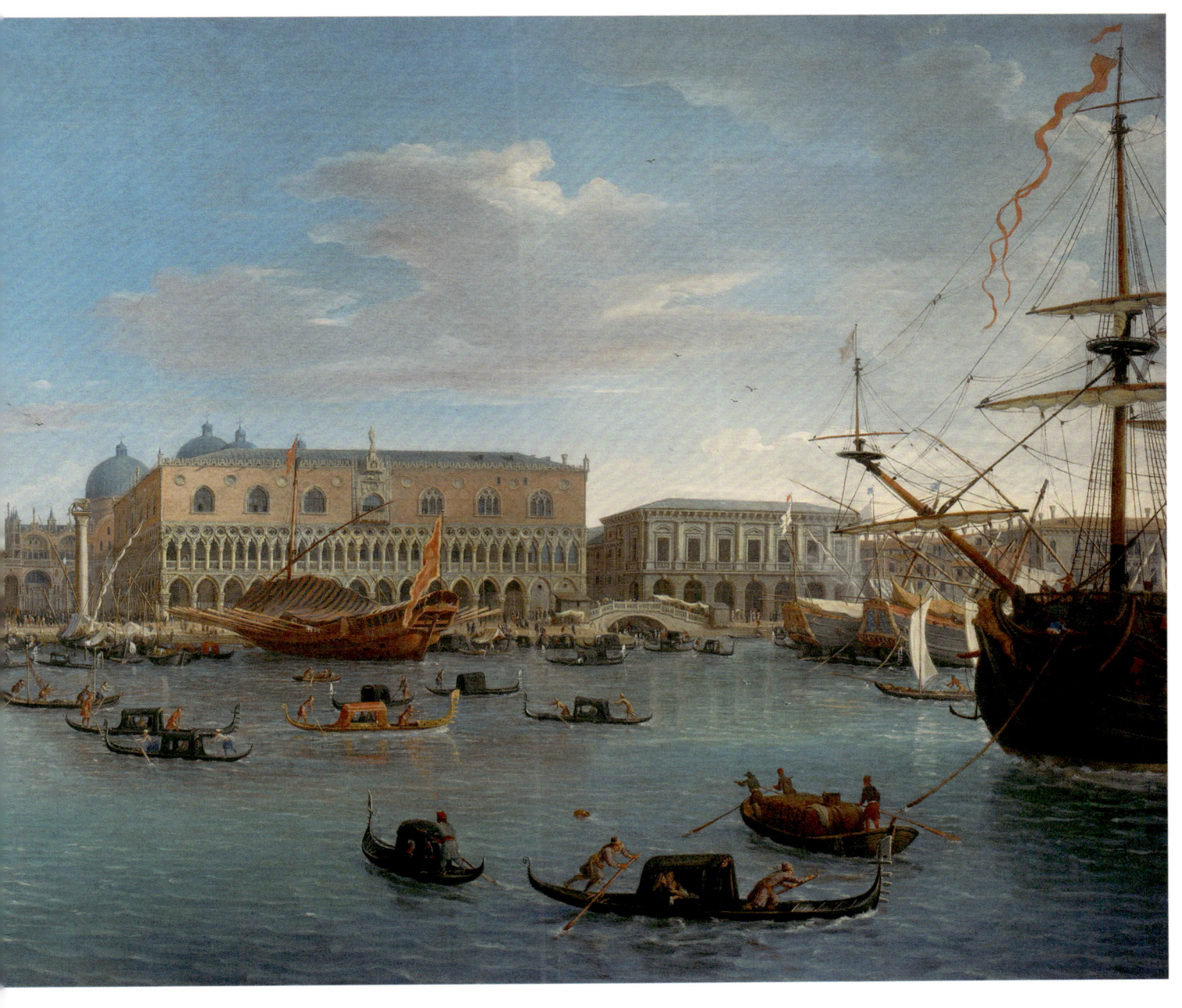

However, Carlevarijs took an innovative approach. He did not limit himself to recording the event, but opened out the scene's perspective so that the city itself became the spectacular protagonist. In this new type of work, he combined the narrative tradition of Venetian painting with the originally Dutch views that Van Wittel had introduced into Italy.

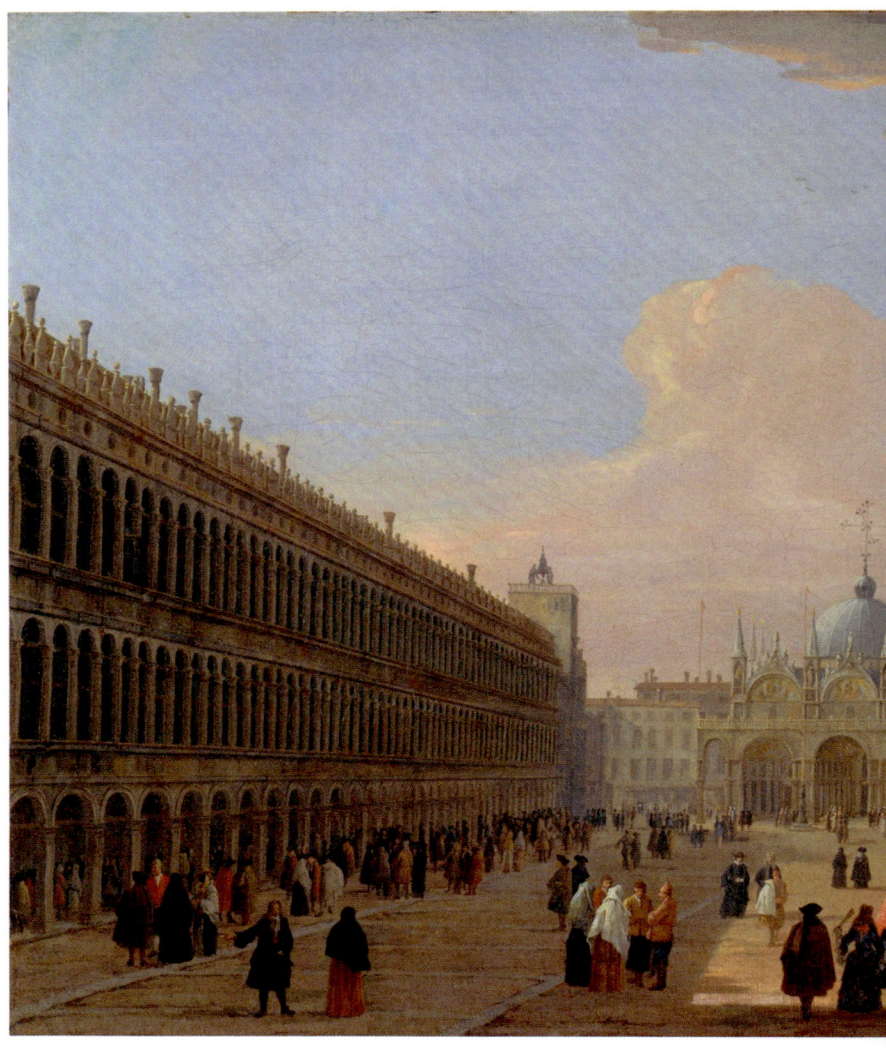

As is well known, *vedutismo* did not originate in Venice, but it reached
its peak in the city in the eighteenth century, with large numbers of painters
employed in this field. A formerly minor genre met with unexpected and
increasing success. The circumstances that produced this positive trend
can be identified as the constant presence of foreigners, who came to the city
in large numbers for the Carnival or for the mandatory stop on the Grand
Tour. Additionally, the absence in Venice of a hierarchical structure such
as the Accademia, which only came into being officially in 1756 – when in
Italy there were already nine such institutions – led to a flexible market that
had few restrictions but was also aggressively competitive. This encouraged
artists to seek innovations that would help them stand out from their peers.

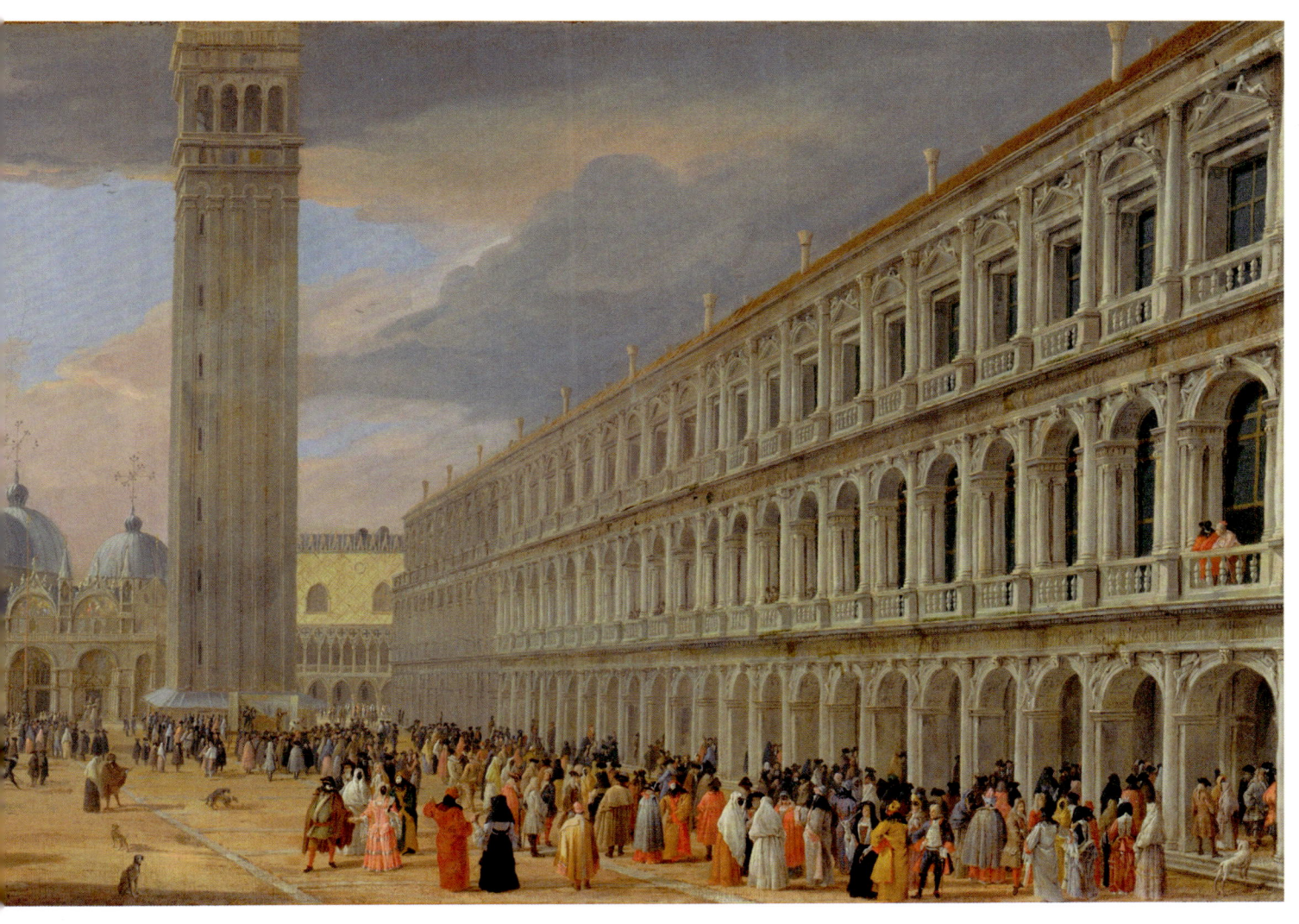

Above all, for the first time, in the eighteenth century the city itself was regarded as a true work of art, worthy of being portrayed.

'As I glided over the lagoons in the brilliant sunshine and saw the gondoliers in their colourful costume, gracefully posed against the blue sky as they rowed with easy strokes across the light green surface of the water, I felt I was looking at the latest and best painting of the Venetian School.'[3]

In about 1720, the Venetian School of painting became an established force in Italy and Europe.

[3] GOETHE, Johann Wolfgang von – *Italian Journey 1786–1788*, p. 79.

While the key figures of Rococo painting became successful abroad as great decorative artists, in Venice a small number of artists were experimenting with very different stylistic formulas. Their points of reference were the masters of mid-seventeenth-century realism: Rembrandt and an artist who was untypical among others from Emilia, Giuseppe Maria Crespi. The result was a ground-breaking form of painting characterized by extreme contrasts between light and shade, the whole resolved through the depiction of human figures in the foreground against a dark and indistinct background. There is no decorative dimension, no warm sensuality: this painting consists of images that have a strong plastic and expressive emphasis, with dramatic gestures and colours. The leading figure in this trend was Giambattista Piazzetta (cats. 31–32), an artist who could not have been more different from Sebastiano Ricci: untravelled, unassuming, introverted and slow in his work.

There were other figures who worked in the same vein, less well known but equally compelling and perhaps even more extreme in their stylistic choices: Giulia Lama (another woman to follow in the footsteps of Rosalba Carriera) and Federico Bencovich. Fascinated by this radical, uncompromising stylistic choice, two very young artists, born within a year of each other – Giambattista Tiepolo and Antonio Canaletto – achieved dazzling results, in which light acquired a fundamental and structural significance. Tiepolo took this to new heights, if such were possible, in strongly dynamic and dramatic compositions, painted with a rapid, aggressive brushstroke.

Canaletto, on the other hand, applied it to the painting of *vedute*, producing realistic, concrete interpretations of the city. He was very young when he began his career as a theatrical scene painter, working alongside his father and uncle, familiarizing himself with perspective and the optical 'tricks' which would be crucial to his subsequent career. In 1719, he 'solemnly abandoned theatre'[4] as is recorded in early texts, and dedicated himself to the painting of *vedute*. He made a sensational start to his career. The tension in his chiaroscuro recalled the stormy effects of Carlevarijs's etching, but surpassed him in intensity and atmosphere. This quantum leap in relation to Carlevarijs's work was immediately noticed by his contemporaries, as is demonstrated in a letter Alessandro Marchesini sent to Stefano Conti in July 1725:

'But now the subject has truly come alive, were it not surpassed in our estimation by Signor Antonio Canale, who astonishes everyone in this country who sees his works, which are of the same type as those of Carlevari, but you can see the sun shining in them.'[5]

Canaletto's *vedute* are wide-angle views, highlighting Venice's unique status as the 'city of water' and celebrating its spectacular qualities, making them even more imposing. As well as the usual repertoire of *vedute*

4 Original text: 'scomunicò solennemente il teatro' (ZANETTI, Anton Maria – *Della pittura veneziana e delle opere pubbliche…*, p. 463).

5 Original text: 'Ma adesso veramente vive il soggetto, se non fosse superato di maggior stima dal signor Antonio Canale, che fa in questo paese stordire universalmente ognuno che vede le sue opere, che consiste sul ordine di Carlevari, ma vi si vede lucer entro il sole' (HASKELL, Francis – *Mecenati e pittori. Studio sui rapporti tra arte e società italiana nell'età barocca.* 2nd edition. Florence: Sansoni, 1985, p. 353). Our translation.

centred on the Piazza San Marco, Canaletto added new views, illustrating not only the Grand Canal but also less familiar corners of Venice. He also stands apart from all the artists who preceded him in terms of the quality of his execution (cat. 2).

From the early 1730s, the dark tones and sharply contrasting light in the works of Canaletto and Tiepolo dissolved into warm tints and coloured shadows. The style of both artists became more controlled and crisp, while the chromatic range settled into a richer and brighter tonality. By now an established artist, Canaletto substantially changed his way of painting. He used a more extended brushstroke on his canvases, while clearer colours enabled him to render details and figures more vividly. His paintings acquired a crystalline luminosity with airy, transparent shadows. Canaletto was the first to experiment with the effect of sunlight in his paintings, following Newton's new discoveries. At that time, these were spreading through Europe, following the publication of a book by another Venetian, Francesco Algarotti, which was intended for a wide public: *Il Newtonianismo per le dame* (published in English as *Newtonianism for Ladies*).

This change was echoed in all Venetian art, from Tiepolo to Piazzetta. The 'sun's luminosity', or 'lume solivo',[6] as observed by contemporaries, found its way into paintings, brightening the colours and filling them with light. At this time, Canaletto forged even closer links with the British public through Consul Joseph Smith, who became his almost exclusive agent. Prices for his work were by now exorbitant and he developed a reputation for being an intractable artist: 'He's a covetous, greedy fellow & because he's in reputation people are glad to get anything & at his own price.'[7] In 1735, he published a series of 14 engravings with the title *Prospectus Magni Canali Venetiarum*. A second edition followed in 1742, enriched with a further 24 *vedute* reproducing paintings he had sold to British collectors. This was the peak of his success, noted by Charles de Brosses on his travels to Italy (24 November 1739):

> 'painting has entirely degenerated. Solimena in Naples, Trevisani in Rome, and Canaletto in Venice, these are the only painters with any reputation left in Italy; and of these three, the first two are so old that they have not been fit to work for some time. As for Canaletto, his job is painting views of Venice; in this genre he surpasses everything that has gone before. His manner is bright, gay, lively, in perspective and with admirable detail. The English have spoilt this artisan so much, offering him three times more than he himself has asked for his paintings, that it is no longer possible to do business with him.'[8]

As the 1730s drew to a close, cracks began to appear for the first time in Canaletto's monopoly. Michele Marieschi made his appearance on the Venice art market: younger than his rival by thirteen years, Marieschi's first

6   Original text: 'lume solivo' (*COMPENDIO DELLE vite de' pittori veneziani istorici più rinomati del presente secolo con suoi ritratti tratti dal naturale delineati ed incisi da Alessandro Longhi veneziano*. Venice: [S.n.], 1762).
7   SWINY, Owen – 'Letter to John Conduitt concerning a proposed memorial to Newton'. 16–27 September 1730. Available at: <https://www.newtonproject.ox.ac.uk/view/texts/normalized/OTHE00007>.
8   *LE PRÉSIDENT de Brosses en Italie, lettres familières*. Paris: Didier, 1869, p. 345. Our translation.

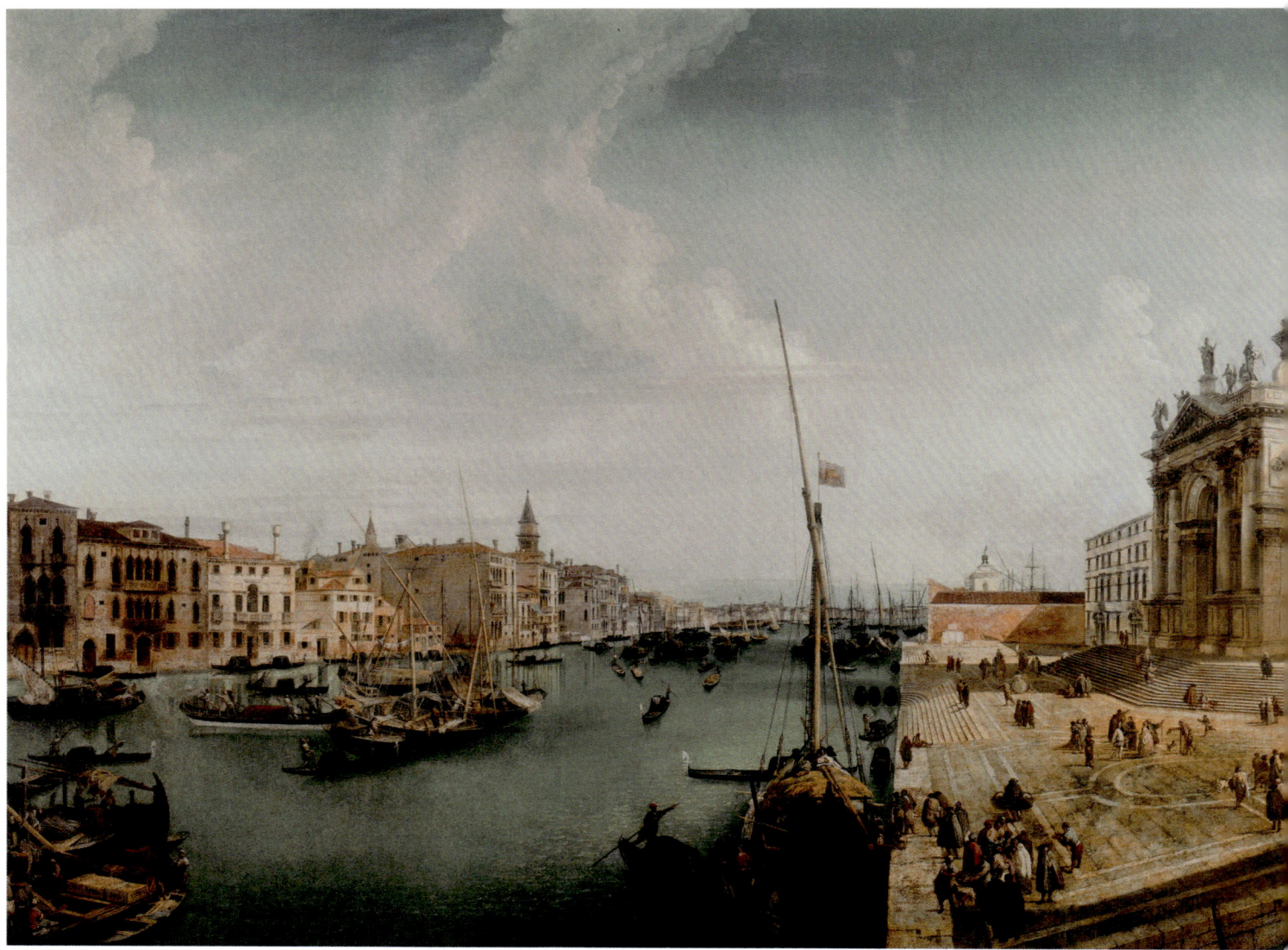

training was also as a scene painter, but he soon switched to the painting of *vedute*, which was certainly regarded as more remunerative. In 1741, it was his turn to publish a collection of engravings depicting views of Venice, taken from his own paintings: the *Magnificentiores Selectioresque Urbis Venetiarum Prospectus.*

Compared to other imitators of Canaletto, Marieschi had an independent temperament, producing new images of the city in his own material style, recalling that of the young Canaletto himself (fig. 4). However, he died prematurely in 1743, leaving the field open to his rival.

In this same period, Canaletto's nephew, the very young Bernardo Bellotto, began working in the master's workshop. His earliest Venetian *vedute* followed his uncle's example but even then revealed an independent personality in their dazzling light and cold tonality, as well as in the crisp definition, achieved through extensive use of black and dark pigments. In 1747, when he was only 25 years old, Bellotto left Venice for good and

Fig. 4
Michele Marieschi (1696–1743), *The Entrance to the Grand Canal and the Basilica of Santa Maria della Salute in Venice*, c. 1740. Oil on canvas. Musée du Louvre, Paris, inv. 162.

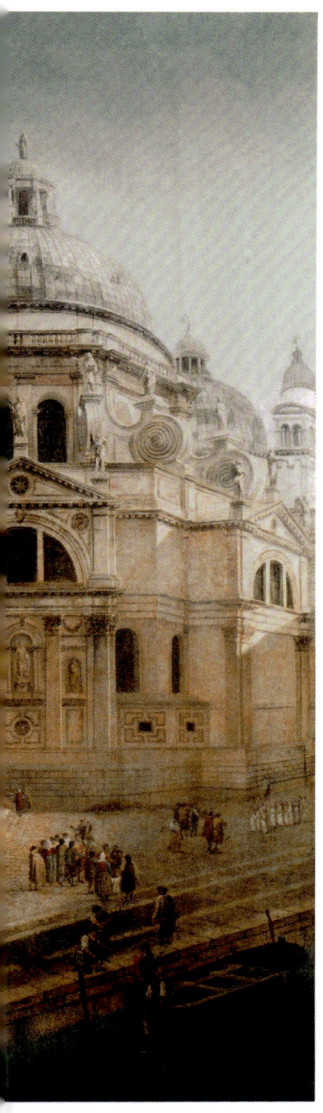

went to Dresden. He later moved to other capitals in northern Europe, where he could find the light he had always preferred. Although both died well before the end of the Venice Republic, Bellotto and Giambattista Piranesi would influence the most vibrant Venetian art of the next century, favouring the 'sublime', which was becoming a new aesthetic trend. Their professional careers were mostly spent abroad, although whenever possible both described themselves proudly as Venetians (cat. 28).

Meanwhile, in the 1740s, Giambattista Tiepolo reached the peak of his maturity. His career was increasingly marked by frenetic and ceaseless activity, whether he was engaged in fresco decorations or in the production of sacred and mythological paintings. He was in demand at almost all the European courts, and wherever he did not appear in person, he sent ceiling canvases and altarpieces. His painting continued to grow more complex, becoming enriched with a strong monumental quality created through an unprecedented focus on classical architecture – perhaps as a result of meeting Francesco Algarotti – while he chose a clear, sharp light over the warm colours of the 1730s: 'erudition was added to pictorial taste.'[9] This high style, powerful yet elegant, can be seen in his fresco masterpieces in the Palazzo Labia in Venice and in the Archbishop's palace in Würzburg. Towards the end of his career, Tiepolo delved deeper into the expression of feelings, bringing new emotional accents to the principal figures in his works. His previously clear colours became laden with darkness, while facial expressions acquired a deeply poignant aspect. Like the most skilful and shrewd composers, he always identified a supremely appropriate poetic and expressive register: dramatic, heroic or languid. This is exemplified in *The Death of Hyacinthus* (fig. 5), produced for an extremely idiosyncratic patron, Wilhelm Friedrich Ernst zu Schaumburg-Lippe, probably in memory of a deceased friend.

In 1741, Pietro Longhi introduced a new genre in Venetian painting. He started depicting scenes from contemporary life. Younger than Tiepolo by five years and Canaletto by four, Pietro Longhi trained with Antonio Balestra, who unsurprisingly, moved to Verona. Longhi's original aspirations to be a history painter had encouraged him to tackle the decoration of the grand staircase in the Ca' Sagredo, but he was conscious both of his own limitations and competition at the highest level from artists such as Sebastiano Ricci, Gaspare Diziani, Giambattista Piazzetta and Giambattista Tiepolo. He therefore adopted a different register and devoted himself to the exploration of genre paintings. It was these that would make his name. The principal subjects were members of the Venetian aristocracy, not portrayed in grand, formal paintings, but going about their daily activities. This was the first time that Venetian aristocrats, normally very reserved, had revealed themselves in an intimate context, intent on their diversions, in an attempt to promote an idea of themselves that differed from official images. In this context, there was no one able to gain access to the private sphere and illustrate it better than Pietro Longhi, who was attentive to the wishes of his aristocratic patrons (cat. 33).

9 Original text: 'l'erudizione si somma al gusto pittoresco' (ALGAROTTI, Francesco – *Il Newtonianismo per le dame*. Naples: [S.n.], 1737).

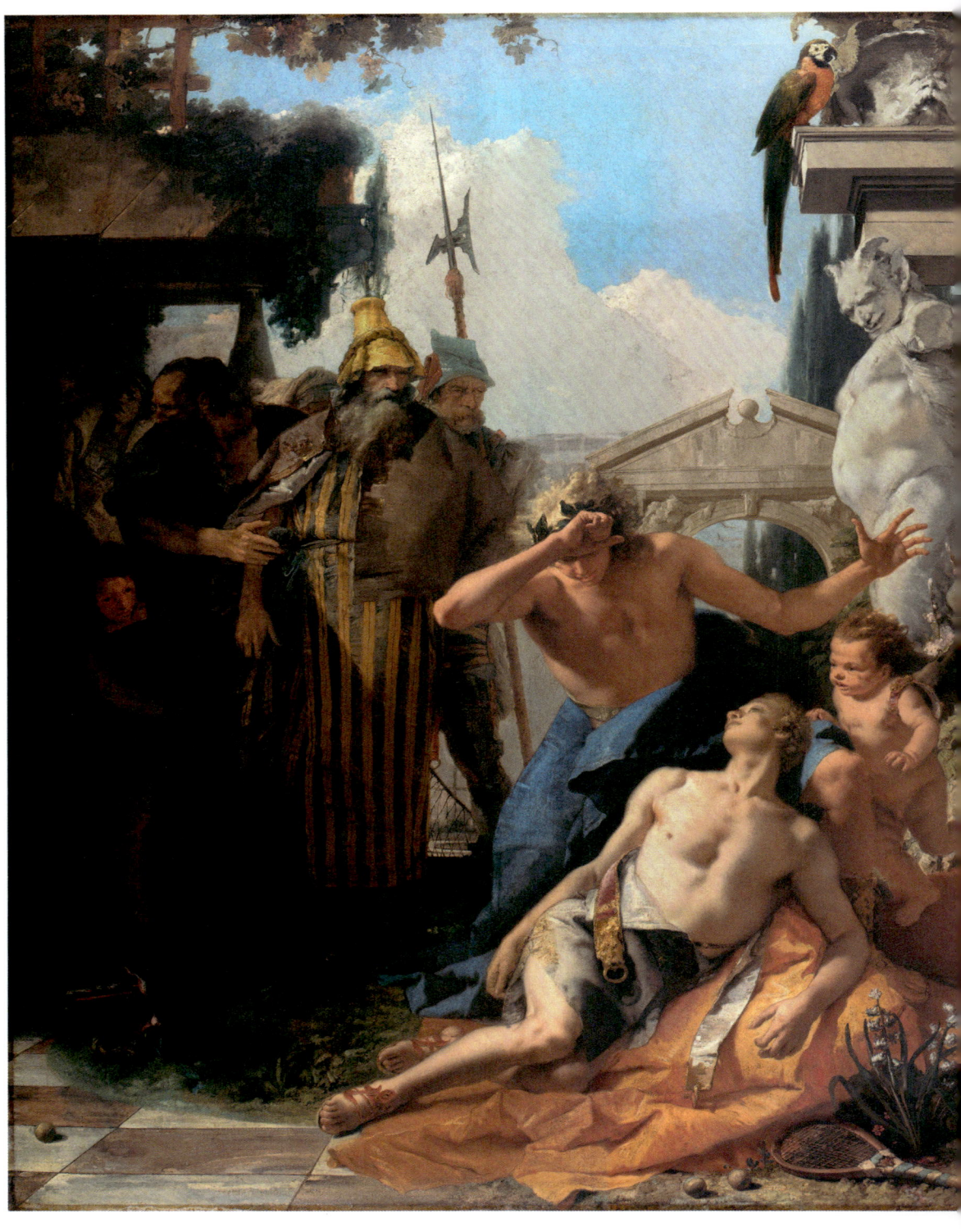

The popularity of Venetian *vedutismo* among foreign collectors encouraged many artists to work for non-Italian clients. Canaletto himself travelled to England twice between 1746 and 1755. Upheavals in Europe resulting from the War of the Austrian Succession (1741–48) reduced the flow of travellers, putting an end to that rich seam of wealthy clients – mainly English – which had brought substantial earnings to Canaletto and to his agent Joseph Smith. In May 1746, at the age of 49, Canaletto travelled to London at Smith's suggestion, carrying several letters of introduction and references. Meanwhile, many artists in Venice decided to latch onto the new genre, taking advantage of Canaletto's absence. These included the less well-known members of the Canal family: Bernardo Canal, Canaletto's father, and Pietro Bellotti, Bernardo Bellotto's brother (who would move to Toulouse). Others have recently been reappraised: the 'Langmatt Master', now identified as Apollonio Domenichini, Francesco Tironi, Jacopo Fabris, Giambattista Cimaroli and Antonio Joli from Modena.

This group also included one of the most original artists of the whole eighteenth century: Francesco Guardi. He began working in the field of history painting, the most highly regarded genre, but in its most humble form, as a copyist. Only when he reached full maturity, at roughly 40 years old, did he move away from the family tradition in search of new avenues. It could be said that he began by looking at Venice from the inside, perceiving the originality of Longhi's 'new manner', which became very popular in the middle of the century. The few known examples by him in this field include *Il Ridotto* (a gaming house) (fig. 6) and *The Parlor of the Nuns at San Zaccaria*, now in the Ca' Rezzonico Museum. These two paintings are classic examples that 'tell a story', containing all the familiar elements of the eighteenth-century Venetian world: masks, a pair of lovers, a carefree lifestyle, anecdotal detail.

Guardi chose a worldly, sophisticated interpretation of such scenes, focusing almost exclusively on masquerades, a genre liable to appeal to foreign visitors. Only about a dozen of these paintings exist, suggesting that this approach did not turn out well.

It is not known for certain when Francesco Guardi began painting views, but it may have been around 1755, when he was already over 40 with a disappointing career as a figure painter behind him. His decision to devote himself to the painting of *vedute* seems to have been a last desperate attempt to turn his fortunes around.

Guardi's personal and professional background was very different from that of Canaletto. He was trained in a modest family workshop where everyone was a painter: his father Domenico as well as his brothers Nicolò and Antonio. None succeeded in achieving a degree of material comfort, much less success:

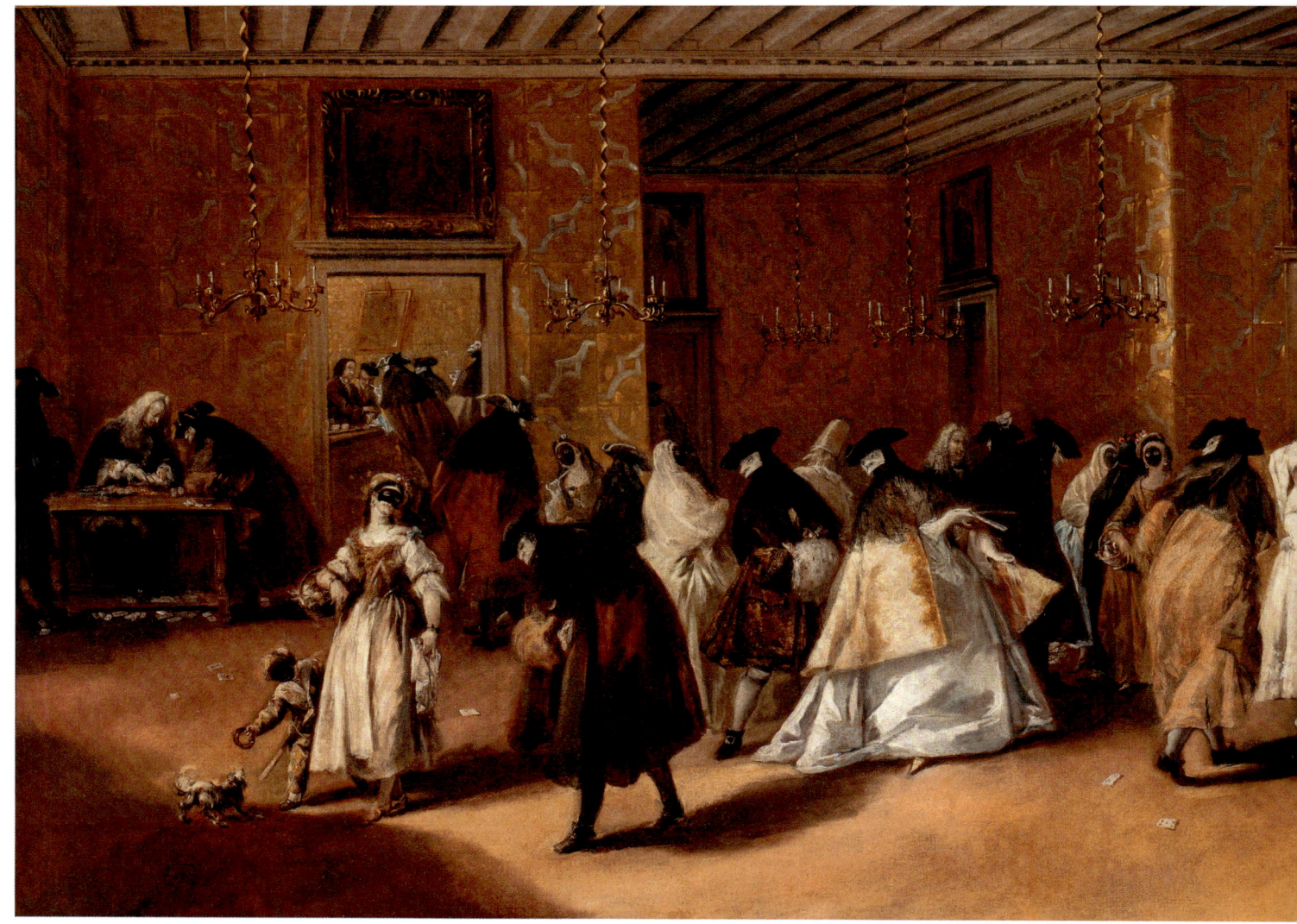

'You know, however, that this artist worked for his daily bread, bought reject canvases with atrocious priming, and used very oily colours to carry out his work quickly, very often painting *alla prima* [wet-on-wet]. Whoever buys his works must resign themselves to losing them before long, and I would not guarantee them lasting more than another ten years.'[10]

Thus wrote Pietro Edwards to Antonio Canova, recording not only the artist's wretched living conditions but also his lack of care for the materials he used, which has resulted in the 'burnt' appearance of many of his paintings. In his early views, he used the same working method that he had used as a figure painter: he took iconographic prototypes from the huge range of engravings of Venice (especially those published almost twenty years earlier by Canaletto and Marieschi, as well as the earlier editions by Carlevarijs and Lovisa) and produced a 'colour' version. This might give the impression that they were pale imitations, but in fact they were brought to life with a lively execution all his own and a palette that

[10] HASKELL, Francis – 'Francesco Guardi as vedutista and some of his patrons'. In *Journal of the Warburg and Courtauld Institutes.* Vol. XXIII, No. 2-3, December 1960, p. 257.

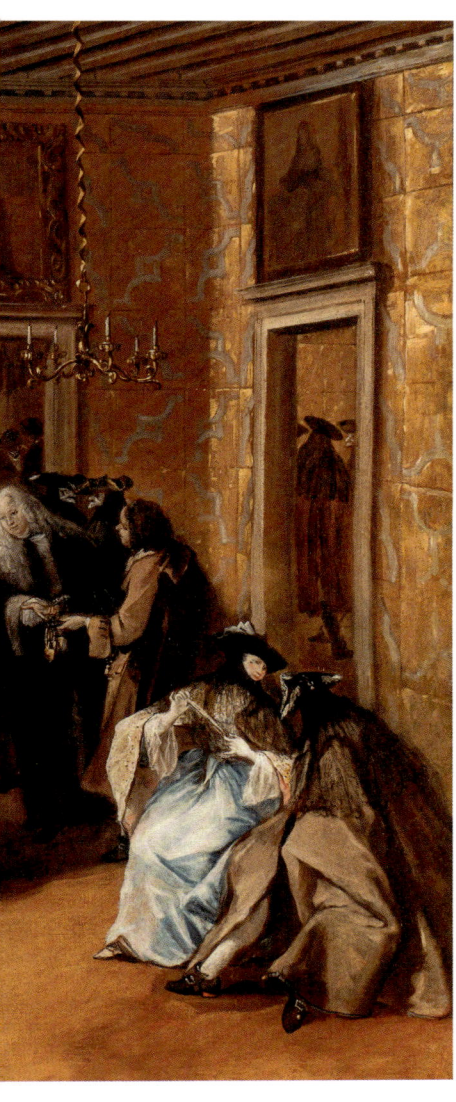

Fig. 6
Francesco Guardi, *Il Ridotto*,
1746–50. Oil on canvas,
108 × 208 cm. Ca' Rezzonico,
Museo del Settecento
Veneziano, Venice.

was far from ordinary. A clear indication that he had a far more refined
sensibility than that of a mere supporting actor can be seen in some
paintings depicting the lagoon and its islands. These are truly original
works, showing a wide panoramic view in which clear, still stretches
of water and sky prevail. They suggest a virtuoso musician tuning his
instrument for a dress rehearsal.

The first commissions for these views came from British aristocrats
on the Grand Tour: Sir Brook Bridges, John Montagu and Richard Milles,
who were all in Venice between 1758 and 1760. Many of these works
are signed, an indication that the artist must have been proud of his
achievements – or simply that he was seeking to promote himself
to those who would see the paintings in England. The course of Guardi's
artistic career becomes even more intriguing when one considers that
the success of his figurative painting, for which he may quite rightly be
numbered among the greats, was only achieved in the last years of his life,
when his very individual style found its full expression in freer and more
allusive views. Far from Canaletto's sunlit geometric certainties, he depicts
buildings corroded by the light, adopting a trembling pictorial idiom
that has been interpreted as evoking a crumbling Venice, reflecting
the Republic's political and social disintegration.

Francesco Guardi was the last to immortalize the celebrations
and ceremonies that took place in La Serenissima. However, much of his
production in this area was not associated with specific events, nor were
his compositions original. This is apparent in *Ducal Celebrations*, where
the artist has 'interpreted' earlier figurative models. His first real attempts
to capture contemporary events came very late. In 1782, when Guardi was 70,
he was presented with a great opportunity to heighten his profile: between 18
and 25 January, the Grand Duke Paul Petrovich Romanov, heir to the throne
and future emperor of Russia, was staying in Venice with his wife Sophie
Dorothea of Württemberg and he was invited to record the festivities.
A few months later, between 15 and 19 May, Pope Pius VI arrived in the
city on his way back from a difficult diplomatic mission in Vienna. In a
contract dated 21 May 1782, Guardi was asked to produce four paintings
commemorating the Pope's visit. At last, at the age of 70, the artist had
received an official commission. It might be thought that this was a
prestigious way of recognizing the last painter of *vedute*; but in fact
the contract terms were humiliating, betraying the low esteem
in which he was held in Venice.

His last commission was of a different type. It was not a public
ceremony but a private event: the wedding between Armand Jules Marie
Héracle, son of the Duc de Polignac, and Idalie Johanna von Neukirchen,
which took place on 6 September 1790 in the Villa Gradenigo at Carpenedo.
The commission does not seem to have been fulfilled: all we have are the
extraordinary preparatory drawings for the paintings. In the last years of his

life, Guardi's very individual style became even freer and more allusive: the proportions between the various elements are loosely aligned and arbitrarily altered, while the perspective structure is elastic. The architectural elements in his views are increasingly 'compressed', at last reduced to simple lines marking the separation between sky and water – it is these that occupy most of the painting's space. Figures and boats are no more than spots of colour, a rapidly executed white squiggle or a trembling dot of black. As was also true of his nephew Giandomenico Tiepolo, Guardi began to look increasingly behind the times, belonging to a culture that was now outdated and in decline, marginalized by the neoclassical taste that was now dominant. However, this disregarded and isolated position gave both artists a special viewpoint from which to focus, with detachment, on the world around them. In this isolation, which soon became existential as well as professional, these two painters created some of the masterpieces of European art.

Giandomenico, who returned from Spain in 1770, found that the cultural climate in Venice had changed profoundly. Commissions were thin on the ground and he retired to his family villa in Zianigo, where he frescoed the rooms purely for his own personal pleasure and produced a series of drawings featuring the figure of Pulcinella. Through this Commedia dell'Arte character, the artist imagined a future both tragic and comic: he juxtaposed the fatuous contemporary world with a brand new society, inhabited by an irreverent community of Pulcinella figures, their freedom and equality a homage to the maxims that were at that time coming out of revolutionary France.

In those same years, Francesco Guardi gradually modified his repertoire. He increased his production of *capricci* – paintings which combine real and imagined places, ancient and modern architecture. This delightful eighteenth-century genre could have been created especially to satisfy Guardi's imagination. Taking Canaletto's etchings as his starting point, he breathed new life into the genre, transferring ancient ruins, now without any classical references, to the shores of the lagoon. The artist also specialized in *capricci* showing views through porticos, with a dark covered walkway framed in the foreground and glimpses of landscape and imagined architecture beyond.

Alongside the familiar views of the Grand Canal and the Basin of San Marco at John Strange's request he also painted several splendid images of villas in the verdant Venetian countryside. He was drawn to neglected corners of Venice, which he illustrated in paintings such as the *Rio dei Mendicanti* and the *Punta di Santa Marta*. In these two works, Guardi widened the horizons of Venetian *vedutismo* until they dissolved into vast expanses of water and sky.

Finally, he paid more attention than other painters of *vedute* to the city's transitory aspects, such as regattas and *The Feast of Ascension in the Piazza San Marco* (cat. 5), the culmination of the celebrations for the festival of the Ascension, called *Sensa* in Venetian. Various stalls were set up in the Piazza San Marco for the occasion, in specially built temporary structures. In this case, the impressive wooden structure houses many stalls [*botteghe*], arranged on either side. True to his practice, Guardi took some liberties with the rendering of the structure and perspective in a painting that prioritizes a virtuoso execution, leaving aside any theoretical canon.

Above all, he took a curious interest in current events and unusual natural phenomena: the flight of the hot air balloon built by Francesco Pesaro, Procurator of San Marco, on 16 April 1784; the freezing of the lagoon in the winter of 1788–89; the fire in the oil warehouse at San Marcuola on 28 November 1789; and the new façade of the Teatro La Fenice. Once again, his natural inclination for unique, imaginative interpretations of the facts enabled him to capture the most original aspects of Venice, dwelling – for the first time – on material reality in a way that was inadvertently modern.

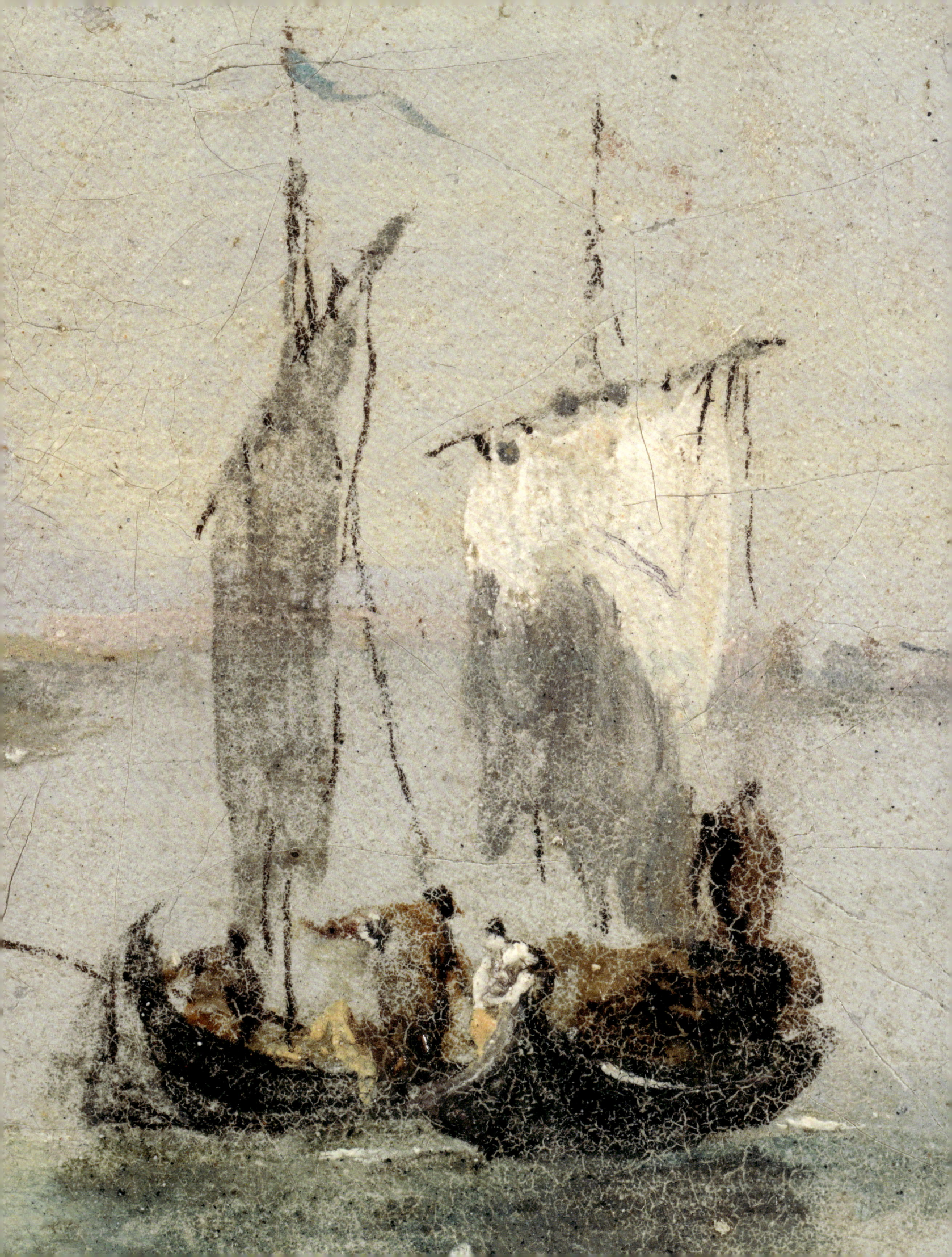

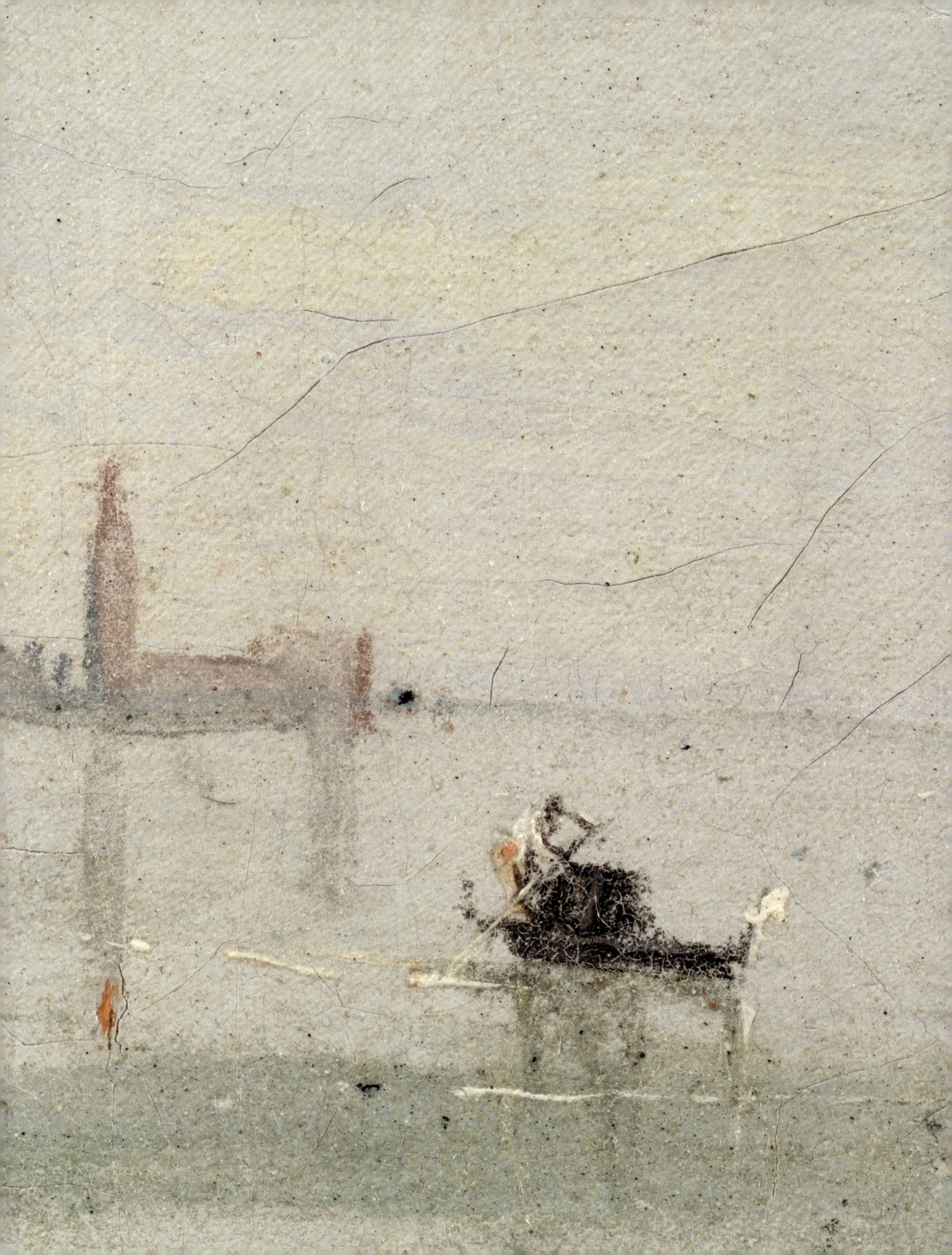

The catalogue is arranged
by the date of birth of the artists
or the motif represented.

CAT ALO GUE

Luísa Sampaio

01
GIOVANNI ANTONIO CANAL (1697–1768), KNOWN AS CANALETTO

The Piazza San Marco in Venice

Venice, c. 1723–24

Oil on canvas

141.5 × 204.5 cm

PROVENANCE Prince of Liechtenstein Collection, Vienna; Thyssen-Bornemisza Collection, Lugano, 1956; on loan at the Museo Thyssen-Bornemisza, Madrid, 1992; Museo Thyssen-Bornemisza, Madrid, 1993. Museo Nacional Thyssen-Bornemisza, Madrid, inv. 75 (1956.1)

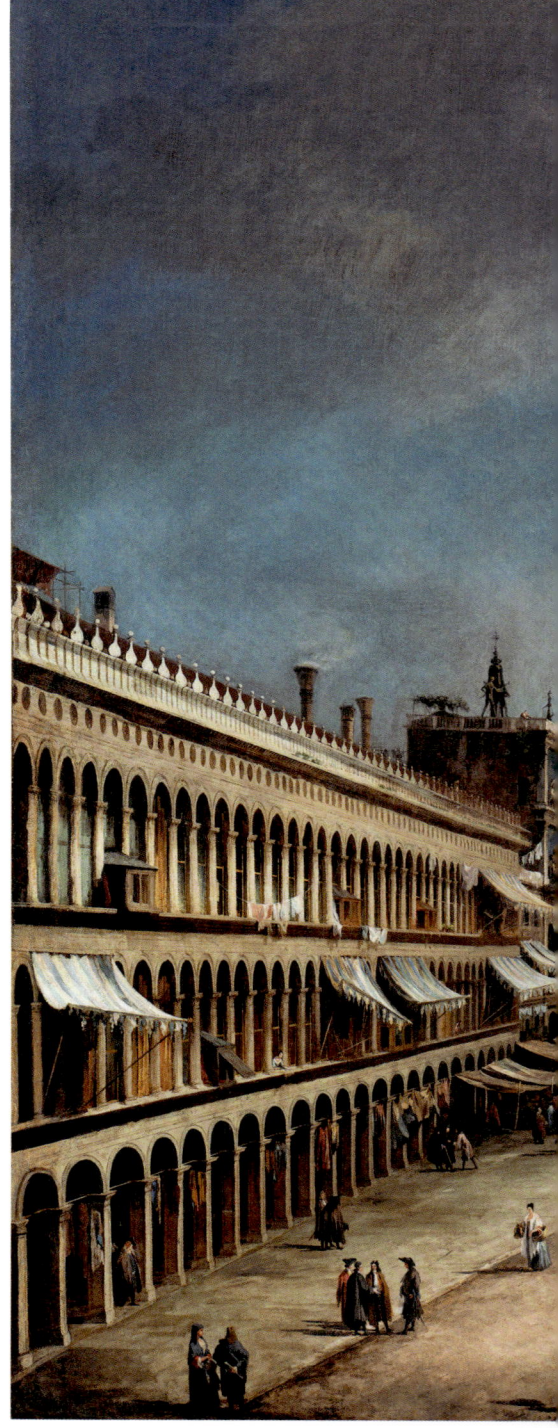

The genre known as *veduta*, or view painting, was introduced to the city of Venice by painters from northern Europe, such as Caspar van Wittel (1653–1736), with Luca Carlevarijs (1663–1730) producing the first topographical landscapes by an Italian artist.

This youthful work by Venice's most famous *vedute* painter of the 1700s, Giovanni Antonio Canal, known as Canaletto, shows the timeless image of Piazza San Marco seen from an elevated viewpoint at the old Church of San Geminiano, which was destroyed during the Napoleonic occupation. The perspective converges on Basilica of San Marco and the verticality of the Campanile, whose impressive 98.6-metre-high tower rises in the background of the composition, partially concealing the Doge's Palace. Two converging diagonals are defined by the meticulous design of the procurator buildings, with the Procuratie Vecchie bathed in light and the Procuratie Nuove in shadow. The atmospheric effect created by the configuration of the clouds, rising in a cross-sectional movement over the buildings, emphasises the sense of depth.

The painstaking realism that characterised Canaletto's work has allowed a reliable date for the painting to be established, since the Piazza San Marco paving is depicted at a time when it was being replaced, in around 1723-24. Designed by the architect Andrea Tirali (1660–1737), the area was undergoing work next to the procurator buildings at the time of the painting. The central geometric decoration, unfinished here,

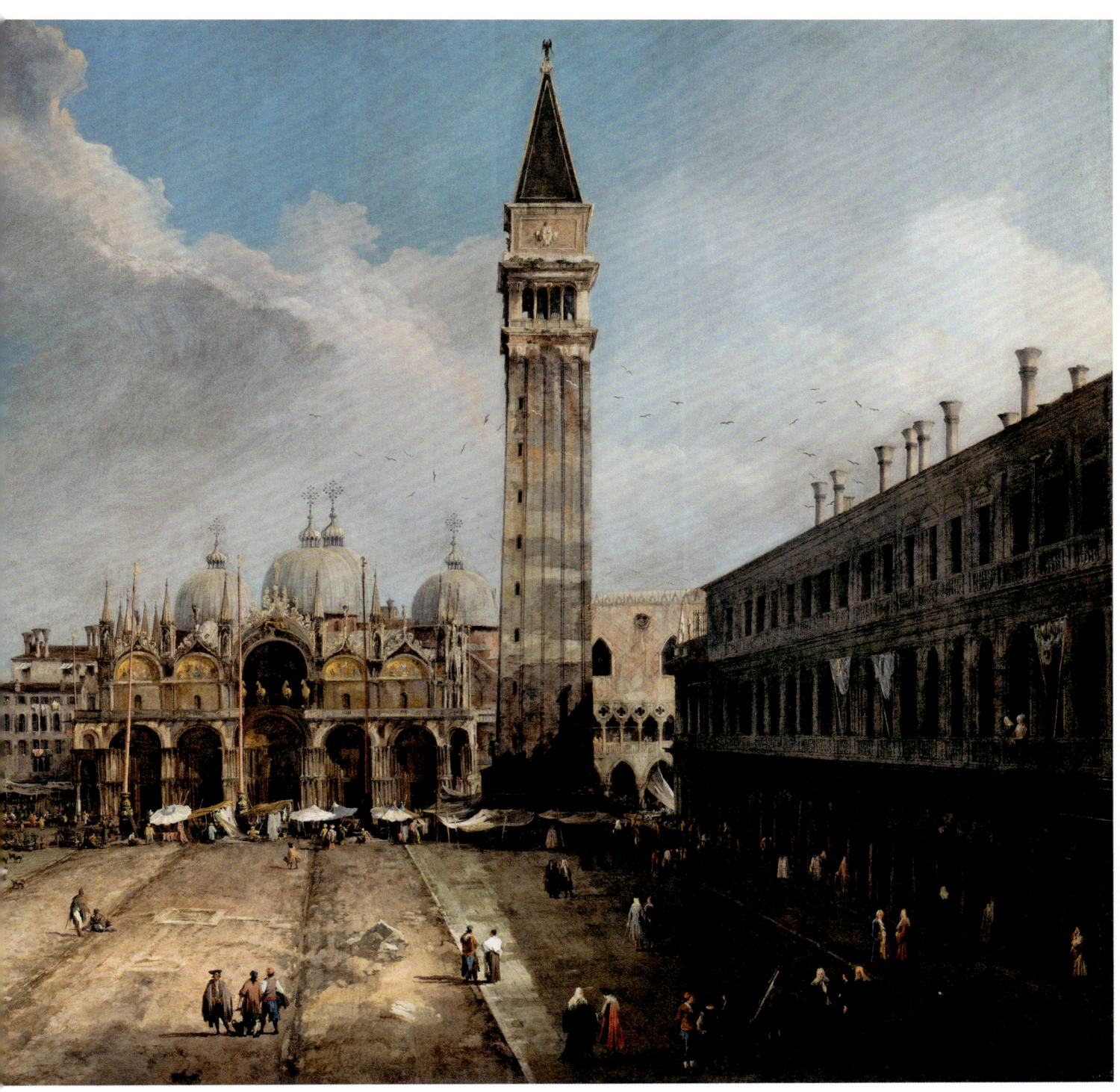

appears later in a painting by Canaletto from the 1730s that belongs to the Duke of Bedford's Collection (Woburn Abbey, Bedfordshire).

This painting is part of a set of four compositions produced by the artist, which includes *The Grand Canal from San Vio, Venice* (cat. 2).

BIBLIOGRAPHY

BOROBIA 2009, p. 494; CONSTABLE 1989, vol. II, pp. 187–88, no. 1; HEINEMANN *et al.* 1969, vol. 1, pp. 55–56, no. 50; KOWALCZYK 2012, pp. 84–85, no. 10; *VENICE* 2010, p. 75, no. 10.

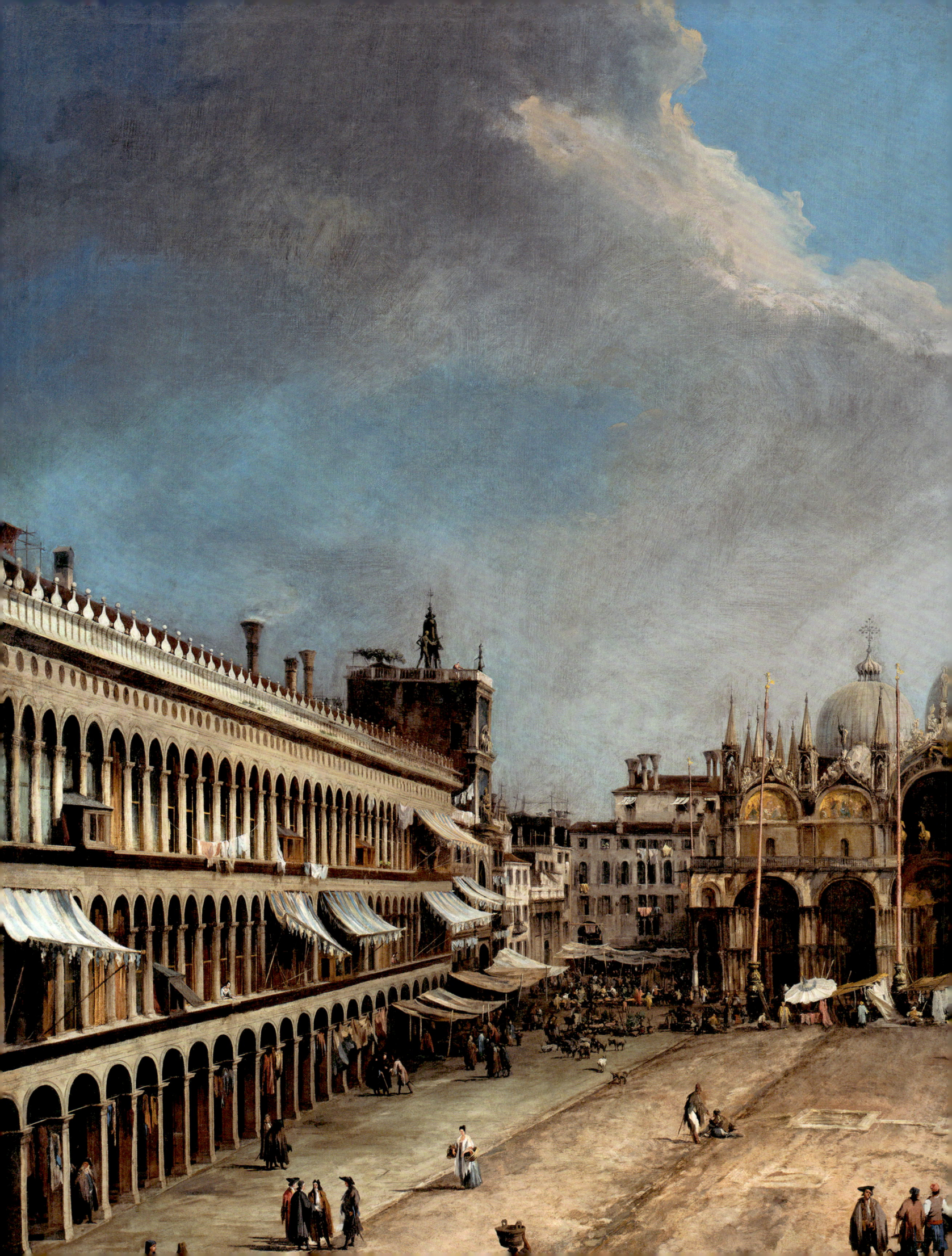

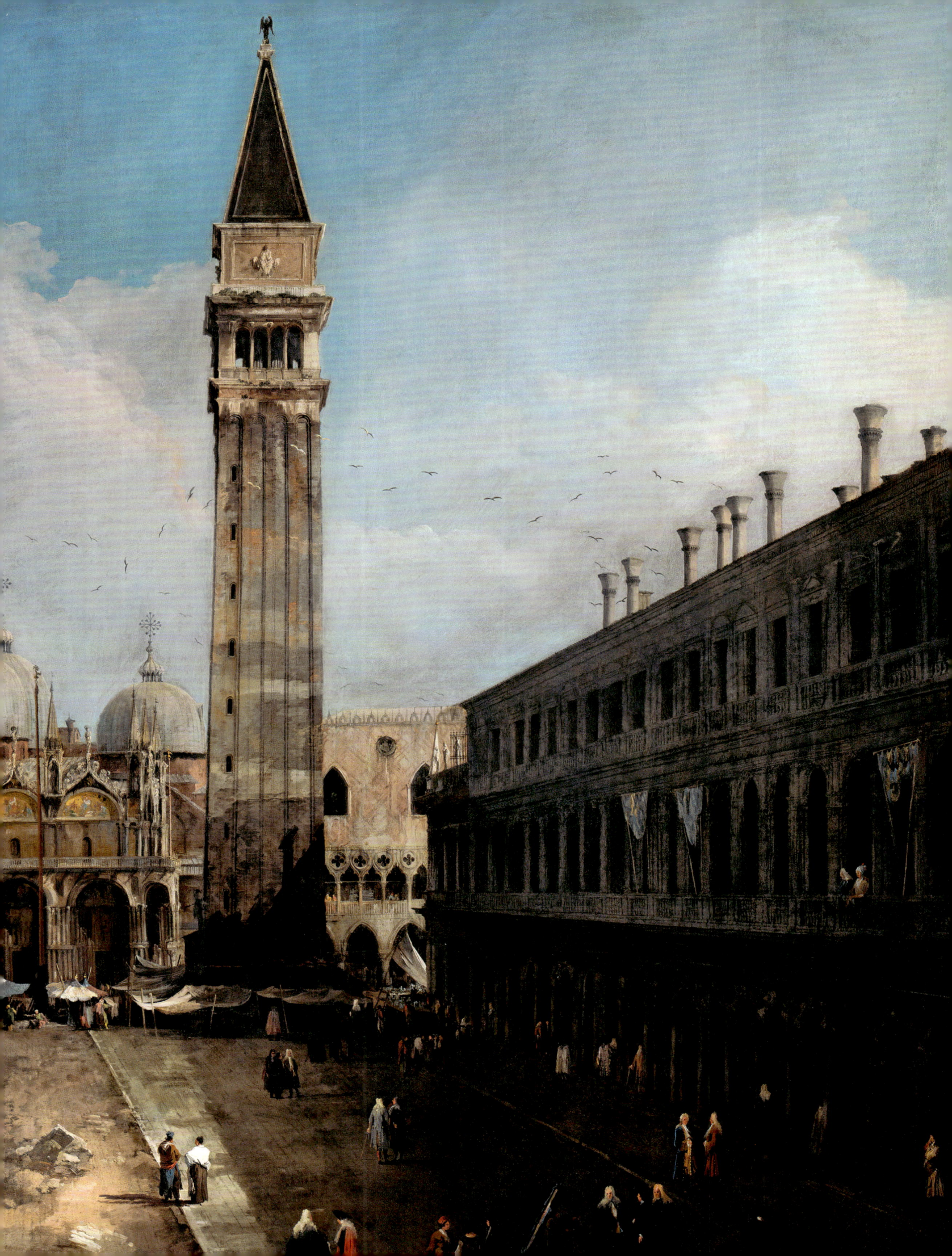

02
GIOVANNI ANTONIO CANAL (1697–1768), KNOWN AS CANALETTO

The Grand Canal from San Vio, Venice

Venice, c. 1723–24
Oil on canvas
140.5 × 204.5 cm

<u>PROVENANCE</u> Prince of Liechtenstein Collection, Vienna; Thyssen-Bornemisza Collection, Lugano, 1958; on loan at the Museo Thyssen-Bornemisza, Madrid, 1992; Museo Thyssen-Bornemisza, Madrid, 1993. Museo Nacional Thyssen-Bornemisza, Madrid, inv. 76 (1958.8)

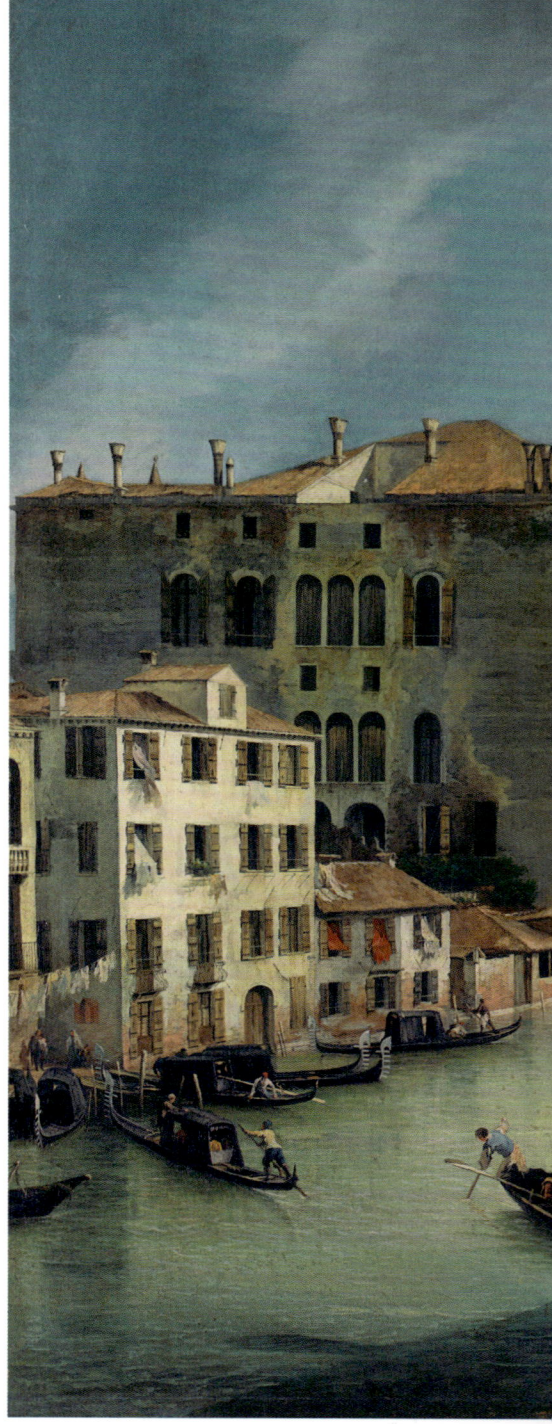

As is the case with *The Piazza San Marco in Venice* (cat. 1), this painting is part of a series of four works from the collection of the Prince of Liechtenstein (Vienna). The other canvases in the series, *View of Rio dei Mendicanti* and *View of the Grand Canal from Palazzo Balbi towards the Rialto*, are currently housed in the Ca' Rezzonico Museum in Venice.

The viewpoint for this work is the Church of San Vio, next to the San Vio River in Dorsoduro, with the bank of the Grand Canal seen at the vanishing point of the composition. On the right-hand side of the piece is the Palazzo Barbarigo, a Renaissance building constructed in the sixteenth century, in which a female figure can be seen at the window. On the side of the building, facing the Campo de San Vio, appears the outline of a large ship. In the foreground, Canaletto depicts the daily life of the local population, with the dome of Santa Maria della Salute visible in the background on the right. On the opposite side is the Renaissance façade with the three-arched portico of Palazzo Corner della Ca' Grande, designed by the architect and sculptor Jacopo Sansovino (1484–1570).

The work retains the atmospheric qualities present in the other views in the series, and the contrast between the greenish tones of the canal water and the blue of the sky, to which the clouds impart a dynamic movement, is particularly efective. The use of canals as a setting (the painter was trained by his father, Bernardo Canal,

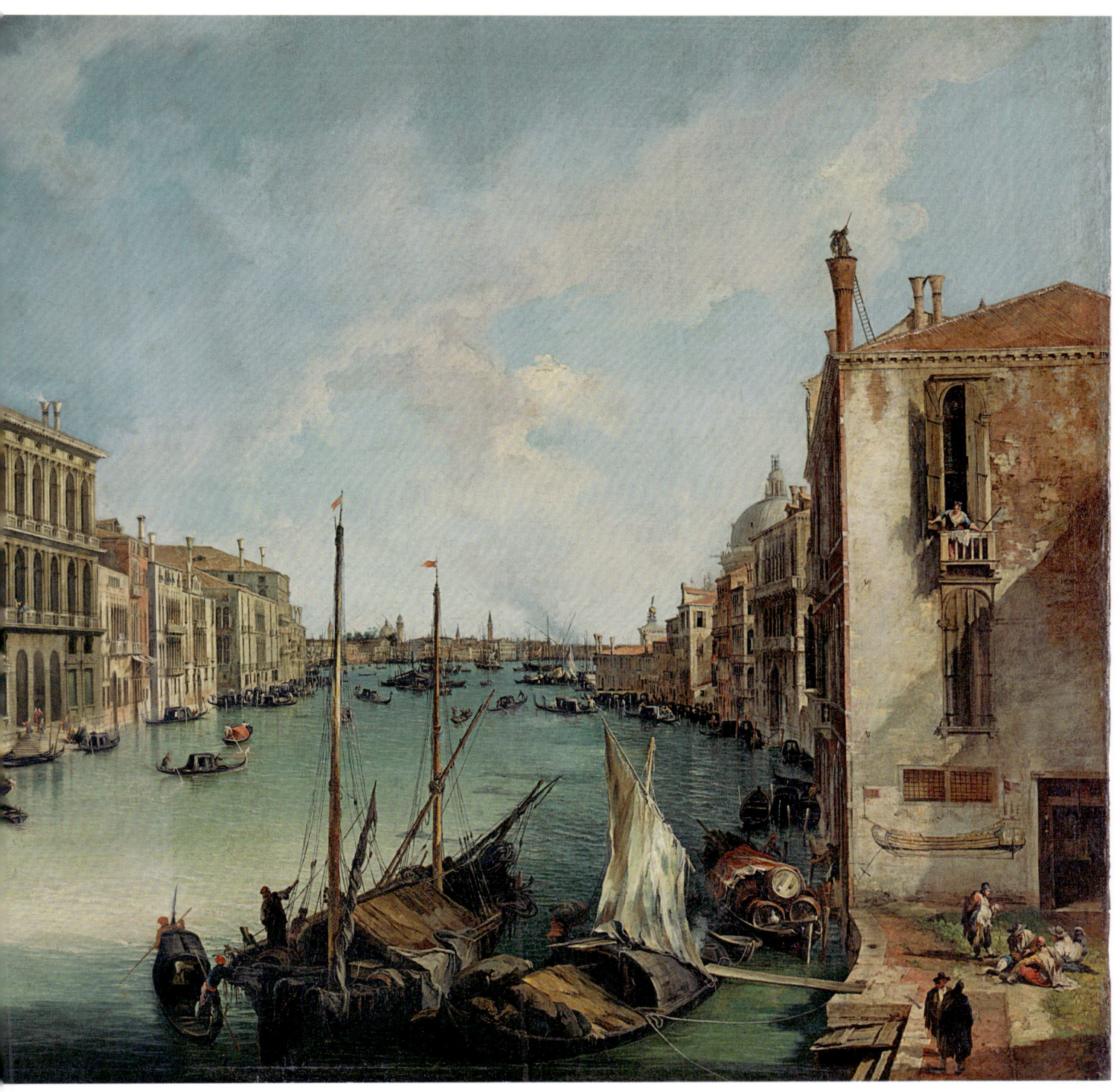

a theatre set designer) is of course a favourite theme
of Canaletto's, as illustrated by two other works
in this set from the early 1720s, which add lesser-known
aspects of the city in large format to the repertoire of
Venice's most famous buildings that cemented its fame.

BIBLIOGRAPHY

BOROBIA 2009, p. 495; CONSTABLE 1989, vol. II, p. 274, no. 182.

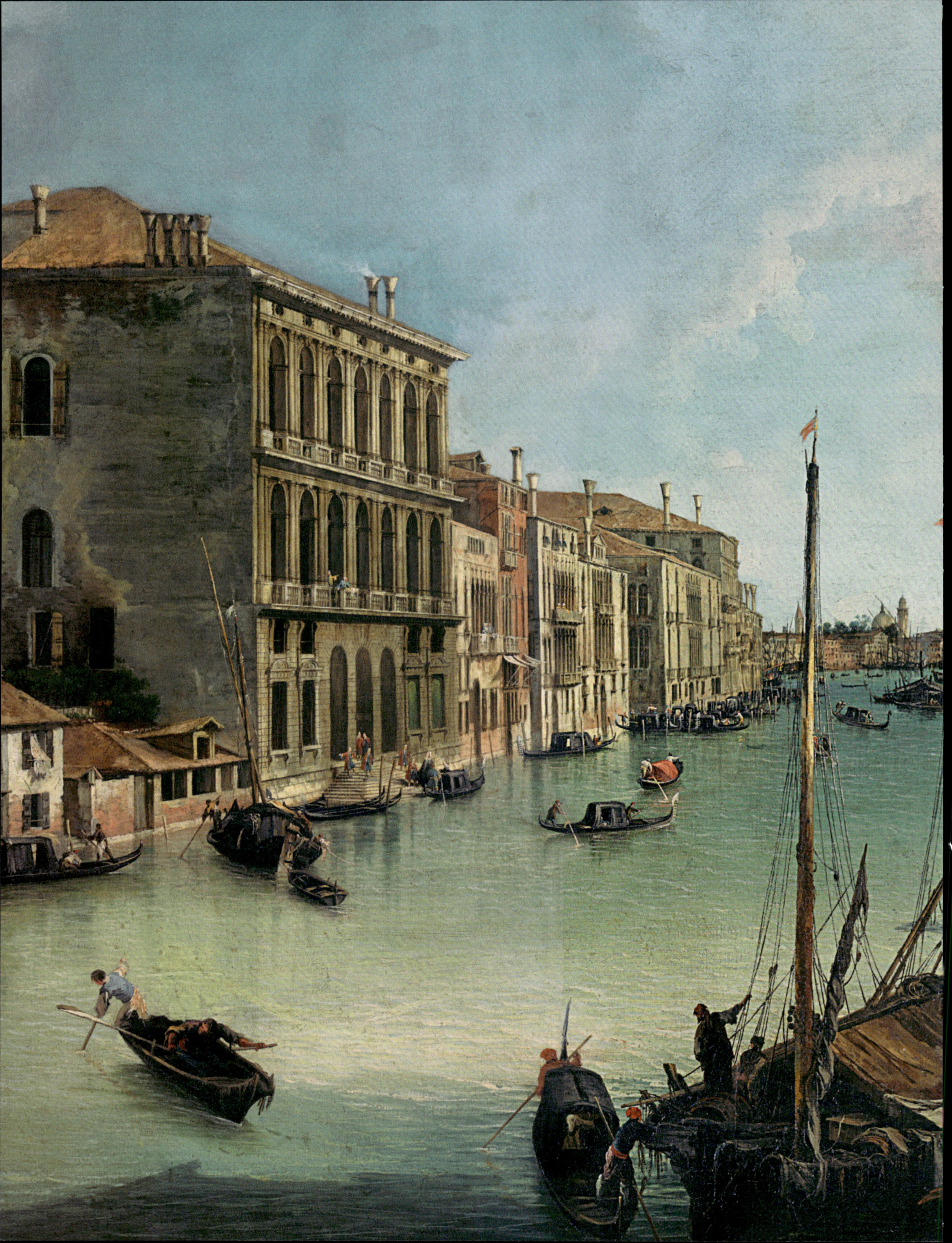

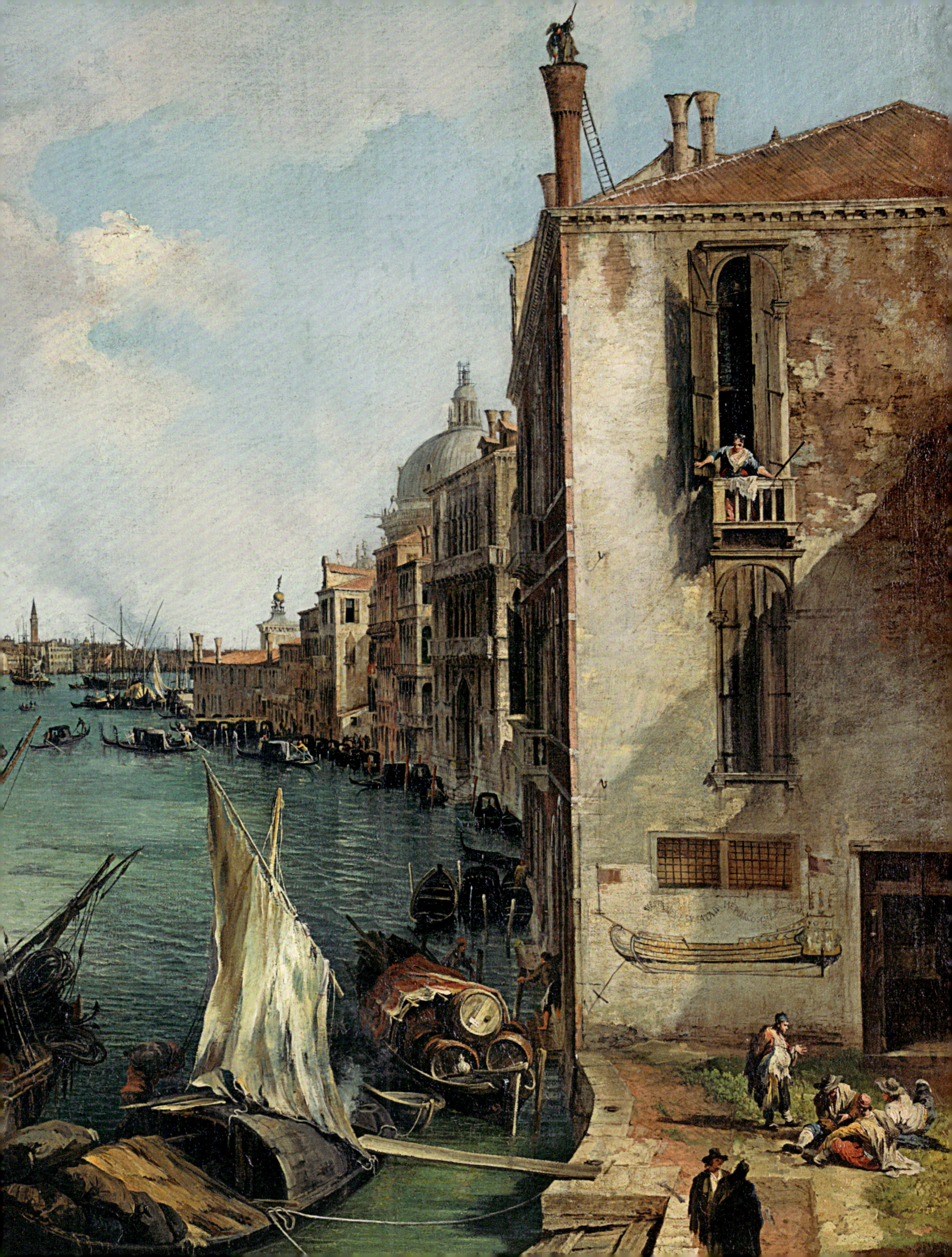

03
GIOVANNI ANTONIO CANAL (1697–1768), KNOWN AS CANALETTO

The Bucintoro

Venice, c. 1745–50

Oil on canvas

57 × 93 cm

<u>PROVENANCE</u> Henry Reveley of Bryn y Gwyn(?) Collection, Wales; Hugh John Reveley Collection, 1876; Mrs A. L. Snapper Collection, London, Sotheby's sale, London, 14 June 1961, lot 52; Agnew's, London; Thyssen-Bornemisza Collection, Lugano, 1962; on loan at the Museo Thyssen-Bornemisza, Madrid, 1992; Museo Thyssen-Bornemisza, Madrid, 1993. Thyssen-Bornemisza Collection, long-term loan to the Museu Nacional d'Art de Catalunya, Barcelona, inv. MNAC 212851-000

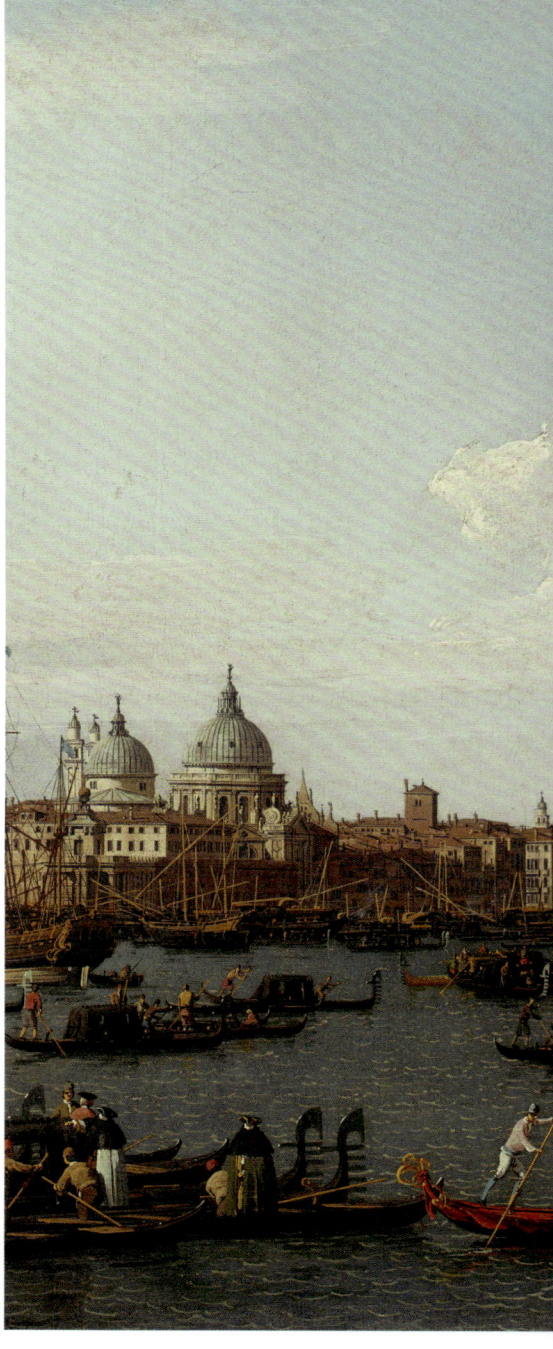

The canvas depicts the *Bucintoro* ceremonial galley moored in front of the Piazzetta, having returned to the Piazza San Marco with the Doge on board. An iconic symbol of the Serenissima, decorated in red and gold, this splendid vessel carried local officials, distinguished guests, ambassadors and the papal nuncio on Ascension Day as they gathered to celebrate Venice's symbolic marriage to the Sea. The boat was heading for the Lido, to Church of San Nicolò, where the Patriarch of Saint Peter's would be waiting for the Doge to bless the ceremonial ring and cast it into the sea as an allusion to the city's naval power over the Adriatic. Once Mass was over, the guests would gather for an immense banquet in the Doge's Palace.

The vessel depicted by Canaletto in this painting was a popular theme among the most renowned Venetian painters of the eighteenth century, such as Francesco Guardi (cat. 8). Operated by Arsenal workers and commanded by three admirals, it was destroyed in 1798 by Napoleonic troops and dismantled in 1824. This *Bucintoro*, the last to be built in the Arsenal shipyards, was decorated by the sculptor Antonio Corradini (1688–1752), who placed a Lion of Venice and an allegory of Justice on the prow.

Canaletto addresses the theme by constructing a panoramic view of the city, allowing the Campanile, the Doge's Palace, the Marciana Library and the Zecca to be seen, with the silhouette of Santa Maria della

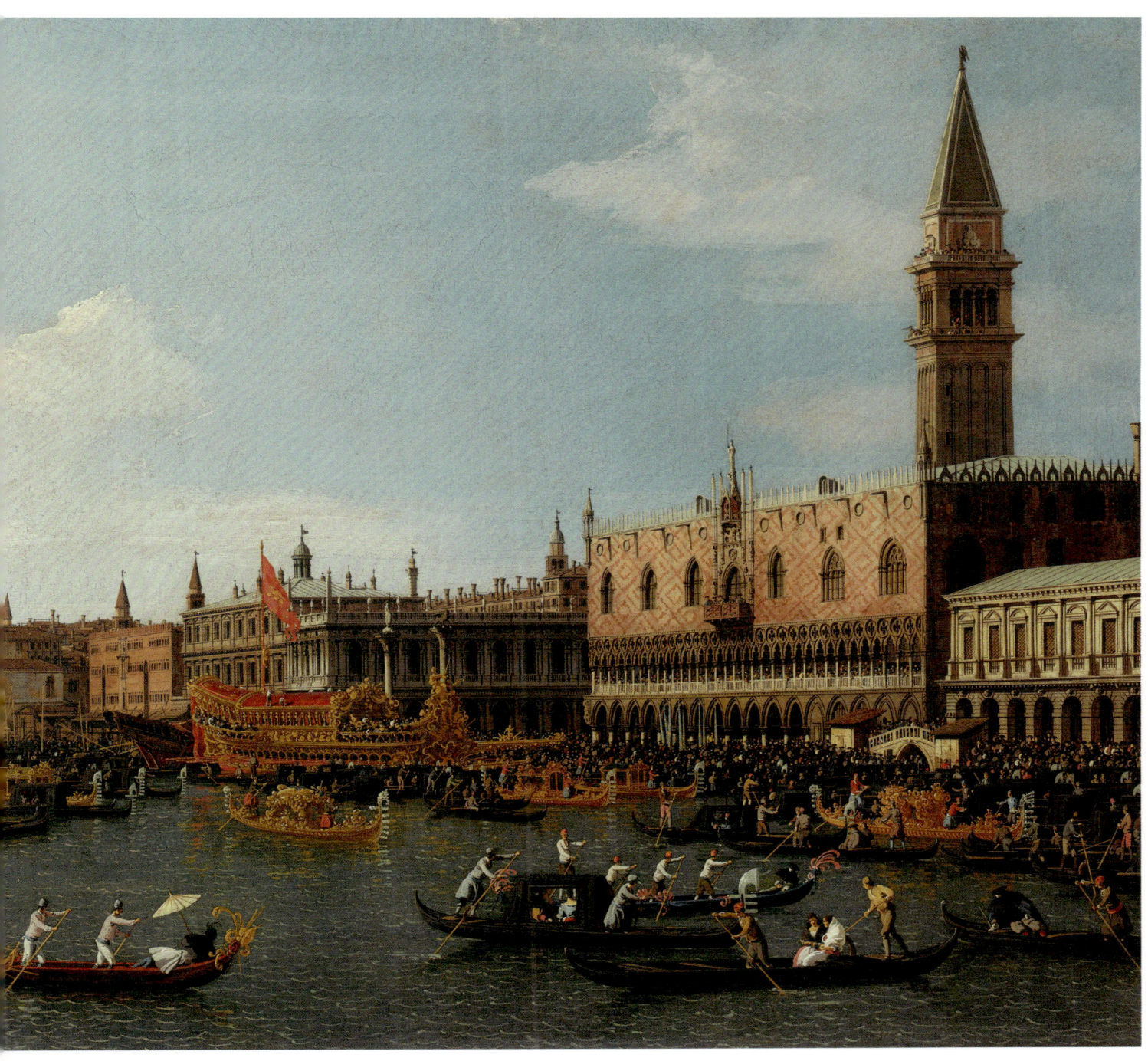

Salute at the edge of the field of vision. The painting, meticulously rendered and imbued with the city's radiant ambience, has been associated with a similar *veduta* housed at Woburn Abbey (Bedfordshire), with certain changes to the details. Extremely popular with the clientèle of the time, the motif gave rise to a dozen known versions.

BIBLIOGRAPHY

BOROBIA 2009, pp. 495–96; CONSTABLE 1989, vol. II, p. 361, no. 340 (aa); HEINEMANN *et al.* 1969, vol. I, p. 59, no. 52; *VENICE* 2010, pp. 91, 183, no. 24.

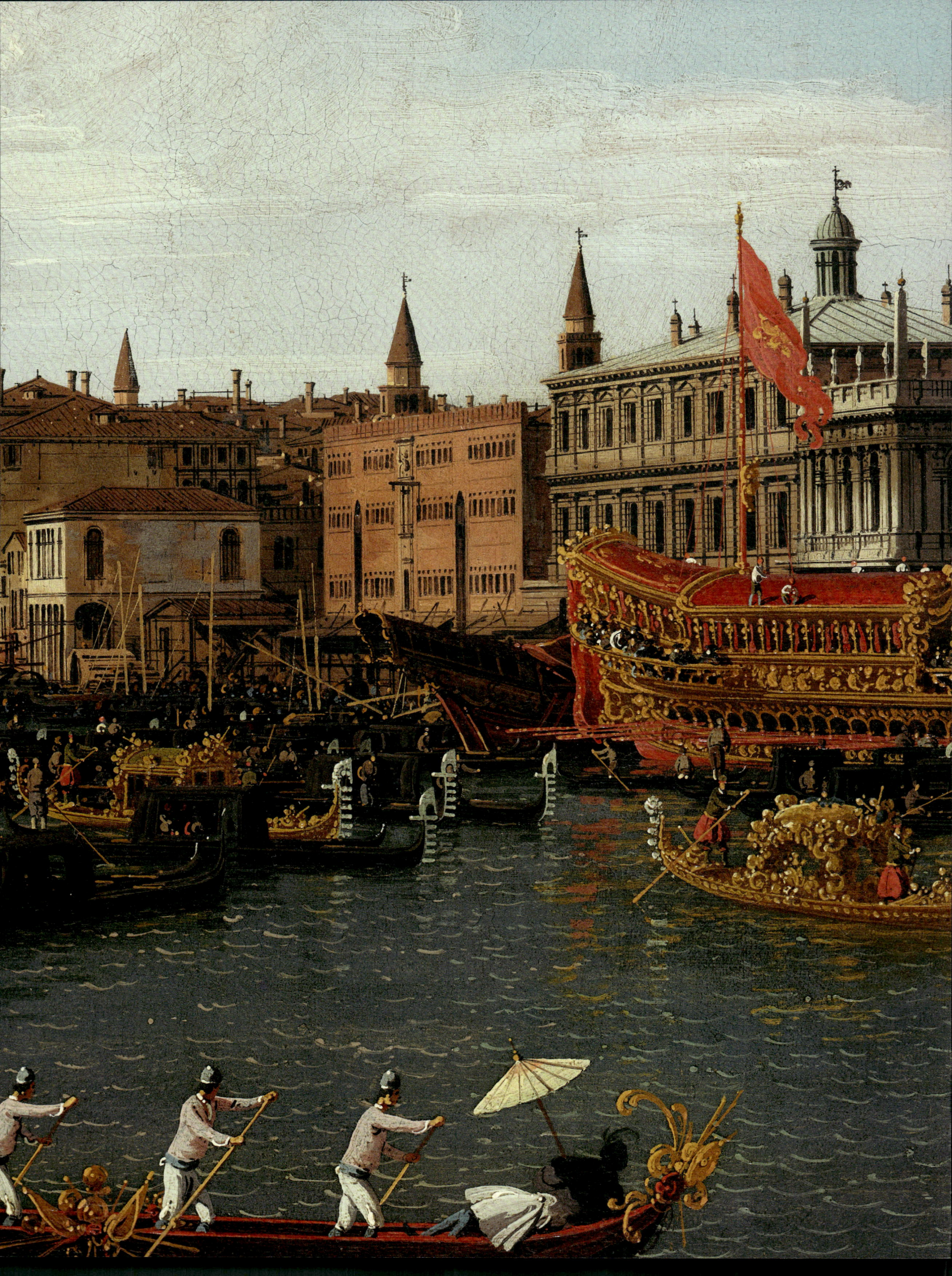

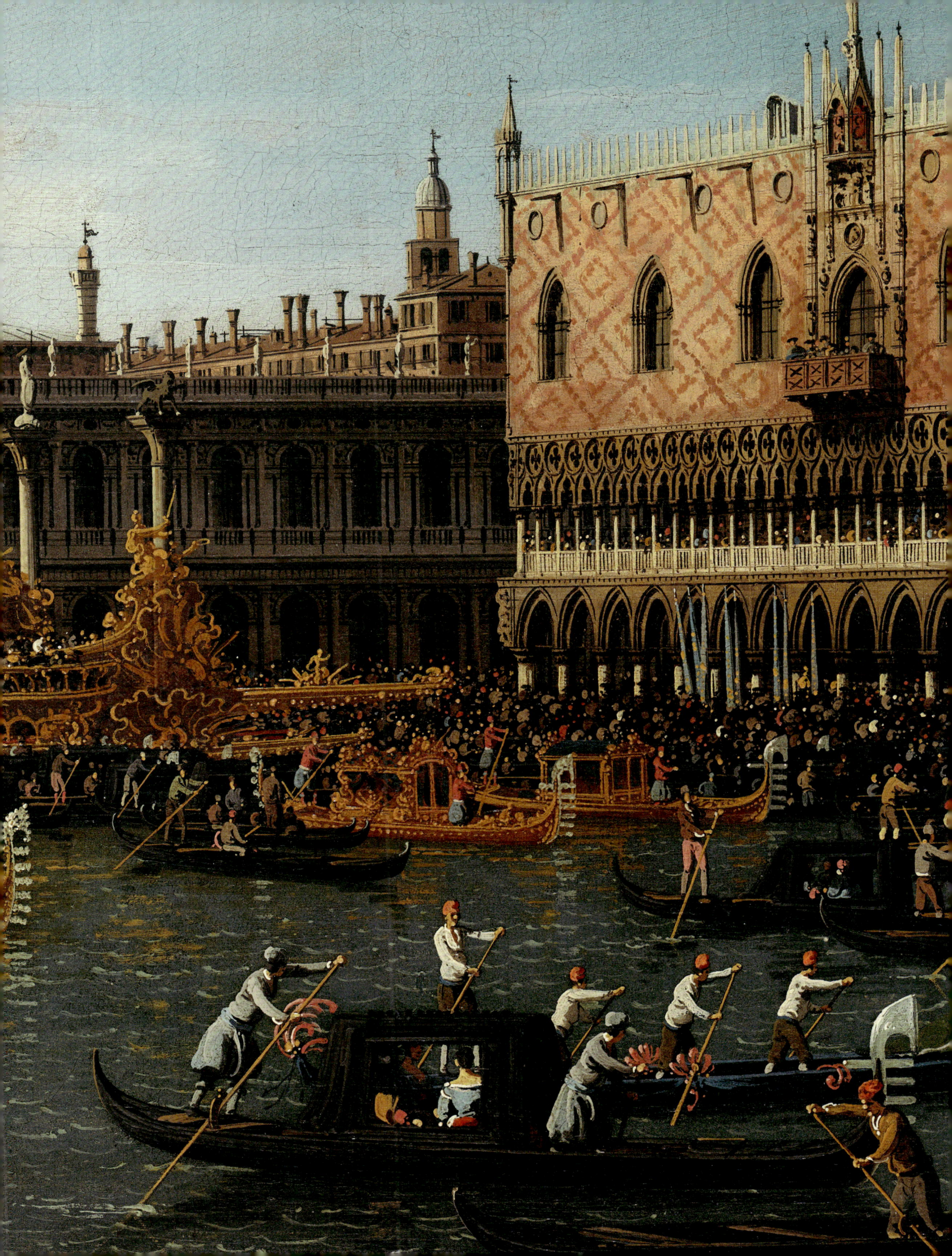

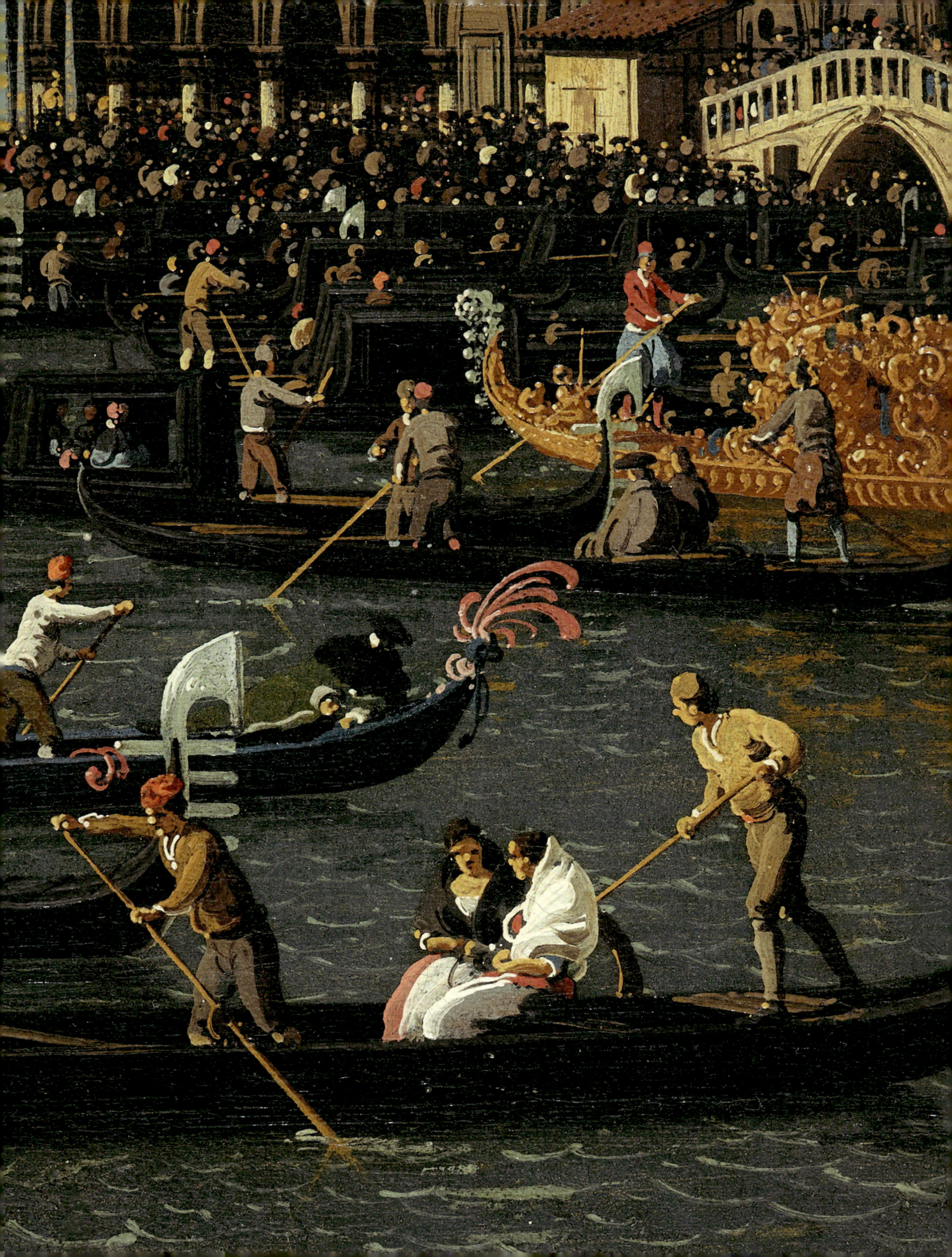

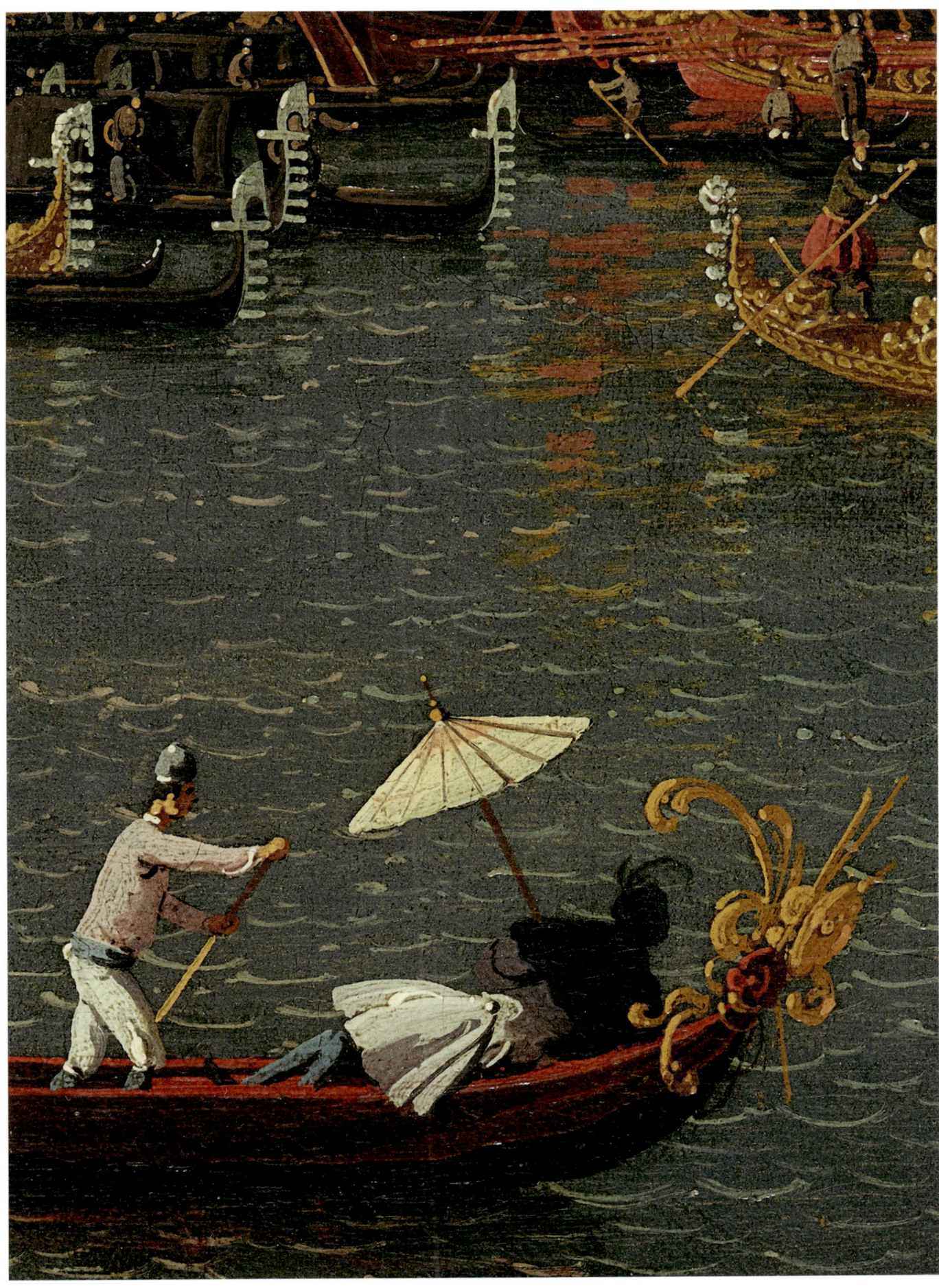

04
MICHELE MARIESCHI
(1710–1743)

The Grand Canal with Santa Maria della Salute

Venice, c. 1738–40

Oil on canvas

83.5 × 121 cm

<u>PROVENANCE</u> Dimitri Tziracopoulo Collection, Athens; Thyssen-Bornemisza Collection, Lugano, 1970; on loan at the Museo Thyssen-Bornemisza, Madrid, 1992; Museo Thyssen-Bornemisza, Madrid, 1993. Museo Nacional Thyssen-Bornemisza, Madrid, inv. 281 (1970.9)

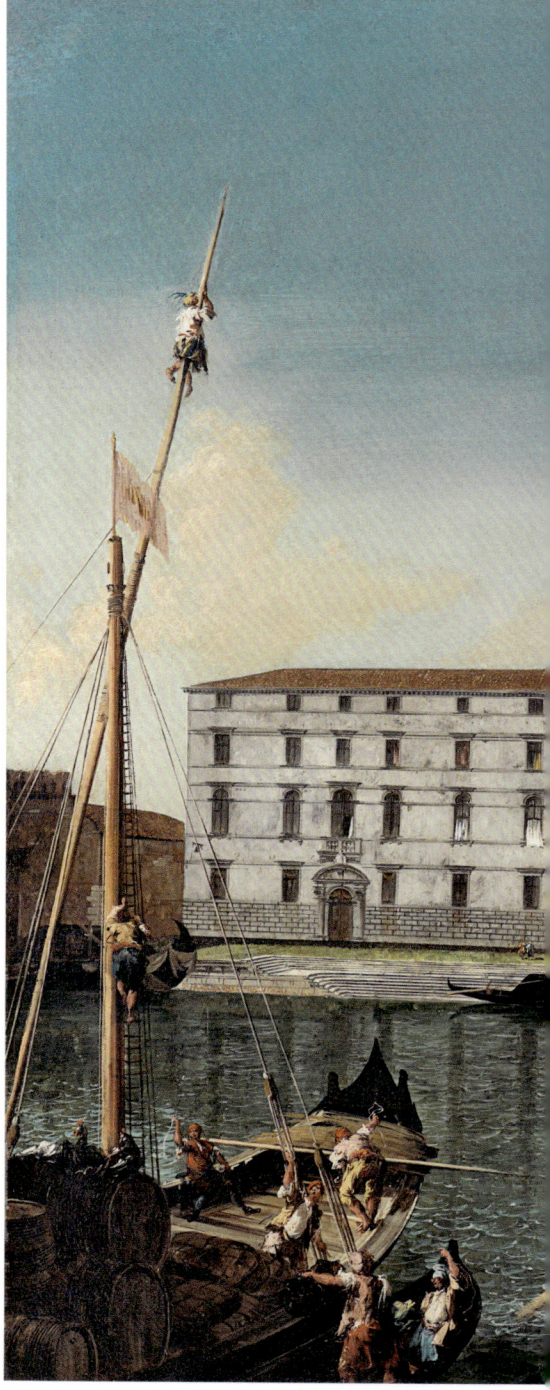

Undoubtedly influenced by Luca Carlevarijs (1663–1730), the pioneer of the Venetian *veduta*, a genre that became widespread in the eighteenth century, Michele Marieschi, who died at a very young age, devoted himself to creating *capricci* and views of Venice, having been encouraged by the success of his contemporary Canaletto.

Here the artist depicts the Basilica of Santa Maria della Salute on the Punta della Dogana, set on the opposite bank of the entrance to the Grand Canal. The piece is enlivened by the foreground, with gondolas and other boats in motion, one of which, on the right, displays a banner with an image of the Virgin. The Baroque basilica, built by the Venetian Senate in 1630 during a plague epidemic, was completed in 1687, long after the death of its architect, Baldassere Longhena (1598–1682). Drawing on the models of Antonio Palladio (1508–1580), Longhena designed the building in an octagonal shape to evoke the crown of the Virgin, to whom the basilica was consecrated.

The frontal depiction of the Salute, in a luminous palette, with its impressive dome and façade facing the viewer, emphasises the grandeur of the building, in which the portal decorated by four Corinthian columns also stands out. This perspective also includes the Seminario Patriarcale on the left and the Abbazia di San Gregorio on the right. There is another frontal version of this group of buildings at the Art Institute of Chicago. Marieschi's viewpoint was revisited by

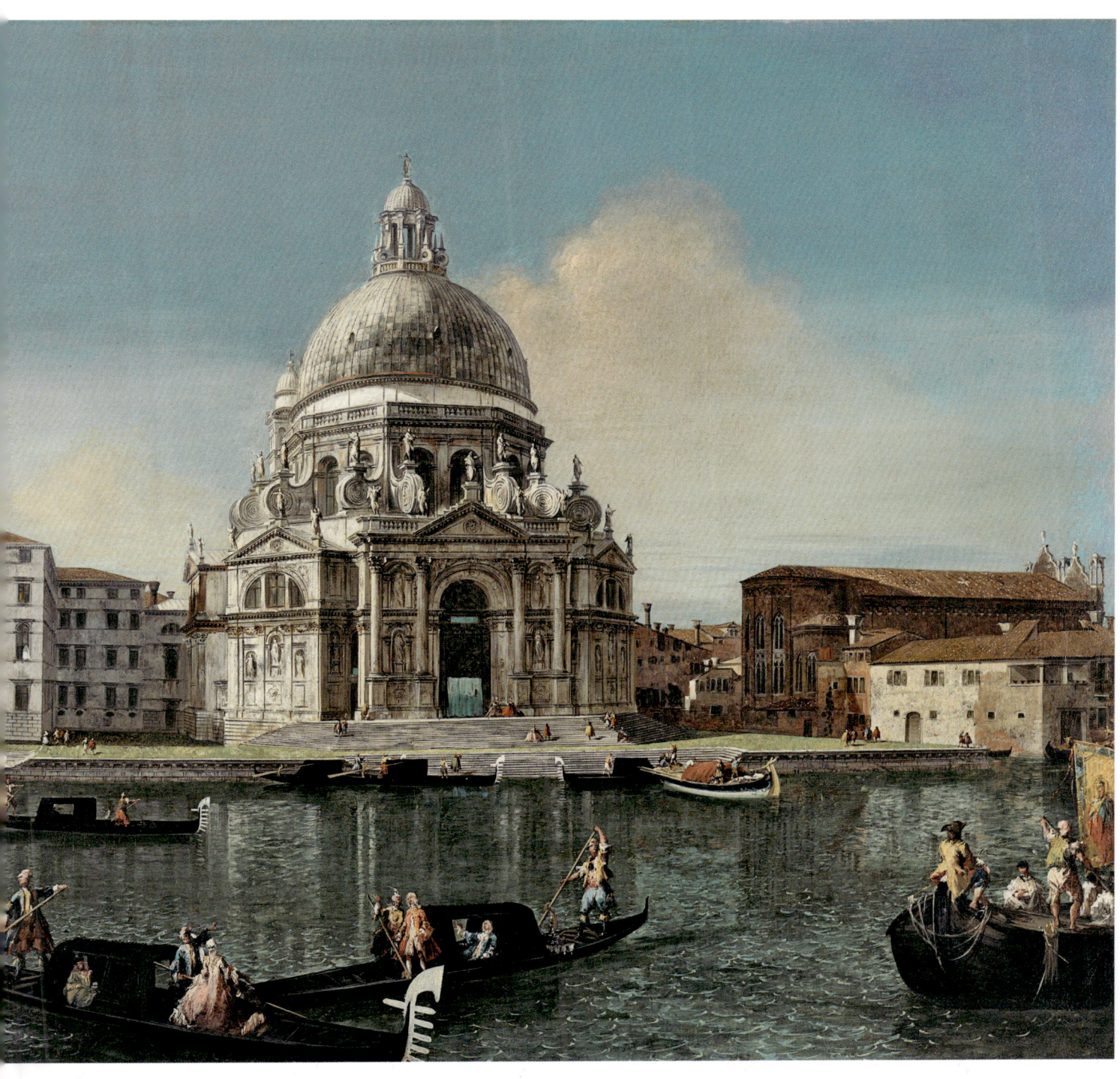

Francesco Guardi (1712–1793) in two paintings, which are now in the Academy of Fine Arts Vienna and the Baltimore Museum of Art.

BIBLIOGRAPHY

BOROBIA 2009, p. 409.

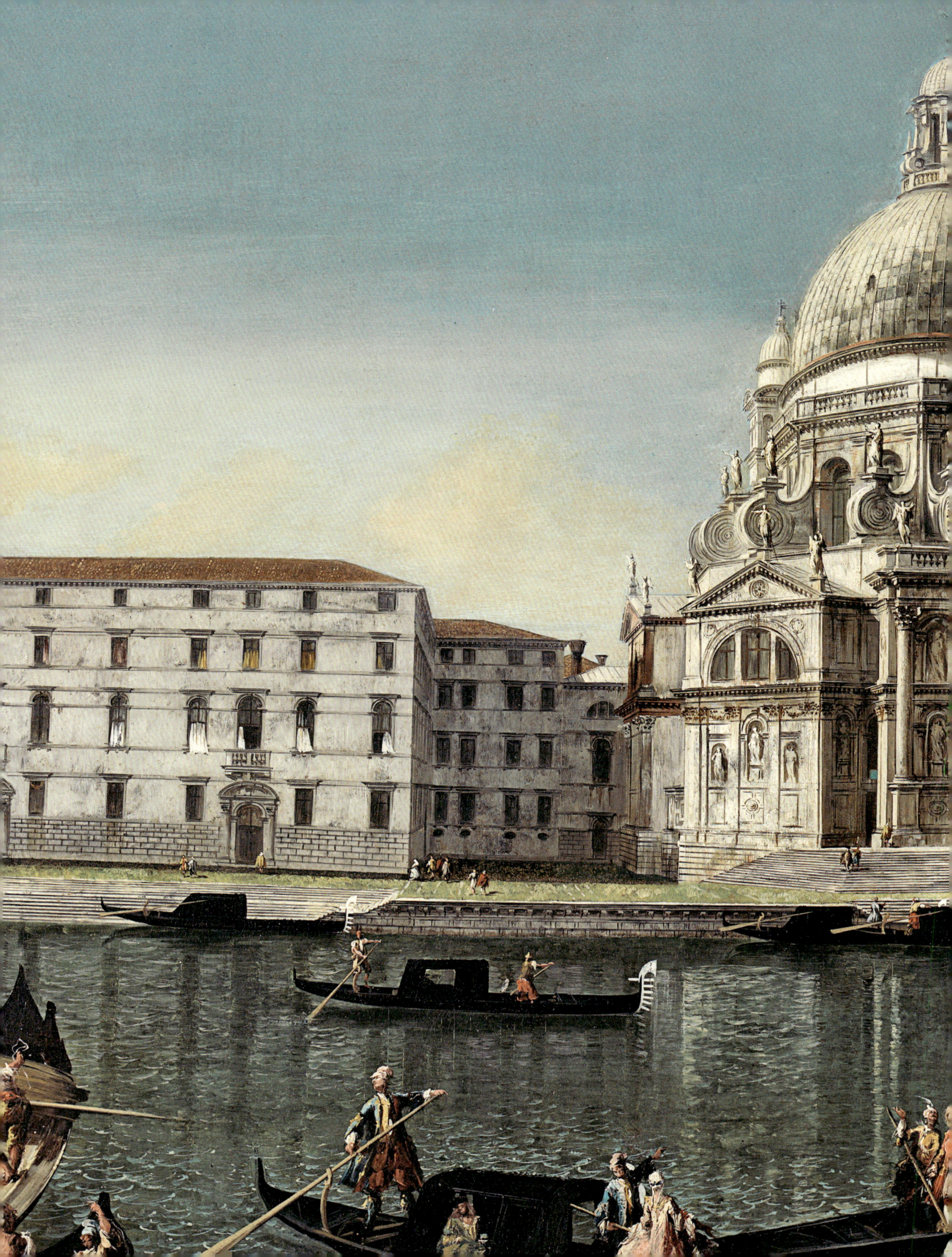

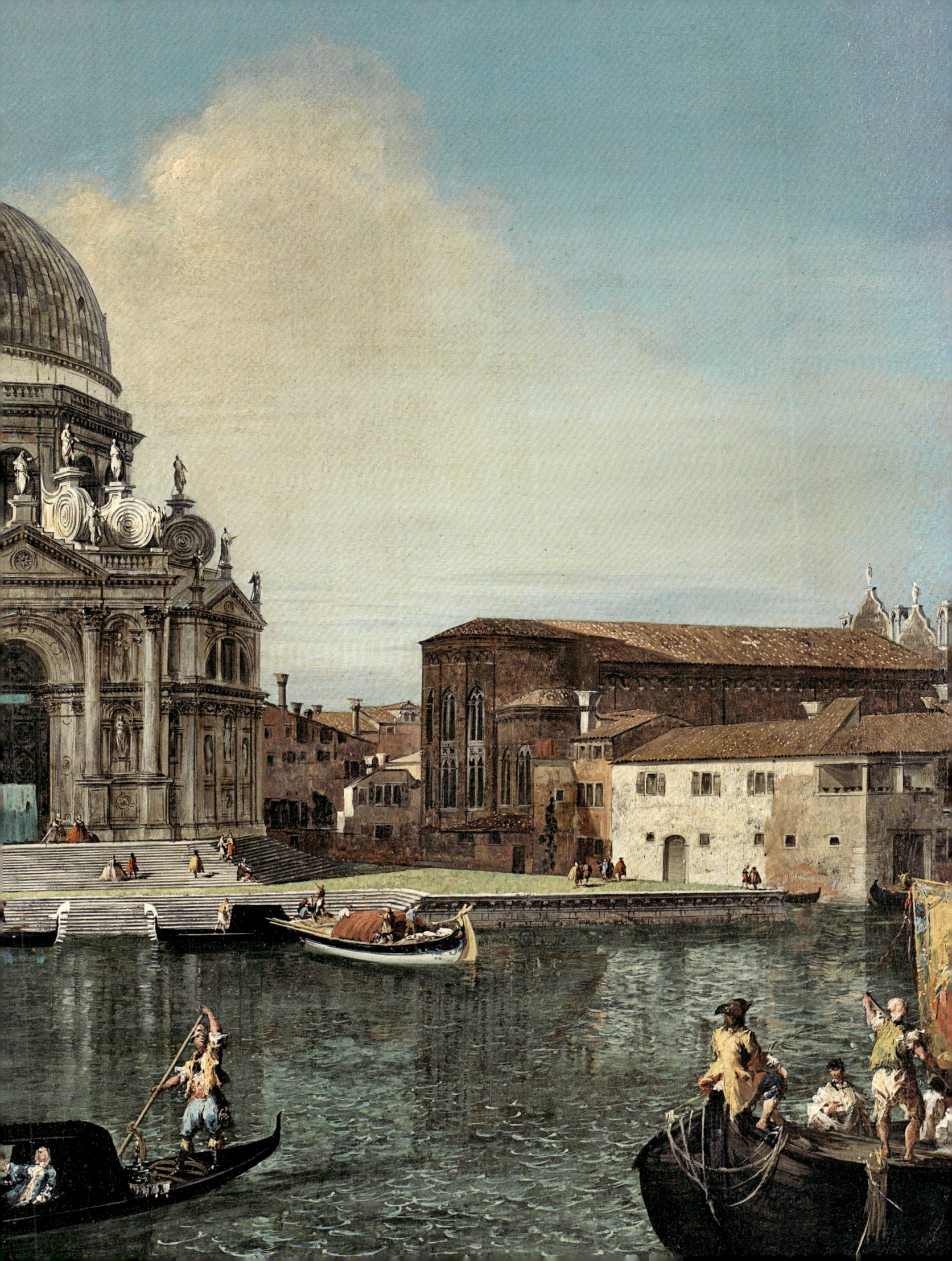

05
FRANCESCO GUARDI
(1712–1793)

The Feast of Ascension in the Piazza San Marco

Venice, c. 1775

Oil on canvas

61 × 91 cm

PROVENANCE Robert Dundas Haldane-Duncan,
1st Earl of Camperdown; Adam Haldane-Duncan,
2nd Earl of Camperdown, 1859–67; Lady Julia Duncan,
Baroness Abercromby, 1867–1915; Georgina Wilhemina
Mercer-Henderson, Countess of Buckinghamshire.
Acquired through Christie's, London, on 8 March 1919.
Calouste Gulbenkian Museum, inv. 390

This *veduta*, the name given to depictions of urban views, shows the Piazza San Marco decorated for the most sumptuous festival in Venice, the Festa della Sensa. On Ascension Day, Venice held a ceremony celebrating the symbolic marriage between Venice and the Sea, an evocation of the ancient victory that had given the city naval control of the Adriatic. The Doge, the city's chief magistrate, would head for the Church of San Nicolò al Lido on board the *Bucintoro*, and once there would cast a ring into the water.

In addition to the Basilica, the painting shows the Campanile, the Clock Tower, the Doge's Palace and, partially covered by temporary arcades, the buildings of the procurators of Saint Mark's, high-ranking officials of the Republic of Venice. In these arcades were the *orefici* and *strazzaruoli* stands, which mainly sold textiles and jewellery. The temporary structure depicted in the painting was used in 1775 and 1776, thus pre-dating the project conceived by the architect Bernardino Maccaruzzi (1728–1798) for the site. This elliptical wooden structure, which could be easily dismantled, was also documented by Guardi in a painting housed in the Kunsthistorisches Museum in Vienna.

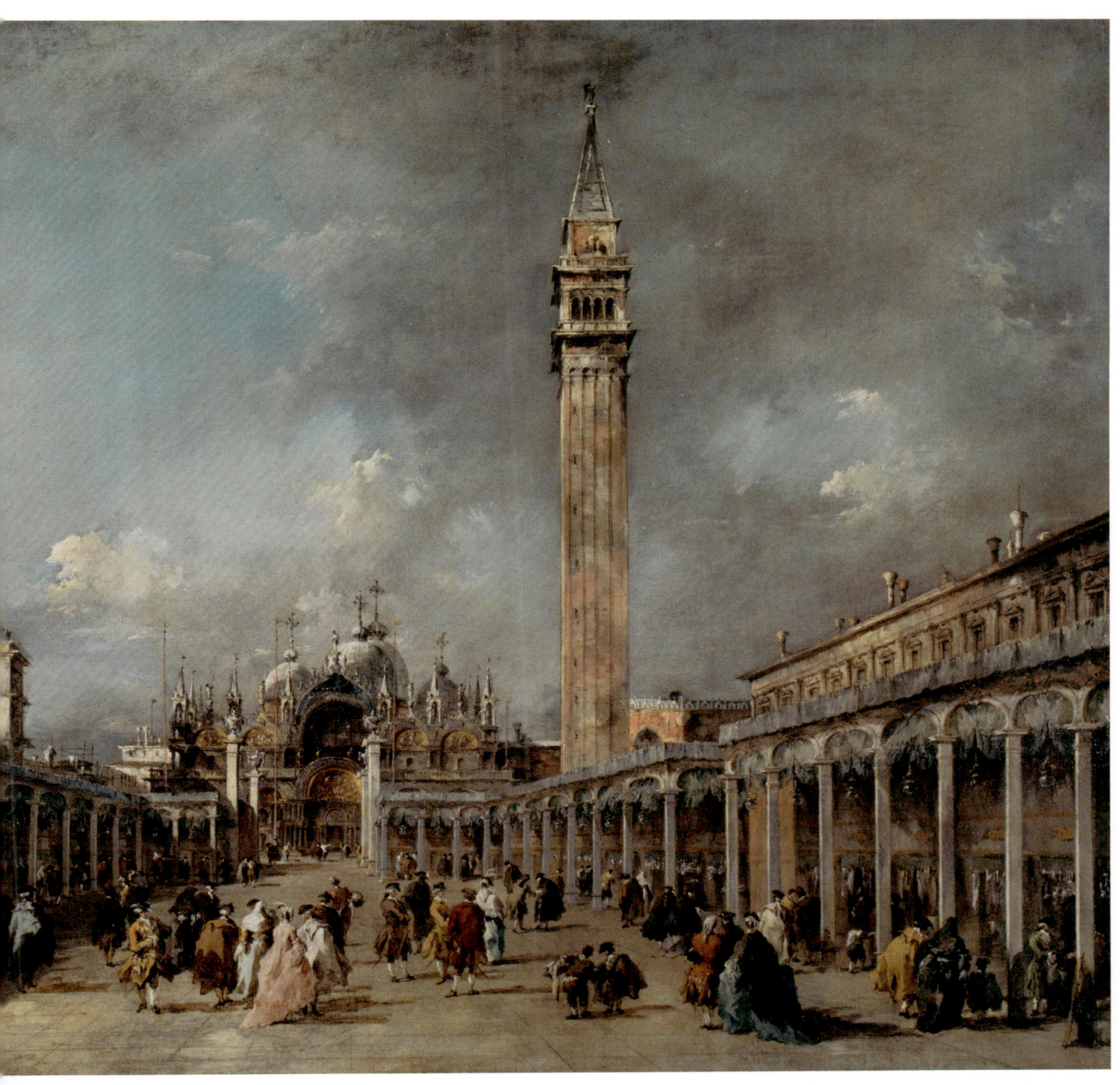

The foreground of the composition, animated by elegant silhouettes, magnificently distributed in the festive setting, adds movement and lively commotion to the ensemble. In this remarkably atmospheric canvas, the artist places the viewer before a fantastic, theatrical space, full of counterpoints, giving an impression of vividness and immediacy.

BIBLIOGRAPHY

CANALETTO 2019, p. 365, no. VII.03; LOISEL 2018, pp. 226–27, no. 160; MORASSI 1993, pp. 187–89, 361–62, no. 277; MURARO 1993, pp. 32–33, no. 8; PALLUCCHINI 1965, no. 3; *VENICE* 2010, pp. 142, 188, no. 59.

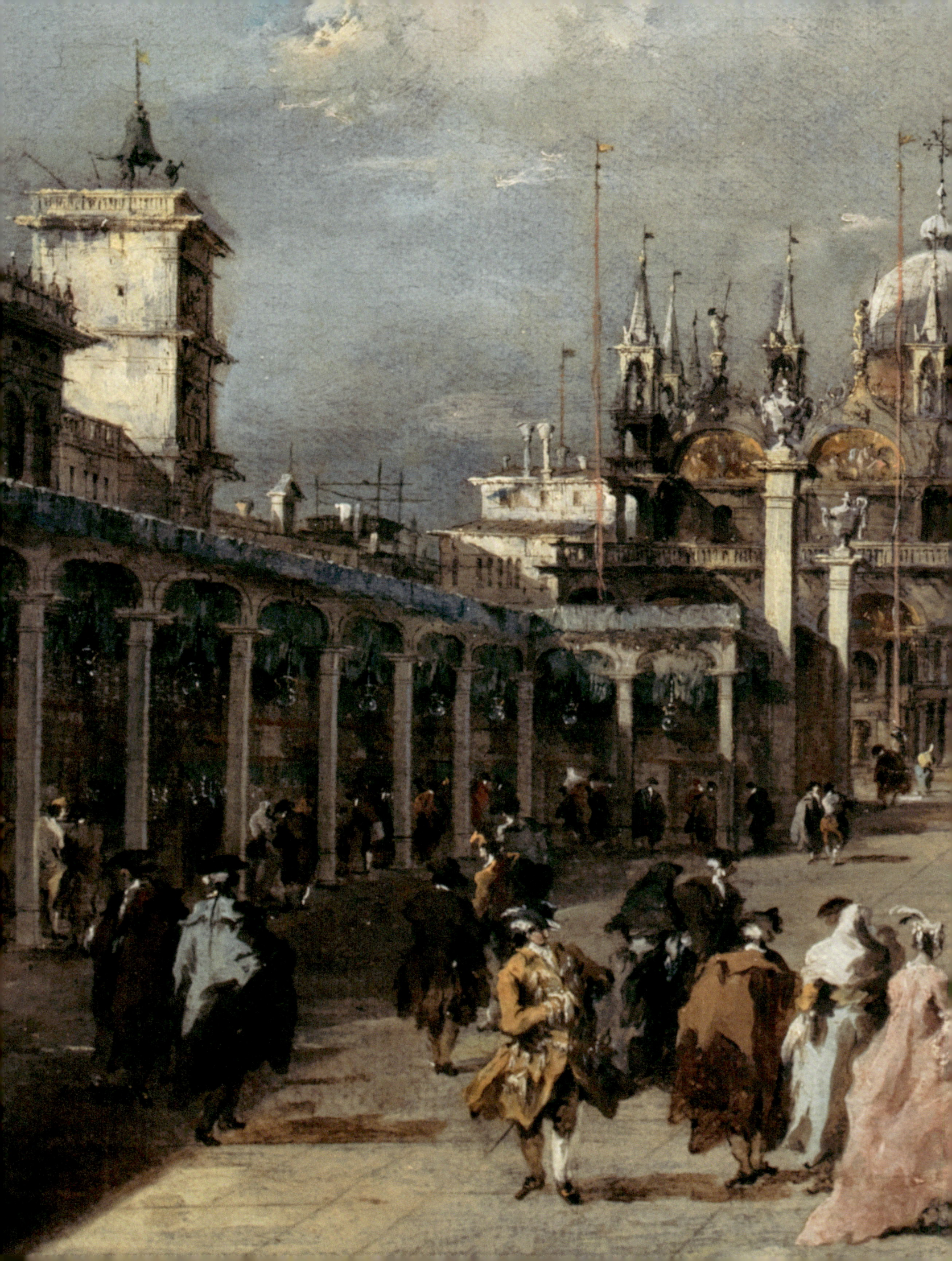

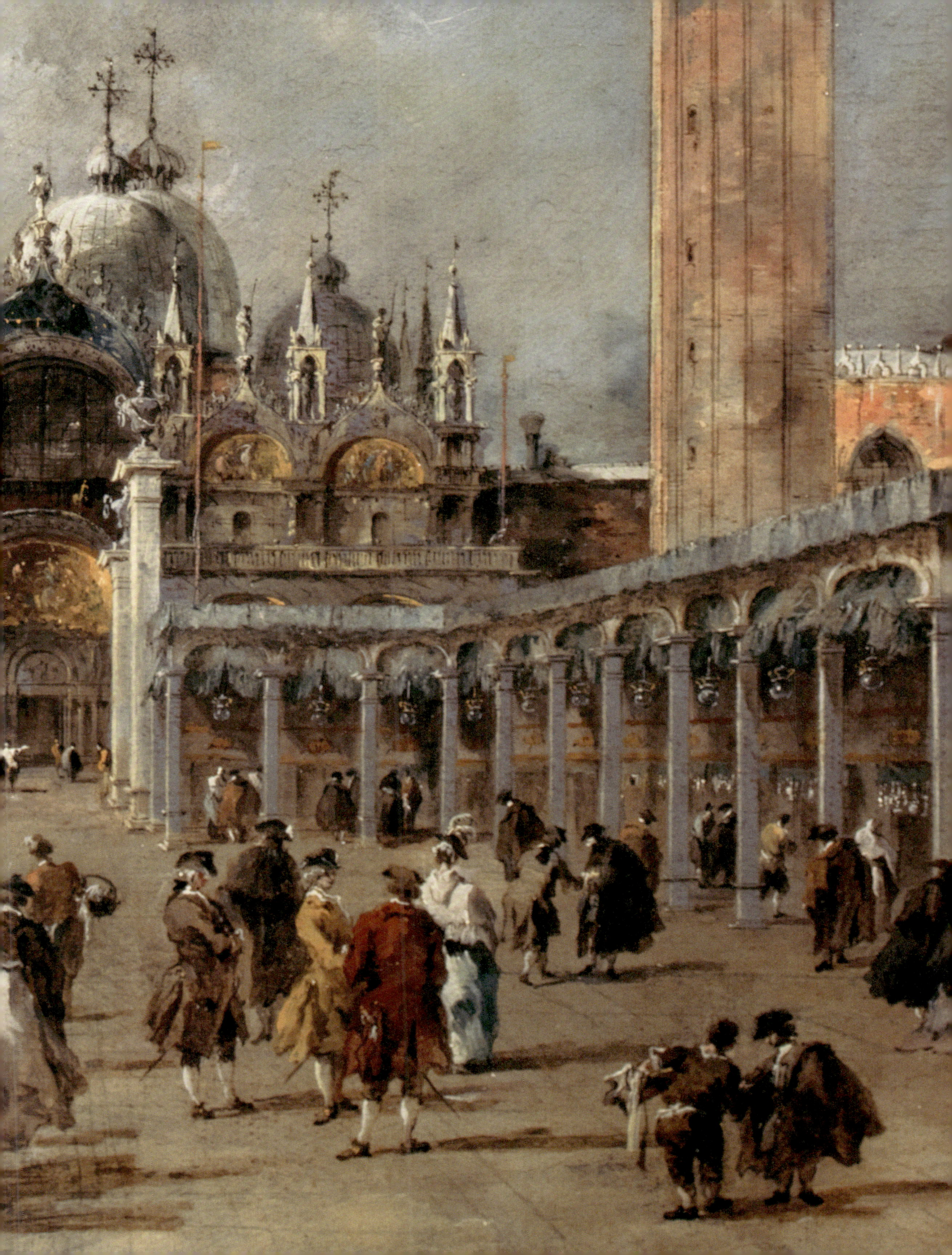

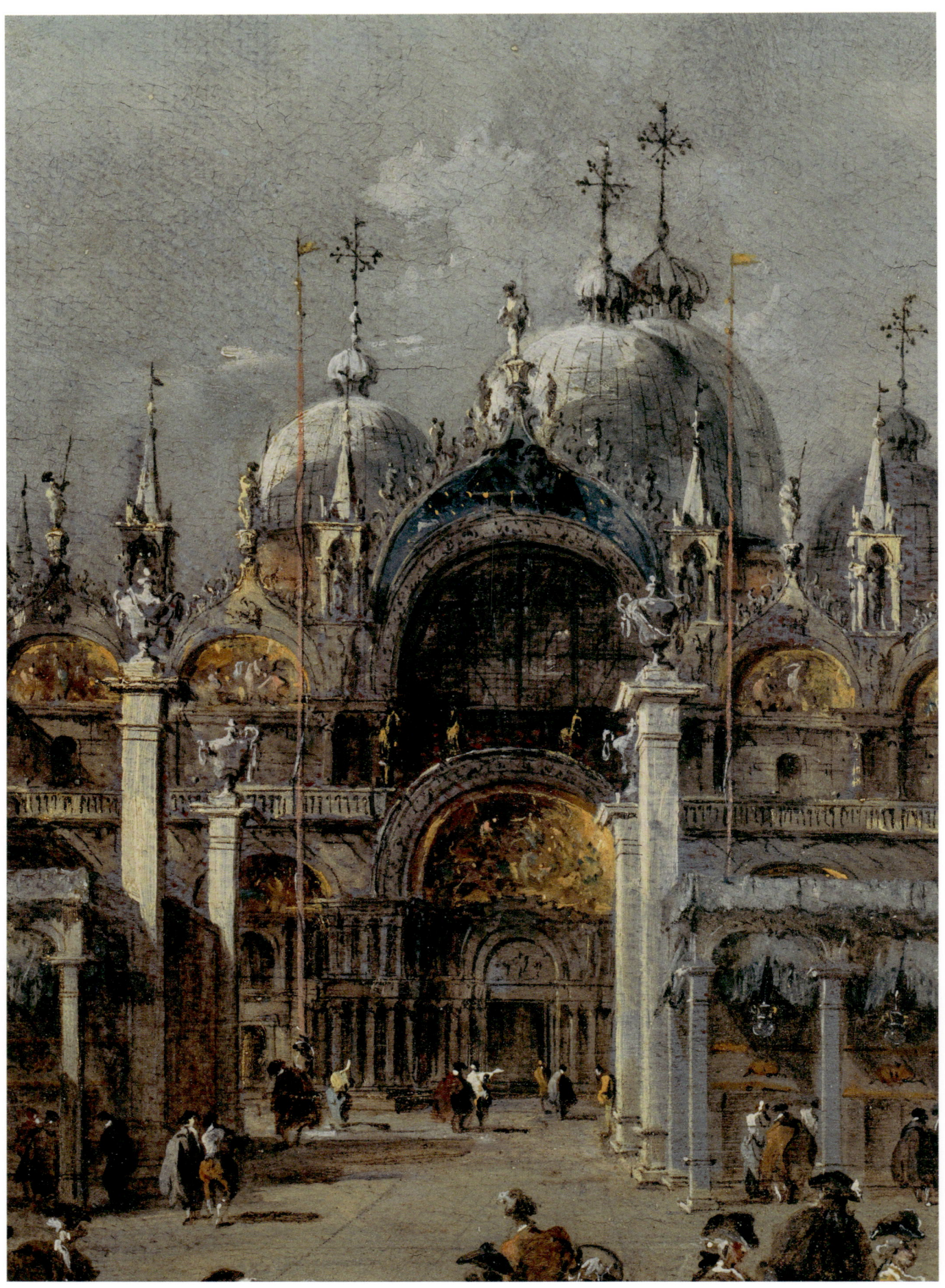

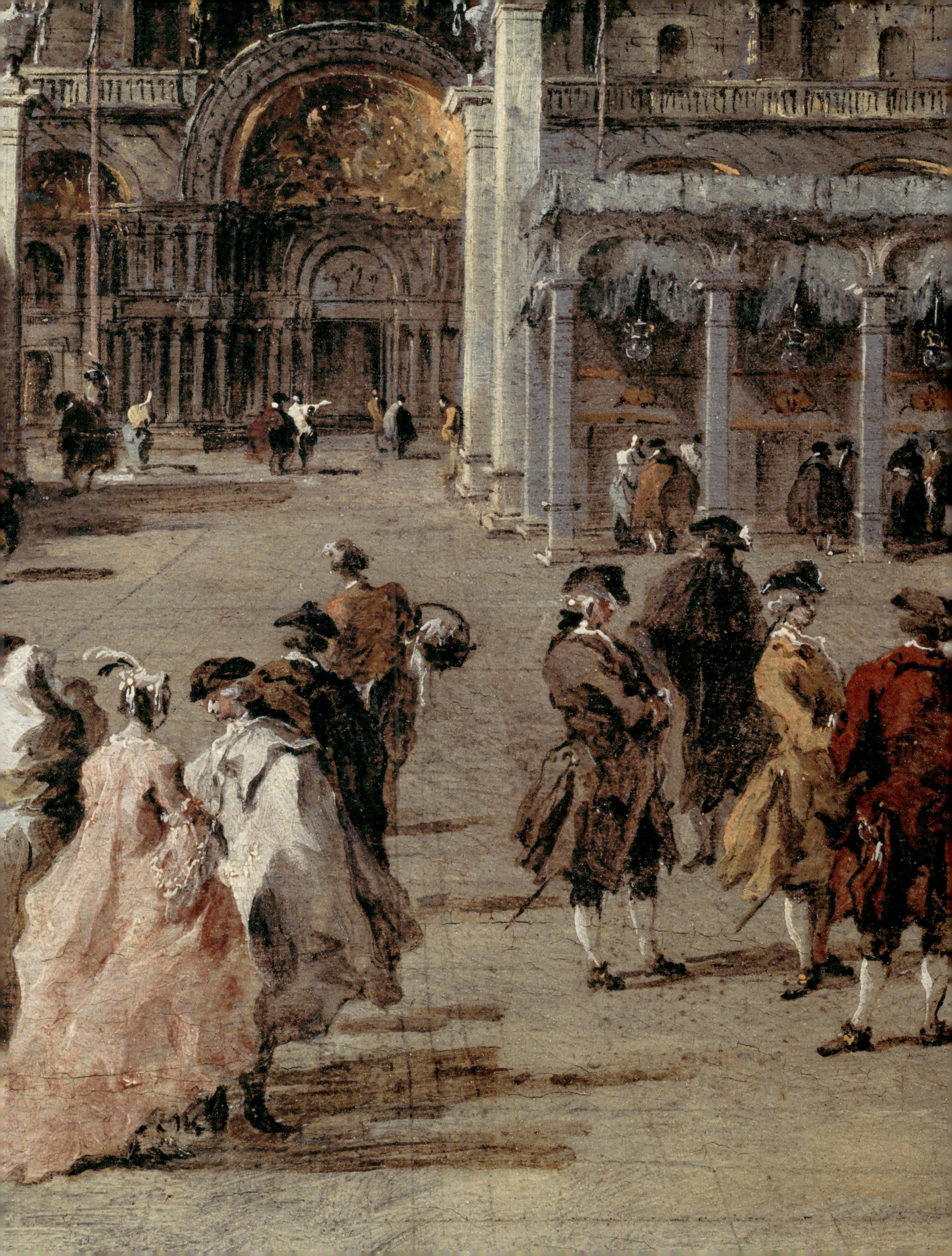

06
FRANCESCO GUARDI
(1712–1793)

Regatta on the Grand Canal

Venice, c. 1775
Oil on canvas
61 × 91 cm

PROVENANCE Robert Dundas Haldane-Duncan,
1st Earl of Camperdown; Adam Haldane-Duncan,
2nd Earl of Camperdown, 1859–67; Lady Julia Duncan,
Baroness Abercromby, 1867–1915; Georgina Wilhemina
Mercer-Henderson, Countess of Buckinghamshire.
Acquired through Christie's, London, on 8 March 1919.
Calouste Gulbenkian Museum, inv. 391

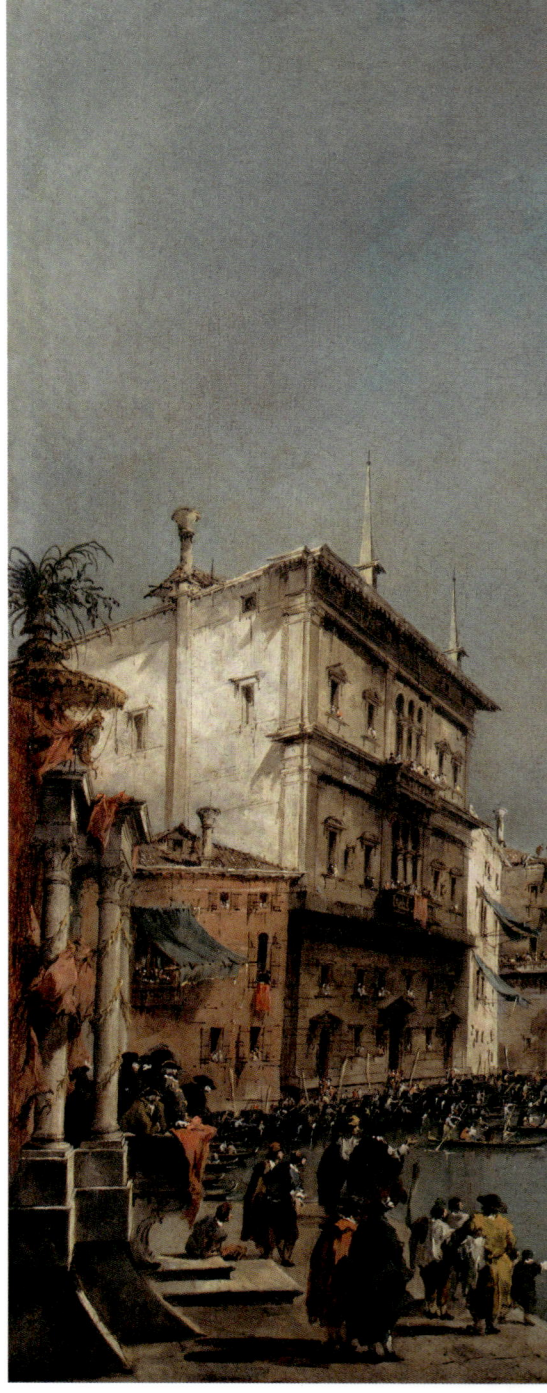

This work is inspired by a Canaletto painting from
the early 1730s called *A Regatta on the Grand Canal*
(Royal Collection, Windsor), whose engraving, made
by Antonio Visentini (1688–1782) and published in 1735,
was widely disseminated. Canaletto's composition was
in turn influenced by Luca Carlevarijs (1663–1730),
one of the forerunners of Venetian *vedute*.

In Guardi, however, the cityscape is constructed
from a more distant point of view and the horizon
line is on a lower plane, aspects that are reflected
in an enlargement of the surface of the sky, resulting
in a magnificent atmospheric effect. The livelier
interpretation of the theme extends to the execution
of the small agitated figures that populate the scene,
animated by vibrant brushstrokes.

The painting centres on a panoramic view of the Grand
Canal, a favourite motif among eighteenth-century
Venetian artists, from a viewpoint located next to
Ca' Foscari, during a regatta. The artist constructs the
space in depth from the tribune near the Balbi Palace,
to the Rialto Bridge, on the edge of the horizon. To the
left is the *macchina*, a floating pavilion where prizes
were distributed to the winners.

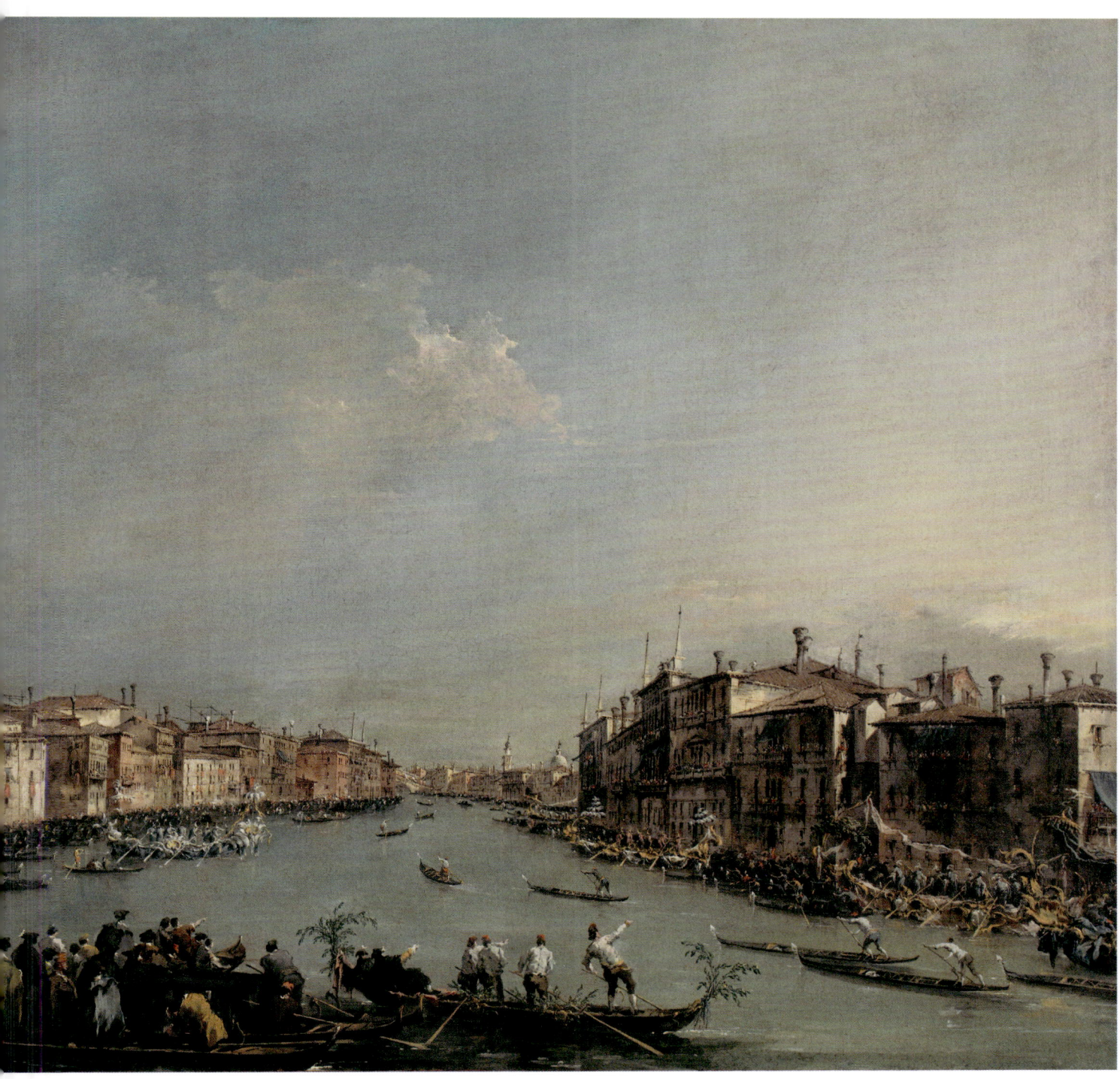

The rich decoration of the fabrics on the balconies and the boats adorned with branches, banners and sea deities, denote gaiety and a suggestion of movement in the Rococo style. The enthusiasm with which the figures in the foreground point out the competing gondolas invites the viewer to participate in the scene.

BIBLIOGRAPHY

CANALETTO 2019, p. 367, no. VII.04; LOISEL 2018, p. 249, no. 163; MORASSI 1993, vol. I, pp. 199, 202, 366–67, no. 299; MURARO 1993, pp. 36–39, no. 9; PALLUCCHINI 1965, no. 4; *VENICE* 2010, pp. 143, 188, no. 60.

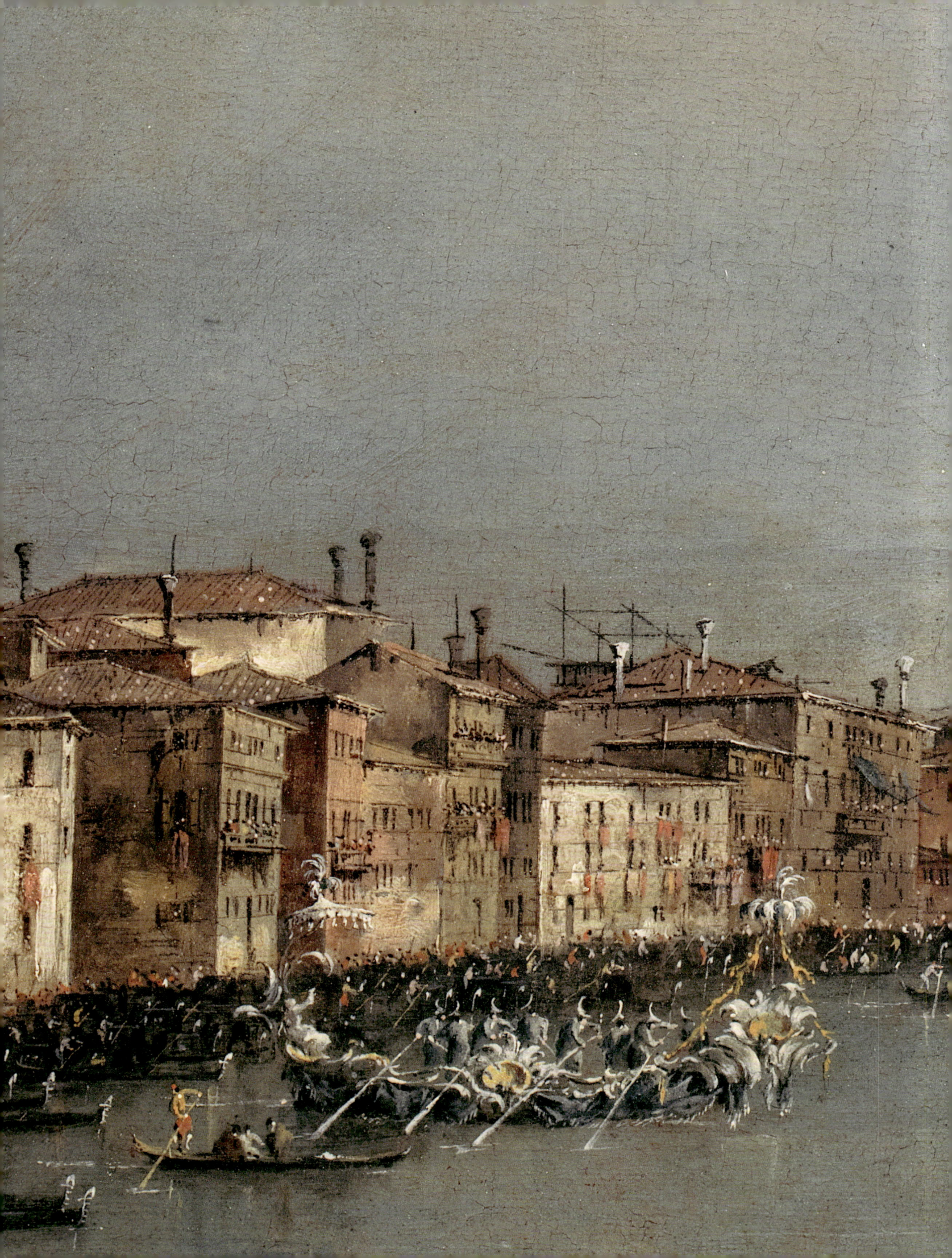

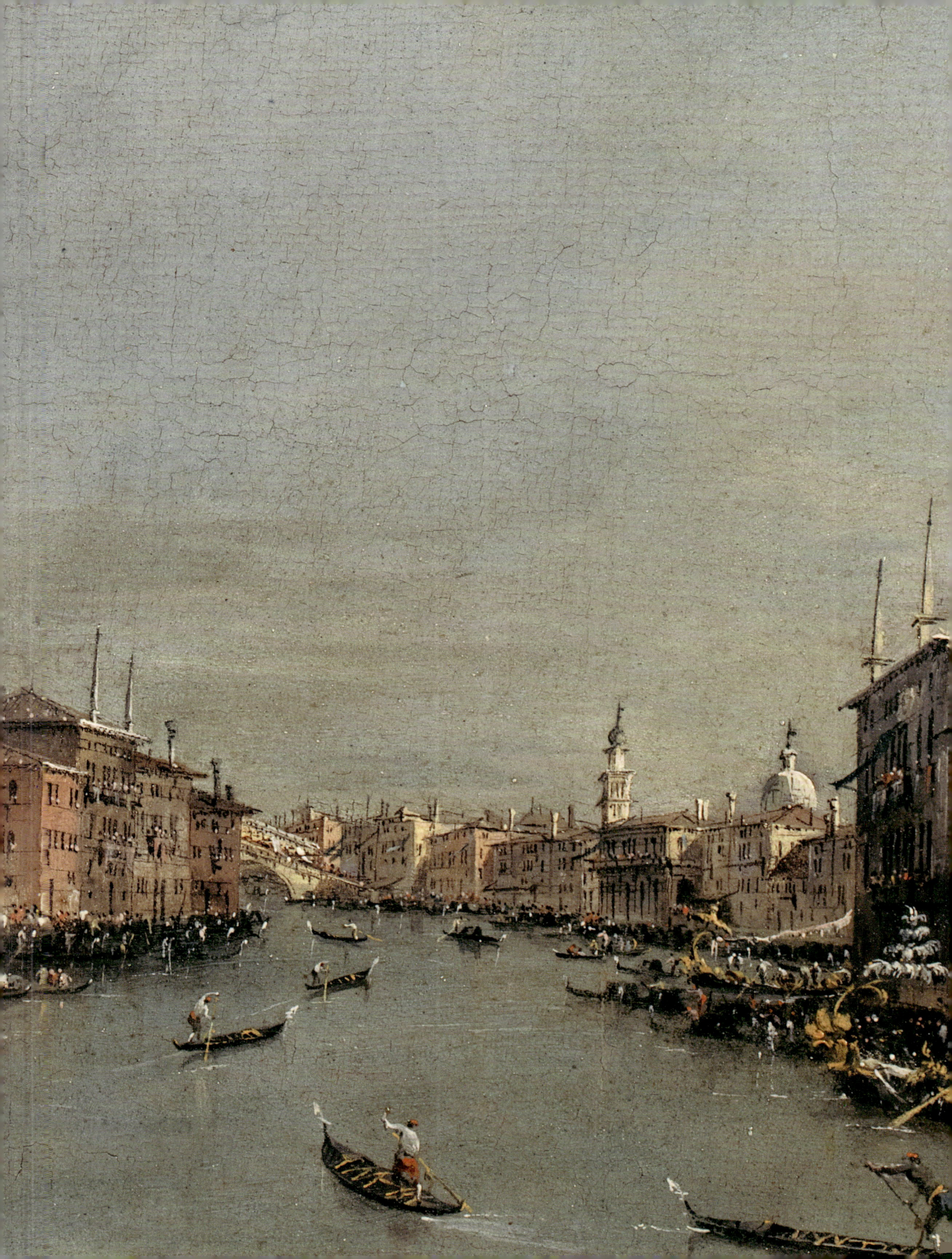

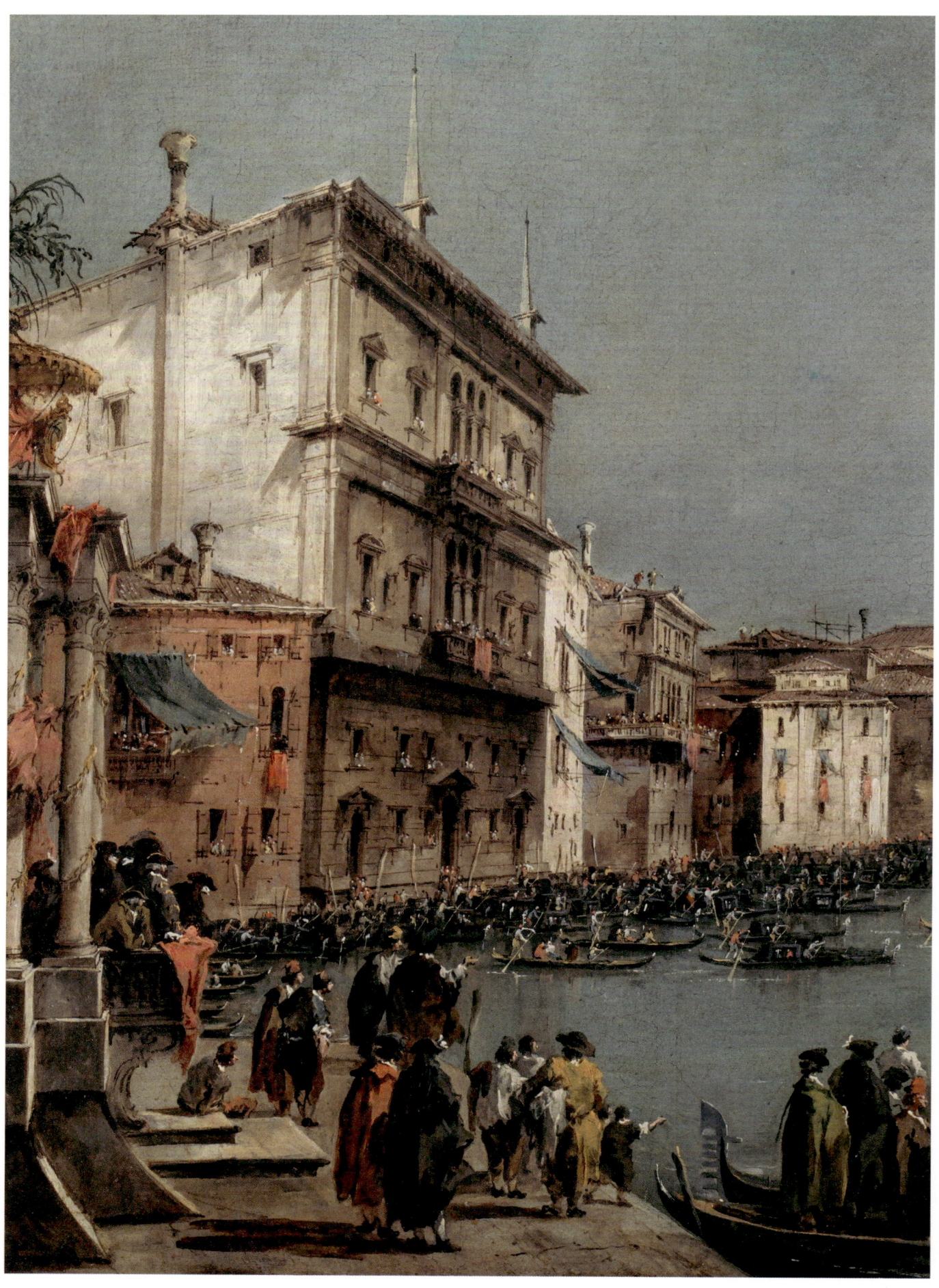

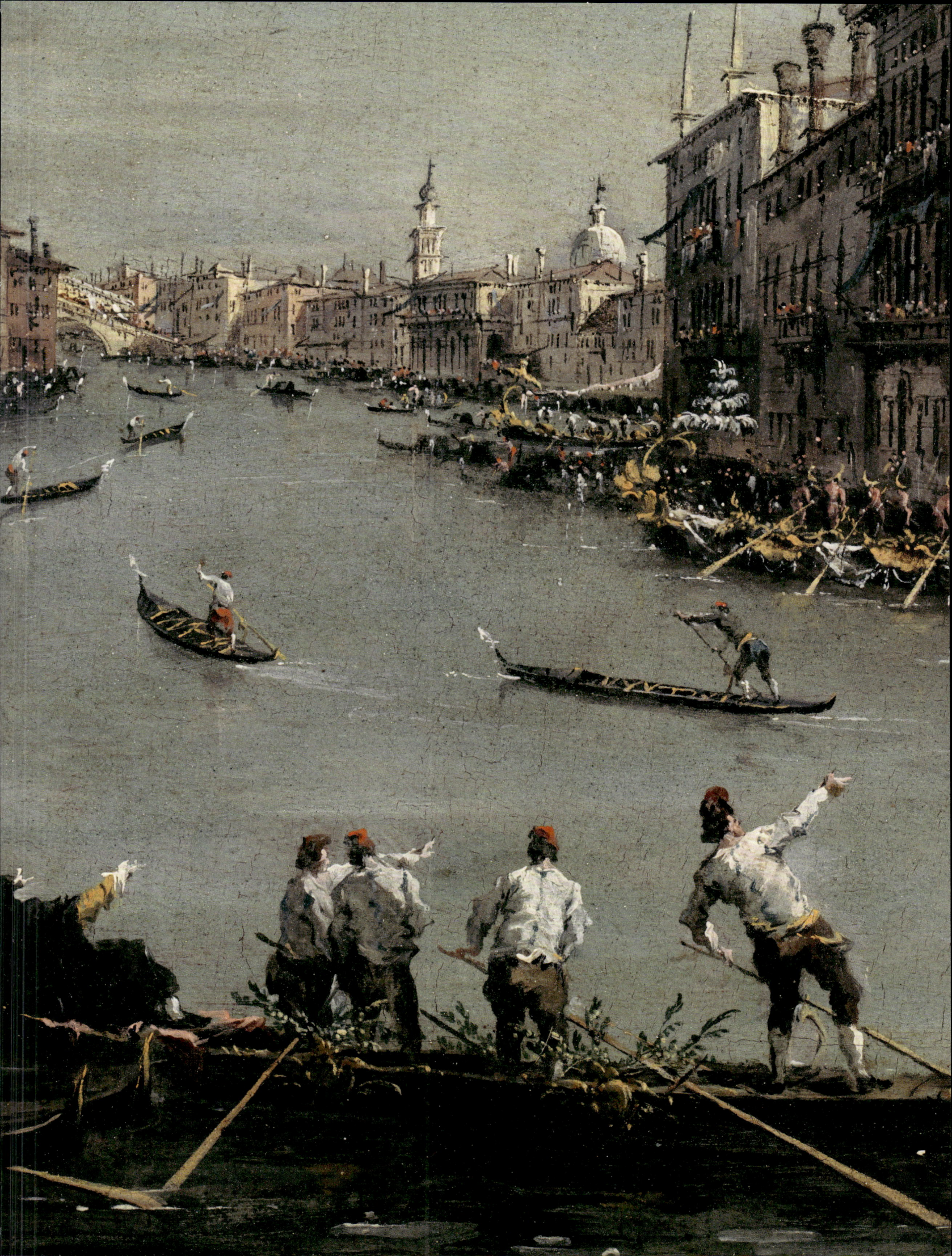

07
FRANCESCO GUARDI
(1712–1793)

*The Feast of Ascension
in the Piazza San Marco*

Venice, c. 1775

Oil on canvas

48 × 78 cm

PROVENANCE John Ashley Collection. Acquired through
Agnew, Christie's, London, on 31 May 1907, no. 88.
Calouste Gulbenkian Museum, inv. 386 A

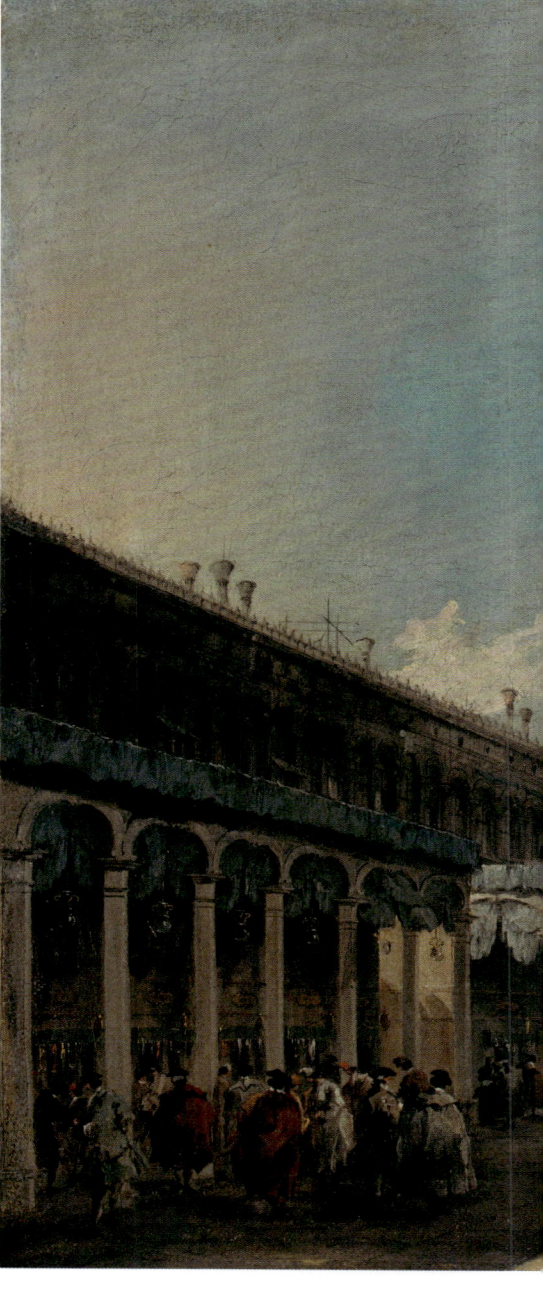

This painting shows the Piazza San Marco decorated
for the Feast of the Ascension, with the Basilica in the
centre, the Clock Tower on the left and the Campanile
on the right. The size of this version, as well as the colour
of the sky and the representation of the figures in the
square, differentiates it from the work of the same title
belonging to the Calouste Gulbenkian Collection (cat. 5).

The Piazza San Marco was naturally a recurring motif
in the work of Francesco Guardi, who depicted the
site more than twenty times from different points

of view. The originality of the paintings in the Calouste
Gulbenkian Museum lies in the fact that they document
Ascension Day, placing them in the category of *feste*,
a genre in which the painter was particularly adept.

The British Museum in London houses the preparatory
drawing for the composition which, if observed closely,
reveals details that are reproduced both in this version
and in the aforementioned work. Although it is not
possible to determine exactly which of the two works
was painted first, this piece is thought to be a replica

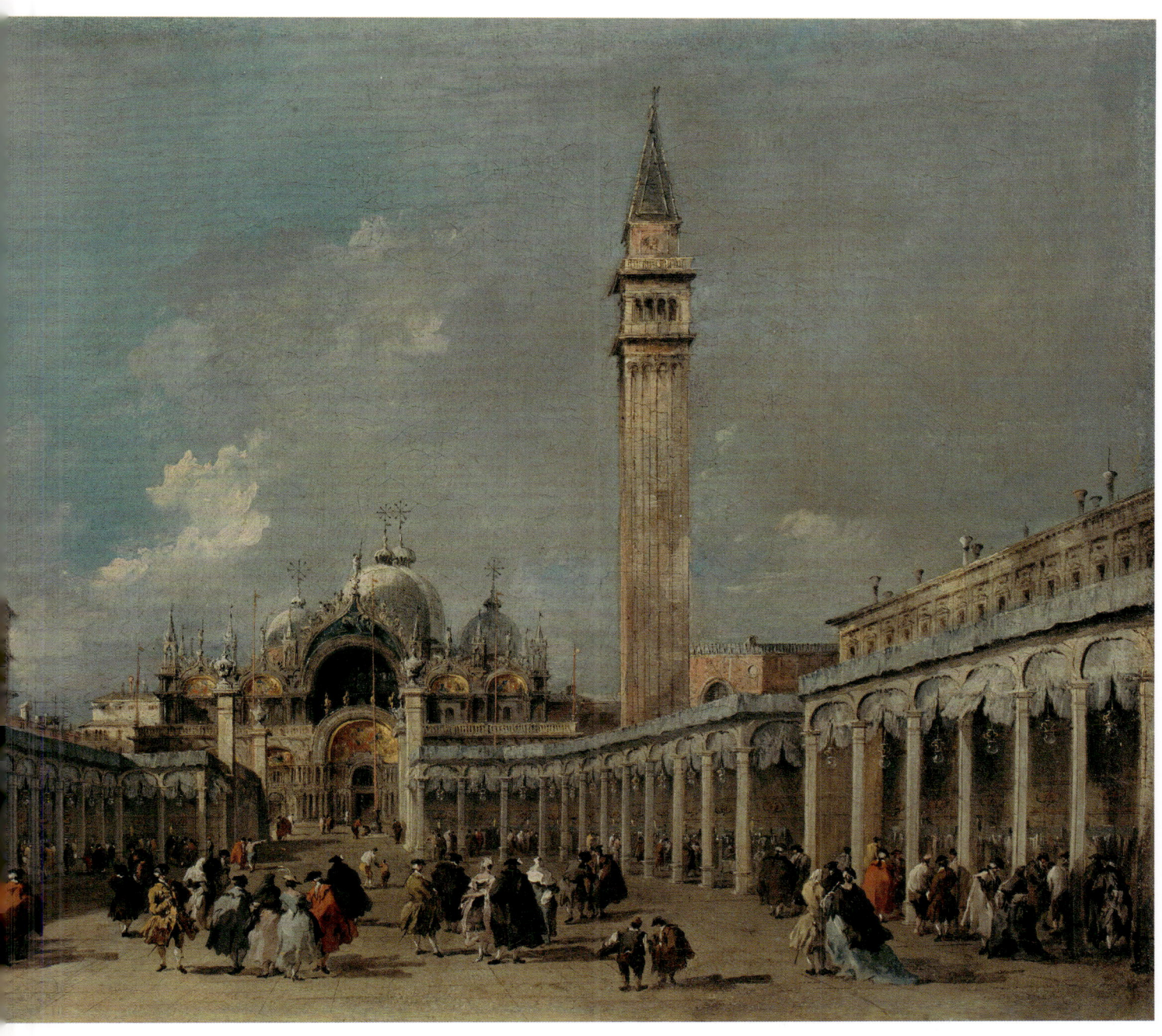

of the same title mentioned above, intended for the thriving art market fuelled by the aristocrats who visited the city on their Grand Tour.

In both cases we can see the temporary structure intended to cover the Procuratie, as it looked before the project for the site was completed by Bernardino Maccaruzzi (1728–1798) in 1776. The new decoration of the elliptical arcades gave rise to another composition by Francesco Guardi, which is now in the Kunsthistorisches Museum in Vienna.

BIBLIOGRAPHY

MORASSI 1993, vol. I, pp. 188, 362, no. 278; MURARO 1993, pp. 32–35, no. 8; PALLUCCHINI 1965, no. 8.

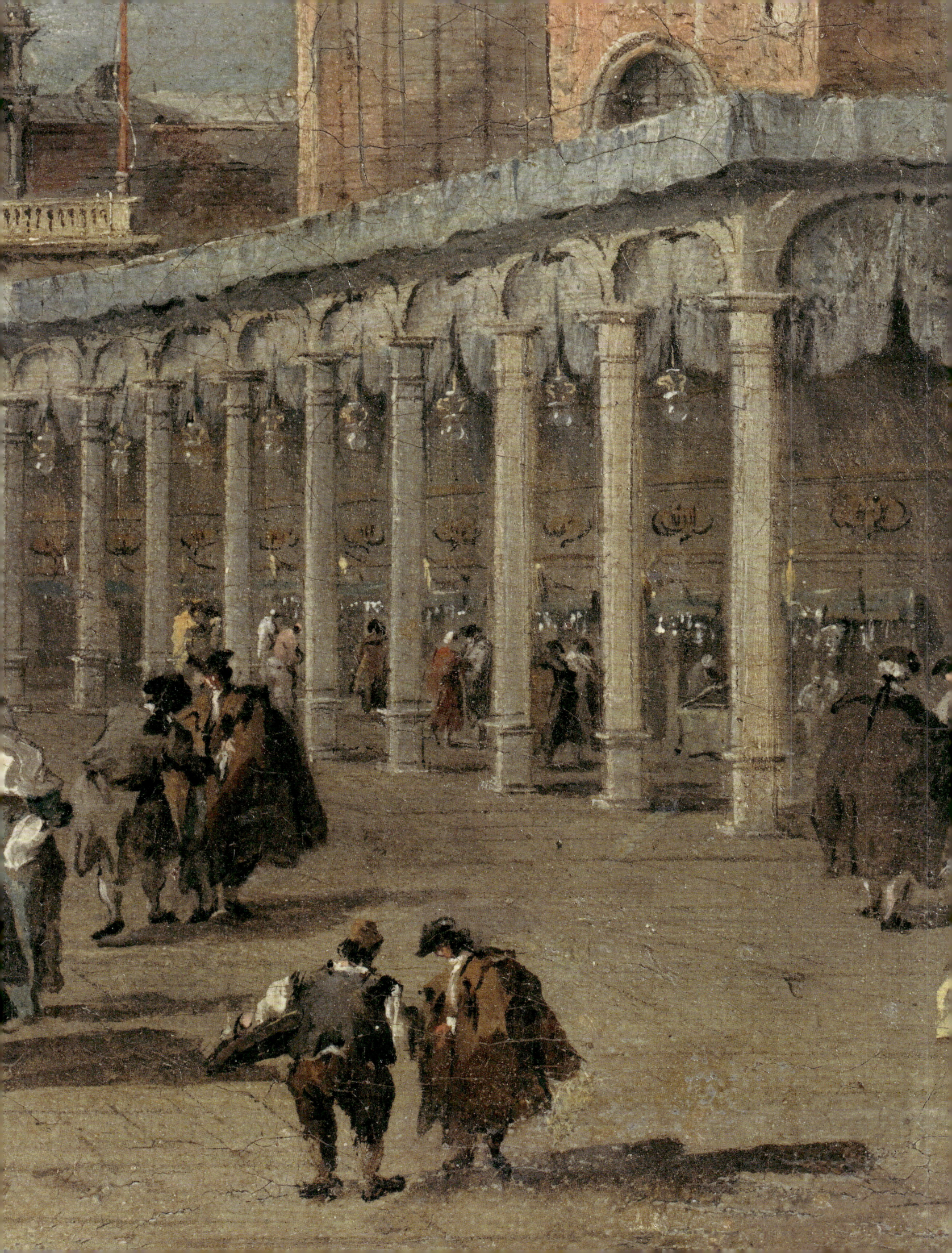

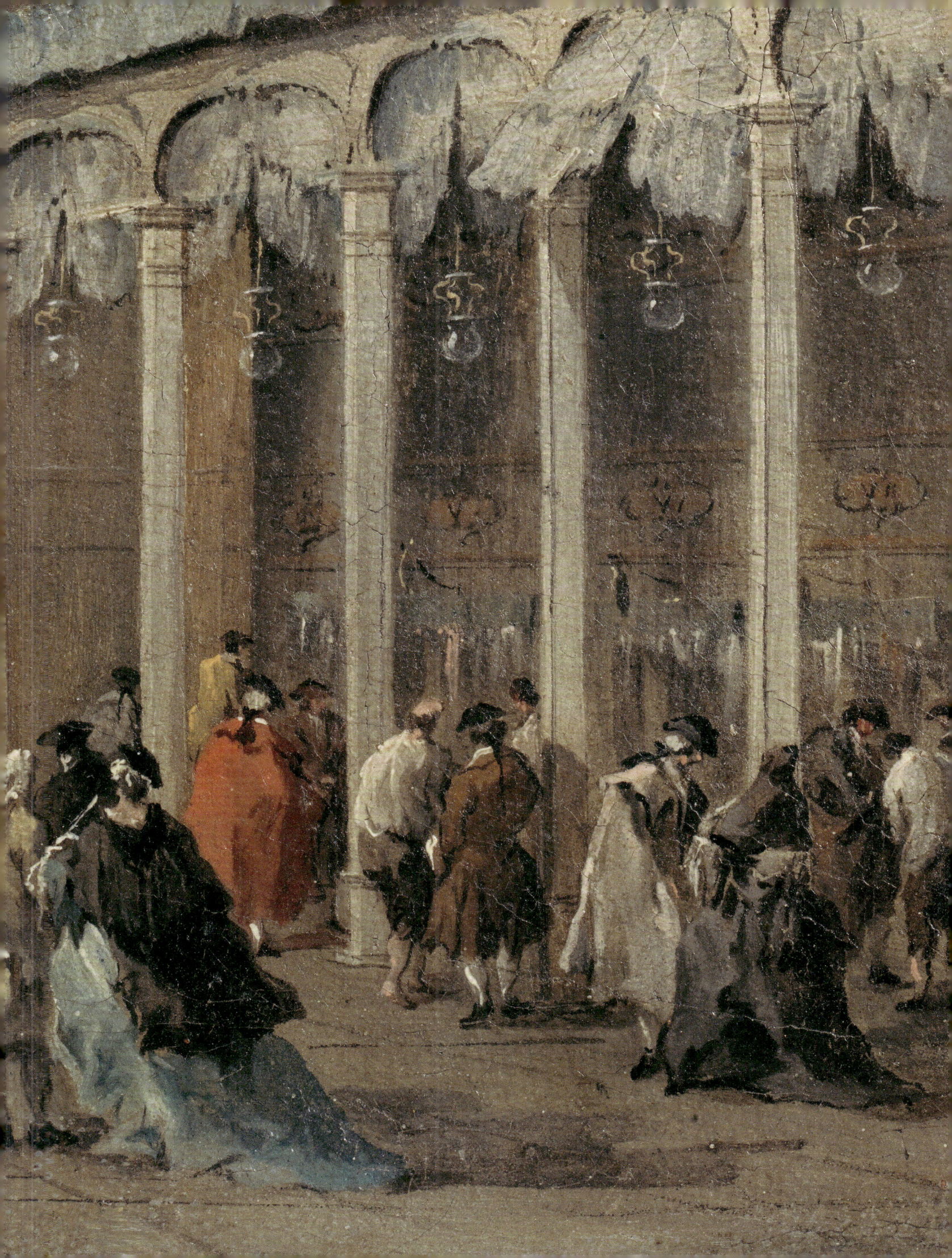

08
FRANCESCO GUARDI
(1712–1793)

The Departure of the Bucintoro

Venice, c. 1765–80

Oil on canvas

61 × 92 cm

PROVENANCE Earl of Camperdown Collection;
Earl of Buckinghamshire Collection. Acquired
through Christie's, London, on 8 March 1919.
Calouste Gulbenkian Museum, inv. 392

This *veduta* depicts the Basin of San Marco as
the *Bucintoro*, the ceremonial barge that carried
the Doge, the chief magistrate of the Republic of Venice
between 726 and 1797, heads towards the Church of
San Nicolò al Lido to celebrate the symbolic marriage
ceremony between Venice and the Sea. On the stern
of the richly decorated ship, the sculptures of Prudence
and Fortitude stand out, while the mast bears the red
and gold banner with the winged Lion of Venice. The
Spozalizio del Mare, as it was known, involved casting
into the water the ring that Pope Alexander III (1105–1181,
pope between 1159–81) had presented to Doge Sebastiano
Ziane (doge between 1171–78) in 1177, in honour of the
naval and diplomatic victories that had given the city
control of the Adriatic. The festivities lasted a fortnight
with regattas and other amusements, reaching their
climax on Ascension Day.

The theatricality of the motif inevitably gave rise
to other compositions by Francesco Guardi, with
the painter documenting this theme of the *Bucintoro's*
journey in different areas, and depicting it from various
points of view. These representations of the barge
include its course in the lagoon, the moment of its
approach to the Church of San Nicolò, or the start
of its return to the heart of the city. This dynamic,
emotive painting, with its vibrant colours, can also
be related to two of the artist's works belonging
to the Calouste Gulbenkian Museum (cats. 9–10),
in which the Molo next to the Ducal Palace stands out,
as it does in this instance, although the grand galley
does not appear in those works. The *Bucintoro*

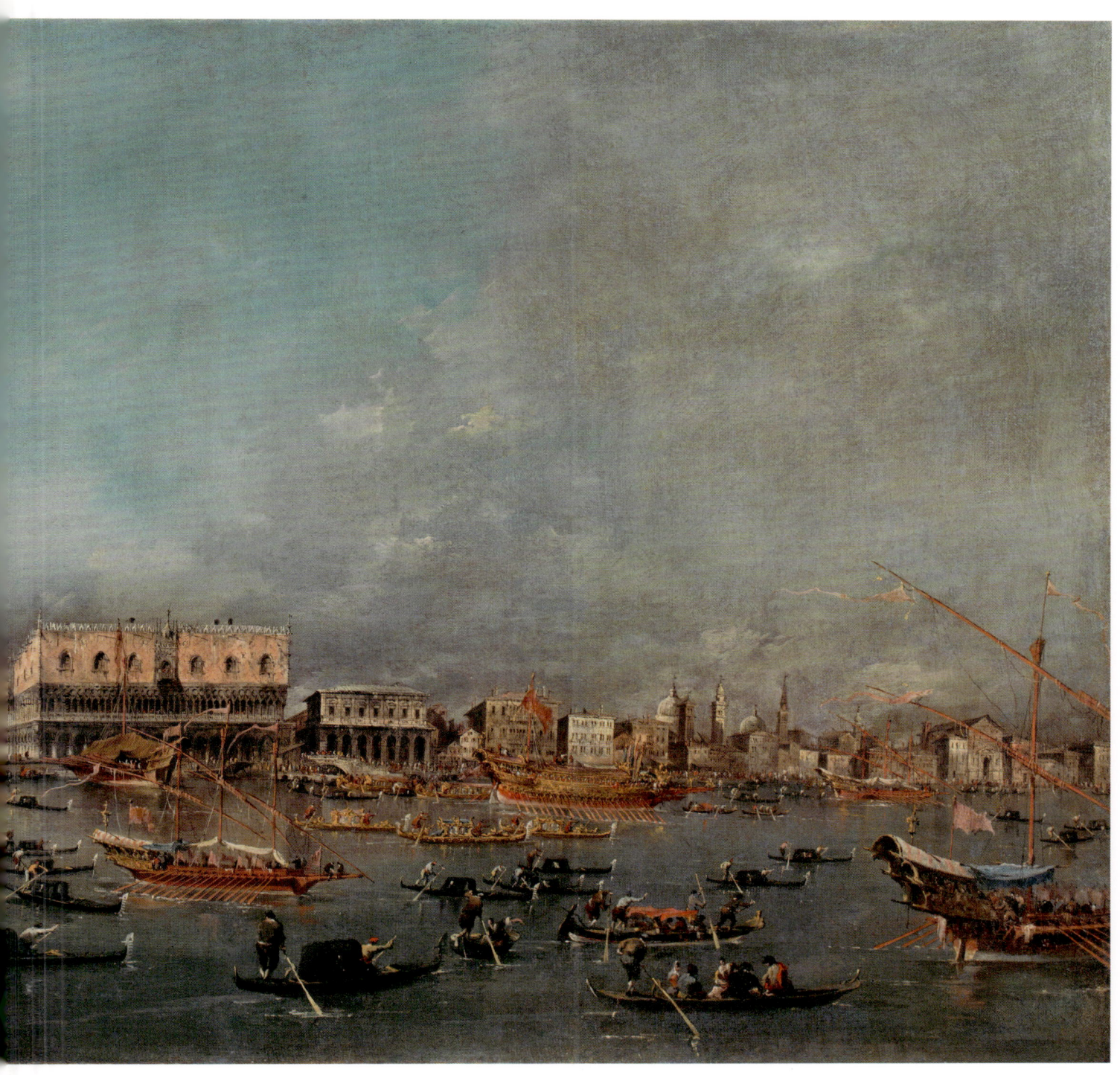

theme had already been explored by Luca Carlevarijs
(1663–1730) in 1710 (Getty Museum Collection, Los
Angeles) and by Canaletto around 1760 (Dulwich Picture
Gallery, London), and like their versions, Guardi conveys
the festive, bustling ambience of the boats, although he
creates a broader and, in this sense, original perspective
of the Basin of San Marco.

BIBLIOGRAPHY

MORASSI 1993, vol. I, p. 386, no. 403; MURARO 1993, pp. 41–43, no. 10;
PALLUCCHINI 1965, no. 5; *VENICE* 2008, pp. 52–53, 216.

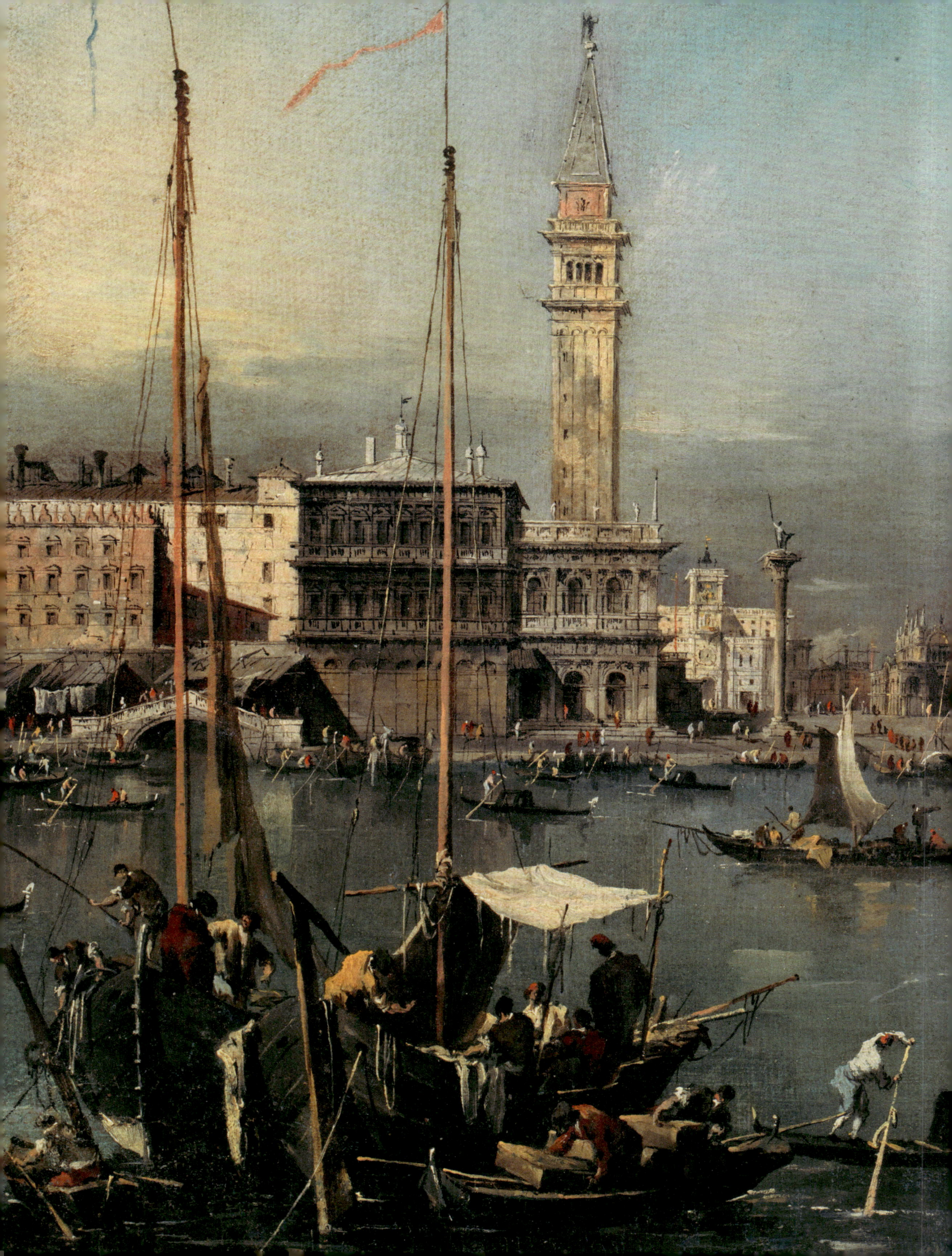

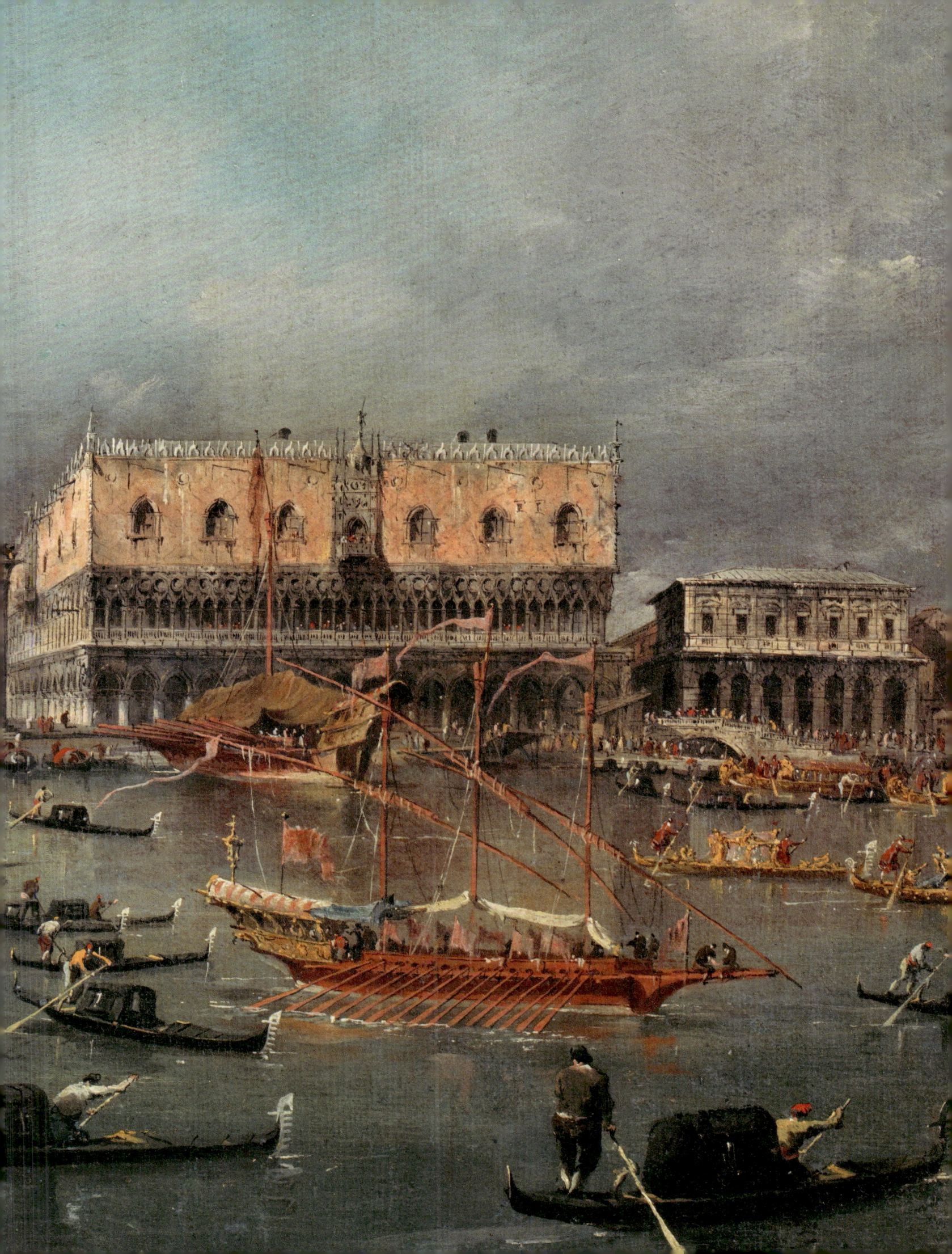

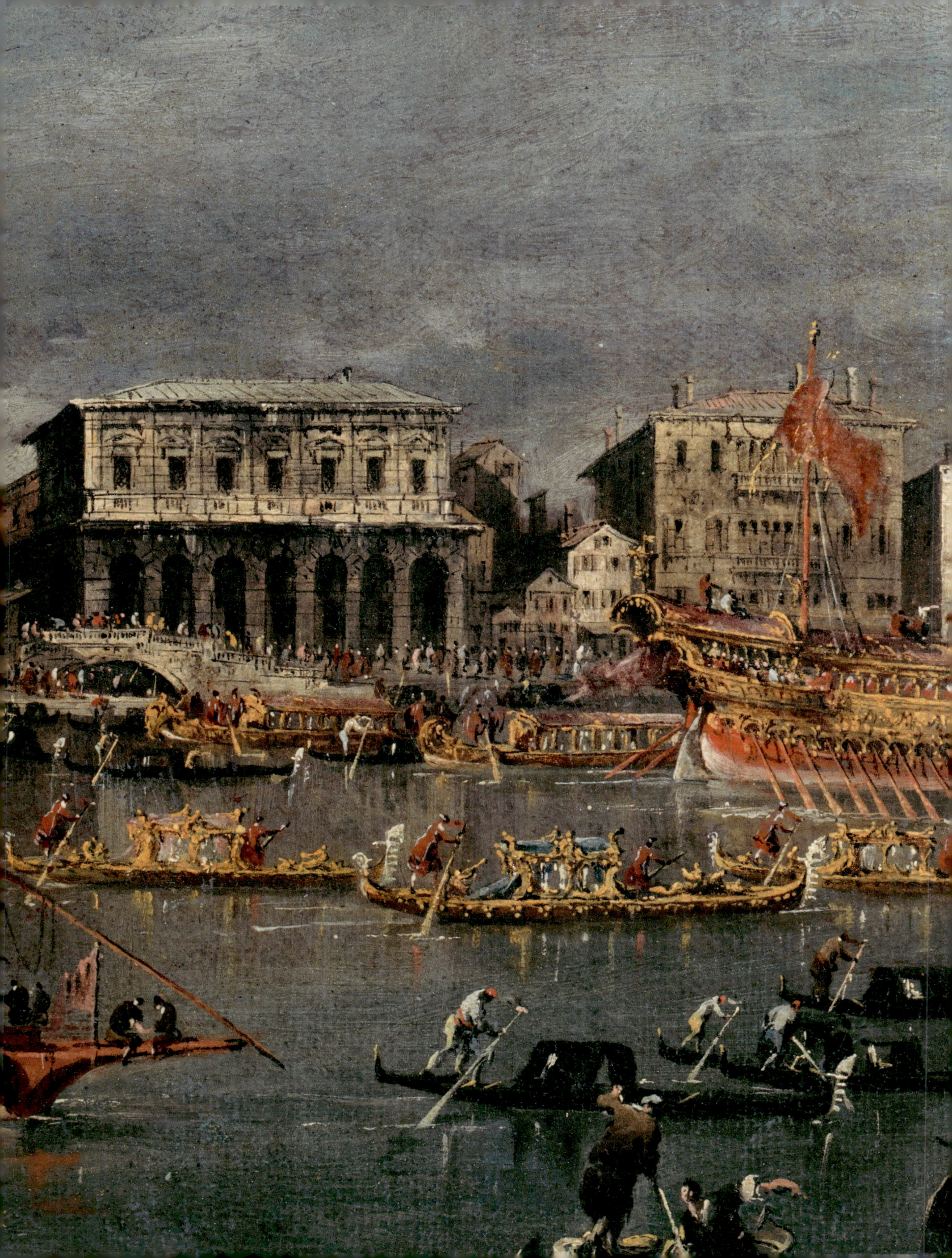

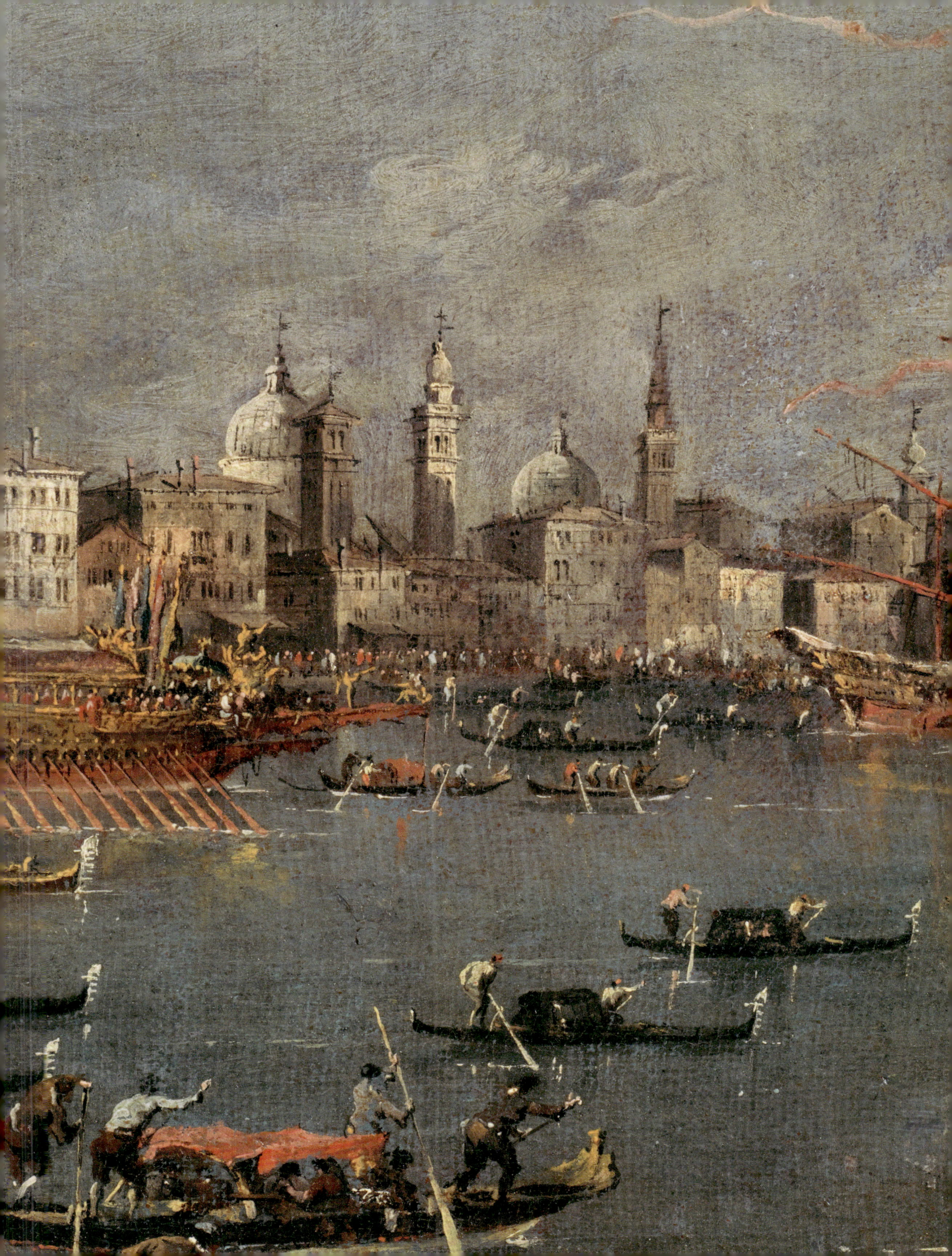

09
FRANCESCO GUARDI
(1712–1793)

View of the Molo with the Ducal Palace

Venice, c. 1780–90
Oil on canvas
48 × 78 cm

PROVENANCE C. Annoot Collection, London. Acquired
through Agnew at the sale of the John Ashley Collection,
Christie's, London, on 31 May 1907, no. 89.
Calouste Gulbenkian Museum, inv. 386 B

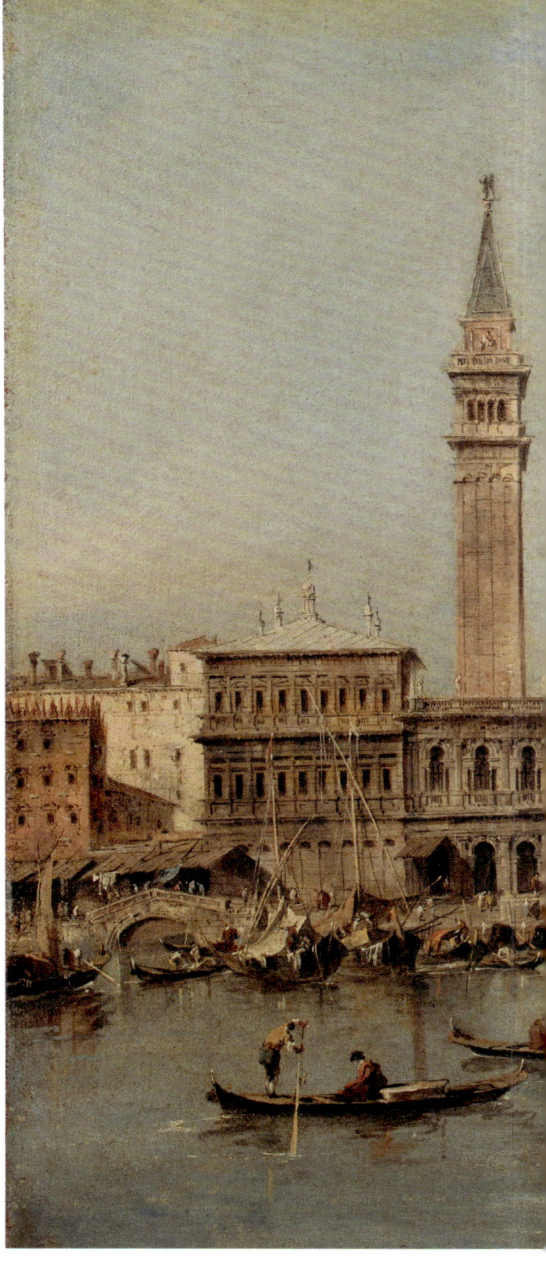

In this *veduta*, Francesco Guardi thoroughly details
the buildings in the heart of Venice, encompassing,
from left to right: the Grain Warehouse, the Zecca,
the Marciana Library, the Campanile, the Clock
Tower, the Piazza, Basilica of San Marco, the Doge's
Palace and the Prison. The motif, recurrent in the
painter's work, gave rise to almost 20 paintings
produced from locations at varying distances from the
wharf, one of which belongs to the Calouste Gulbenkian
Museum collection (cat. 10). The frontal viewpoint is

inspired by Canaletto's painting *The Molo, Seen from the
Bacino di San Marco*, from c. 1730-55 (Musée du Louvre,
Paris), as is the case with other views painted by Guardi.

Unlike the other version in the Gulbenkian Collection,
more focused on depicting a particular atmospheric
effect, this work demonstrates a particular attention
to detail, with a meticulous rendering of the architecture
portrayed. It also reveals a more scenographic vocation,
through the emphasis placed on the animated

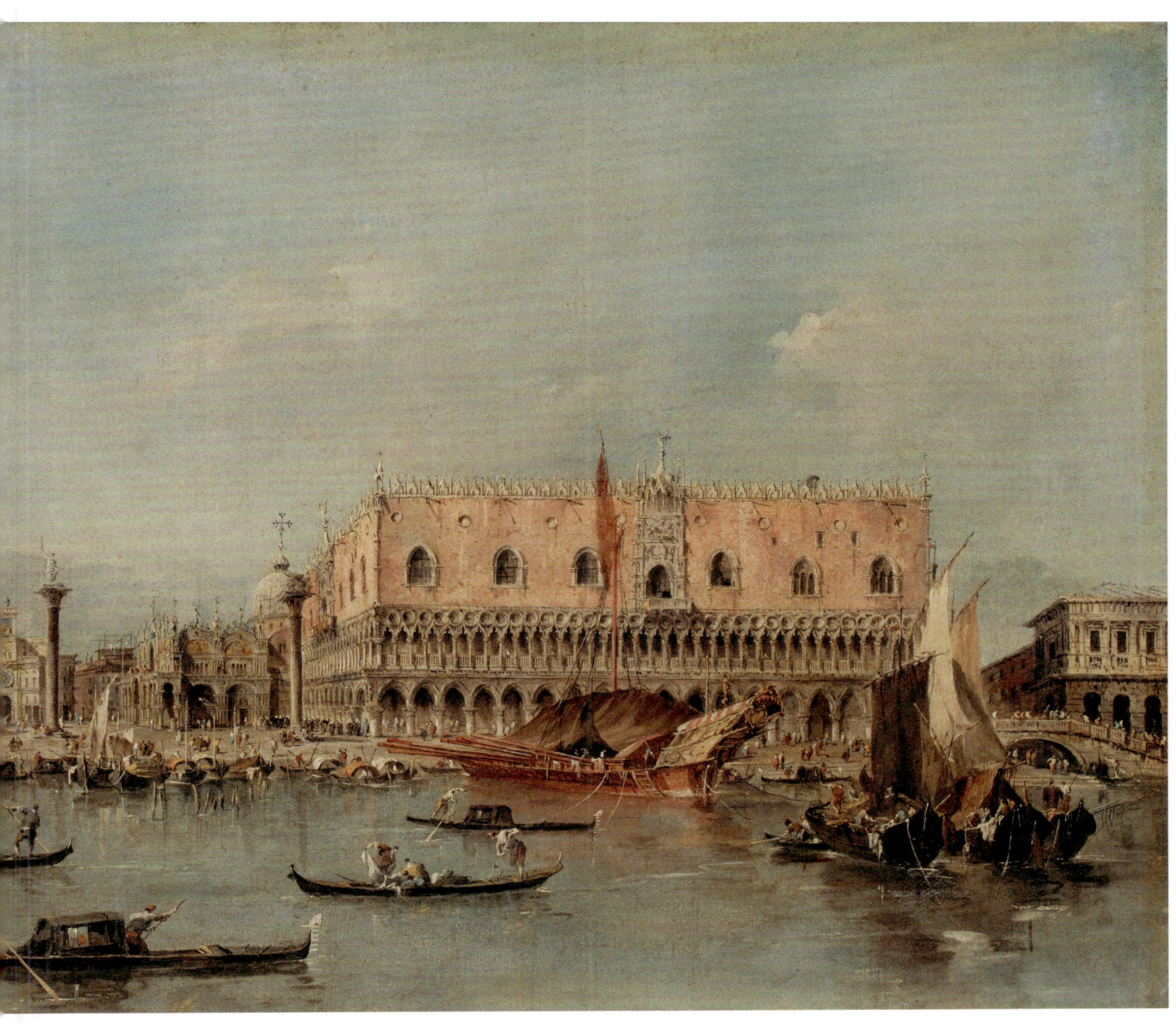

movement of the figures populating the canvas.
Francesco Guardi thus uses tones that, although
muted, accentuate the sharpness of the forms,
an aspect that also extends to the composition's
foreground, where the state galleon with the inscription
'CXC' and a sailing boat, also present in the version
mentioned above, are prominent on the right.

BIBLIOGRAPHY

MORASSI 1993, vol. I, pp. 241, 386, no. 400; MURARO 1993, pp. 44–45,
no. 11; PALLUCCHINI 1965, no. 9.

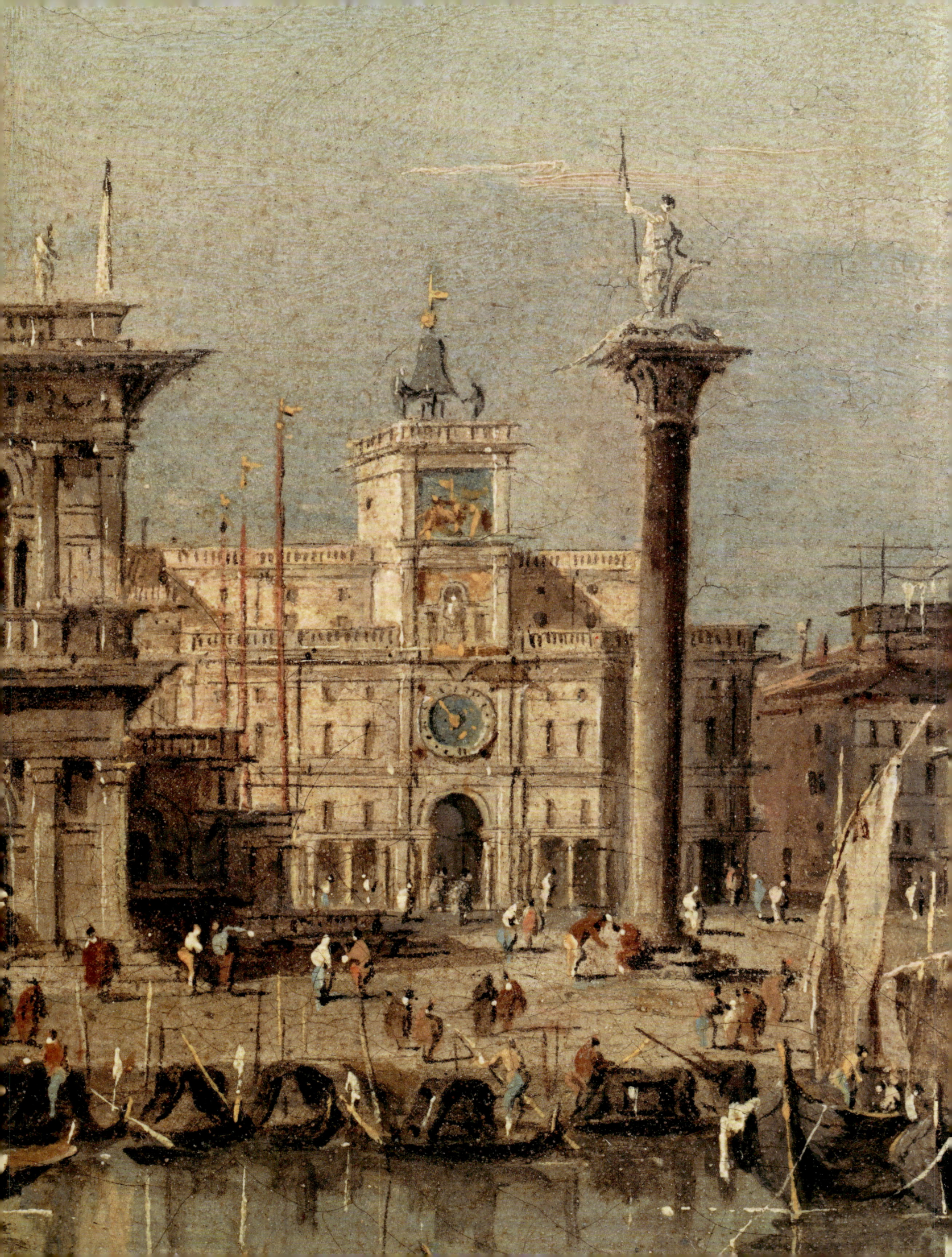

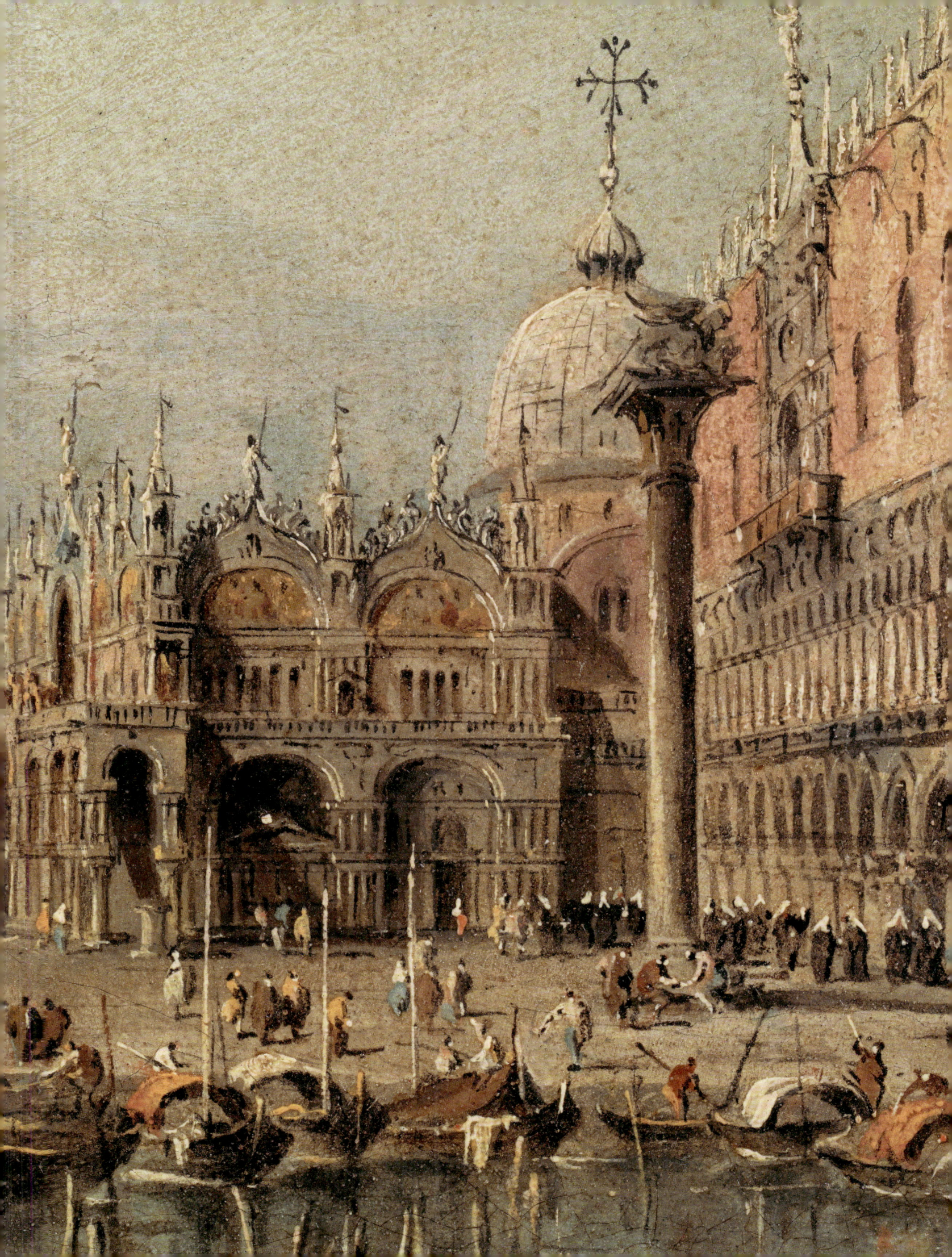

10
FRANCESCO GUARDI
(1712–1793)

View of the Molo with the Ducal Palace

Venice, c. 1790
Oil on wood
25 × 35 cm

PROVENANCE Kaufmann Collection. Acquired
through Agnew, London, on 30 November 1907.
Calouste Gulbenkian Museum, inv. 491

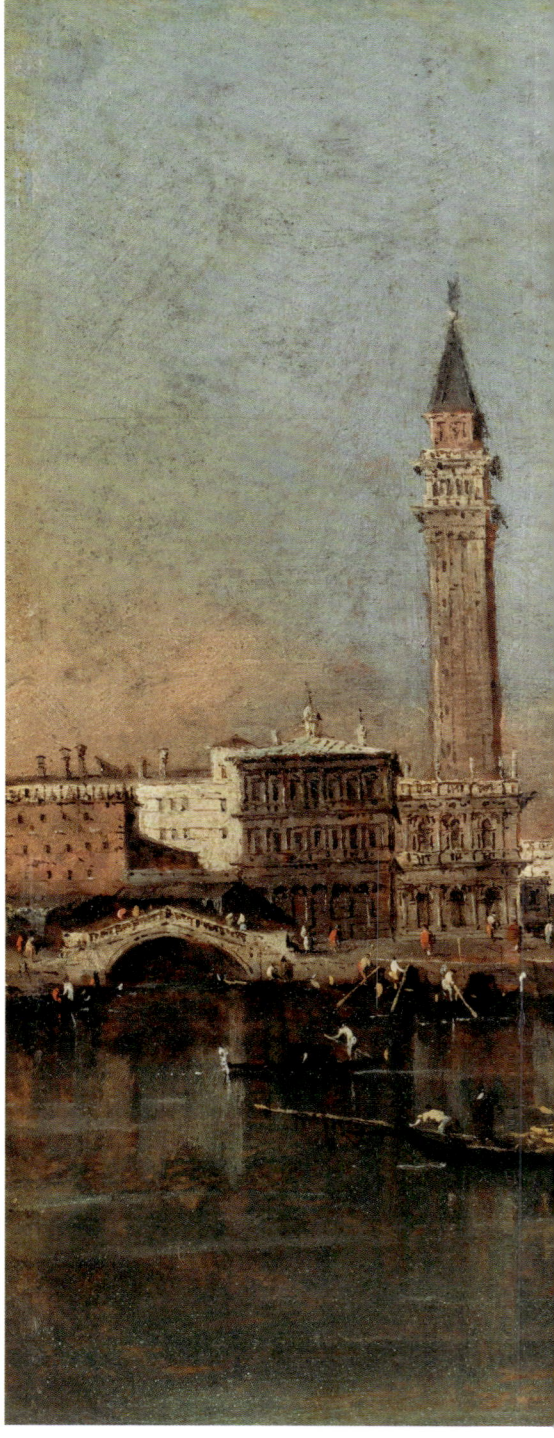

This *veduta* depicts Venice from the Basin of San Marco, where the group of monuments around the Piazzetta, the gateway to the city, stand out. In addition to the Zecca, the mint built between 1536 and 1566, and the Doge's residence, the Doge's Palace, built in 1340, it also includes the façade of the Prison and the beginning of the group of buildings on the Riva degli Schiavoni. In the background, one can also see the Campanile, the Clock Tower and the dome of Basilica of San Marco. In the foreground, the scene is completed by gondolas and boats. This section of the painting distinguishes it from another version of the theme in the Calouste Gulbenkian Collection (cat. 9), which is larger and differs in the treatment of the light.

The warmer tones of this painting, with dense preparation visible in some areas, particularly evident in the depiction of the lagoon and in some sections of the sky, seem to indicate a later work, as with *The Island of San Giorgio Maggiore* (cat. 21), which bears a similar colour treatment. This leads to the conclusion that this is one of the last variations on a motif created

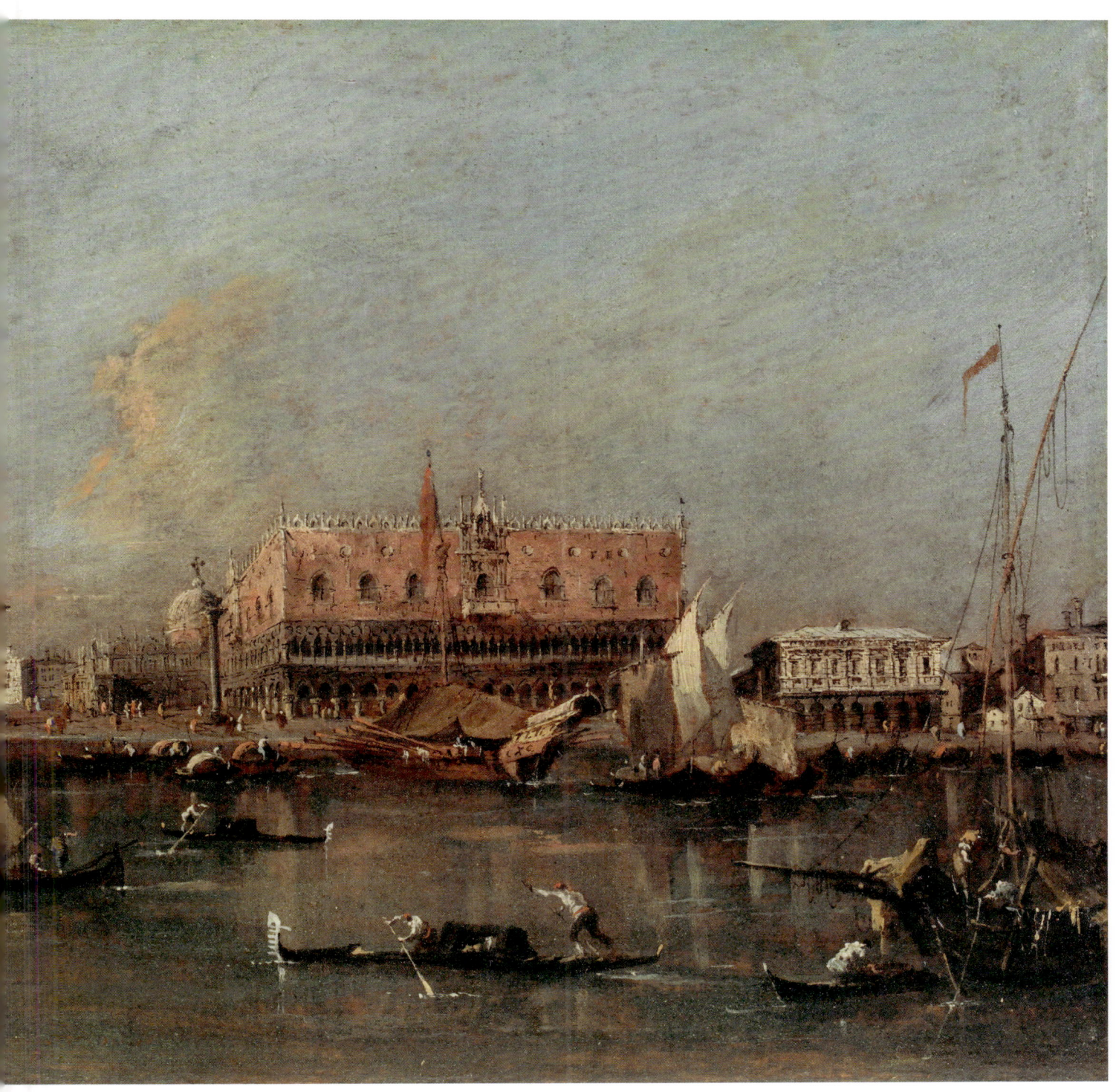

by Francesco Guardi, who produced some 17 versions
of the theme in total, in which the most emblematic
buildings in Venice are seen from the same viewpoint,
at greater or lesser distances from the waterfront.
The considerable number of versions naturally
derives from the success of the *veduta* among
the local clientèle.

BIBLIOGRAPHY

MORASSI 1993, vol. I, p. 386, no. 401; MURARO 1993, pp. 49–51, no. 13;
PALLUCCHINI 1965, no. 17.

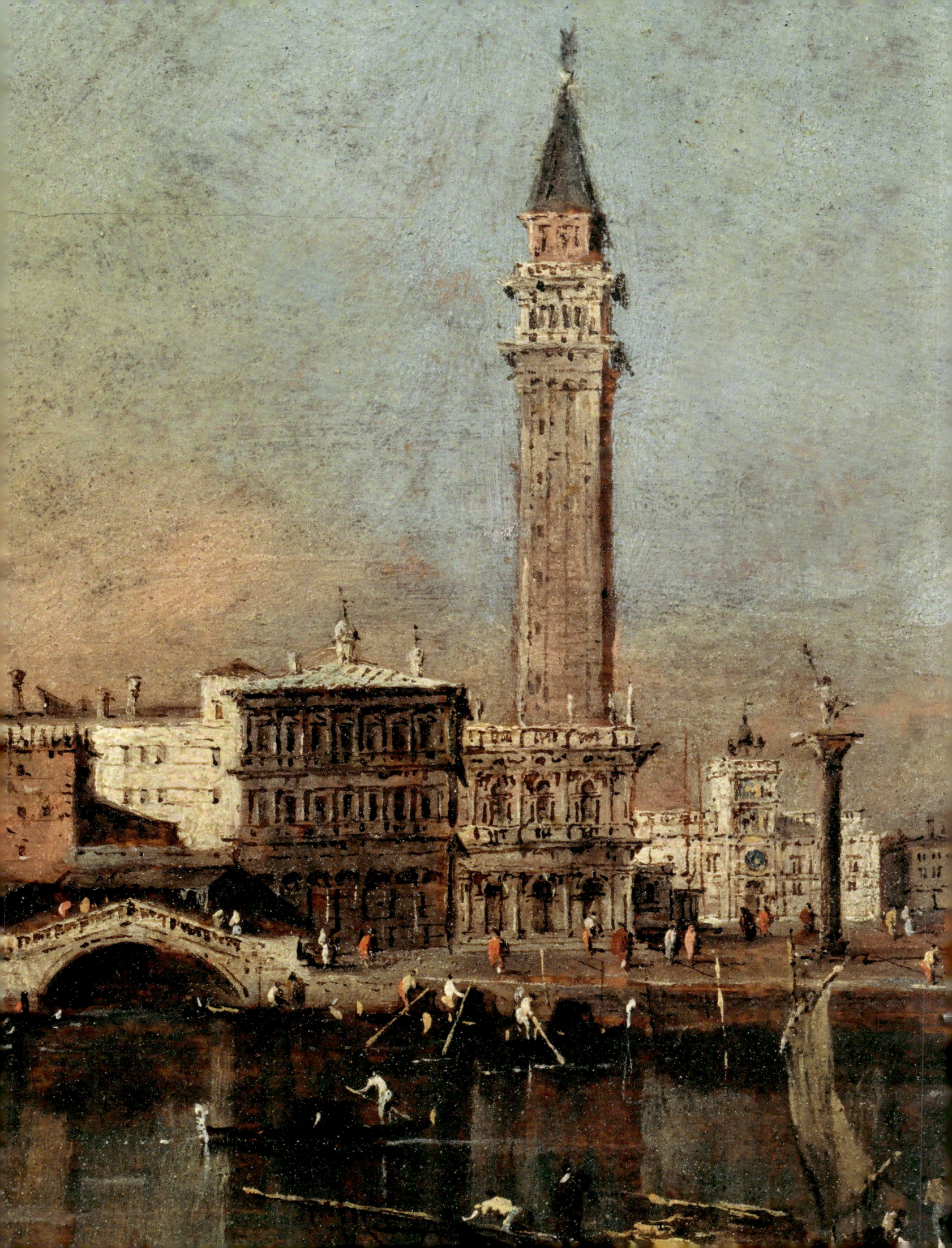

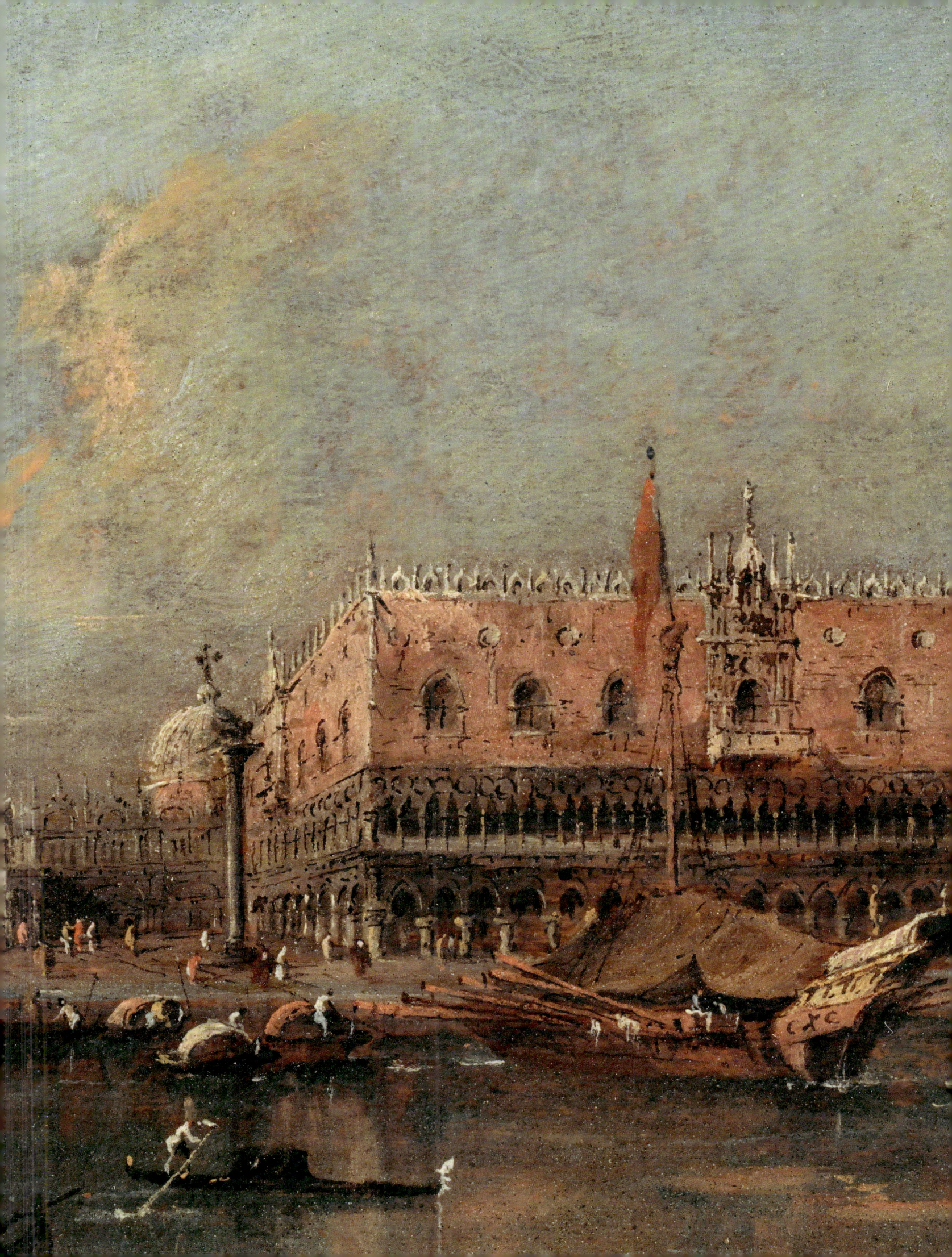

11
FRANCESCO GUARDI
(1712–1793)

The Grand Canal near Rialto Bridge

Venice, c. 1780–90
Oil on canvas
45.1 × 69.2 cm

<u>PROVENANCE</u> George Drummond Collection, Montreal.
Acquired through Knoedler, London, on 1 July 1919.
Calouste Gulbenkian Museum, inv. 389

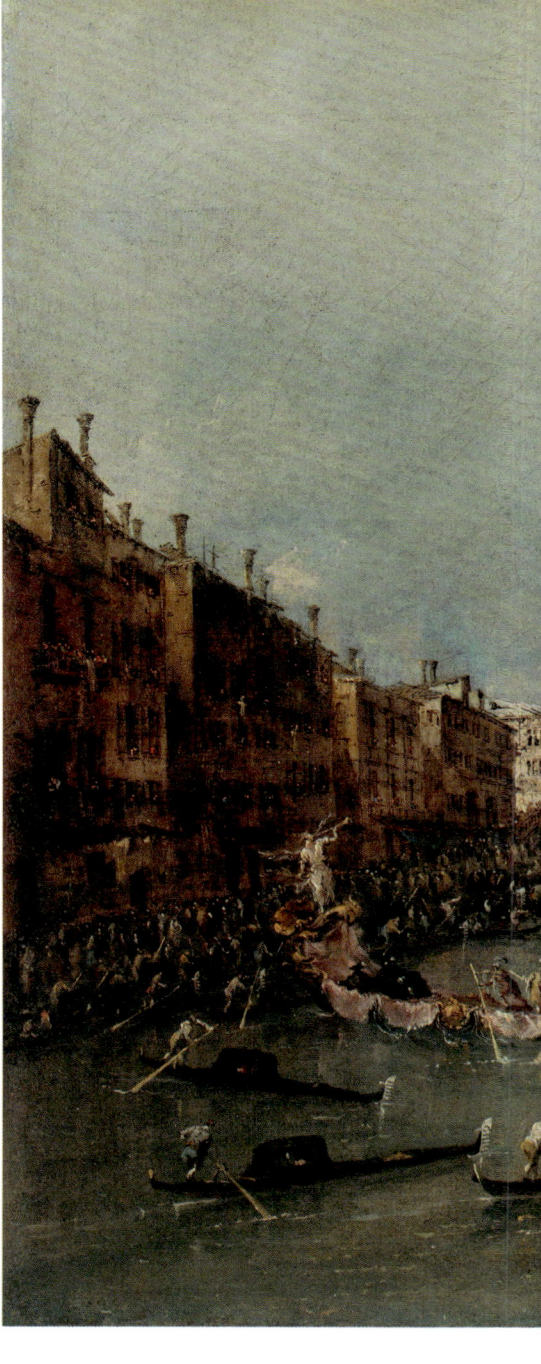

The depiction of regattas on the Grand Canal in Venice was a recurring motif in the work of Francesco Guardi and his contemporaries throughout the eighteenth century. In this composition, the observer's gaze is directed towards the Rialto Bridge, designed by Antonio da Ponte (1512–1595) and inaugurated in 1591, as seen in the painting with the same title, also part of the Calouste Gulbenkian Museum Collection (cat. 6).

This canvas depicts a larger vessel on the left, the *bissona* (a name derived from *bissa*, or water snake), which has an exuberant allegory of Fame sculpted on the stern. This fast and agile boat, made up of eight pairs of oars and specially decorated for festive occasions, was used to closely monitor the regattas. On the opposite side is another *bissona*, also richly decorated. There is another version of the theme at The Barber Institute of Fine Arts (Birmingham).

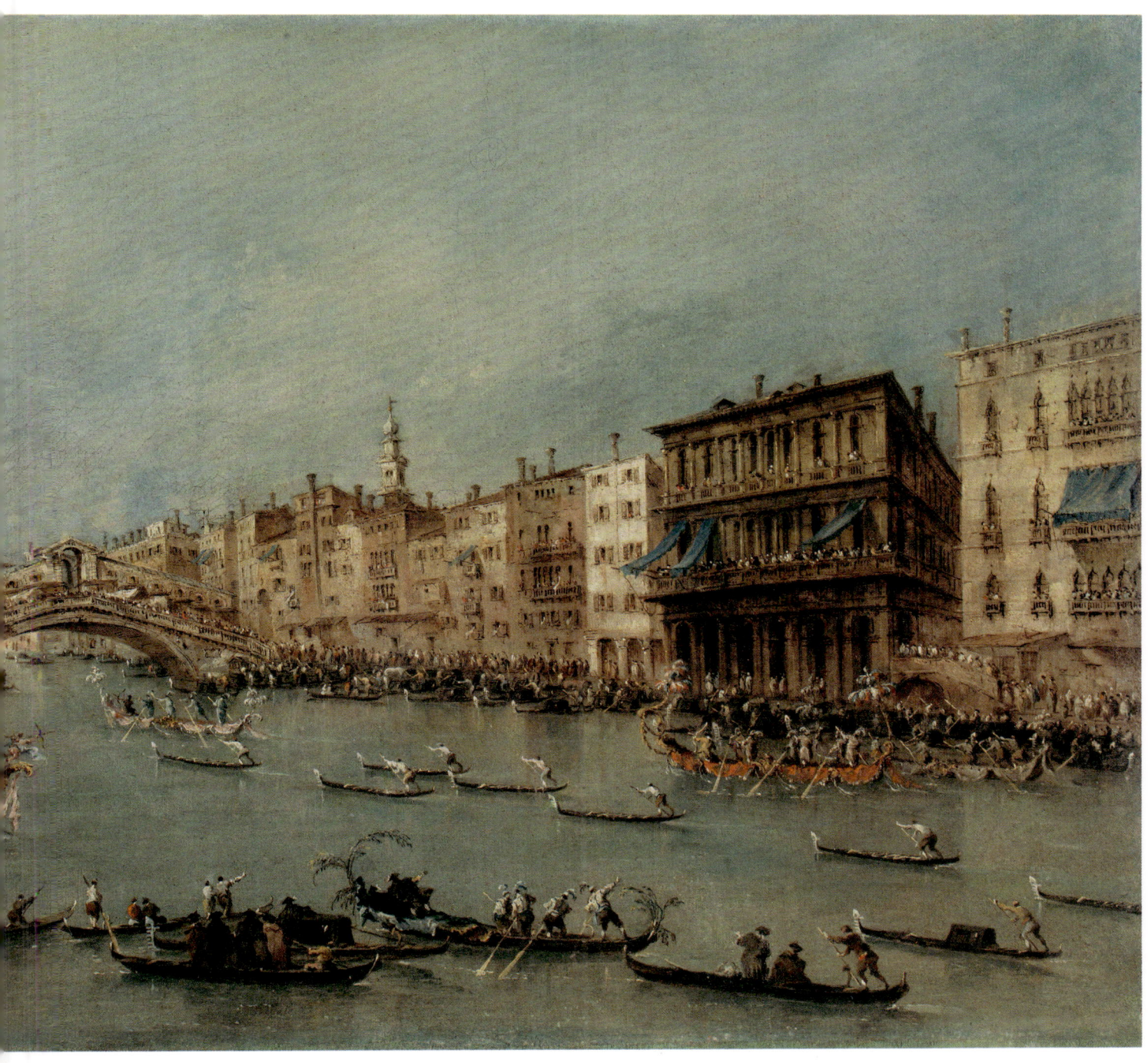

Guardi made two preparatory drawings for the painting, one of which was a detailed study of a *bissona* (Victoria and Albert Museum, London). One possibility that cannot be ruled out is that this work, considered late by most experts, included some collaboration by Giacomo Guardi, the painter's son. This is suggested by the less daring façade of the buildings and the crowd on the banks of the canal, contrasting with the composure demonstrated in the figures on the gondolas in the foreground of the scene.

BIBLIOGRAPHY

BYAM-SHAW 1951, p. 73, no. 54; MORASSI 1993, pp. 203, 268, no. 306; MURARO 1993, pp. 62–65, no. 18; PALLUCCHINI 1965, no. 16.

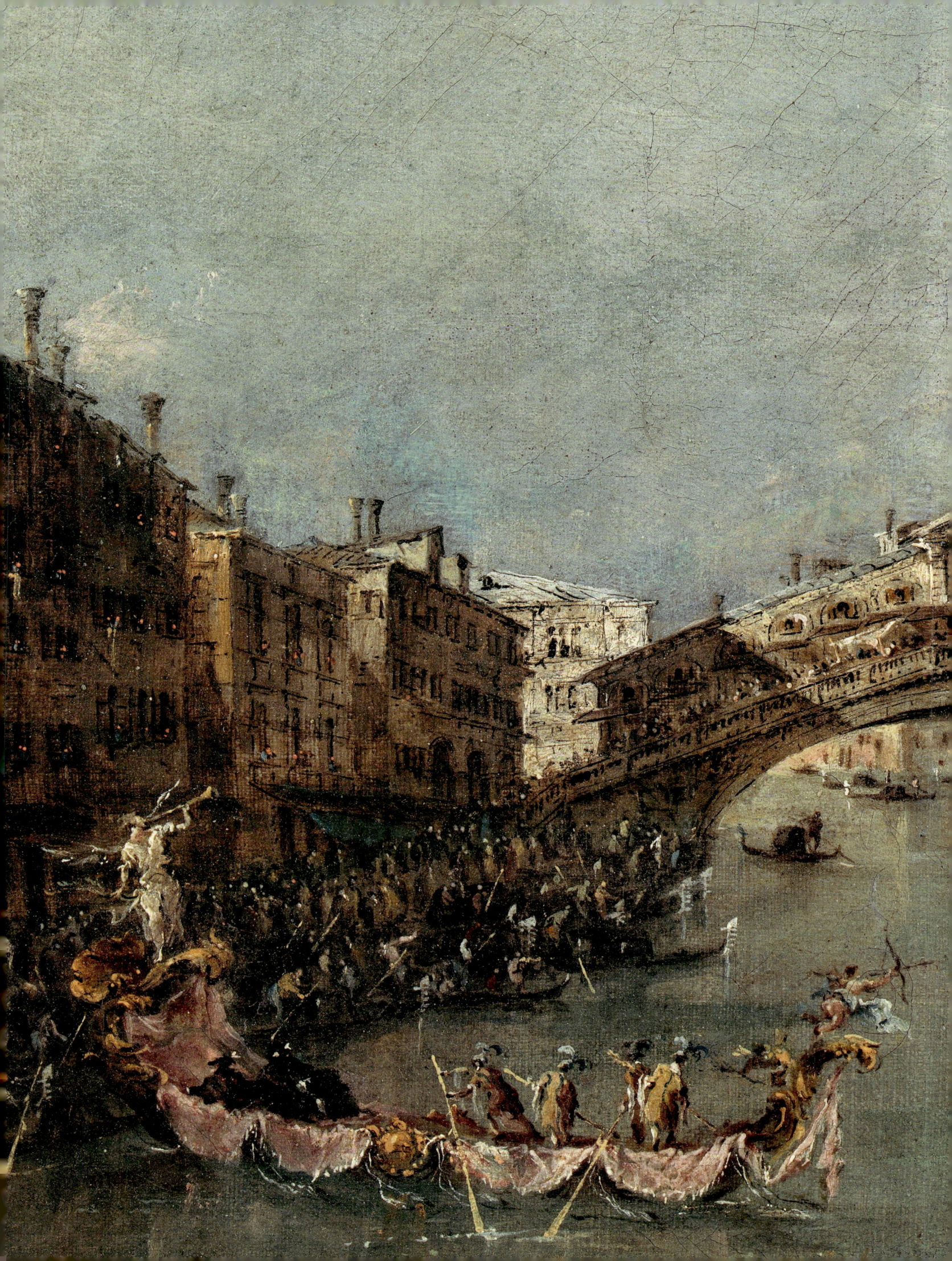

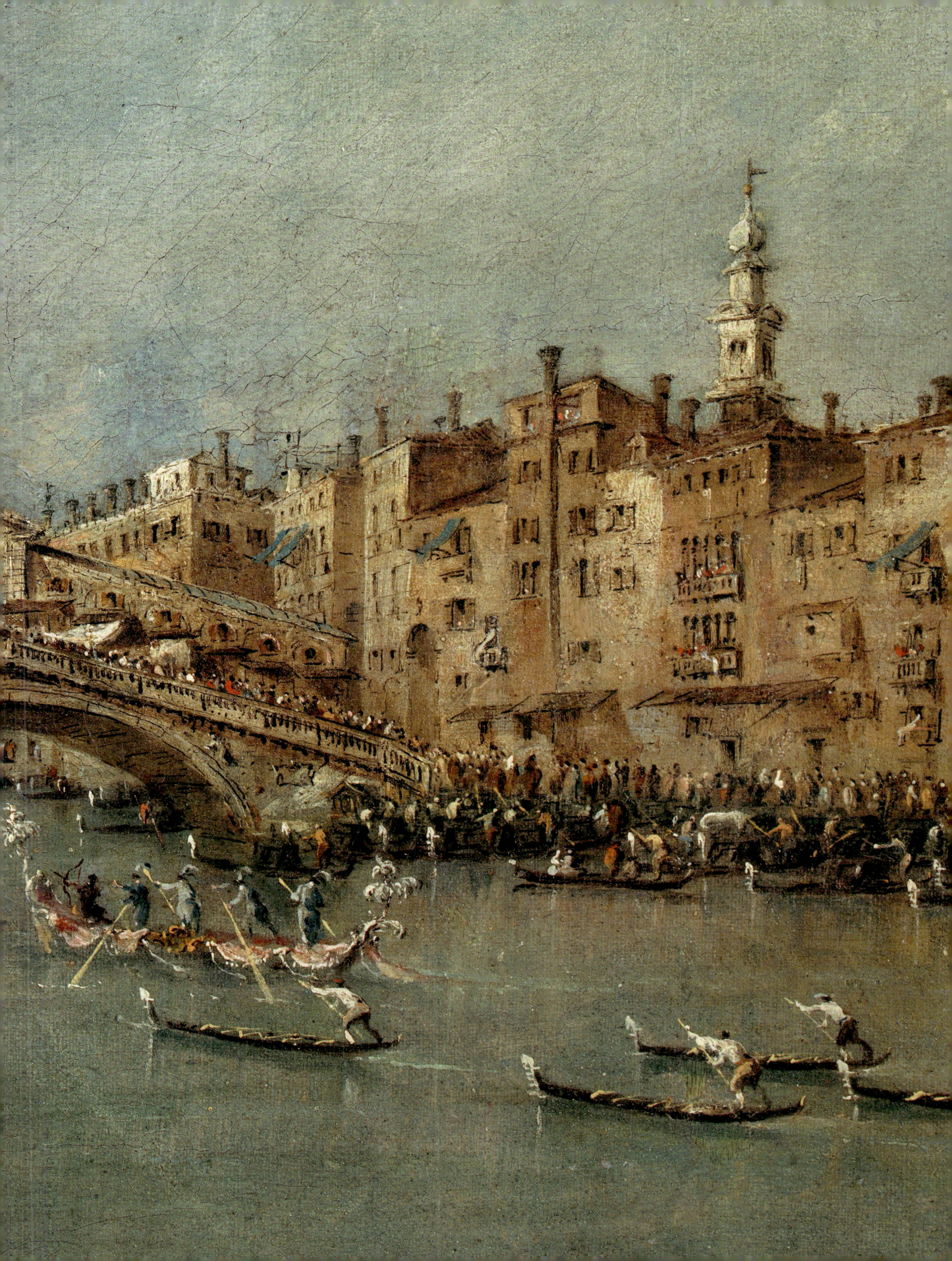

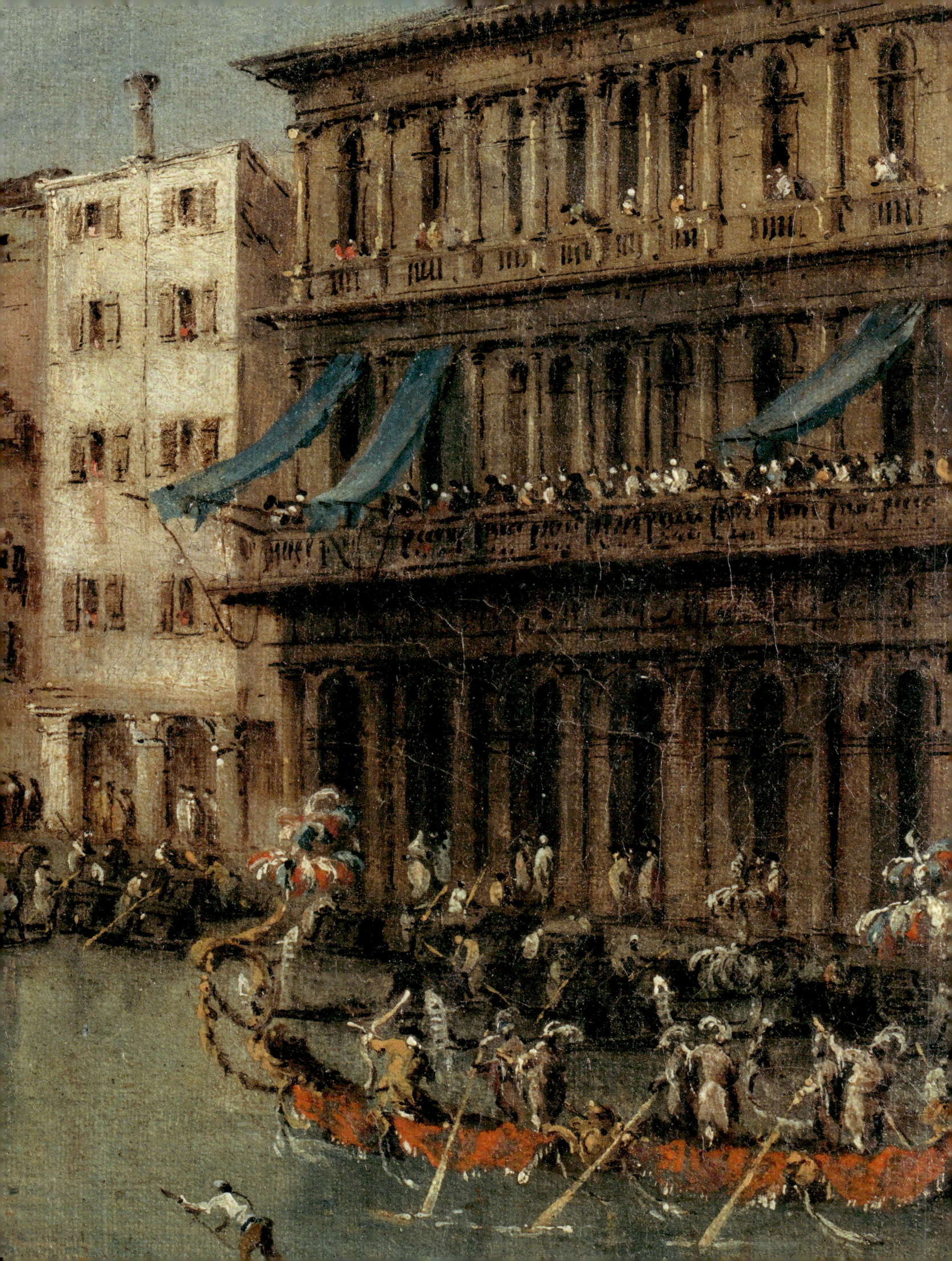

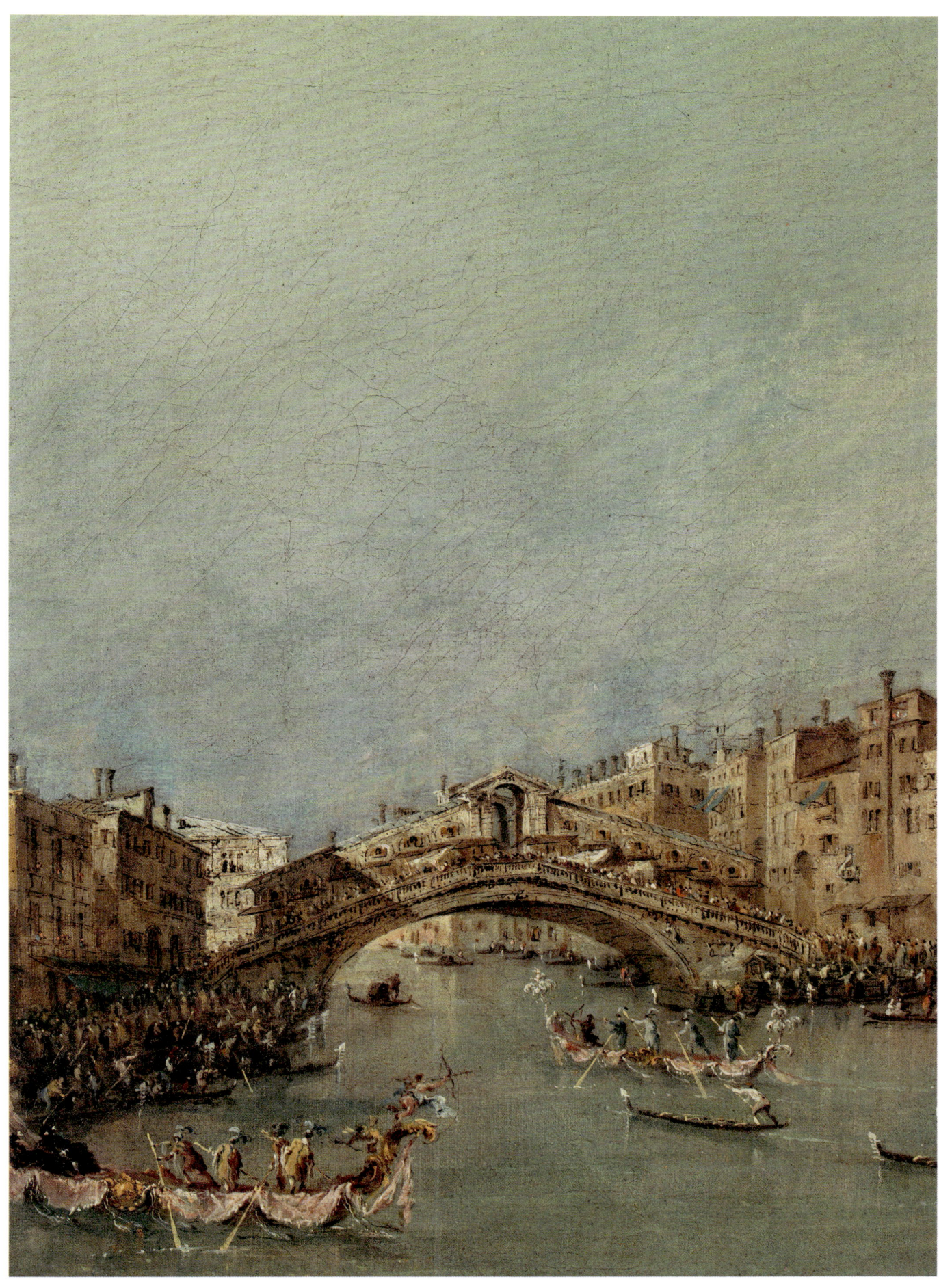

12
FRANCESCO GUARDI
(1712–1793)

Grand Canal at the Rialto Bridge

Venice, c. 1780–90

Oil on canvas

52 × 84 cm

PROVENANCE Rodolphe Kann Collection, Paris.
Acquired through Joseph Duveen, 1907.
Calouste Gulbenkian Museum, inv. 488

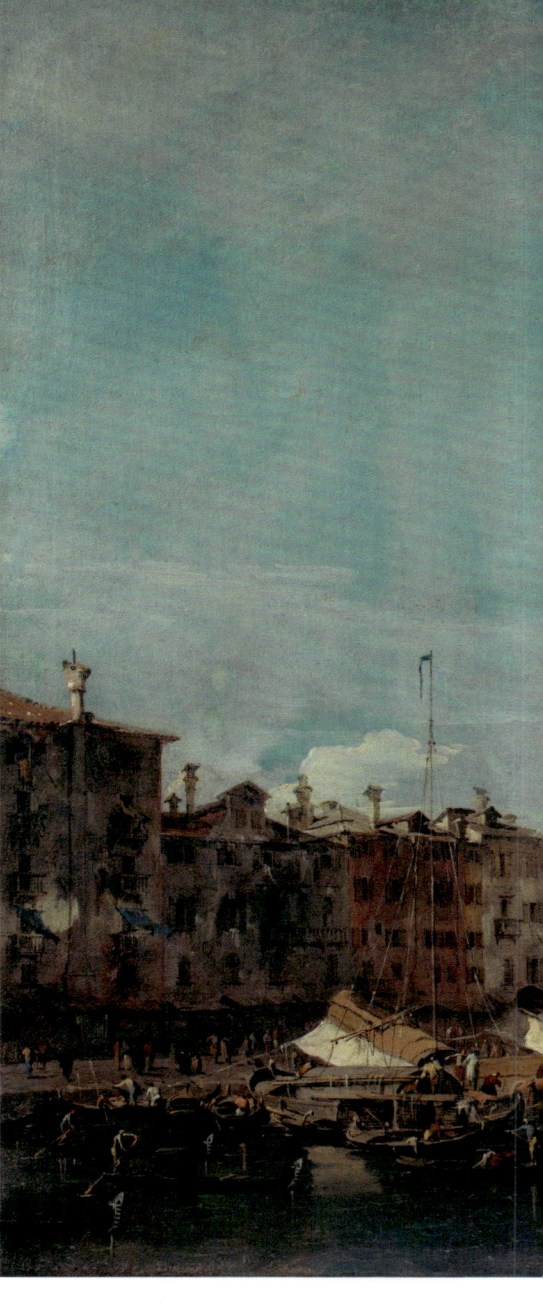

This painting depicts the Rialto Bridge from the Riva del Carbon, next to the Palazzo Dolfin Manin, built in 1536 by the architect and sculptor Jacopo Sansovino (1486–1570), which stands in the foreground on the right-hand side of the composition. This is the only work by Francesco Guardi in the Calouste Gulbenkian Collection that is signed, a detail visible on the notice next to the staircase, where various figures can be seen. On the opposite bank, the Riva del Vin, are the Fondaco dei Tedeschi building and the Palazzo dei Camerlenghi, the seat of the Republic's financial magistrates.

The painting's date has proved difficult to determine, as experts on Guardi's work hold differing positions. While some believe they recognise in the work affinities with Guardi's style at a time when his art was still influenced by Canaletto, i.e. before the 1760s, others seem to see in the depiction of the Riva del Vin the collaboration of his son Giacomo Guardi, which would make the painting's date much later. Supporting the latter hypothesis are the small 'pinhead' figures typical of compositions by the master's son.

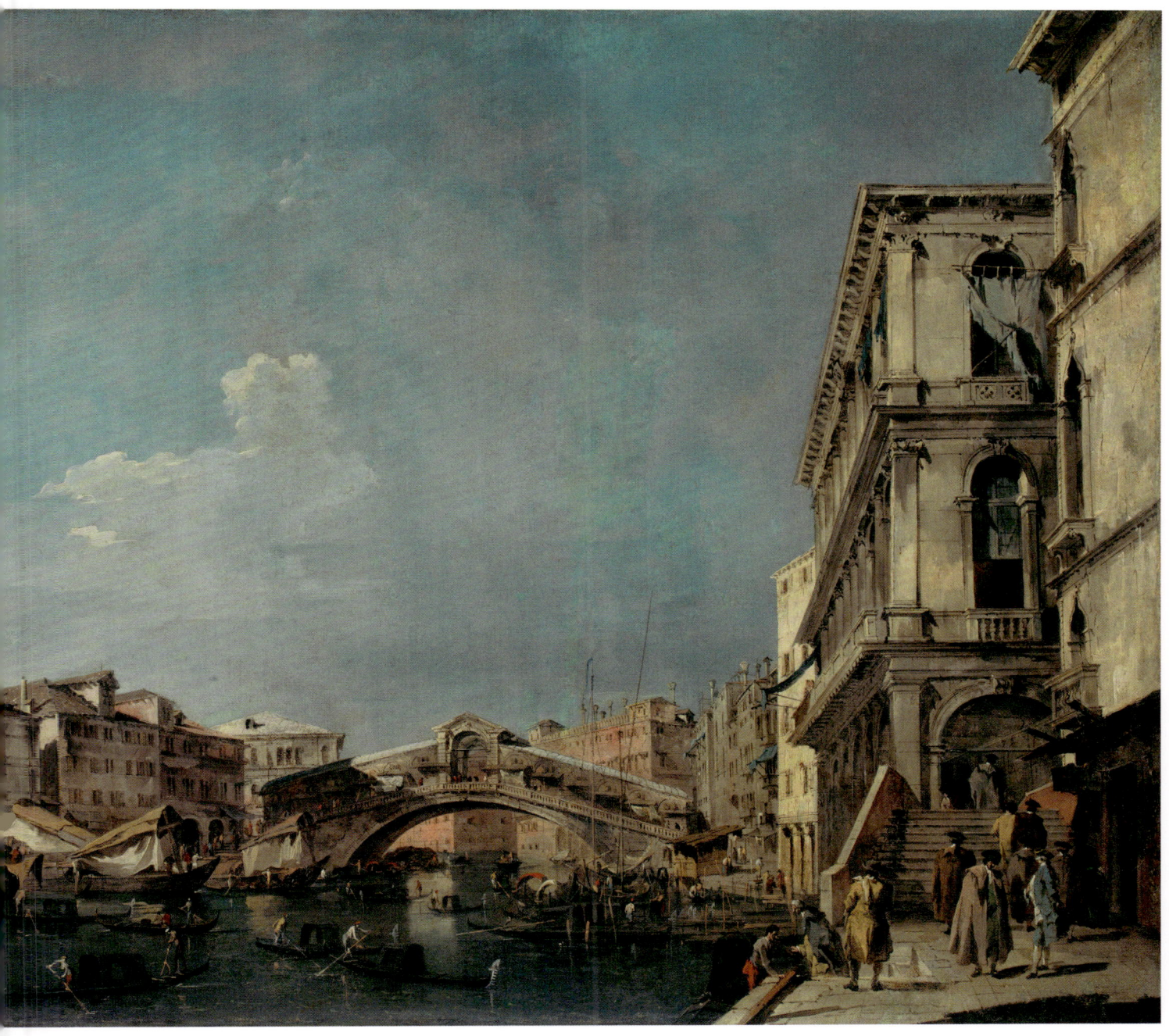

In the Earl of Iveagh Collection in London, there is another version of the theme, taken up by Guardi in around eight compositions with a very similar general configuration. The Musée du Louvre in Paris houses a preparatory drawing for the painting, while the Sperling Collection in New York has a sketch for the two figures in the foreground of the scene.

BIBLIOGRAPHY

MORASSI 1993, vol. I, p. 408, no. 525; MURARO 1991, pp. 32–37, no. 89; MURARO 1993, pp. 66–69, no. 19; PALLUCCHINI 1965, no. 1.

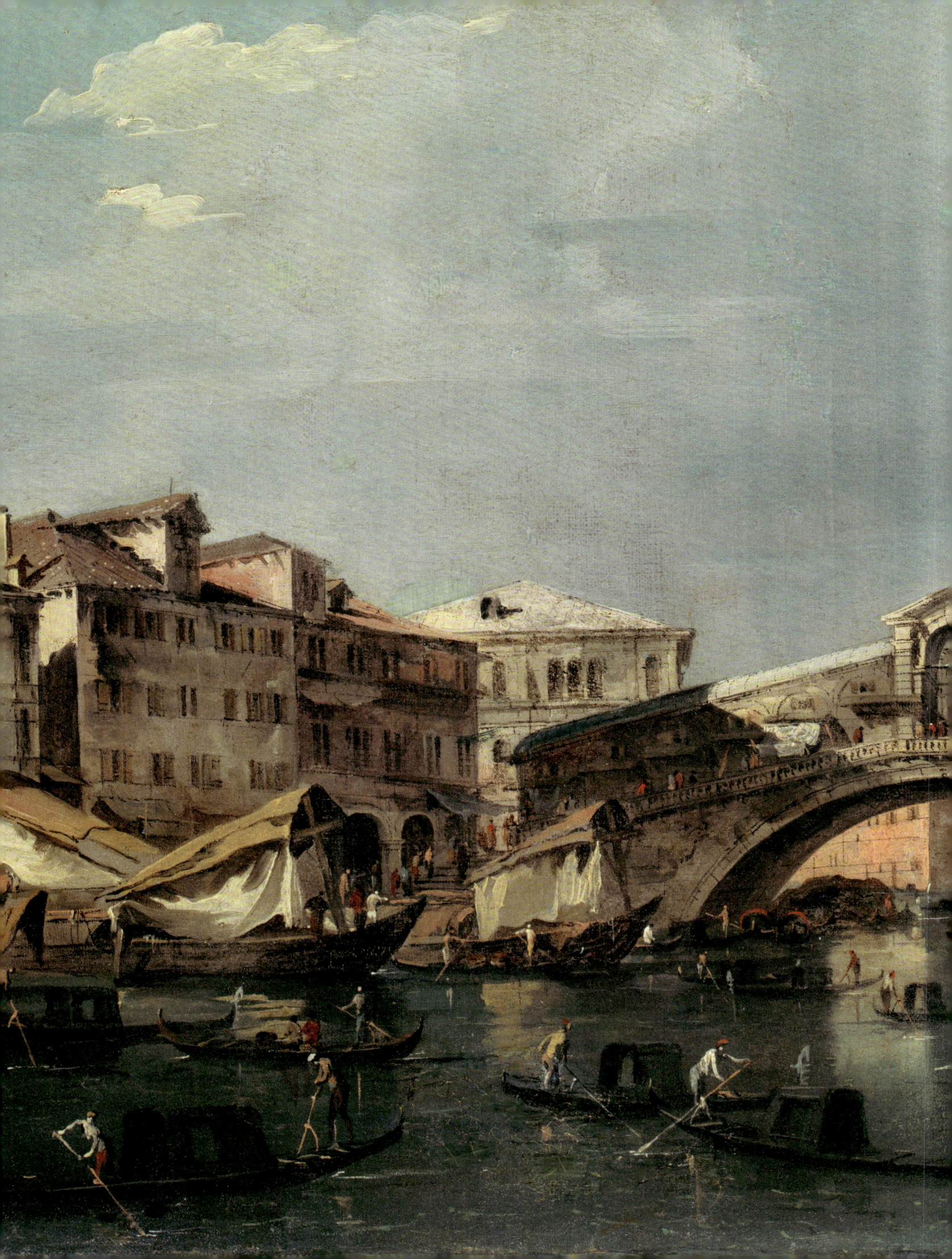

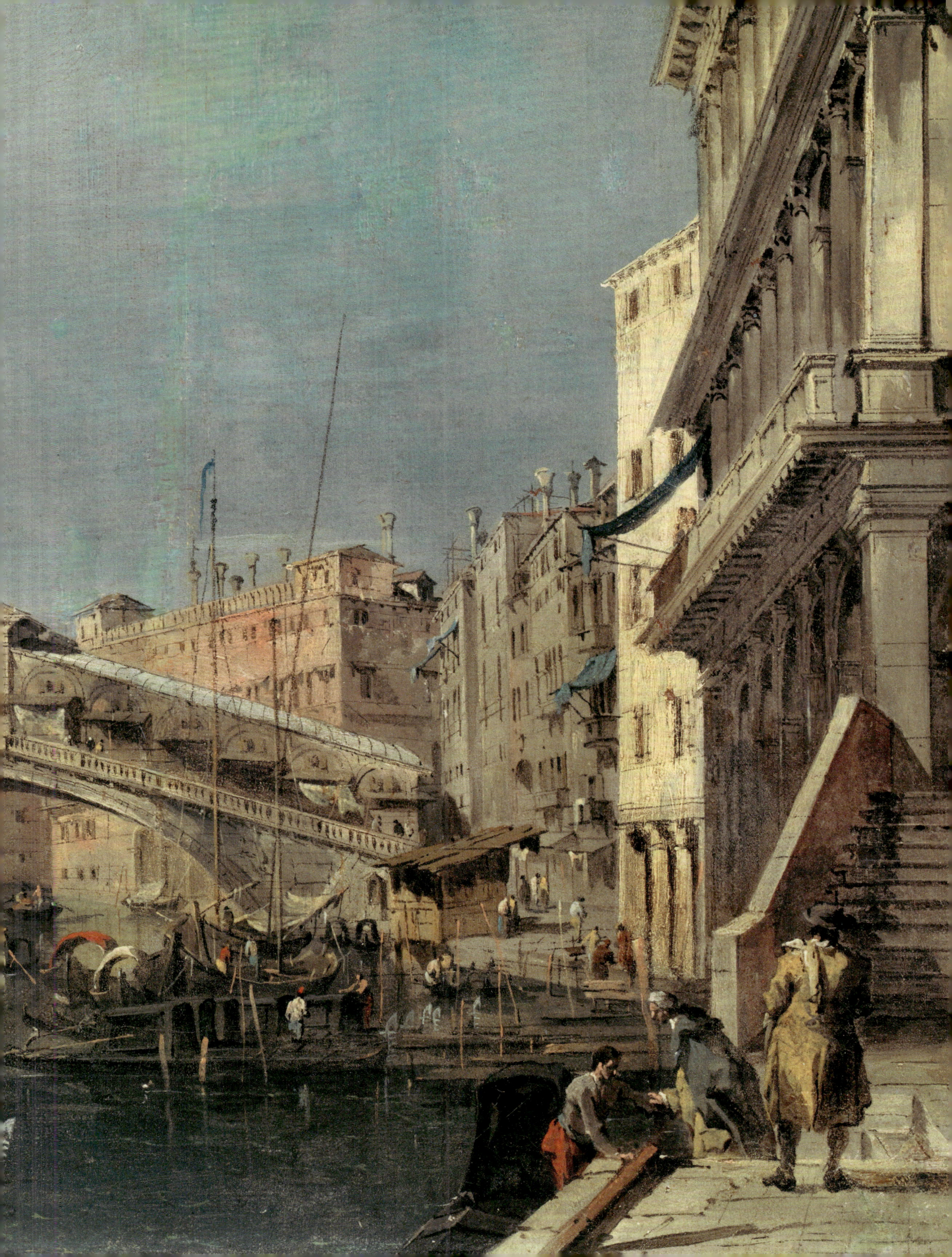

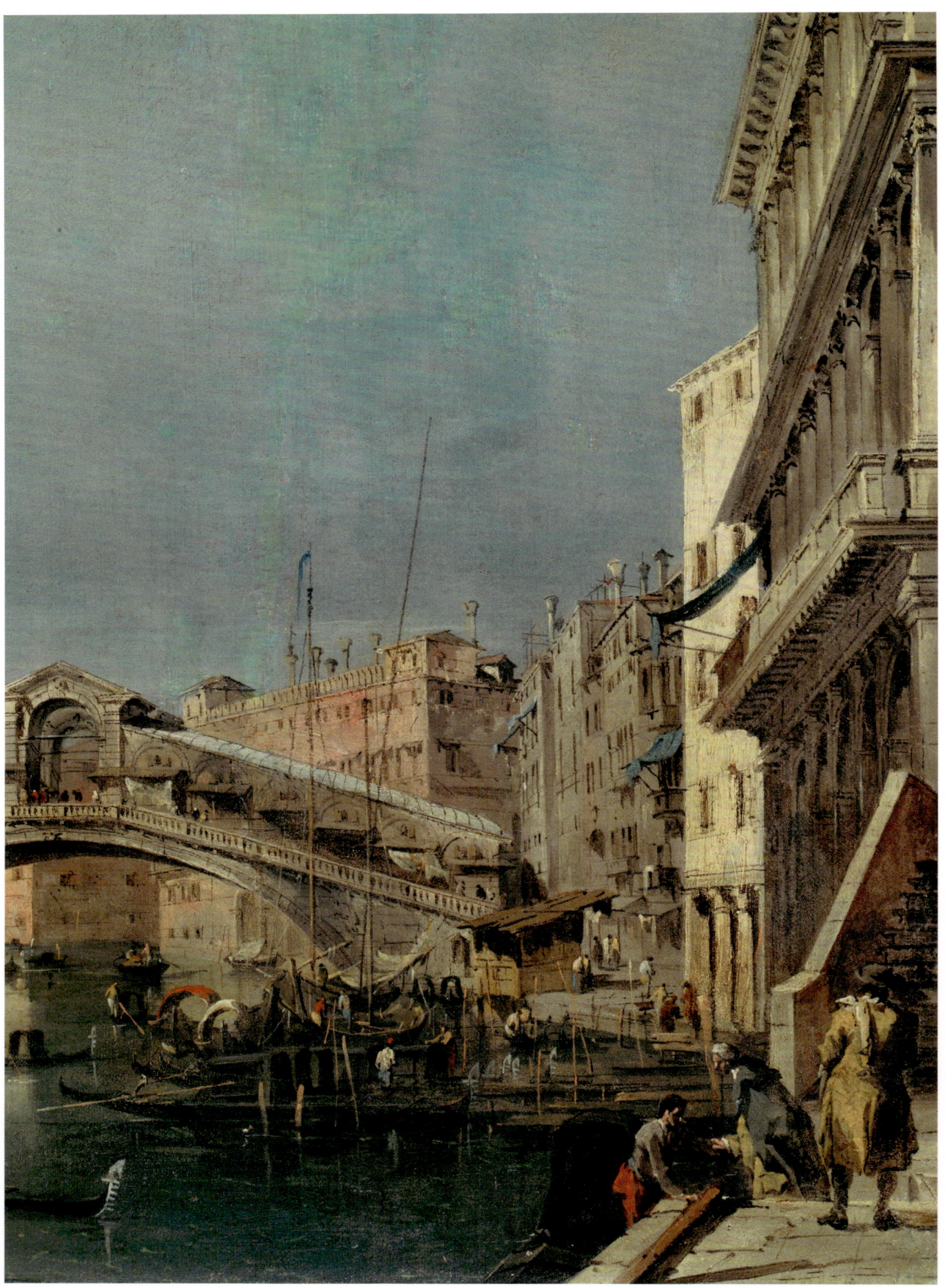

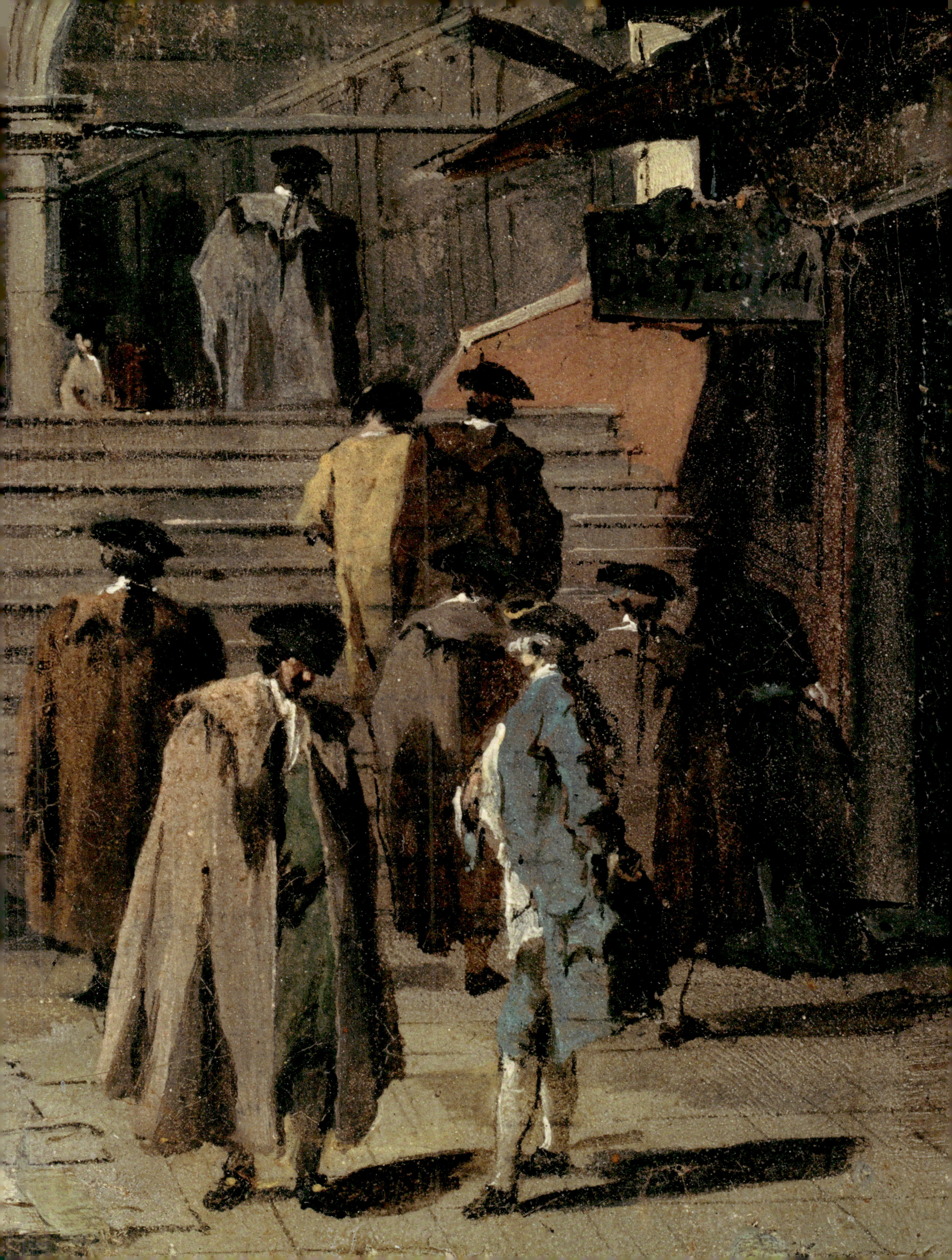

13
FRANCESCO GUARDI
(1712–1793)

The Rialto Bridge after the Design by Palladio

Venice, c. 1770

Oil on canvas

61 × 92 cm

<u>PROVENANCE</u> Earl of Camperdown Collection;
Earl of Buckinghamshire Collection. Acquired
through Christie's, London, on 8 March 1919.
Calouste Gulbenkian Museum, inv. 393

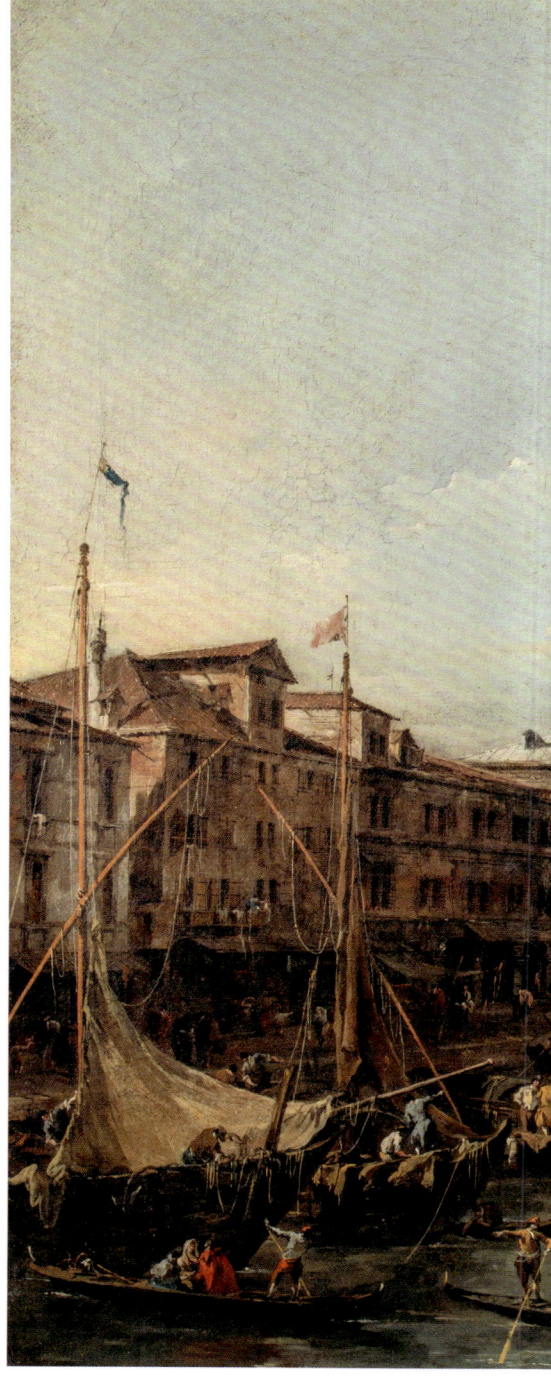

This idealised view of Venice shows the bridge designed
by Renaissance architect Andrea Palladio (1508–1580)
for the Rialto area, a project that never actually came
to fruition. The work was eventually commissioned
to Antonio da Ponte (1512–1595) who, in 1591, was given
the task of replacing the old wooden bridge on the site
with a stone structure.

In this *capriccio*, Francesco Guardi decided to bring
Palladio's project for the Rialto 'to life' by recreating,
next to the classically-inspired bridge, the bustling
movement of the boats and figures that habitually made
their way between the Riva del Carbon and the Riva del
Vin, as portrayed in other *vedute* by him. In this sense,
the painting takes on a tone of almost palpable veracity
in relation to a reality that never actually existed,
yet the integration of these elements gives the scene
a real urban view feel.

The theme had already been explored by Canaletto
in 1742 and c. 1756–59 (Royal Collection Trust, London)
in *Capriccio View with Palladio's Design for the Rialto
Bridge* and *Capriccio with Palladian Buildings*
(Galleria Nazionale di Parma, Parma), respectively,
works that differ in their configuration. Among the
English clientèle, the motif aroused particular interest

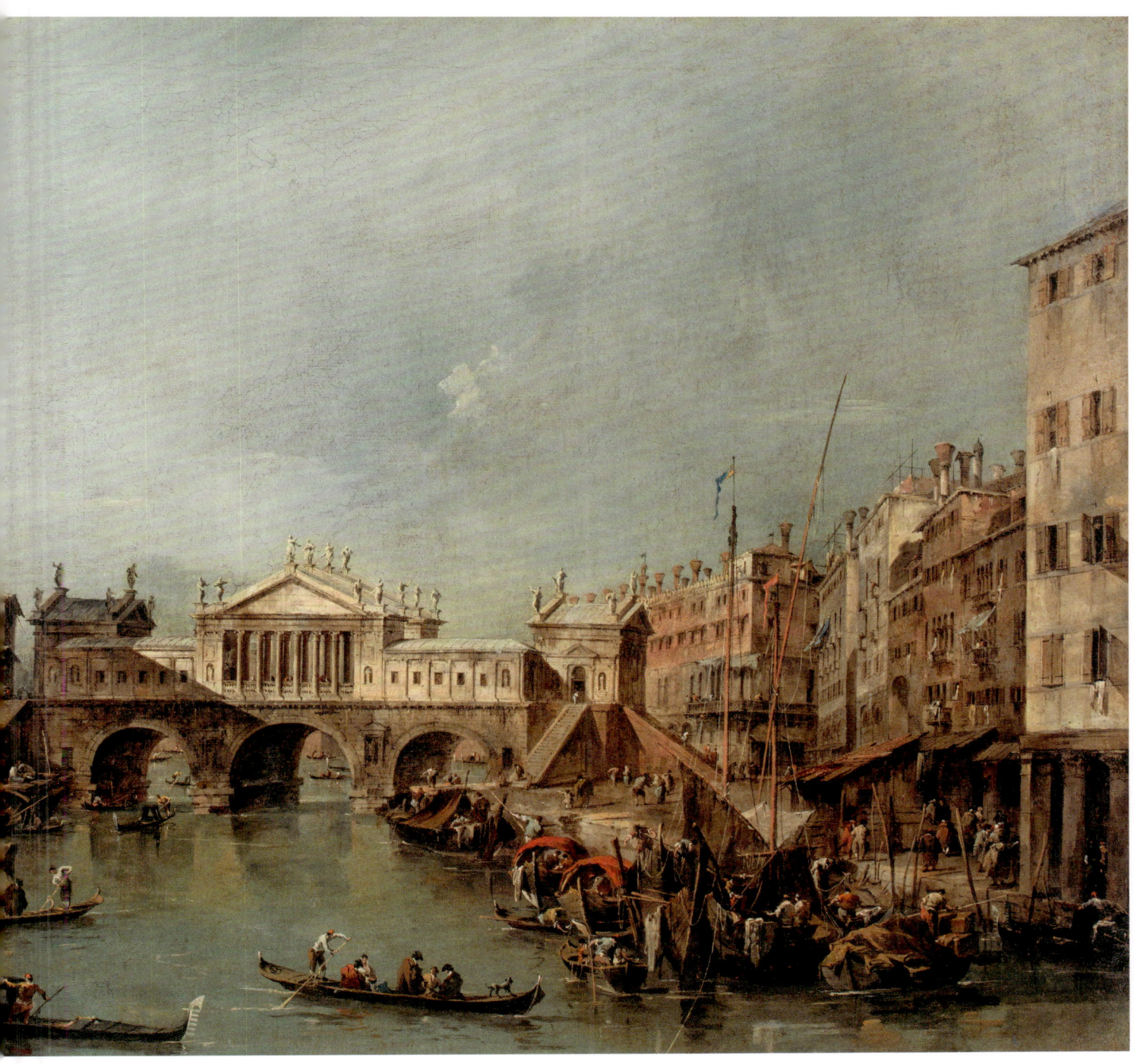

in the eighteenth-century Venetian painters who incorporated elements of Palladian architecture into their compositions, at a time coinciding with the affirmation of neoclassical aesthetics in England. The preparatory sketch for the painting can be found in the Museo Correr in Venice.

BIBLIOGRAPHY

FRANCESCO 1993, pp. 166–67; MORASSI 1993, vol. I, p. 414, no. 559; MURARO 1993, pp. 18–21, no. 3; PALLUCCHINI 1965, no. 6.

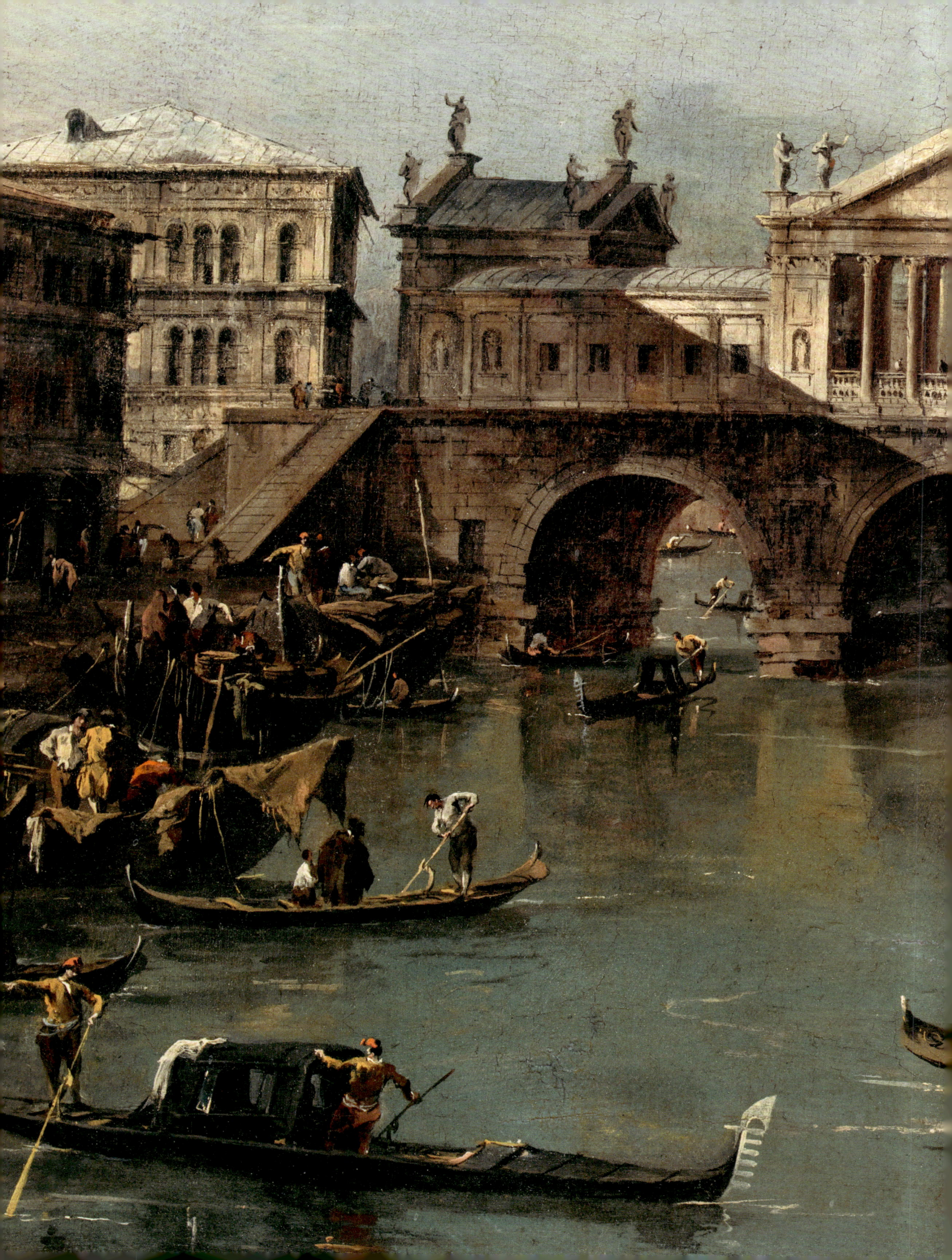

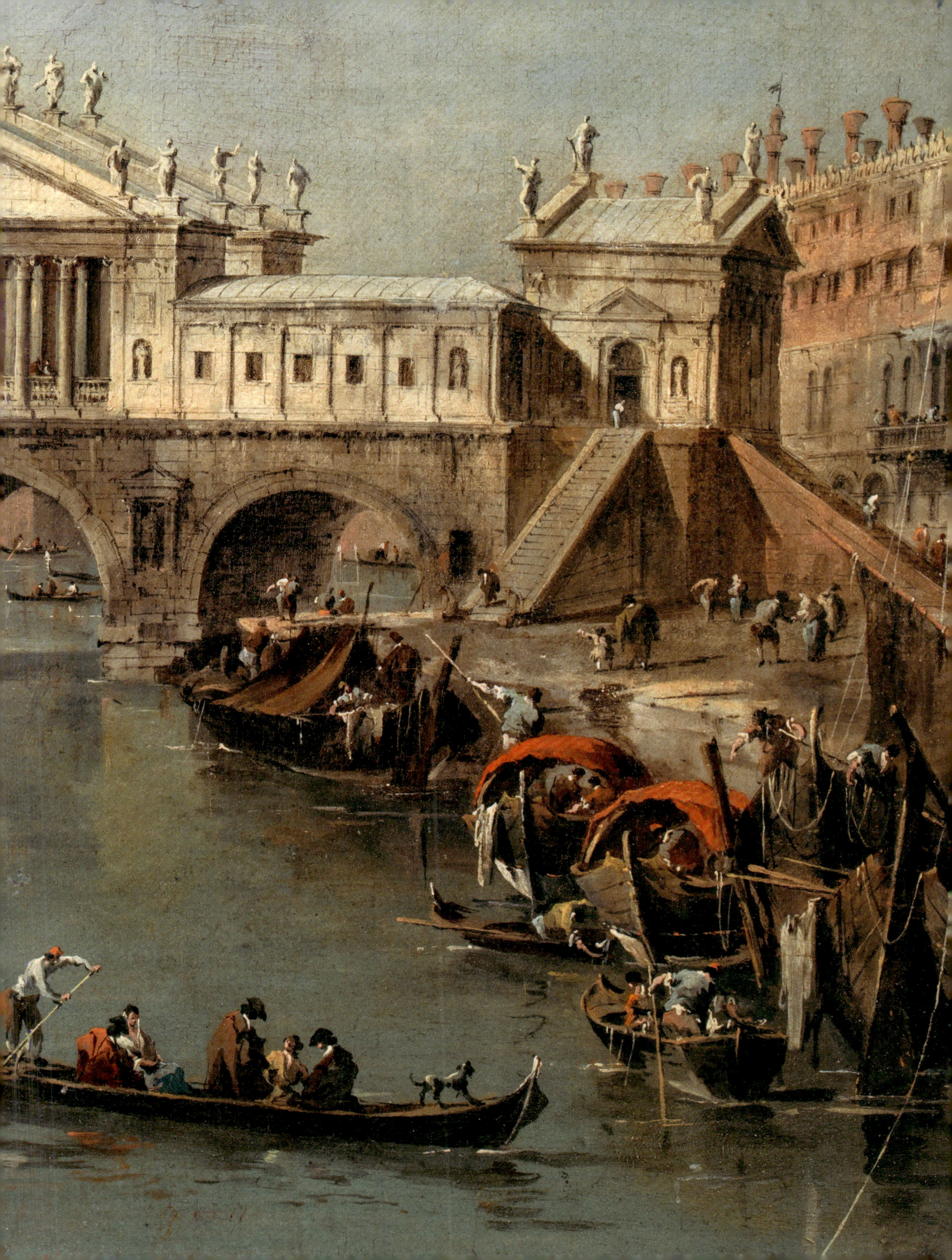

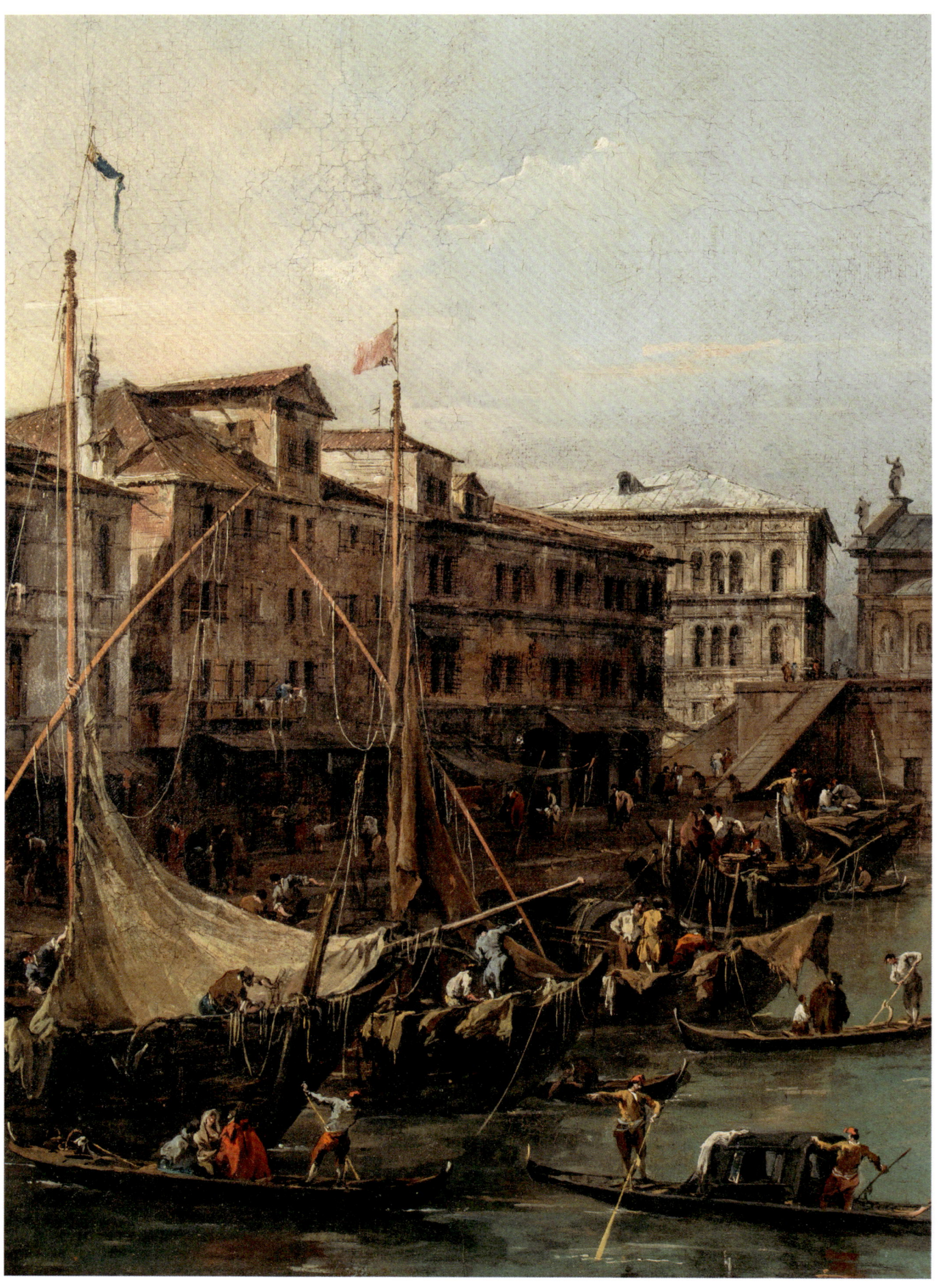

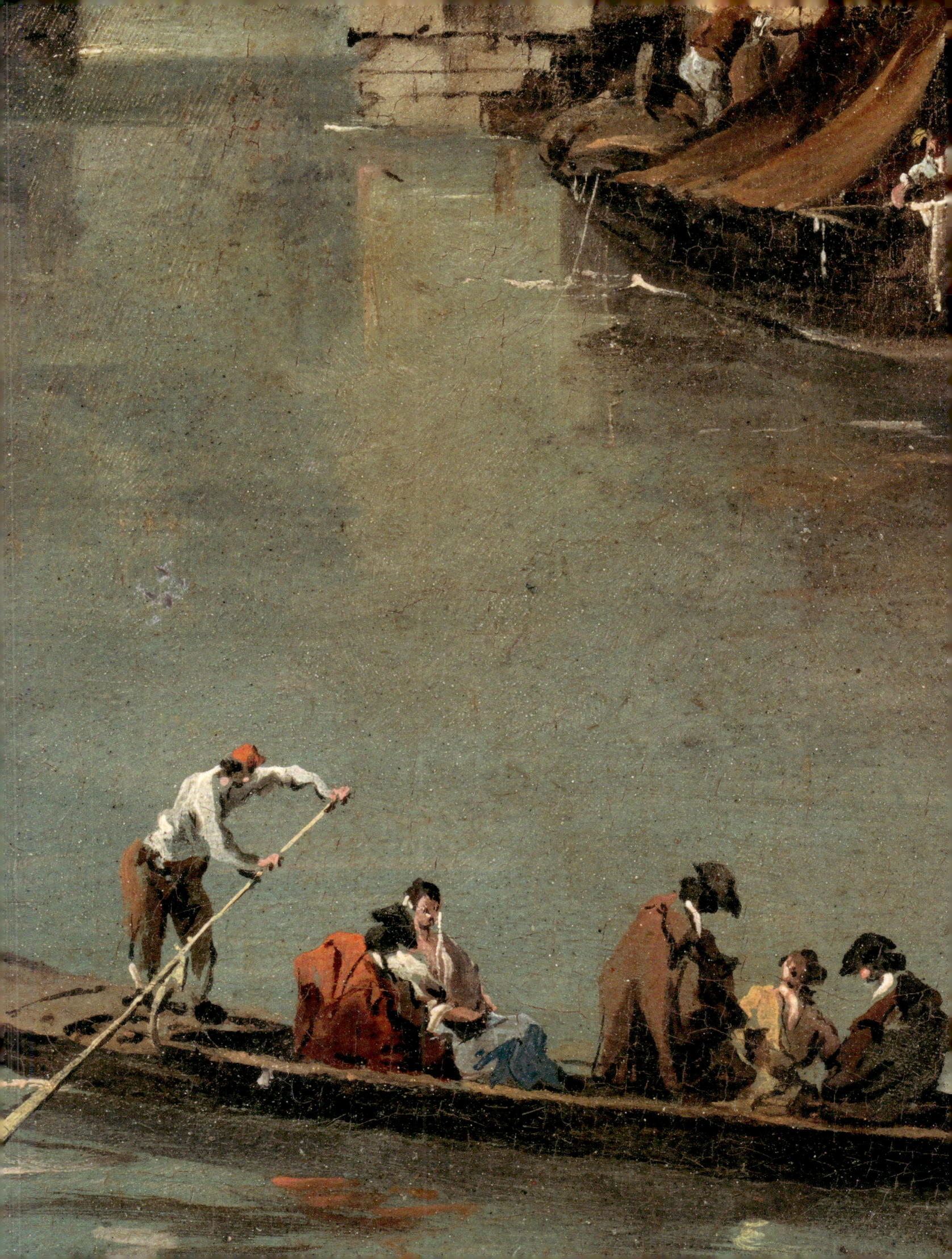

14
GIACOMO GUARDI
(1764–1835)

Regatta on the Grand Canal near the Rialto Bridge

Venice, 1790s
Oil on canvas
49.5 × 83.2 cm

PROVENANCE Acquired from Colnaghi,
London, on 25 January 1921.
Calouste Gulbenkian Museum, inv. 387

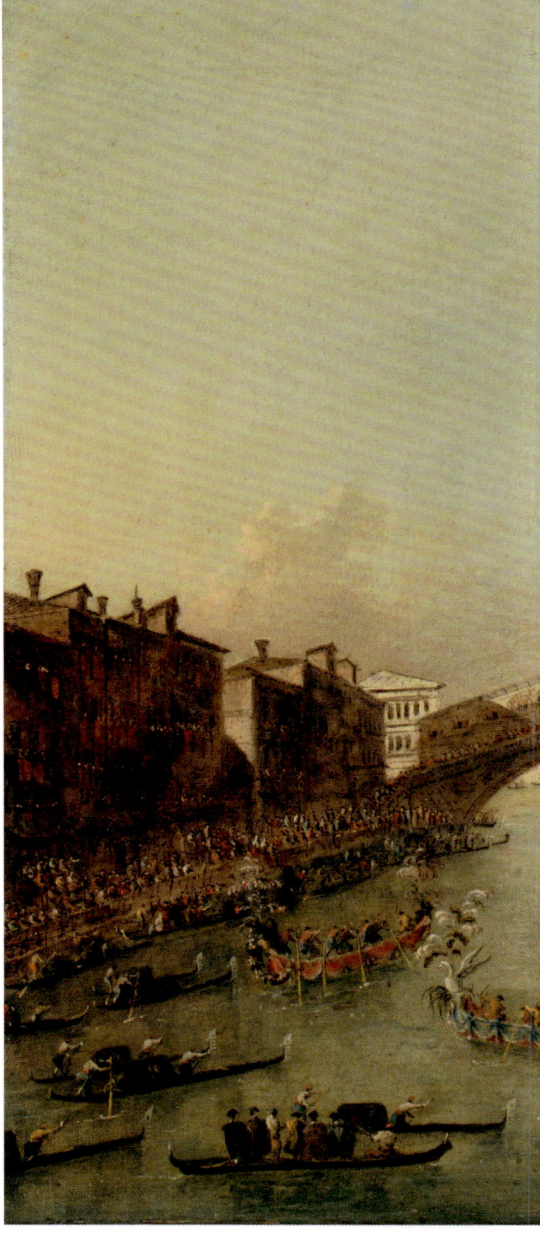

The painting shows obvious similarities to the work in the Calouste Gulbenkian Collection mentioned in cat. 11, although it displays less dynamism in the movement of the boats and the figures in the foreground of the scene. The decoration of the buildings' balconies is also less exuberant and executed more mechanically, indicating the less inventive style of Giacomo Guardi, who, throughout his career, repeated successful motifs previously depicted by his father. The presence of French banners on one of the gondolas seems to confirm that this is indeed a painting produced after the end of the Venetian Republic.

As in the other version in the Calouste Gulbenkian Collection, this painting depicts the *bissona*, a large, richly decorated gondola, which also appears in works from Francesco Guardi's last phase. Unlike another version of the master's work on the same theme (Rijksmuseum, Amsterdam), in which the viewpoint is closer to the Rialto Bridge, this painting emphasises the buildings on the Riva del Carbon, with the San Bartolomeo Bell Tower rising above them.

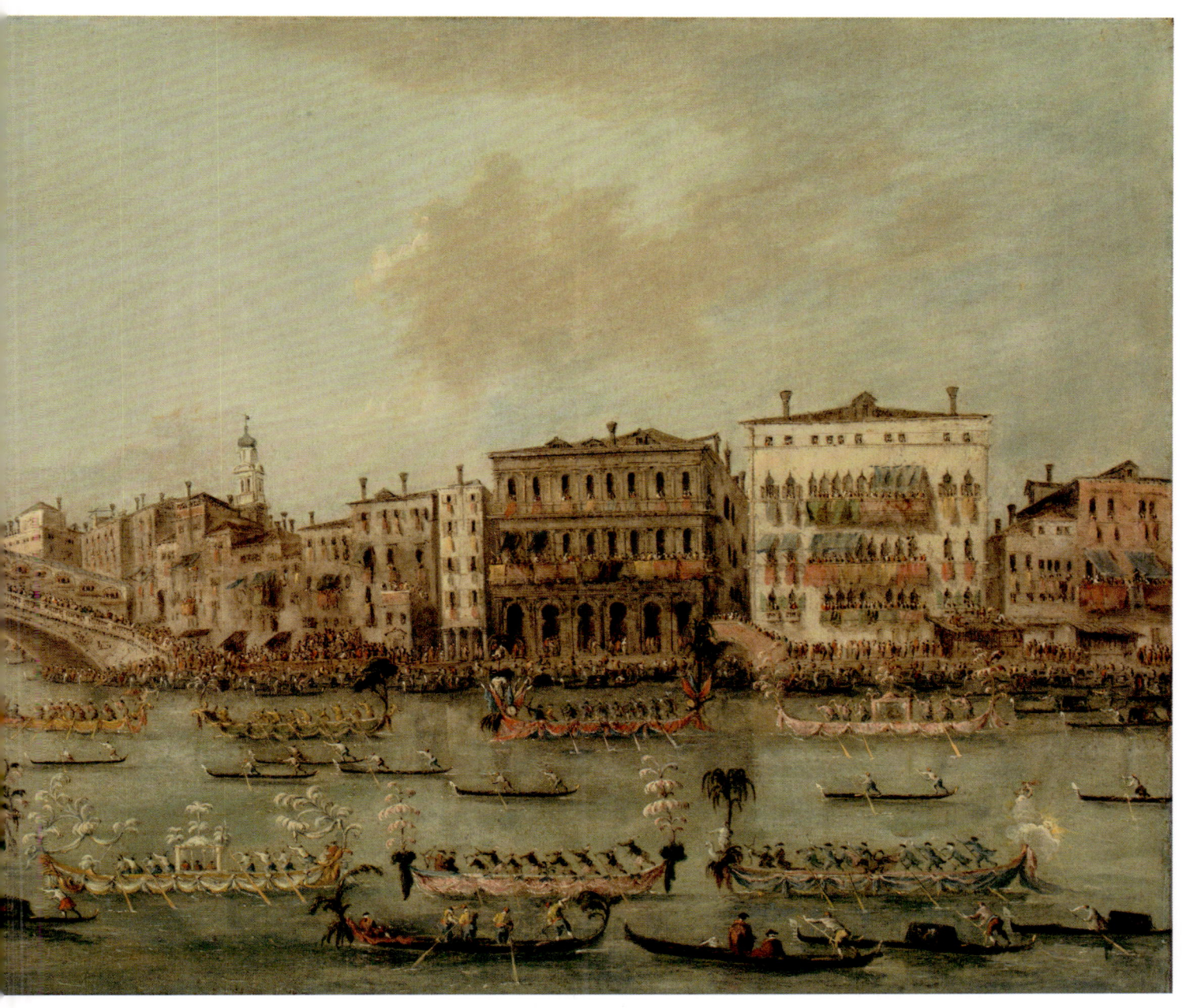

BIBLIOGRAPHY

MORASSI 1993, vol. I, pp. 203, 368, no. 307; MURARO 1993, pp. 70–71, no. 20; PALLUCCHINI 1965, no. 18.

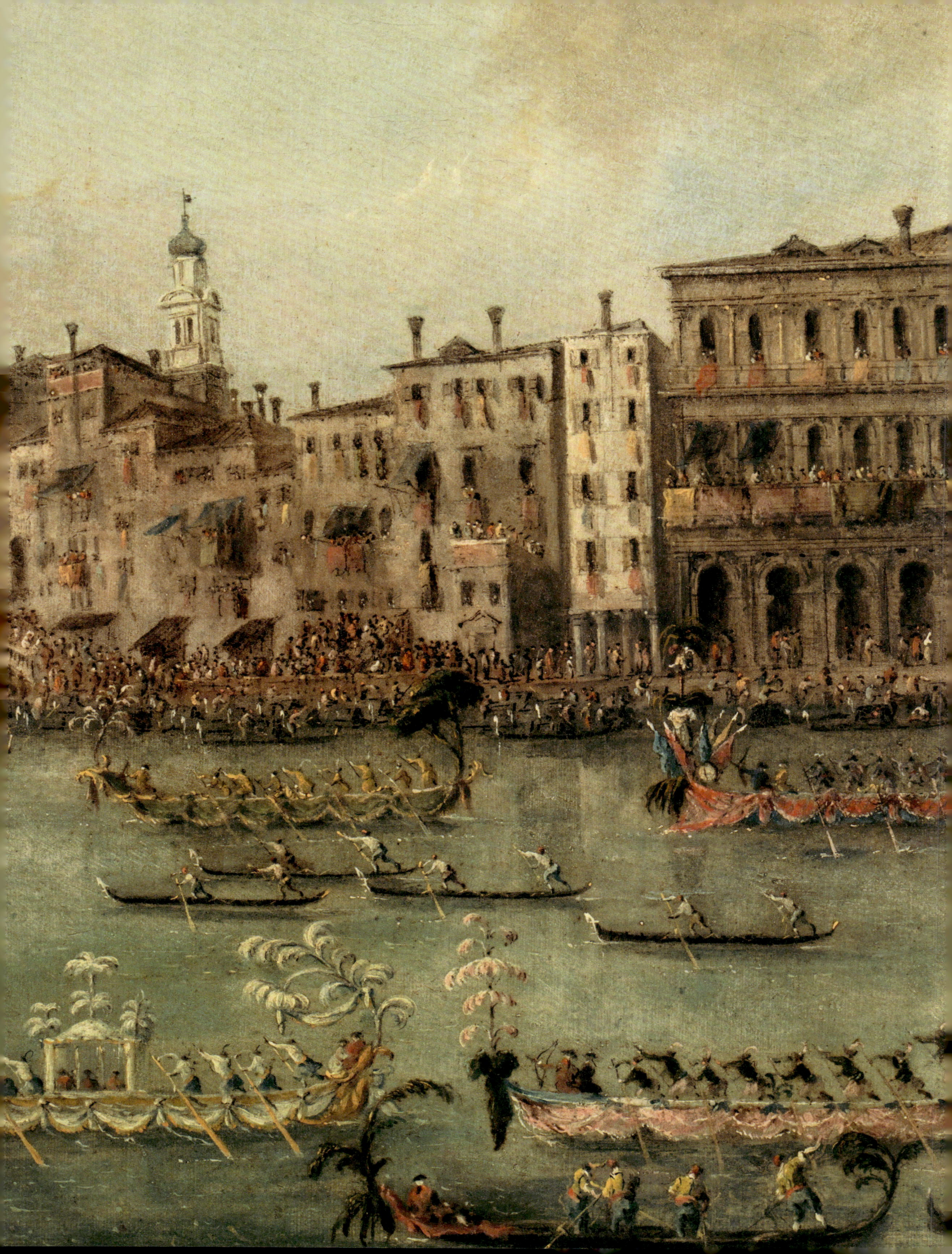

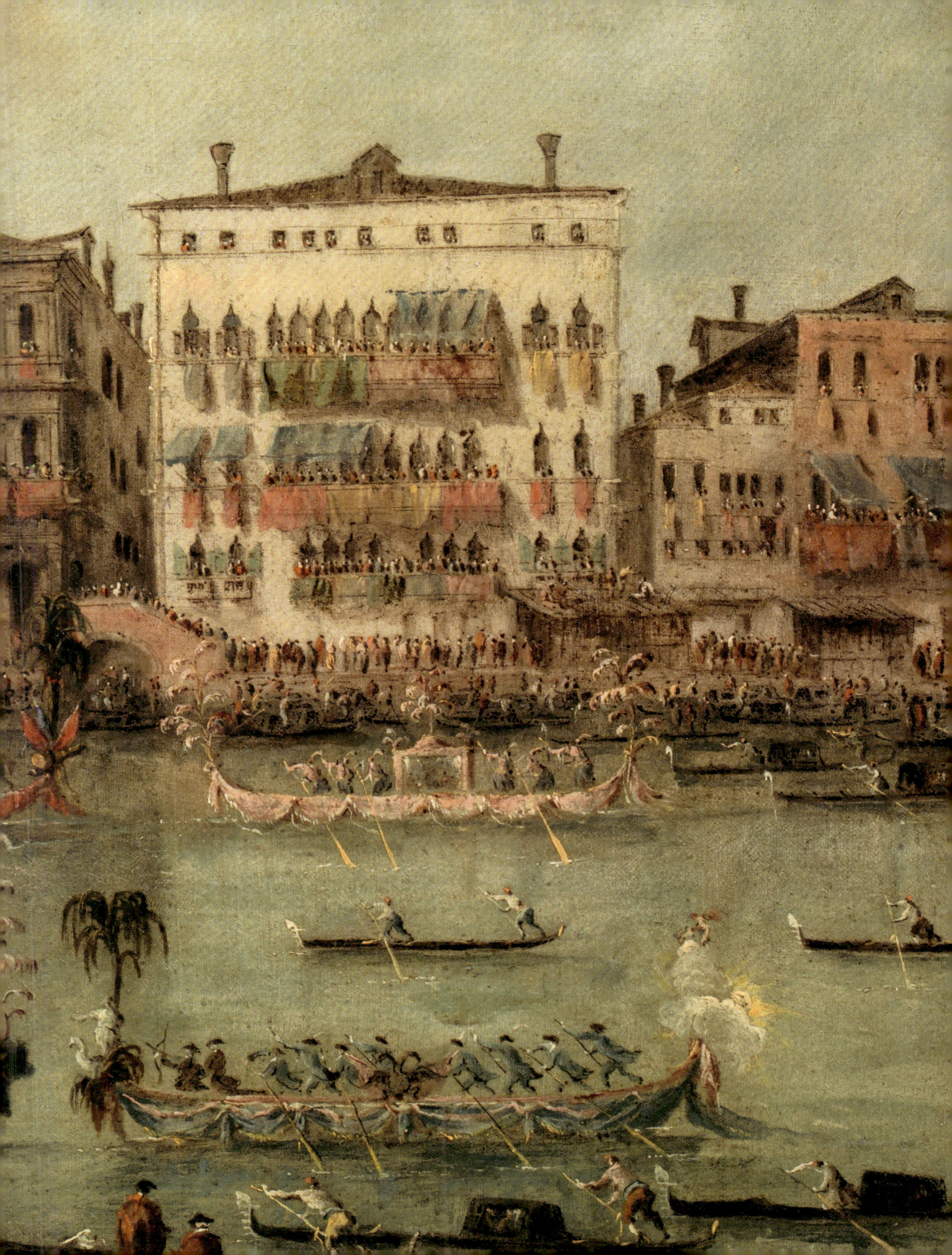

15
FRANCESCO GUARDI
(1712–1793)

The Grand Canal with San Simeone Piccolo and Santa Lucia

Venice c. 1780
Oil on canvas
48 × 78 cm

PROVENANCE Mrs Danbuz Collection, Isle of Wight;
Leonard Gow Collection, Eksan, Craigendoran,
Dumbartonshire; Thyssen-Bornemisza Collection,
Lugano, 1934; on loan at the Museo Thyssen-Bornemisza,
Madrid, 1992; Museo Thyssen-Bornemisza, Madrid, 1993.
Museo Nacional Thyssen-Bornemisza, Madrid,
inv. 175 (1934.7)

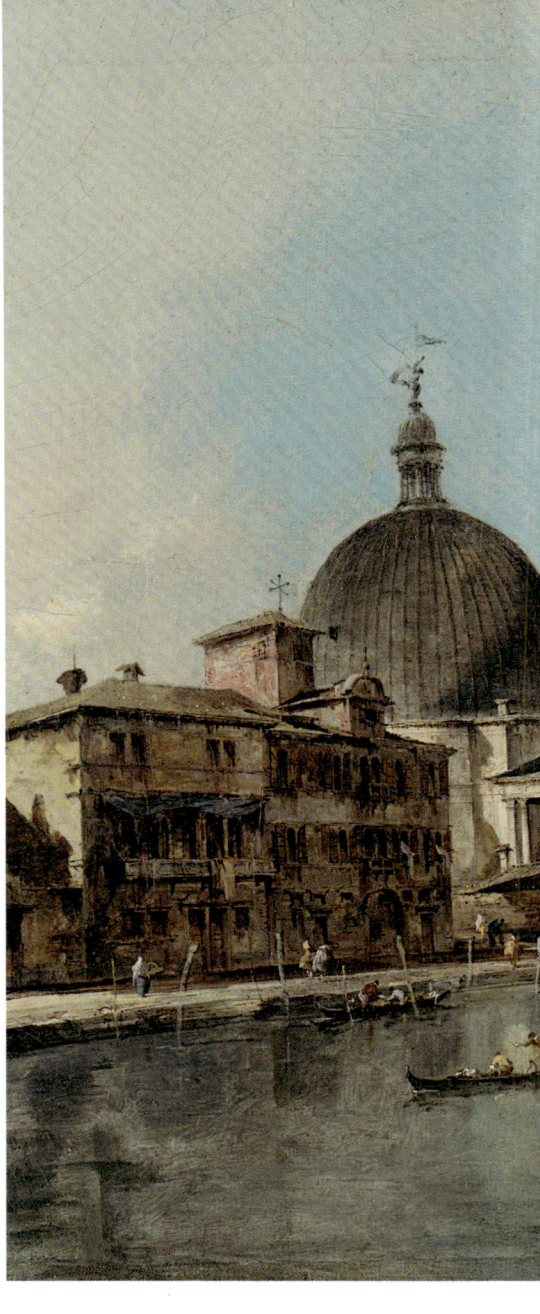

The painting depicts an area of the Grand Canal, on whose bank rises the dome of the Church of San Simeone Piccolo, constructed on a ninth century building and rebuilt in 1718 by the architect Giovanni Scalforotto (1672–1764), who was inspired by the Pantheon in Rome. Next to it is the Palazzo Foscari Contarini, built in the sixteenth century. On the opposite bank, the Church of Santa Lucia is visible, which was demolished in 1861 and was also depicted by Francesco Guardi in the painting *The Grand Canal with Santa Lucia and Santa Maria di Nazareth* (cat. 16), this work's counterpart.

There are six similar compositions of the *veduta* by the artist, with minor variations in detail, such as the larger versions at the Philadelphia Museum of Art and the Academy of Fine Arts Vienna. This canvas differs from those works primarily from a chromatic point of view, as the softer colour palette, in which pastel shades and greyish blue dominate, lends the composition a particularly serene atmosphere. This was a recurring feature of the painter's work, with alterations introduced to compositions whose success with the Venetian clientèle led to repetitions of certain urban views. A very similar *veduta* by

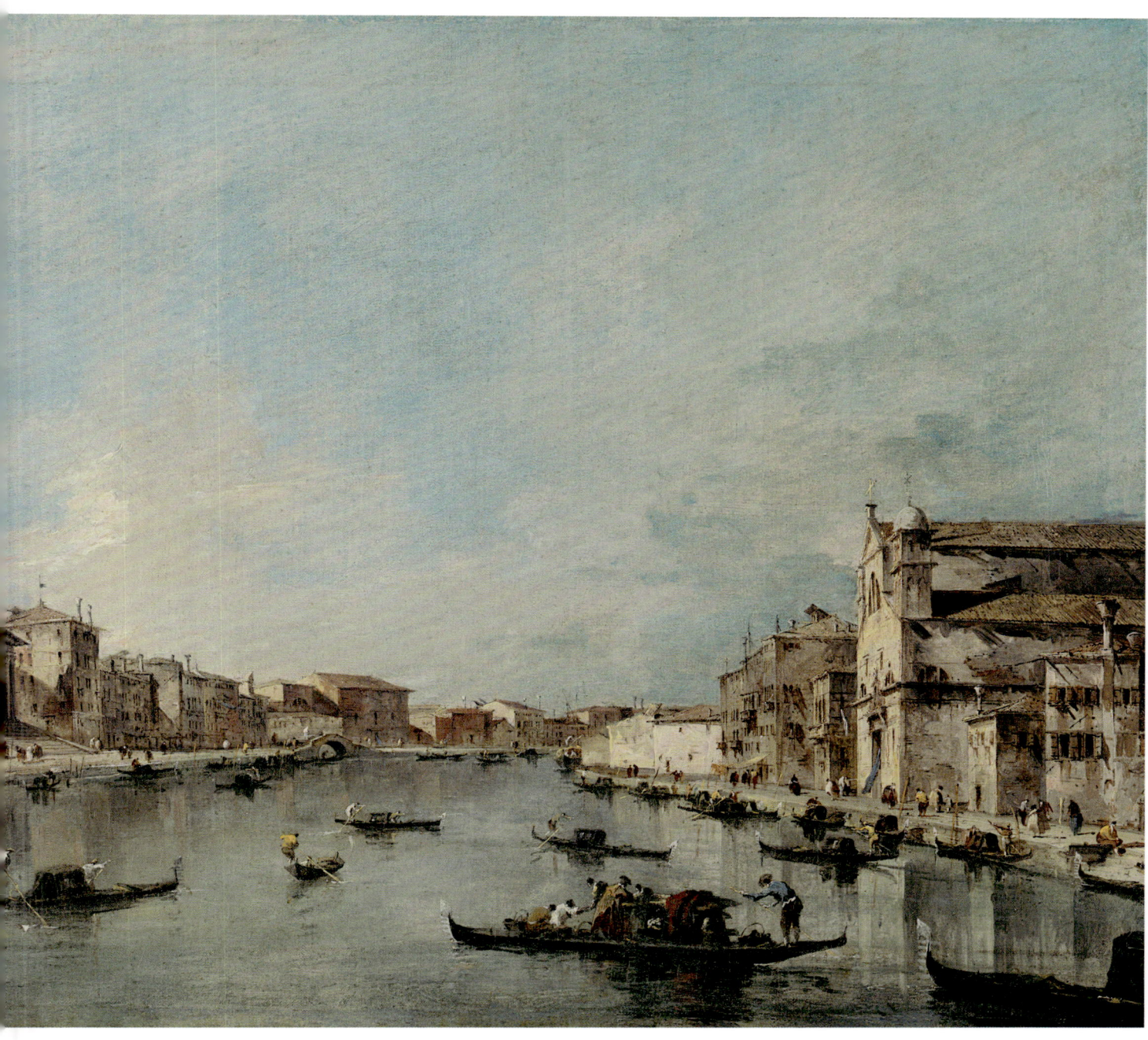

Canaletto from around 1740 (The National Gallery, London) includes the façade of the Church of the Scalzi in the scene, which Francesco Guardi's perspective does not show.

BIBLIOGRAPHY

BOROBIA 2009, pp. 508–9; CRAIEVICH AND PEDROCCO 2012, pp. 251, 276, no. 106; MORASSI 1993, vol. I, pp. 418–19, no. 580.

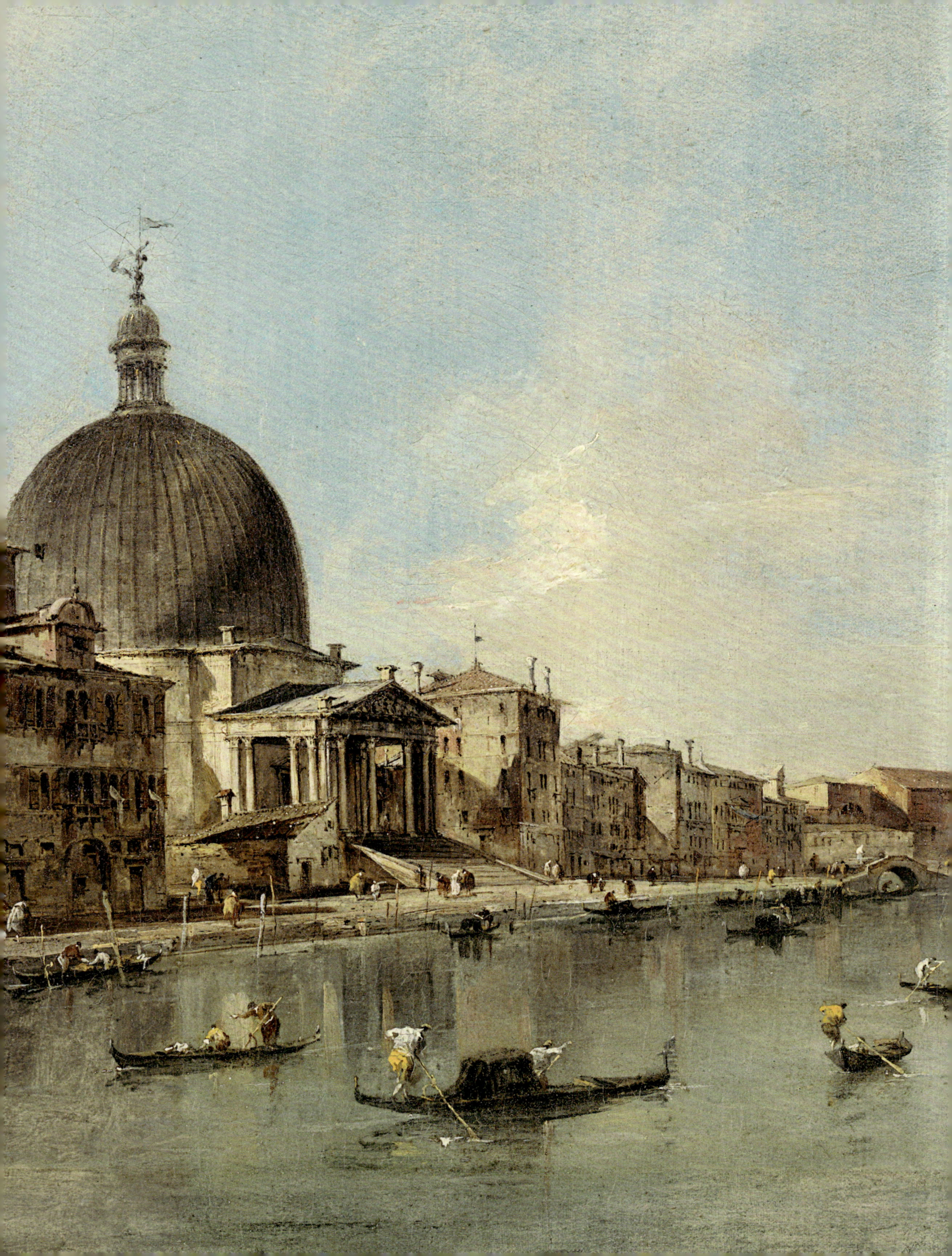

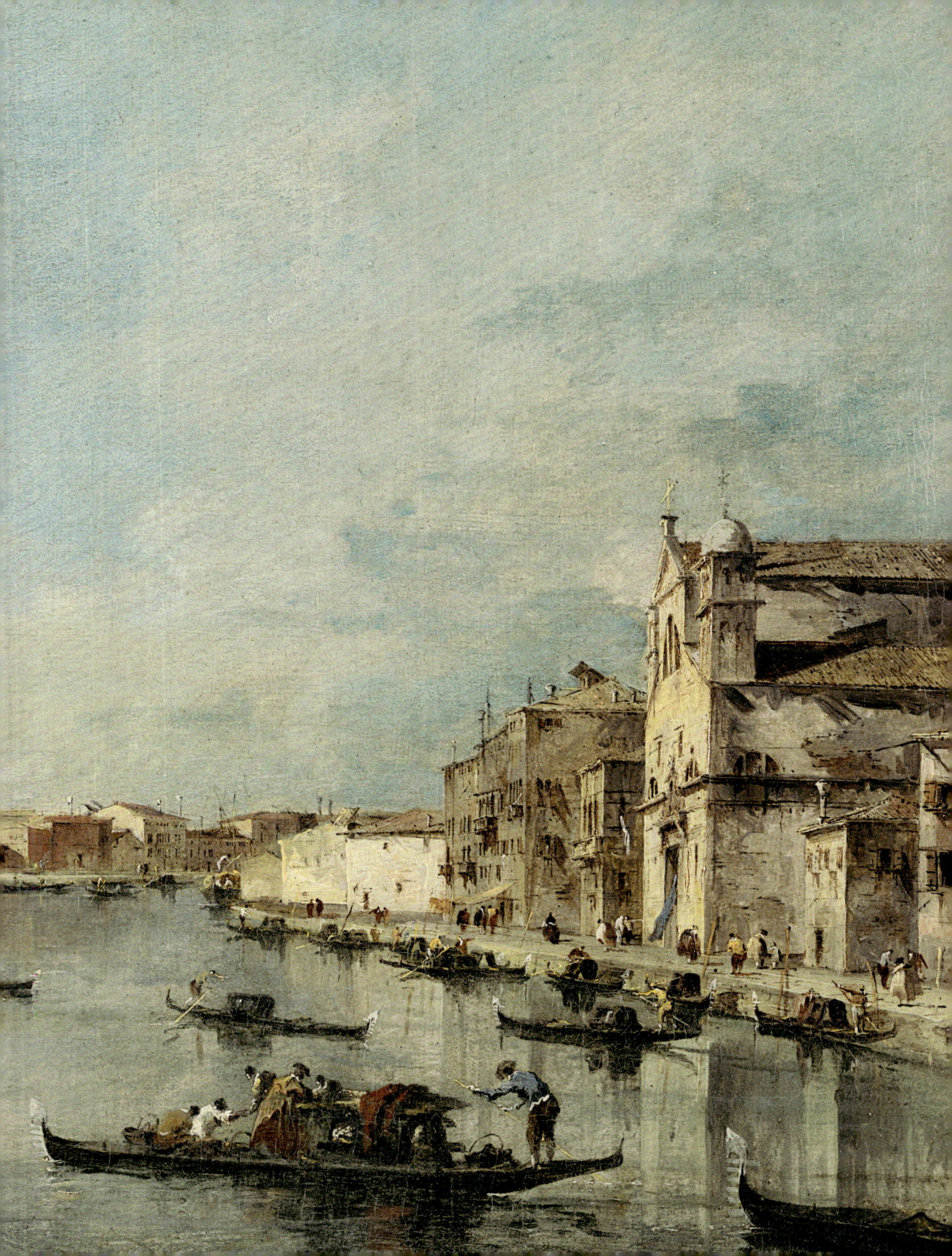

16
FRANCESCO GUARDI
(1712–1793)

The Grand Canal with Santa Lucia and Santa Maria di Nazareth

Venice, c. 1780

Oil on canvas

48 × 78 cm

PROVENANCE Mrs Danbuz Collection, Isle of Wight;
Leonard Gow Collection, Eksan, Craigendoran,
Dumbartonshire; Thyssen-Bornemisza Collection,
Lugano, 1934; on loan at the Museo Thyssen-Bornemisza,
Madrid, 1992; Museo Thyssen-Bornemisza, Madrid, 1993.
Museo Nacional Thyssen-Bornemisza, Madrid,
inv. 174 (1934.6)

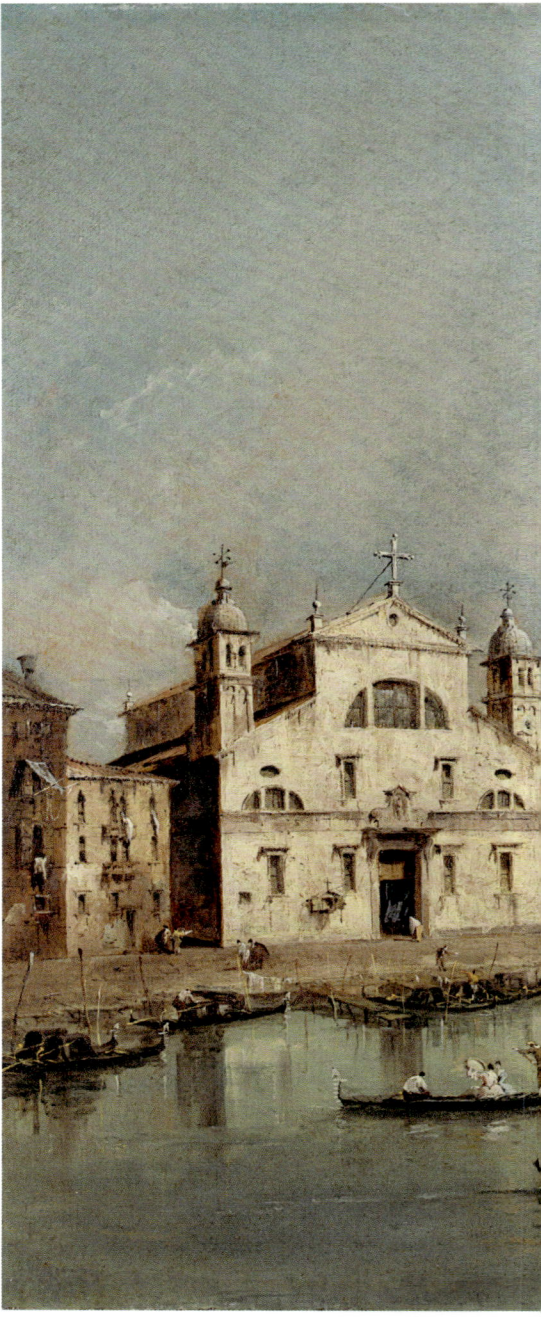

The pair of *The Grand Canal with San Simeone Piccolo and Santa Lucia* (cat. 15), this painting depicts the Grand Canal on the opposite bank to these buildings, with the Church of Santa Lucia standing out on the left, which was demolished in the mid-nineteenth century to make way for a railway station. Visible in the distance is the Church of Santa Maria di Nazareth, known as the 'Chiesa degli Scalzi', a former Carmelite convent rebuilt by the Venetian architect Baldassare Longhena (1598–1682), the man behind the project for the Basilica of Santa Maria della Salute, and by Giuseppe Sardi (1624–1699), who was responsible for designing the façade. The Academy of Fine Arts Vienna houses a very similar version of this city view.

Once again, Francesco Guardi adopts a viewpoint used in a composition by another artist, currently attributed to a disciple of Canaletto (National Galleries of Scotland, Edinburgh), although in this work there is a liveliness in the brushstroke that gives the scene greater expressiveness and a sense of movement. This *veduta*, for which Guardi made a preparatory drawing (Private Collection), forms part of an almost informal record of the daily life of the local inhabitants, as confirmed by

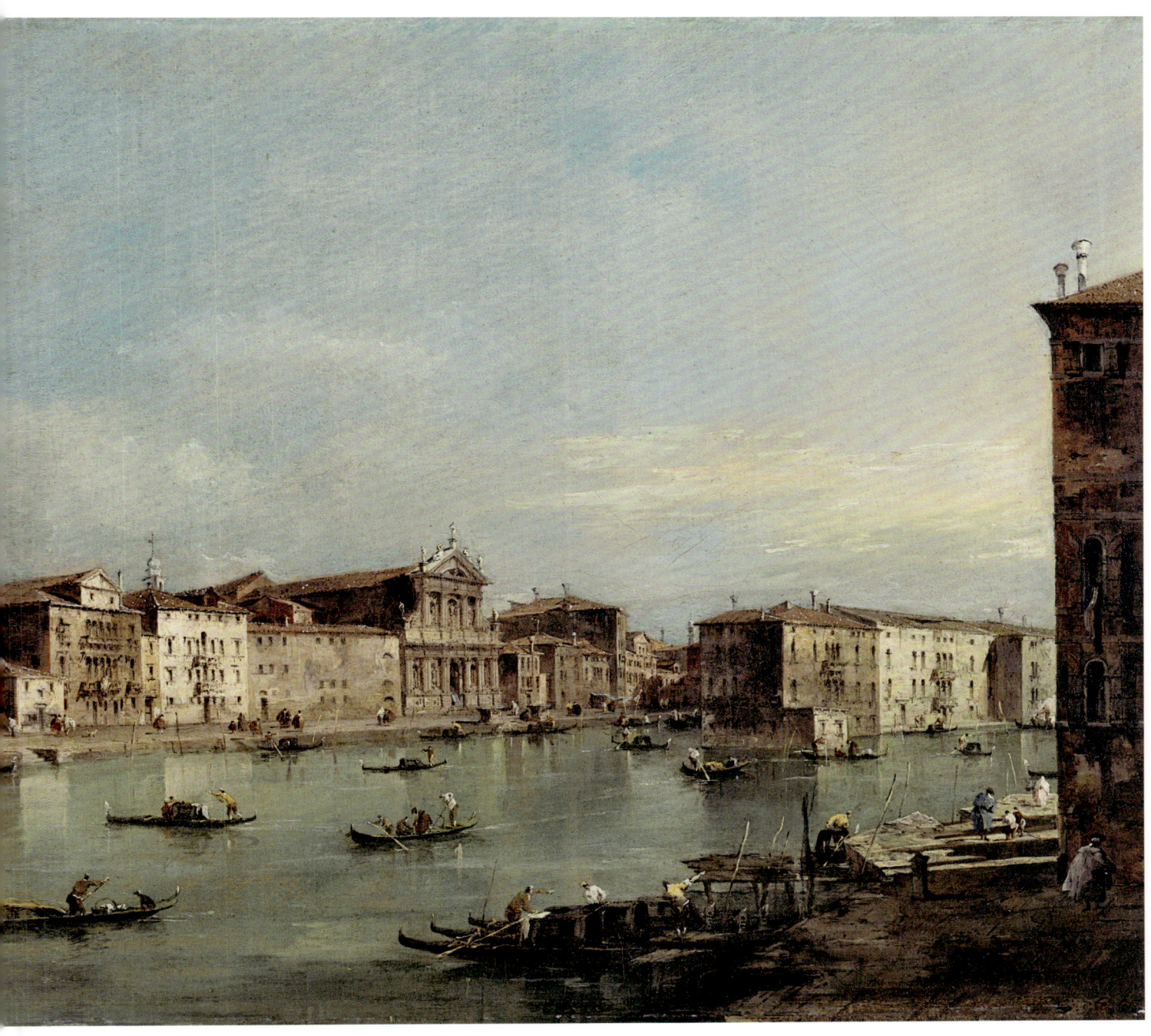

the foreground of the painting, on the right. Although permitting a panoramic view of the site, this portrayal of an ordinary day on the Grand Canal contrasts with the festive evocations of regattas populated by gondolas and the frenzy characteristic of such works produced by Francesco Guardi in remarkable numbers. It is therefore closer to compositions in which the daily routine of Venetians moving around the lagoon or Giudecca areas takes centre stage.

BIBLIOGRAPHY

BOROBIA 2009, pp. 508–9; *CANALETTO* 2019, p. 363, no. VII.01; CRAIEVICH AND PEDROCCO 2012, pp. 250, 277, no. 107; LOISEL 2018, p. 249, no. 162; MORASSI 1993, vol. I, pp. 419–20, no. 585.

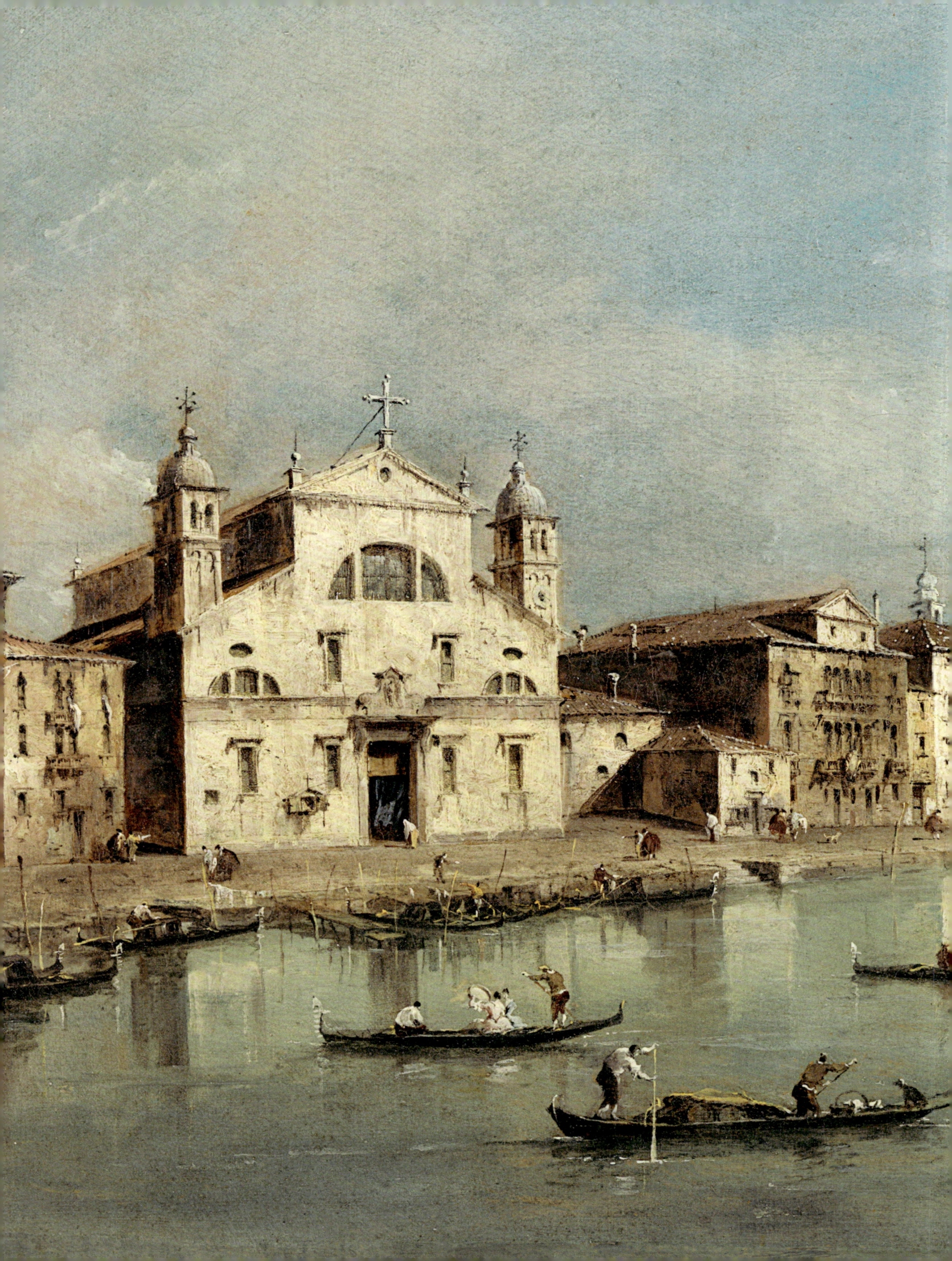

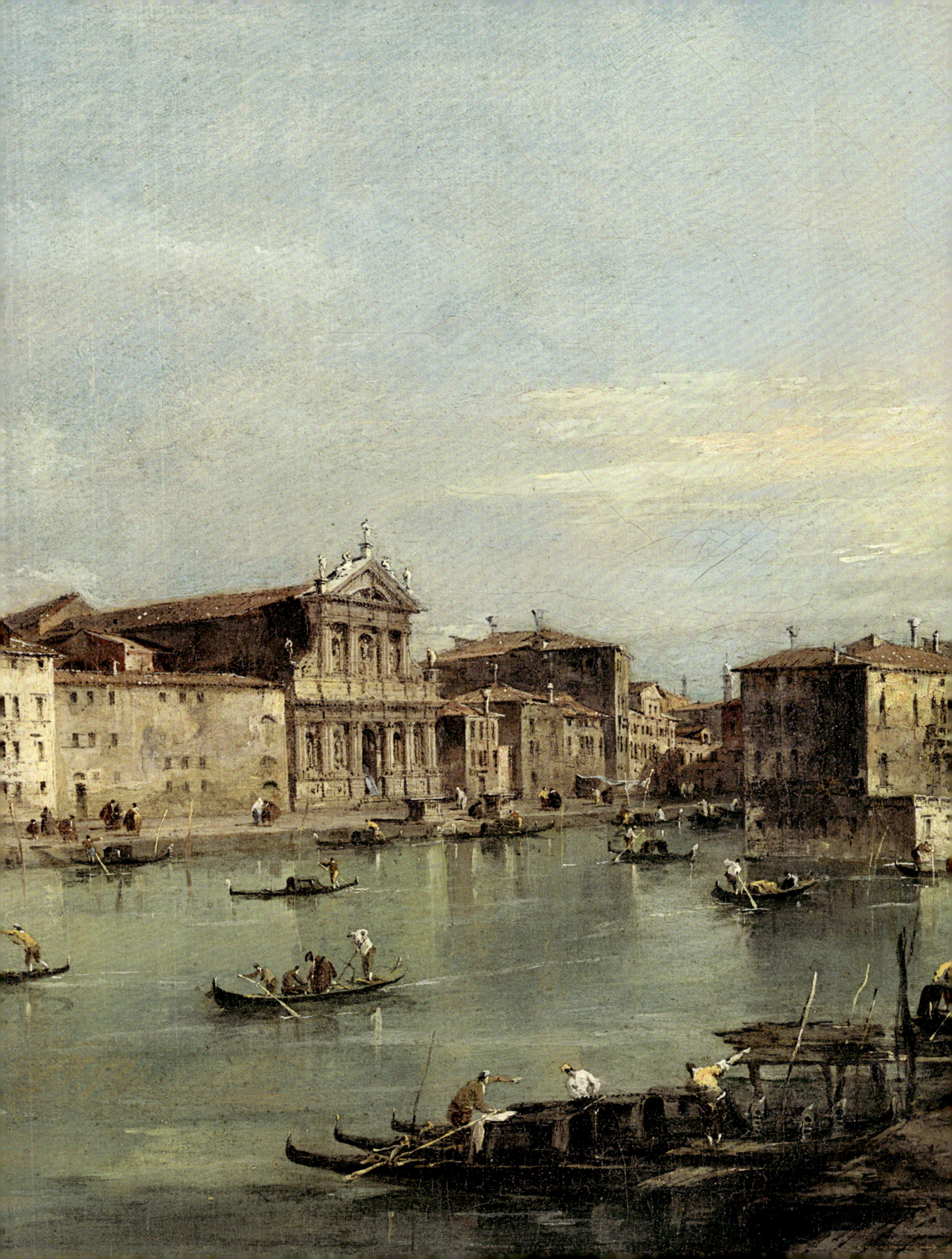

17
GIOVANNI ANTONIO CANAL (1697–1768), KNOWN AS CANALETTO

The School of San Marco

Venice, c. 1765

Oil on canvas

42 × 32.5 cm

PROVENANCE Sotheby Parker Bernet & Co., London, 8 June 1981, lot 10; Thyssen-Bornemisza Collection, Lugano, 1981; Carmen Thyssen-Bornemisza Collection on deposit at the Museo Thyssen-Bornemisza, Madrid. Carmen Thyssen Collection, inv. CTB.1981.38

This painting depicts part of the façade of the Scuola Grande di San Marco, situated in Campo Santi Giovanni e Paolo, whose basilica is not visible in the composition. Constructed in 1260 by the Confraternity of San Marco, the building, destroyed by a fire, was rebuilt in the Renaissance style by Pietro Lombardo (1435–1515), Giovanni Buora (1450–1513) and Mauro Codussi (1440–1504). As with other Venetian buildings, the presence of arches and decorative niches gives it Byzantine overtones.

Two youthful works by Canaletto, produced in the mid-1720s (Staatliche Kunstsammlungen Gemäldegalerie, Dresden and Private Collection, Montreal), offer a wider view of the site, where it is possible to see the Basilica of Santi Giovanni e Paolo and the equestrian statue of Condottiero Bartolomeo Colleoni, by Andrea del Verrocchio (1435–1488). Part of the Ponte del Cavallo over the Rio dei Mendicanti visible here is already finished, which is not the case in the older versions, where it is rendered in wood or merely sketched.

These works both belonged to Luca's ambassador, Stefano Conti (1654–1739). One common feature of all three canvases is the presence of a banner next to the fountain in front of the school.

According to scholars, the work appears to be from Canaletto's mature period in which, instead of creating large panoramic views of the Serenissima, he depicted iconic Venetian buildings in darker tones, with smaller dimensions and an upright format, compatible with the demand of local or European collectors, for whom these easily transportable canvases were excellent souvenirs of the Grand Tour. The pair of paintings from the late 1750s called *Piazza San Marco* (The National Gallery, London), are eloquent examples of this production.

BIBLIOGRAPHY

COLECCIÓN 2004, vol. 1, pp. 192–93; CONTINI 2002, pp. 276–79, no. 58.

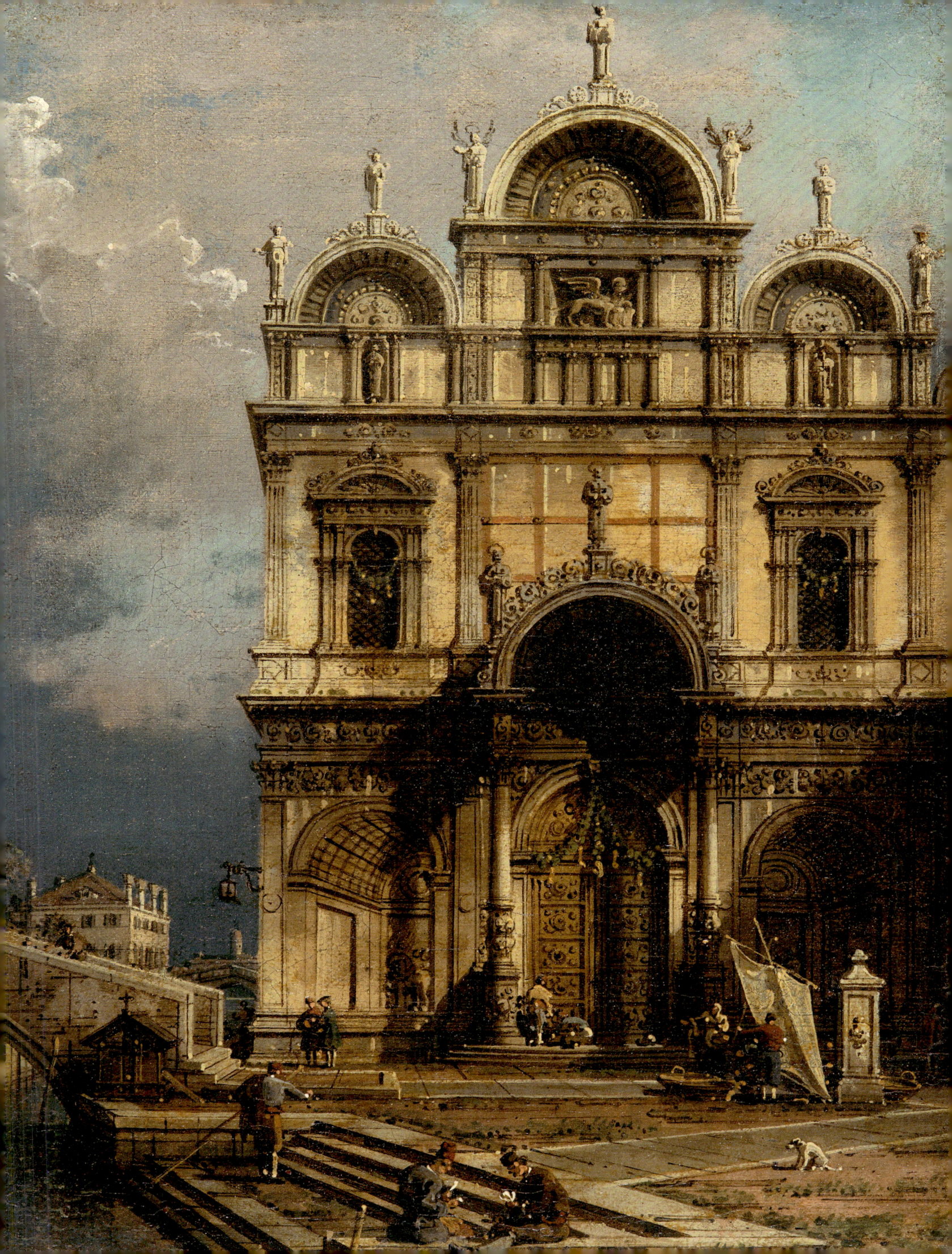

18
GIOVANNI ANTONIO CANAL (1697–1768), KNOWN AS CANALETTO

Capriccio with Colonnade in the Interior of a Palace

Venice, c. 1765
Oil on canvas
42 × 32.5 cm

This work is a variant of a larger canvas (131 × 93 cm) entitled *Perspective View with Portico*, belonging to the Gallerie dell'Accademia (Venice), which Canaletto gave to the institution two years after his election as a member of the Academy of Painting and Sculpture in 1763. The imaginary setting of the work, which places this painting in the *capriccio* category, seems to be inspired by the Ca' d'Oro, one of the most famous Venetian palaces facing the Grand Canal, which was built in the 1420s for the Contarini family.

In both paintings Canaletto creates a bold perspective that allows the viewer to simultaneously see the ground floor and the great hall of the building, with the *portego* and the inner courtyard observed from a recessed viewpoint. The upper floor, defined by the diagonal line of five Corinthian columns, offers a glimpse of a balustrade from which hangs a curtain bearing a coat of arms. The carved wooden coat of arms visible in the Galleries of the Academy of Venice version is almost in profile in this painting. Differences in the interior courtyard, such as the presence of statuary instead of a vase in the style of Piranesi, the departure from the pink colouring of the wall, a different configuration of the staircase, and the distribution of the figures moving around the scene, make it difficult to establish a secure chronology for these canvases, whose creative intent is nevertheless distinct.

This work seems to have been intended to satisfy the demand of the local clientèle, like other late compositions of the same format by Canaletto whose point of view is established from inside the architecture depicted, as is the case with the pair dedicated to the Piazza San Marco seen from inside its arcades (The National Gallery, London).

BIBLIOGRAPHY

COLECCIÓN 2004, vol. 1, pp. 194–95; CONTINI 2002, pp. 280–95, no. 59.

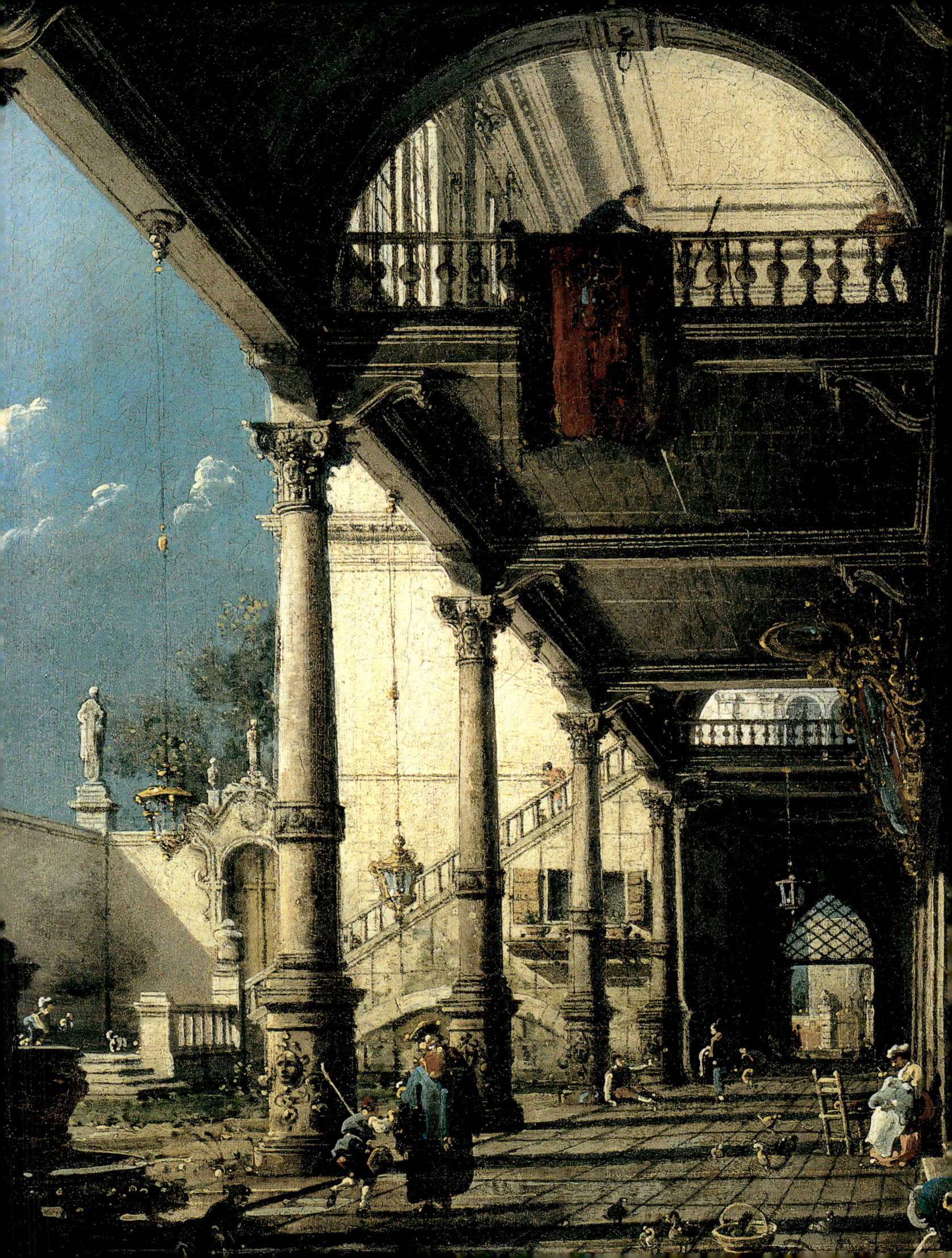

19
FRANCESCO GUARDI
(1712–1793)

Portico with Figures

Venice, c. 1778
Oil on wood
24 × 17 cm

PROVENANCE Prince Alexis Orloff Collection.
Acquired through Graat et Madoulé from the
Georges Petit Gallery, Paris, on 9 April 1920, no. 31.
Calouste Gulbenkian Museum, inv. 93 A

The portico of the Doge's Palace may have served as inspiration for this *capriccio*, although it has been hypothesised that the piece bears similarities to the portico of the Porta della Carta, the ceremonial doorway into the Ducal Palace. The background of the work, a result of the artist's fantasy, is dominated by the entrance to a garden with classical features and a small square. On the right is a religious building with a Gothic aedicule. The work is part of a pair, along with the next painting (cat. 20), both of which can be dated to around the late 1770s.

A larger canvas belonging to the Norton Simon Art Foundation (Pasadena), entitled *A Venetian Capriccio*, is probably an earlier version of the same composition, although the treatment of light and colour differs significantly. In this case, the transition from the light to the dark areas of the painting is smoother, and there is a typically *guardesca* ambience to the painting, in which the forms appear slightly dissolved.

BIBLIOGRAPHY

MORASSI 1993, vol. I, p. 459, no. 803; MURARO 1993, pp. 60-61, no. 17; PALLUCCHINI 1965, no. 19.

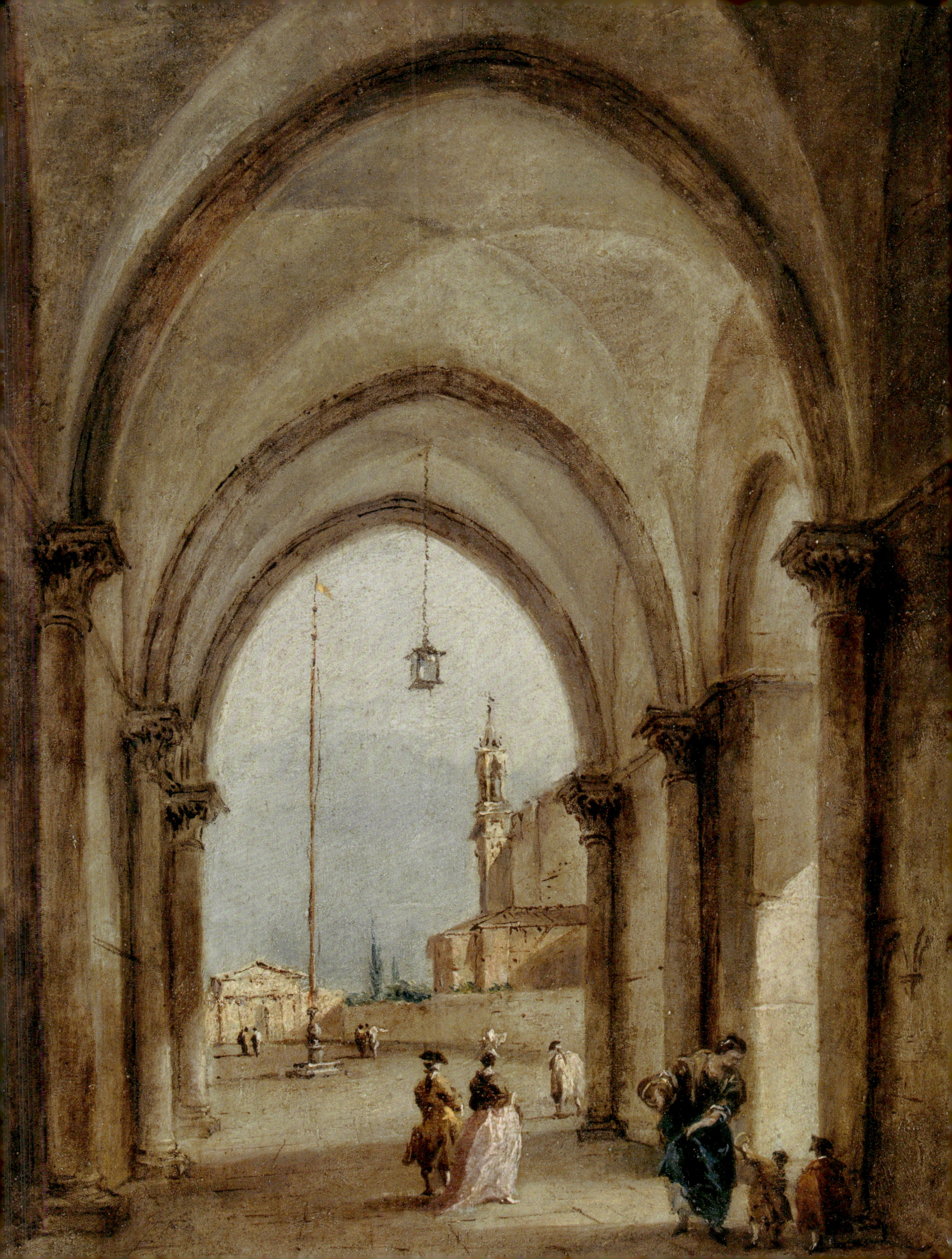

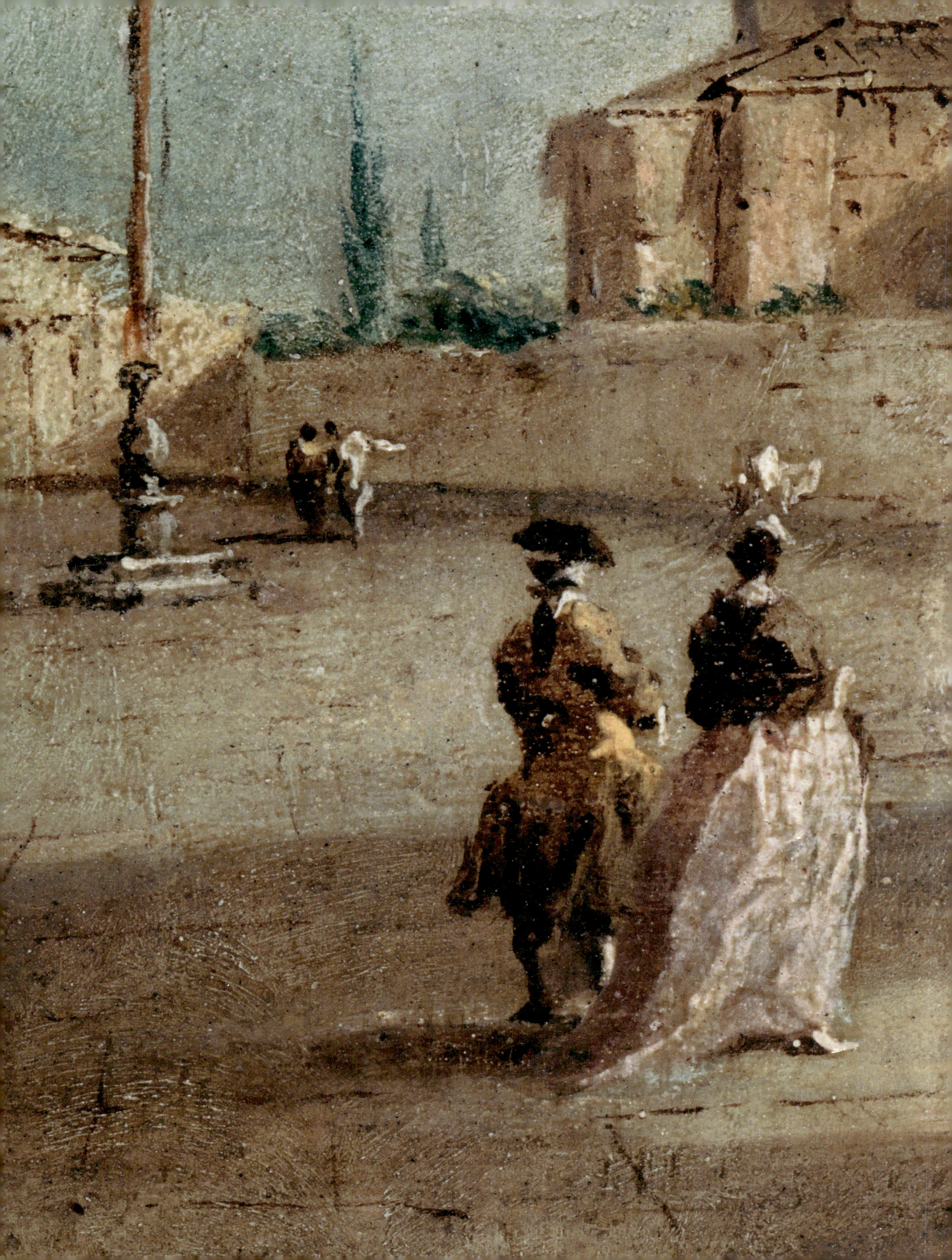

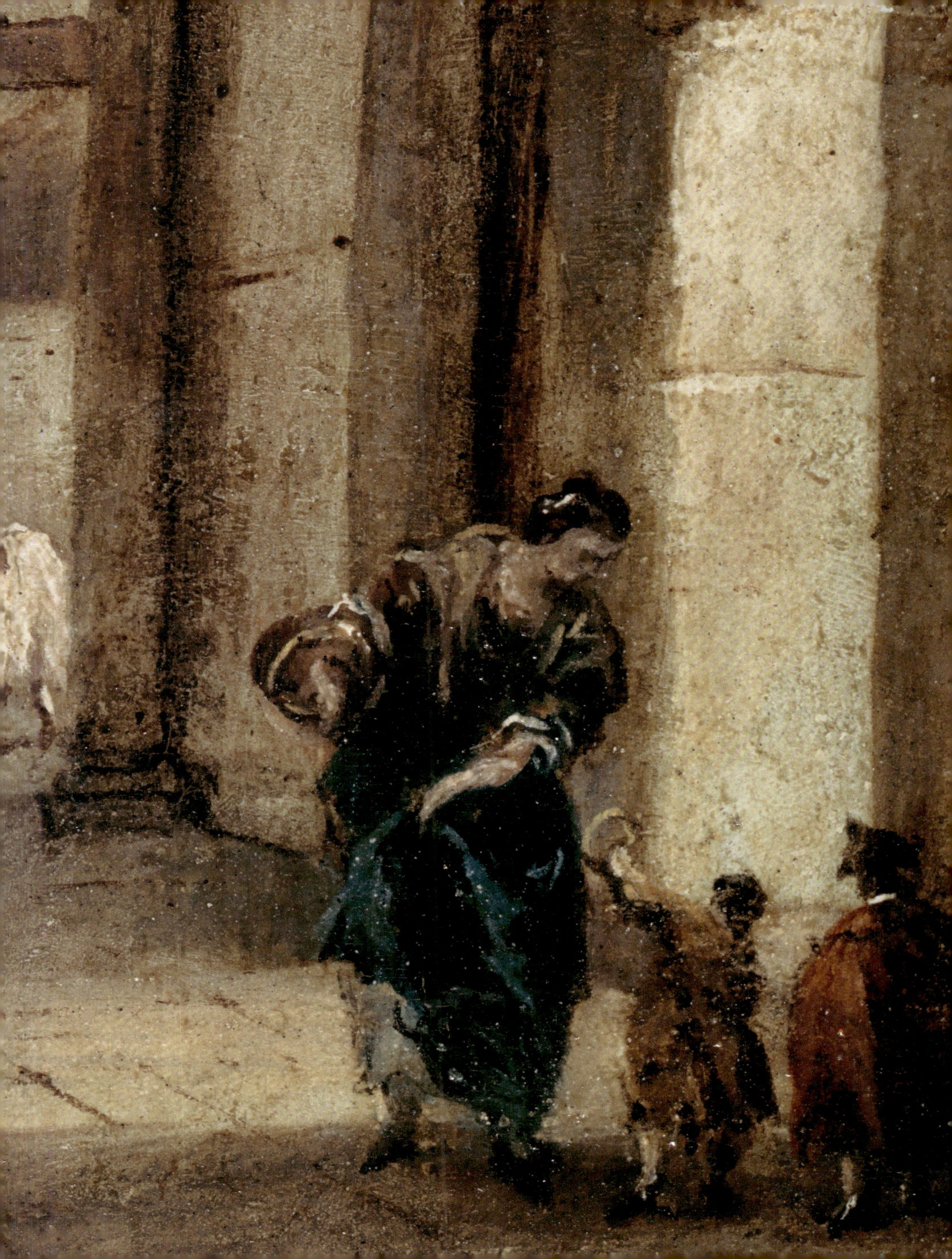

20
FRANCESCO GUARDI
(1712–1793)

The Portico at the Ducal Palace

Venice, c. 1778
Oil on wood
24 × 17 cm

PROVENANCE Prince Alexis Orloff Collection.
Acquired through Graat et Madoulé from the
Georges Petit Gallery, Paris, on 29 April 1920, no. 32.
Calouste Gulbenkian Museum, inv. 93 B

This painting depicts the arcades of the Doge's Palace, a masterpiece of Venetian Gothic, from the side of Piazza San Marco, with some of the buildings on the island of San Giorgio Maggiore visible in the background. Various figures in small groups populate the space and evoke the daily life of the local inhabitants. There is another version of the theme, larger and more elaborate, belonging to the Earl of Normanton Collection (Ringwood), which has some differences in the details.

The motif of the portico of the Doge's Palace gave rise to various compositions by the artist, some of which were fantasised versions of the arcades' architecture, to which he added imaginary features, as can be seen in the previous painting (cat. 19), this work's counterpart. A similar version, but oval in shape, can be found at The Wallace Collection in London.

BIBLIOGRAPHY

MORASSI 1993, vol. I, p. 454, no. 774; MURARO 1993, pp. 58–59, no. 16; PALLUCCHINI 1965, no. 20.

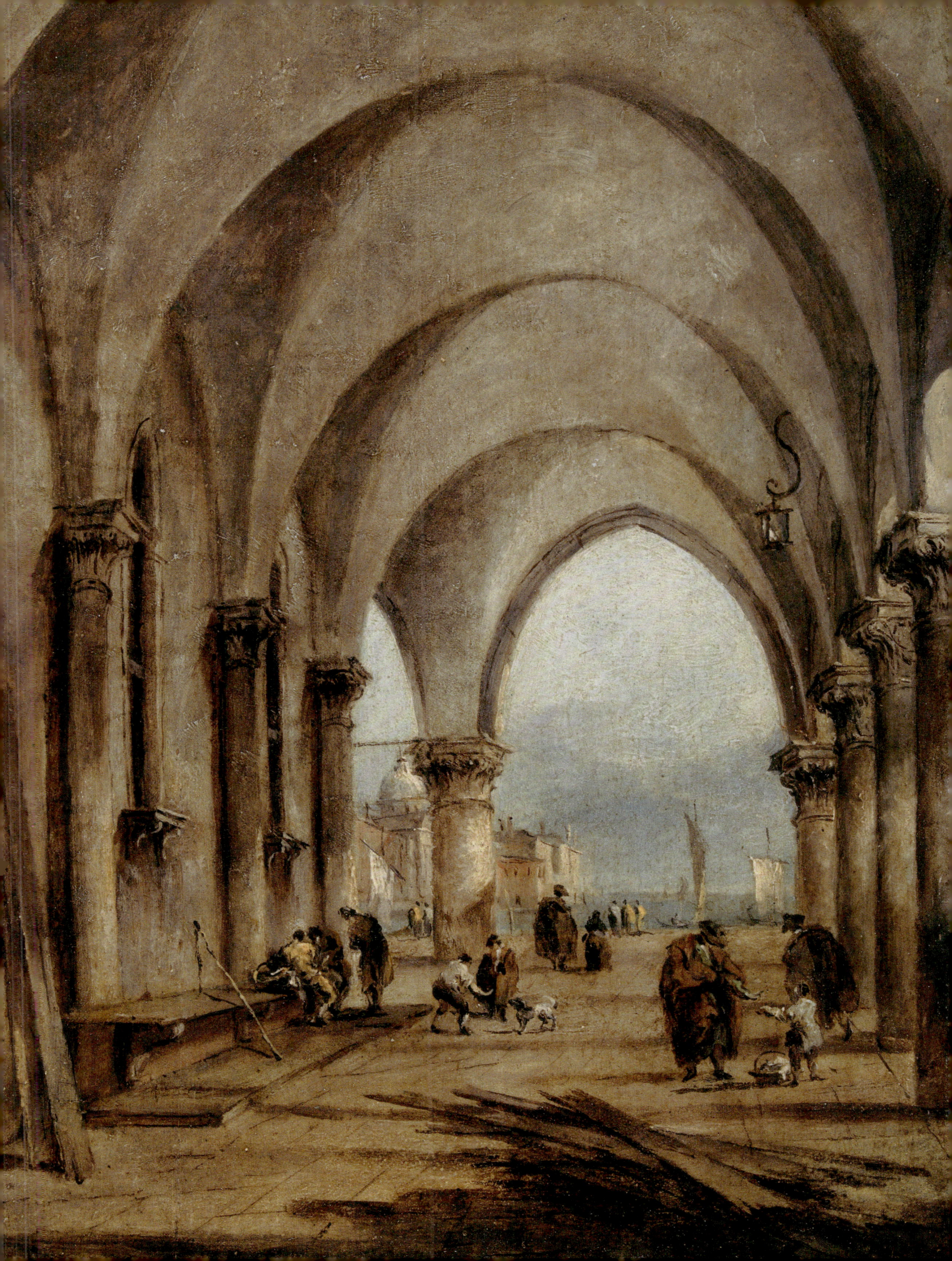

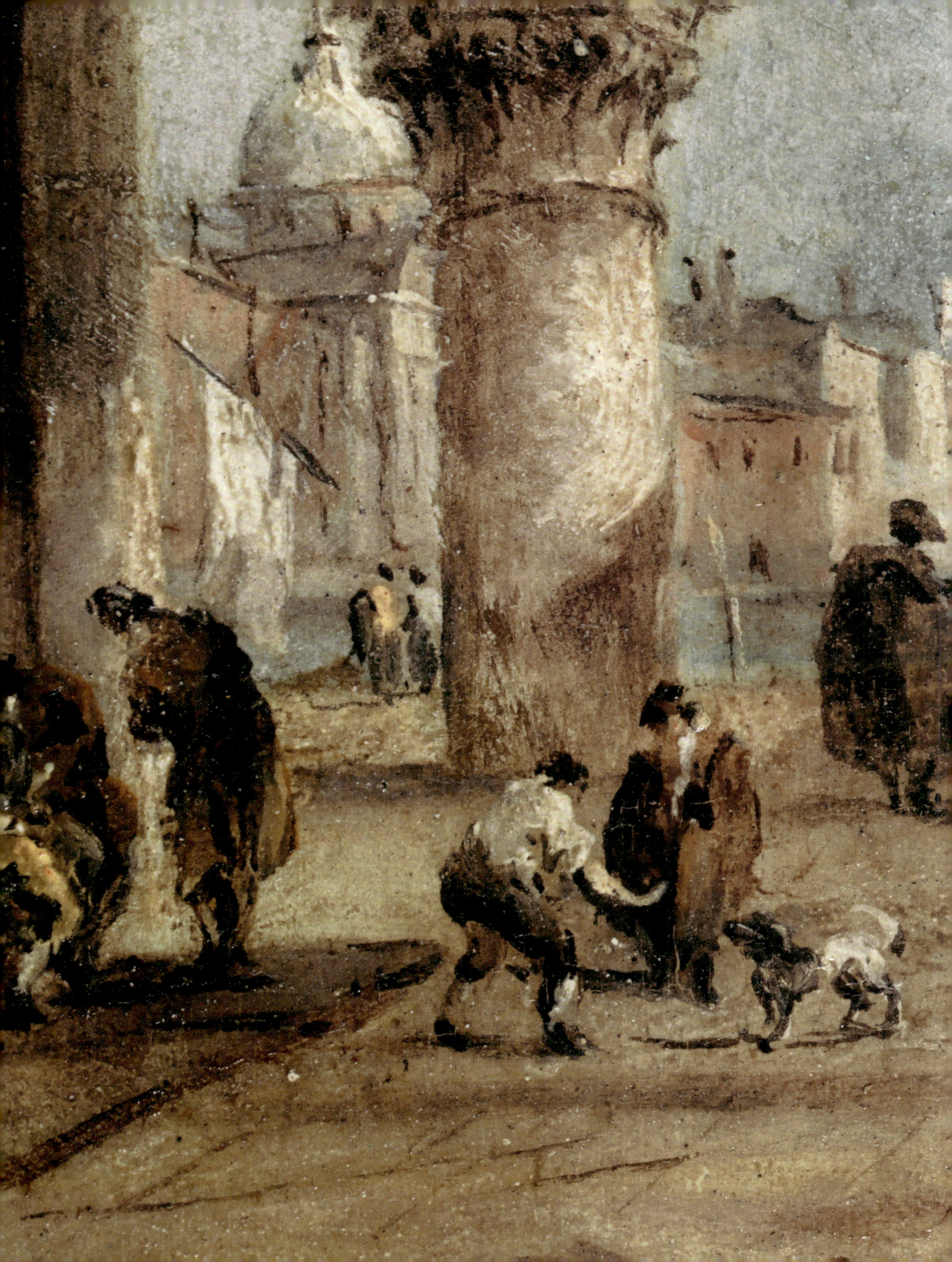

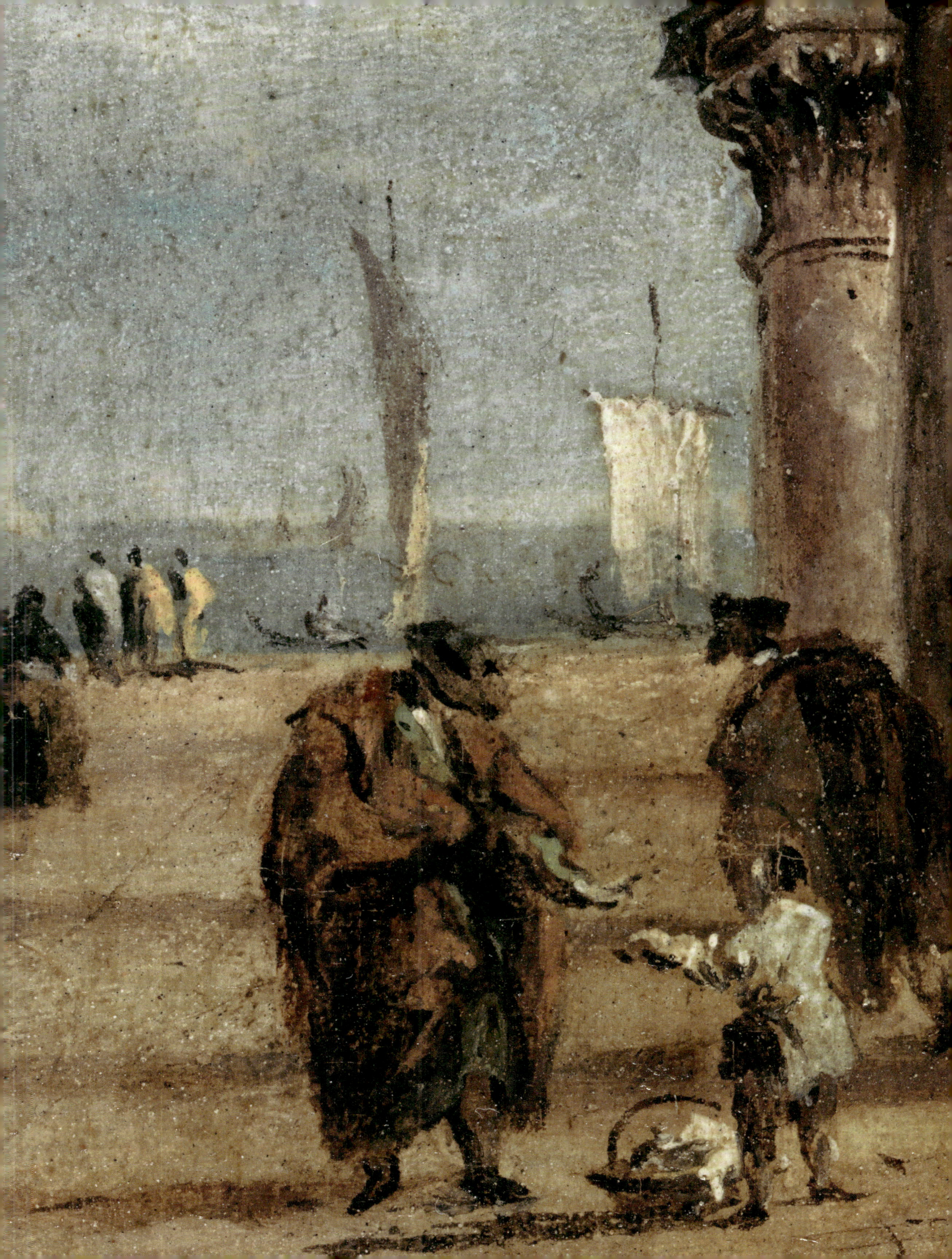

21
FRANCESCO GUARDI
(1712–1793)

The Island of San Giorgio Maggiore

Venice, c. 1780–90
Oil on wood
19.4 × 16.5 cm

PROVENANCE Acquired through Colnaghi,
in London, on 27 September 1918.
Calouste Gulbenkian Museum, inv. 388

This painting depicts the island of San Giorgio Maggiore, in Venice, as it appears when arriving at the Basilica of San Marco from Giudecca. In the foreground are the gondolas and the former Benedictine convent adjacent to the Church of San Giorgio Maggiore, which was designed by Andrea Palladio (1508–1580) and constructed between 1566 and 1610. In the background, some of the buildings along the Riva degli Schiavoni are visible. Guardi depicted the architectural complex from a distance on numerous occasions in compositions featuring San Giorgio Maggiore's façade. The bell tower in this painting, which collapsed in 1774 and was rebuilt in 1791, provides no reliable indication of the work's date, since Guardi chose to include it in other compositions, even after its demise. A work with the same title belonging to The Clark, Williamstown, from c. 1780, would appear to support this hypothesis.

In this case, all the details point towards the work being a fragment of a larger panoramic painting of the type that Guardi produced time and again, which was probably cropped at an undetermined date, for reasons unknown. Indeed, the vagueness of the features on the left seems to indicate that this is the background of one such composition, as is the case with the horizontal painting belonging to The Clark (18.3 × 30.2 cm). In the composition's current format, the sultry evening ambience and humidity of the lagoon take centre stage and offer the viewer an almost poetic pictorial impression of the place.

BIBLIOGRAPHY

MORASSI 1993, vol. I, p. 393, no. 439; MURARO 1993, pp. 52–54, no. 14; PALLUCCHINI 1965, no. 15.

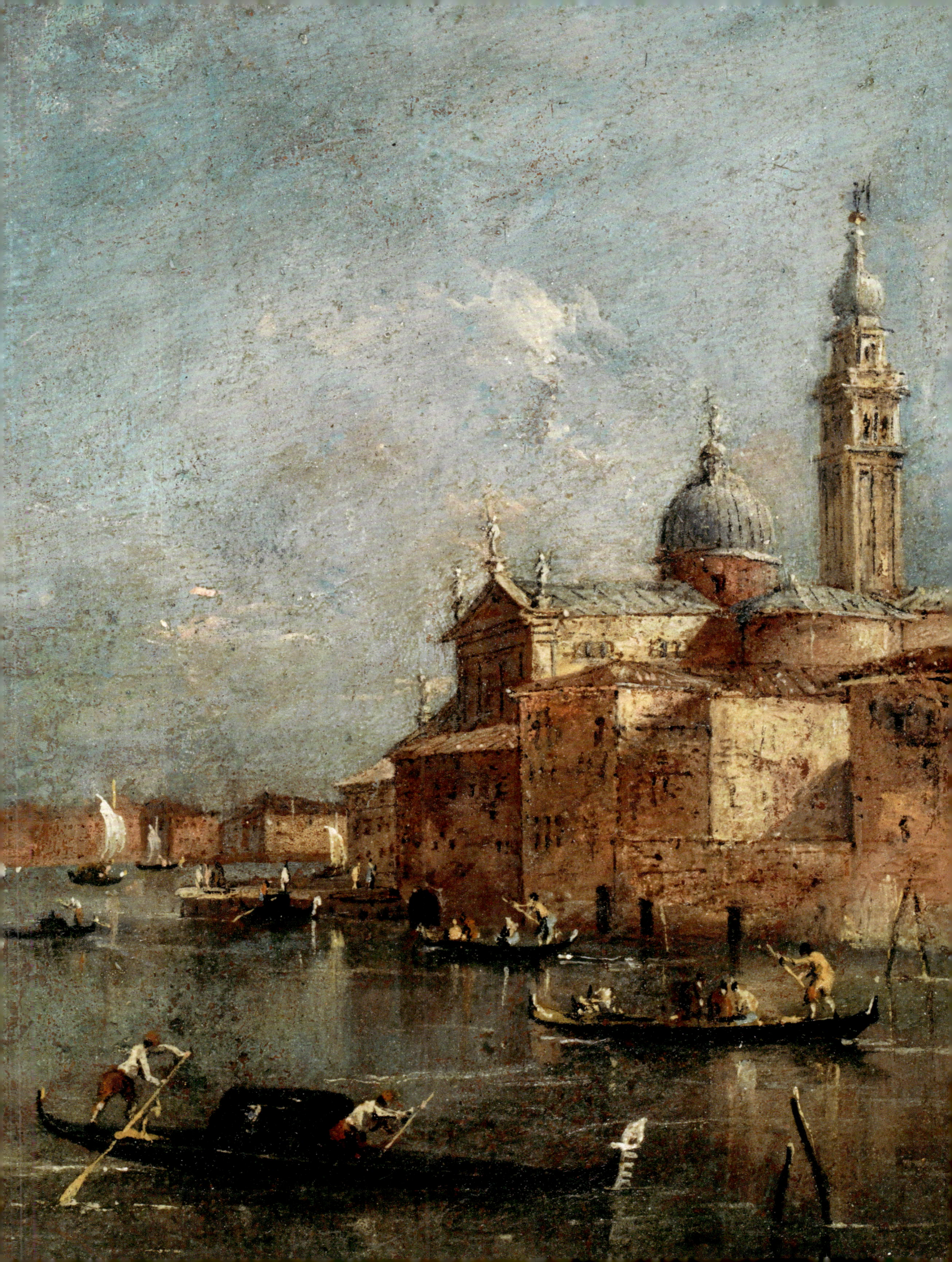

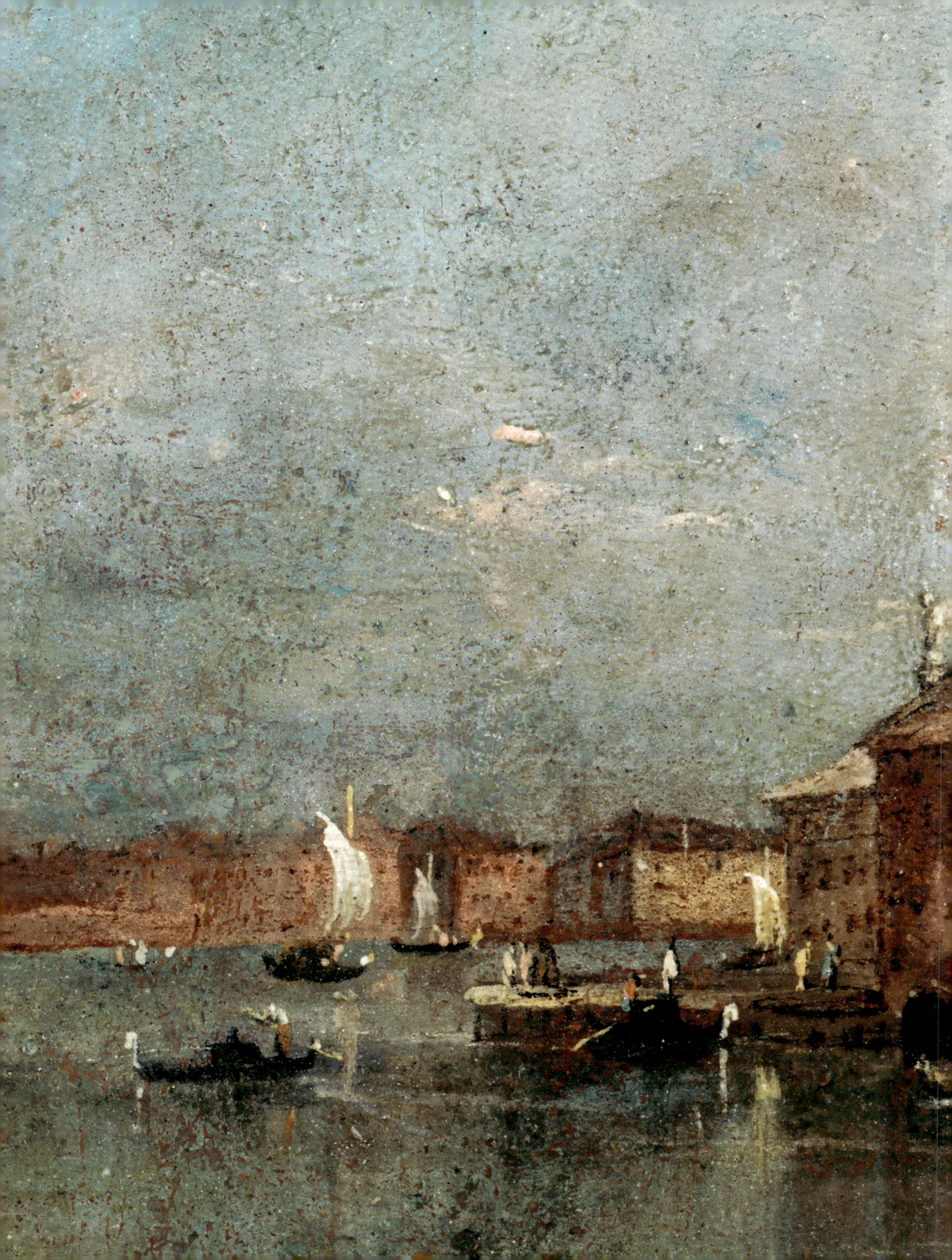

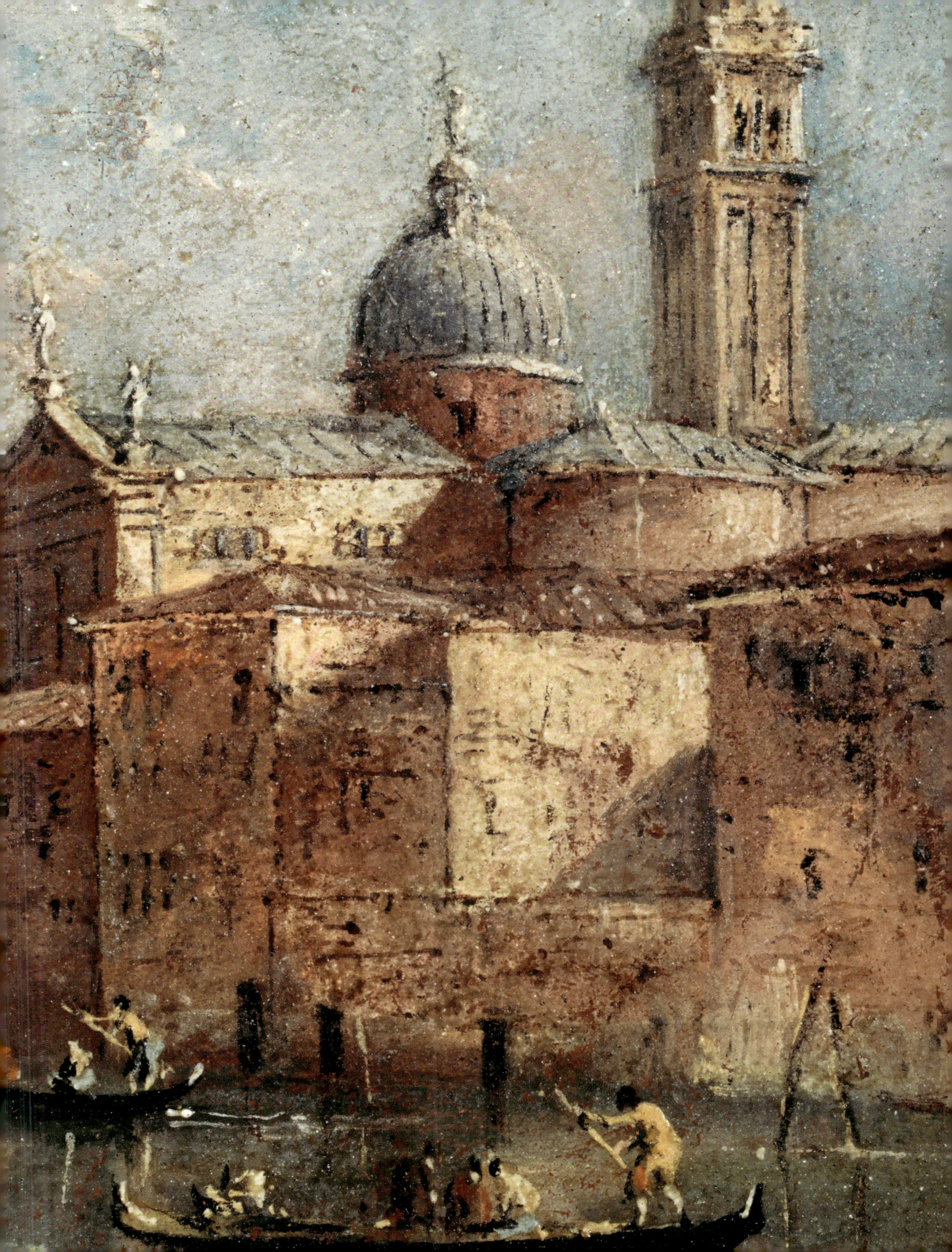

22
FRANCESCO GUARDI
(1712–1793)

The Bridge over the Brenta near the Lock Gates at Dolo

Venice, c. 1770–80
Oil on wood
18 × 14 cm

PROVENANCE Acquired through Colnaghi,
Christie's, London, on 5 July 1920, no. 111.
Calouste Gulbenkian Museum, inv. 385 A

This painting depicts an ancient bridge close to the village of Dolo, near Venice. Francesco Guardi painted some eight variations of the motif, in both vertical and horizontal compositions. In the National Gallery of Victoria (Melbourne), there is a larger canvas version, very similar to the one we see here. The Museo Correr in Venice has a preparatory drawing for the theme in its horizontal format, and this group of works differs little overall.

As in *The Lock Gates at Dolo* (cat. 29), Francesco Guardi's composition captures the daily life of inhabitants in the outskirts of Venice, vividly portraying local scenes. A painting of stark colour contrasts, the work reveals the artist's expressive brushstroke, particularly visible in the movement of the figures that populate the scene.

BIBLIOGRAPHY

MORASSI 1993, vol. I, pp. 254, 435, no. 674; MURARO 1993, pp. 16–17, no. 2; PALLUCCHINI 1965, no. 10.

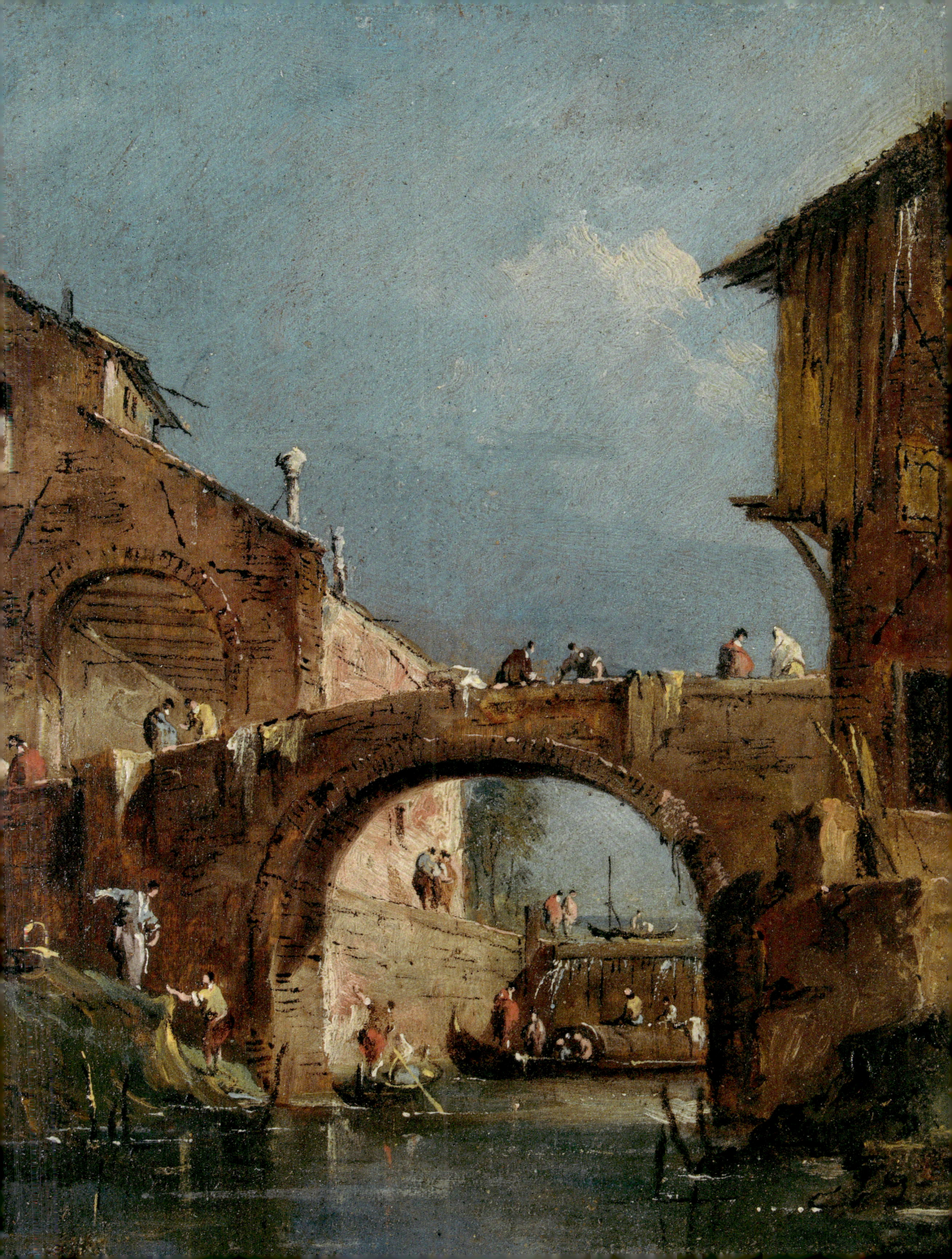

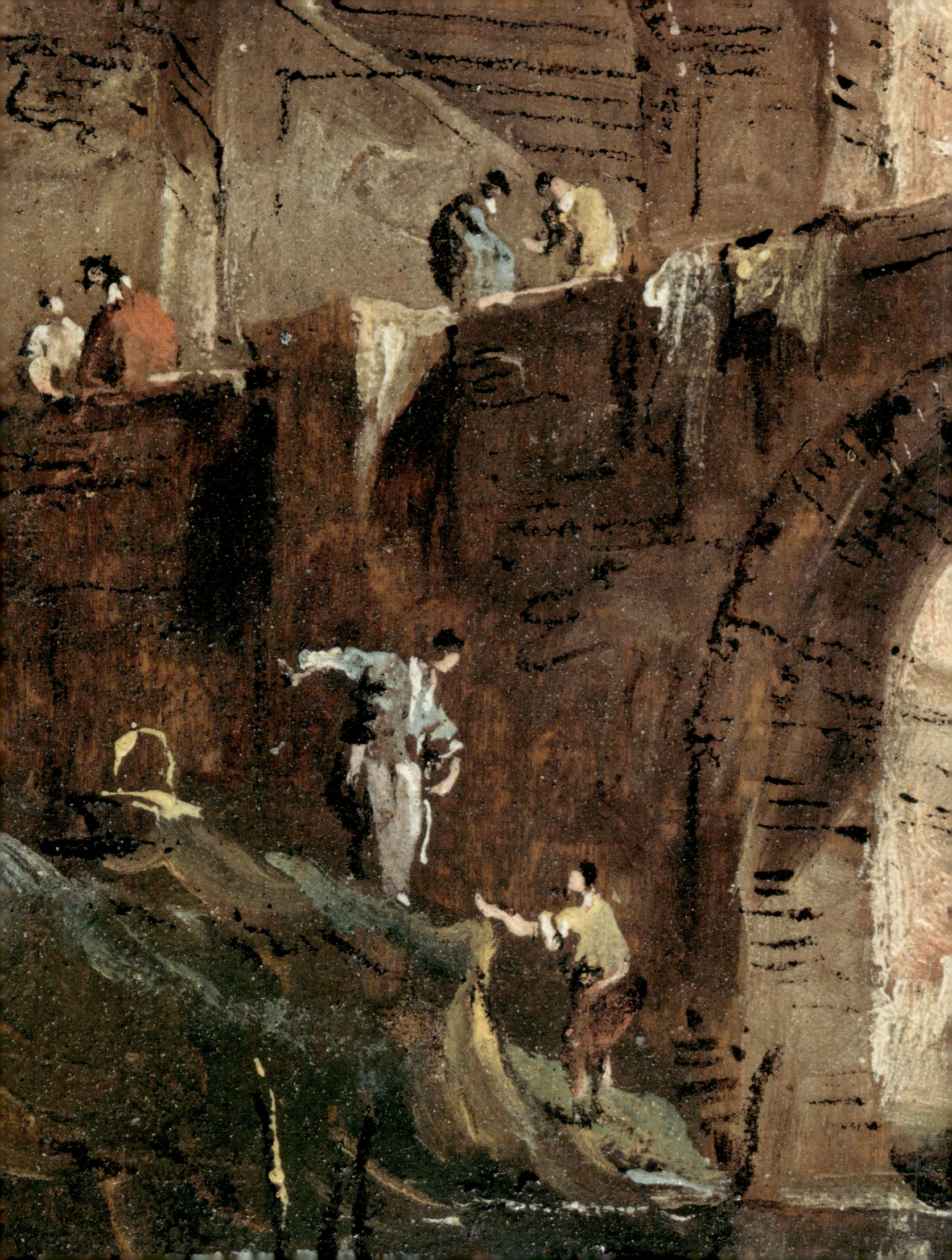

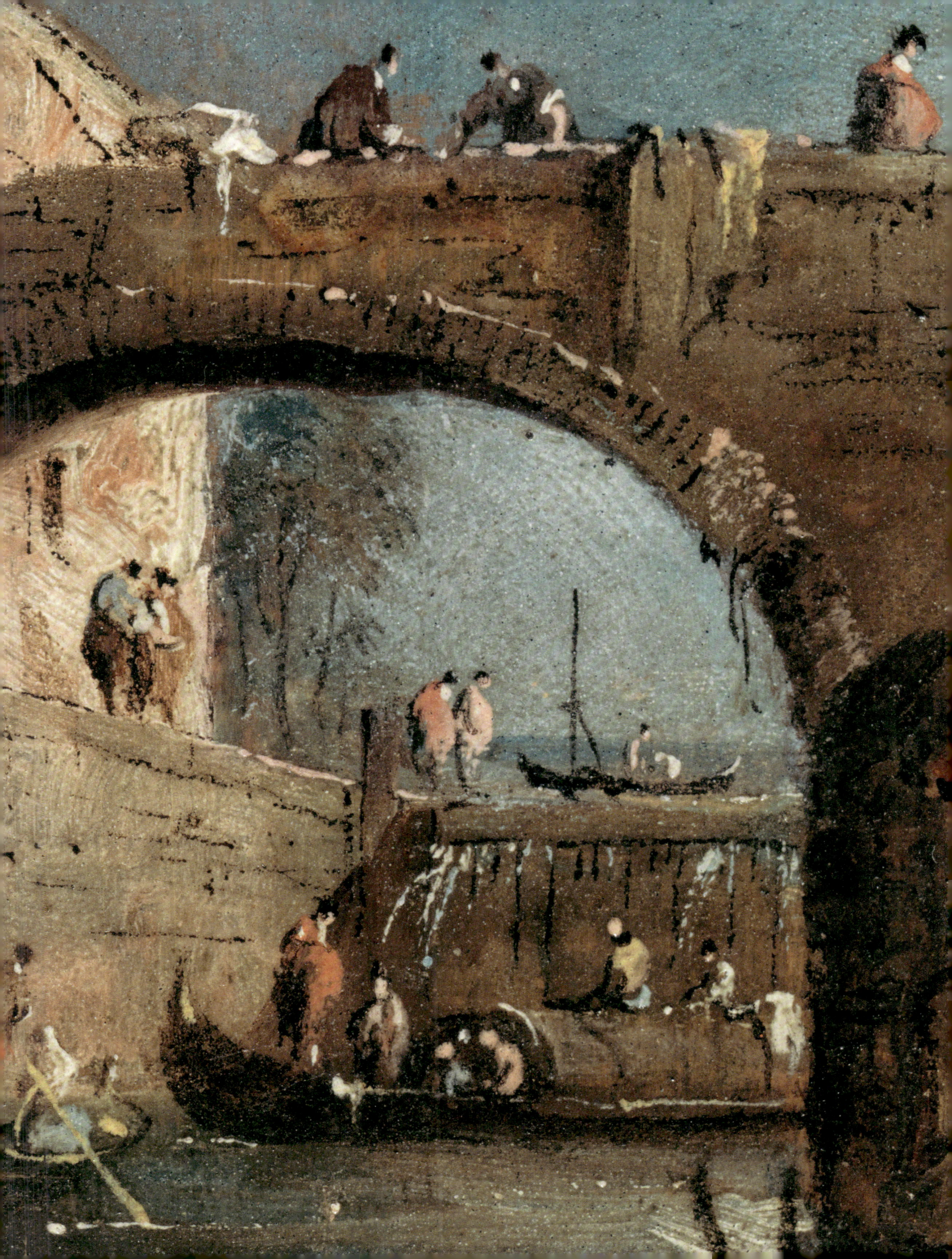

23
FRANCESCO GUARDI
(1712–1793)

Landscape with Ruins

Venice, c. 1770–80

Oil on wood

18 × 14 cm

PROVENANCE Acquired through Colnaghi, Christie's, London, on 5 July 1920, no. 111. Calouste Gulbenkian Museum, inv. 385 B

This idealised scene, in which the influence of Marco Ricci (1676–1730) is visible, depicts the ruins of a temple with an architrave supported by columns, an element reused in varying forms in other works by Francesco Guardi. In the centre of the composition is a classical pedestal decorated with a bas-relief, while a medieval tower occupies the background.

The artist's fantastical vision introduces classical elements into a landscape that evokes the distant tradition of fifteenth-century Venetian art, as evidenced by the mountain at the edge of the horizon. The sky, an intense, expressive, typically *guardesco* blue, points to the painter's mature period. *Architectural Capriccio with Architrave* (Riva Collection, Milan) is perhaps the work that most resembles this composition.

BIBLIOGRAPHY

MORASSI 1993, vol. I, p. 448, no. 743; MURARO 1993, pp. 24–25, no. 5; PALLUCCHINI 1965, no. 11.

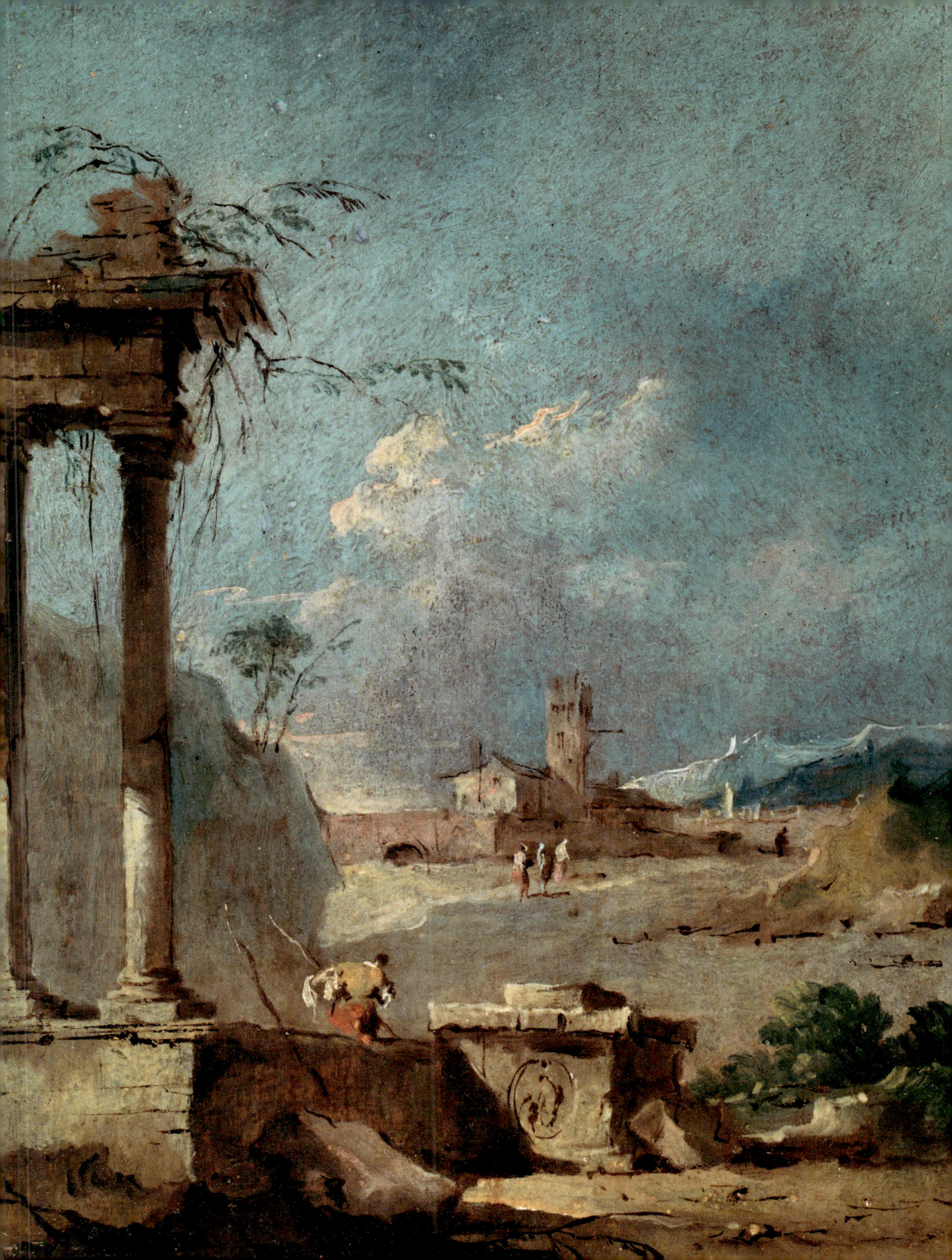

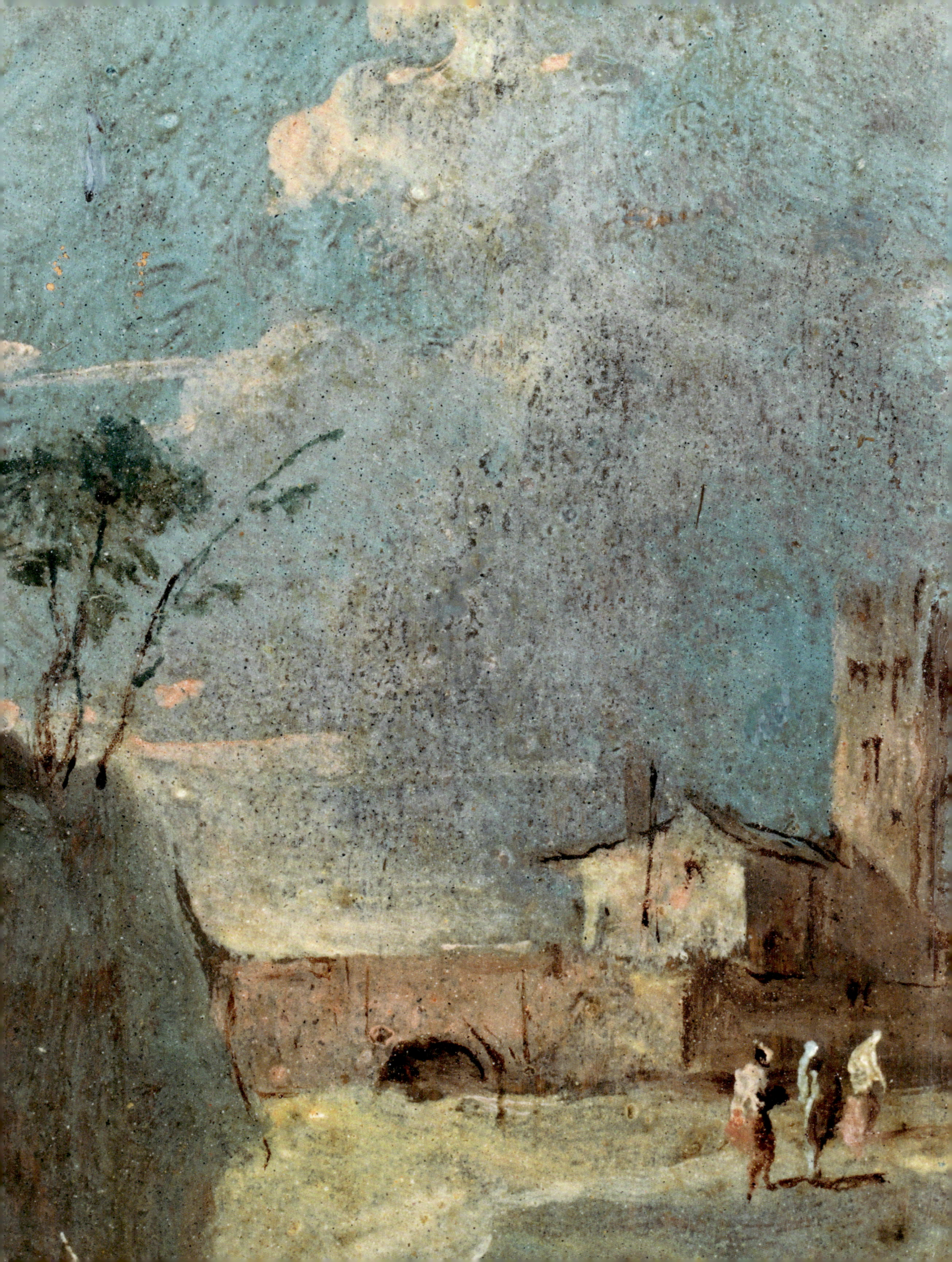

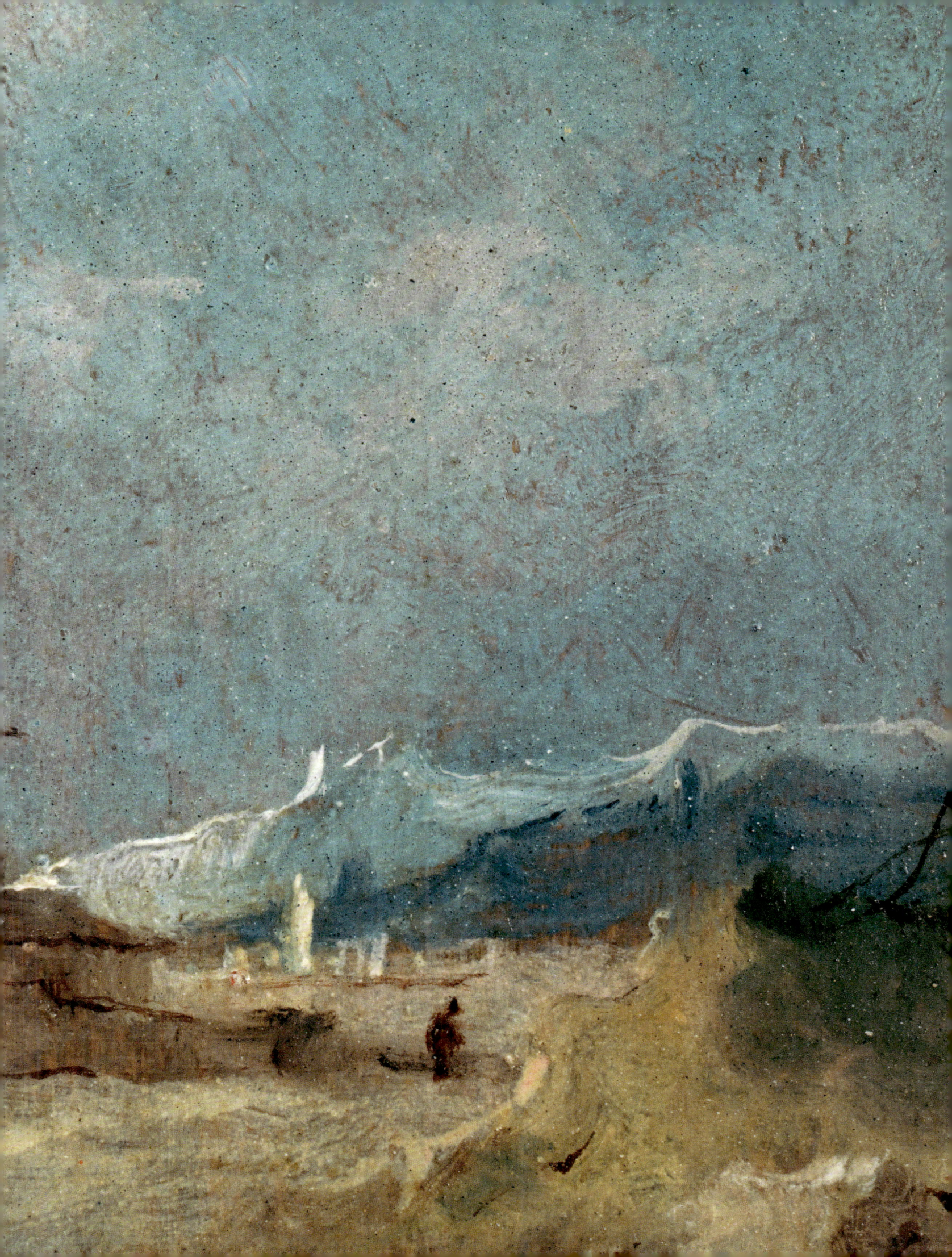

24
FRANCESCO GUARDI
(1712–1793)

Architectural Capriccio

Venice, c. 1770–80
Oil on wood
19 × 15 cm

PROVENANCE Charles Thomas Daniell Crews
Collection. Acquired through Agnew,
Christie's, London, on 2 July 1915, no. 159.
Calouste Gulbenkian Museum, inv. 538

Structured along two diagonals, this imaginary composition, in a deliberately theatrical setting, depicts a staircase on the right leading to a classical portico, decorated with bas-reliefs. To the left is a circular temple with a dome, atrium and classical tympanum. The adjoining building may have been inspired by an unrealised project by Andrea Palladio (1508–1580) for the Rialto Bridge in Venice. A building with arcades, where a group of figures are descending a staircase, occupies the background. These lively figures reveal the influence of the Genoese painter Alessandro Magnasco (1667–1749).

Francesco Guardi painted two versions of this same theme, the second of which is in the National Gallery in London. In this variant, which is slightly larger, the differences are essentially changes to the figures, which nevertheless appear grouped together in the same places. The classical portico on the right displays small differences in detail, but the structure of the composition is identical in both works. There is a preparatory drawing for this motif in the Victoria and Albert Museum (London).

BIBLIOGRAPHY

MORASSI 1993, vol. I, pp. 275–450, no. 754; MURARO 1993, pp. 22–23, no. 4; PALLUCCHINI 1965, no. 14.

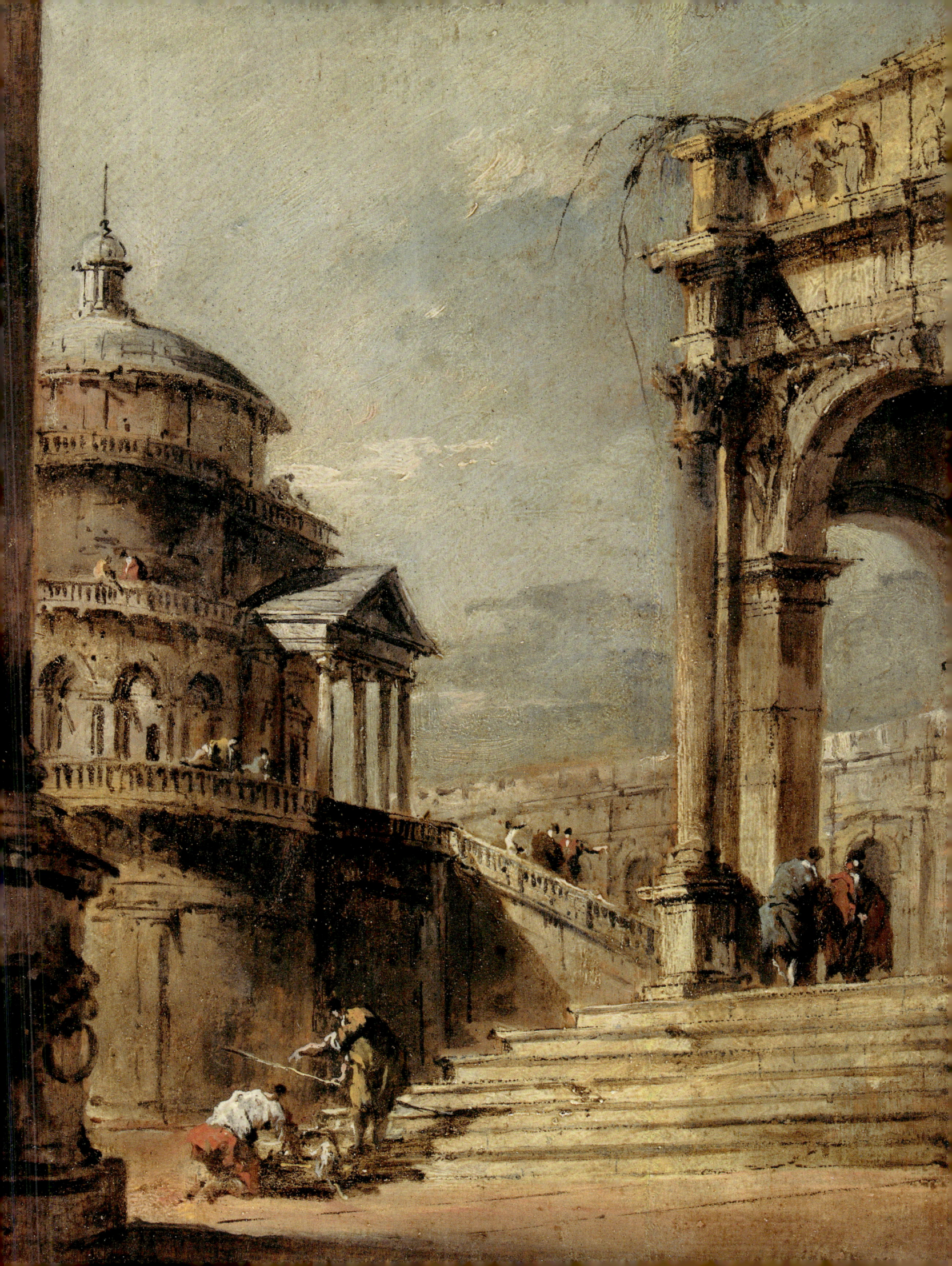

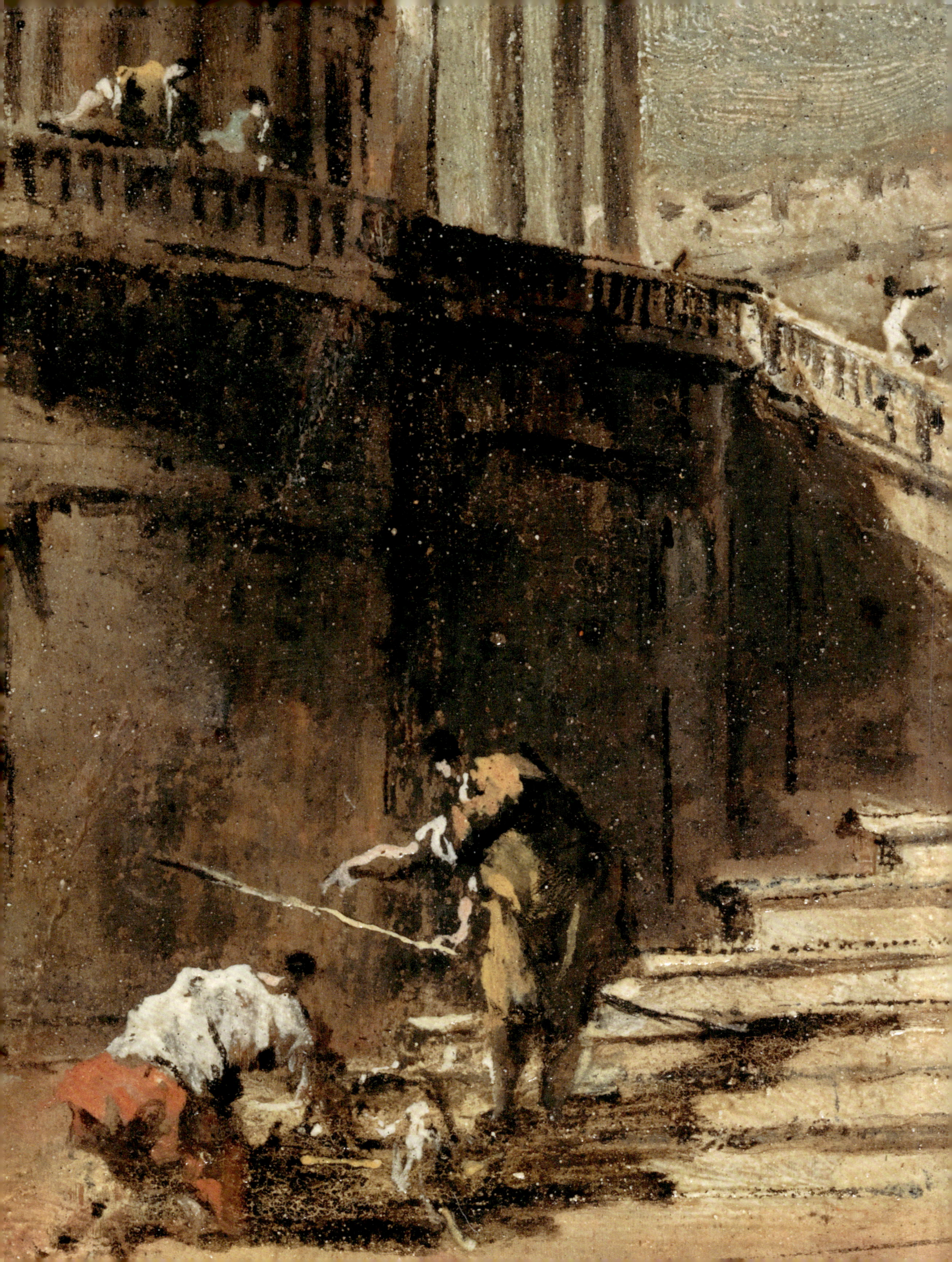

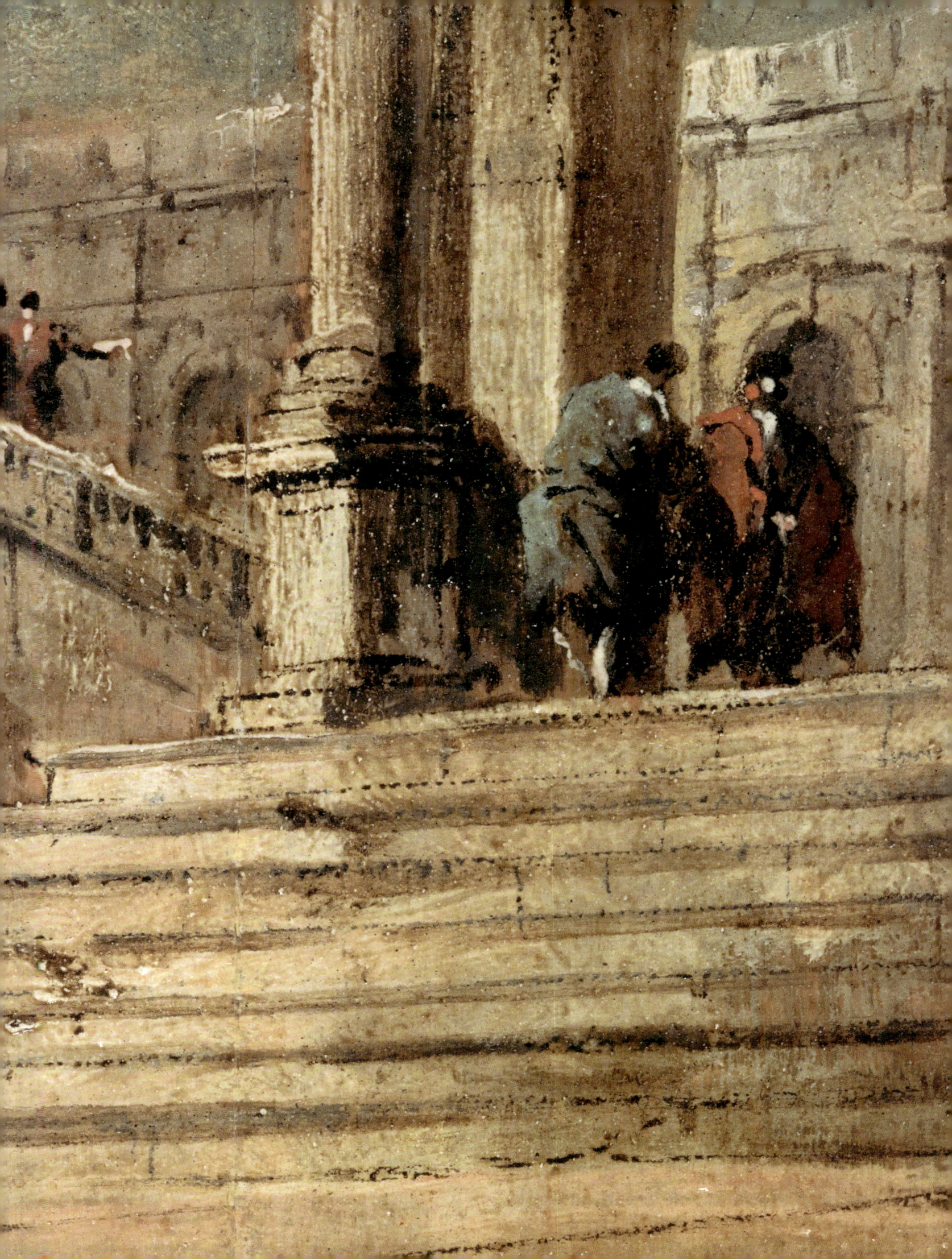

25
FRANCESCO GUARDI
(1712–1793)

Capriccio

Venice, c. 1770–80
Oil on canvas
46 × 34 cm

PROVENANCE Acquired through Agnew,
Christie's, London, on 24 January 1919, no. 56.
Calouste Gulbenkian Museum, inv. 531

Originating in Italy, the *capriccio*, which reached
its apogee with the *vedutisti* of the eighteenth century,
is a type of imaginary landscape that combines
architectural ruins and other classical buildings
in more or less fantastical compositions. In this
capriccio, the result of the artist's imagination,
there is a double arch in ruins next to a watercourse,
with a domed, circular plan temple in the background.
Two figures in the foreground add a certain liveliness
to the scene. *Capricci* in which the main architectural
element, seen from different distances and angles,
comprises one or more arches, are a frequent feature
of Francesco Guardi's work, and two smaller versions
of this theme are known.

On 23 January 2002 at Christie's in New York,
the Calouste Gulbenkian Foundation acquired
the preparatory study for the painting, a sepia pen
and wash drawing (23.1 × 14.7 cm) previously belonging
to the former Duke of Talleyrand Collection (cat. 26).
The two works differ only in the number and distribution
of the figures, which testifies to the close relationship
between the painting and the drawing.

BIBLIOGRAPHY

MORASSI 1993, vol. I, p. 483, no. 934; MURARO 1993, pp. 26–27, no. 6;
PALLUCCHINI 1965, no. 12.

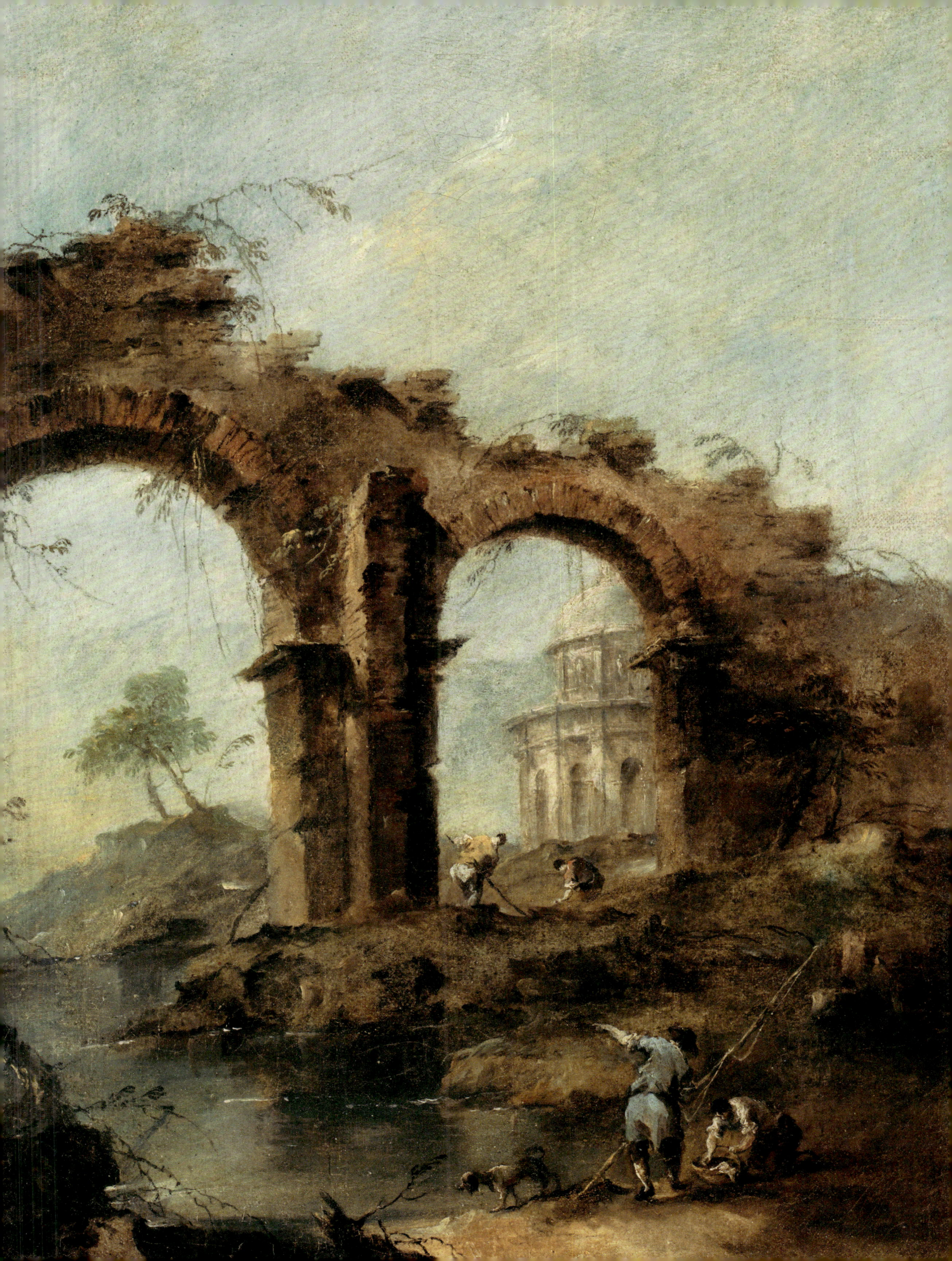

26
FRANCESCO GUARDI
(1712–1793)

Capriccio with Roman Ruined Arch and Circular Temple

Venice, c. 1770–80

Pen and brown ink with grey wash on paper

23.1 × 14.7 cm

PROVENANCE Former Fauchier-Magnan Collection, Paris; Sotheby's, London, 4 December 1935, no. 29; Duke of Talleyrand Collection. Acquired by the Calouste Gulbenkian Foundation through Christie's, New York, on 23 January 2002. Calouste Gulbenkian Museum, inv. 2871

The graphic work of Francesco Guardi, who started out in the family workshop run by Gian Antonio Guardi (1669–1760), a history painter, totals more than five hundred drawings. After his brother's death, Guardi, who had collaborated on religious scenes and figure studies, took over the workshop and began to focus increasingly on landscapes, as reflected in his numerous preparatory studies for this type of composition. This category naturally includes *vedute* and architectural *capricci*, as in the case of this drawing.

The work, acquired in 2002 due to its close connection to the painting *Capriccio* (cat. 25), differs from the latter in some details, such as the absence of the dog next to the figures in the foreground, but there is no doubt that it is a preparatory drawing for that work. The artist made several identical drawings, in which the main feature is an arch, or arches, in vertical or horizontal compositions. Guardi's pen stroke is characterised by a loose, elusive drawing that gives the scene a greater expressiveness and vitality, less evident in the oil version. On the back of the sheet is a study of an interior with columns, garlands, festoons and a sculpture on a pedestal.

BIBLIOGRAPHY

FIDALGO 2014.

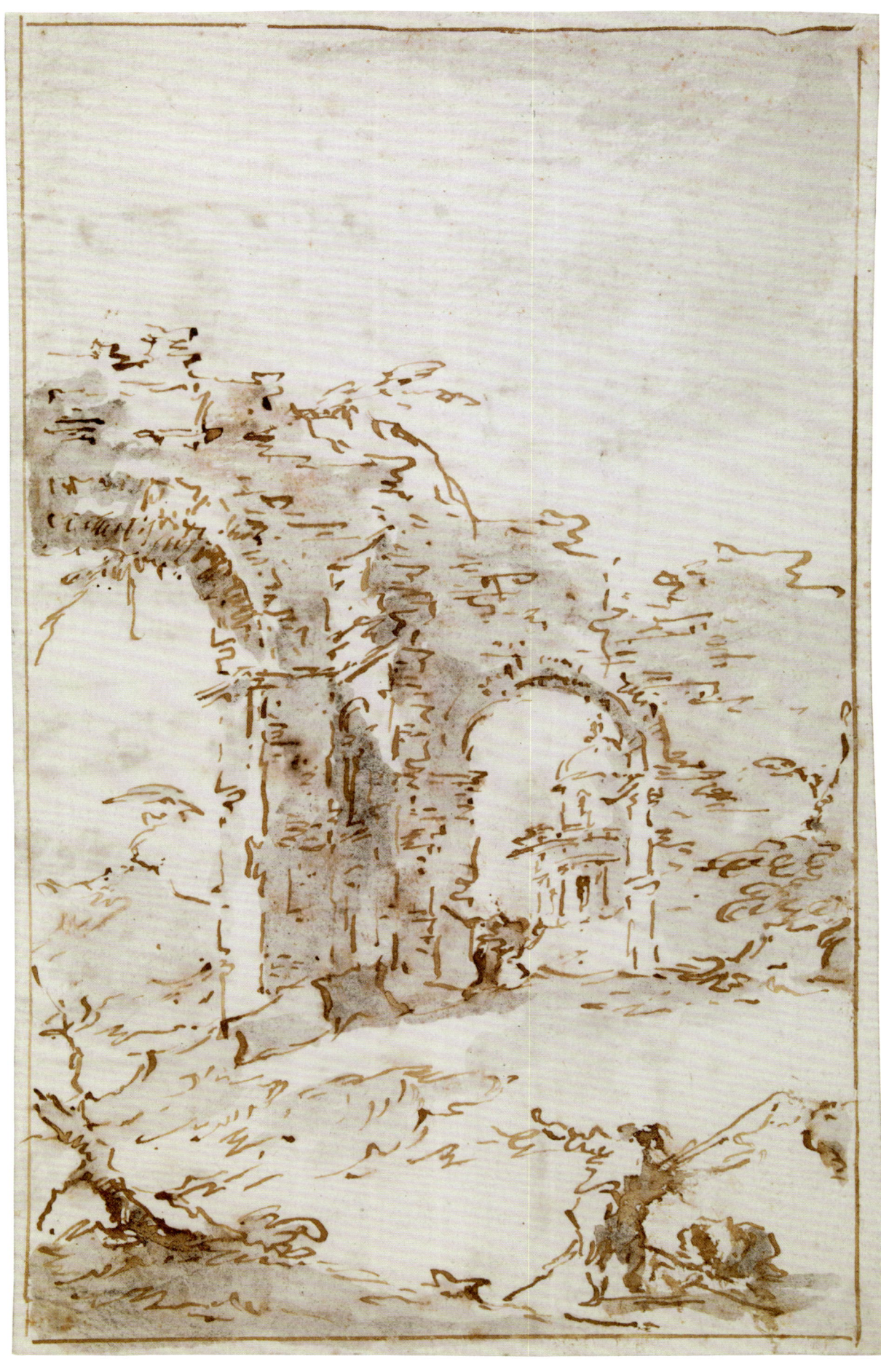

27
GIOVANNI ANTONIO CANAL (1697–1768), KNOWN AS CANALETTO

Porta Portello, Padua

Venice, c. 1760
Oil on canvas
62.8 × 109.2 cm

PROVENANCE Lord Trend; Sotheby's, London, 15 December 1954, lot 87; Speelman; Frank Partridge, London; Walter Dunkels, Sussex; Vera Dunkels; Sotheby's, London, 6 July 1966, lot 16; C. Duits; Mr and Mrs Eugene Ferkauf, New York; Christie's, London, 7 July 1972, lot 98; Private Collection; Christie's, London, 19 April 1996, lot 249; Carmen Thyssen-Bornemisza Collection on deposit at the Museo Thyssen-Bornemisza, Madrid. Carmen Thyssen Collection, inv. CTB.1996.6

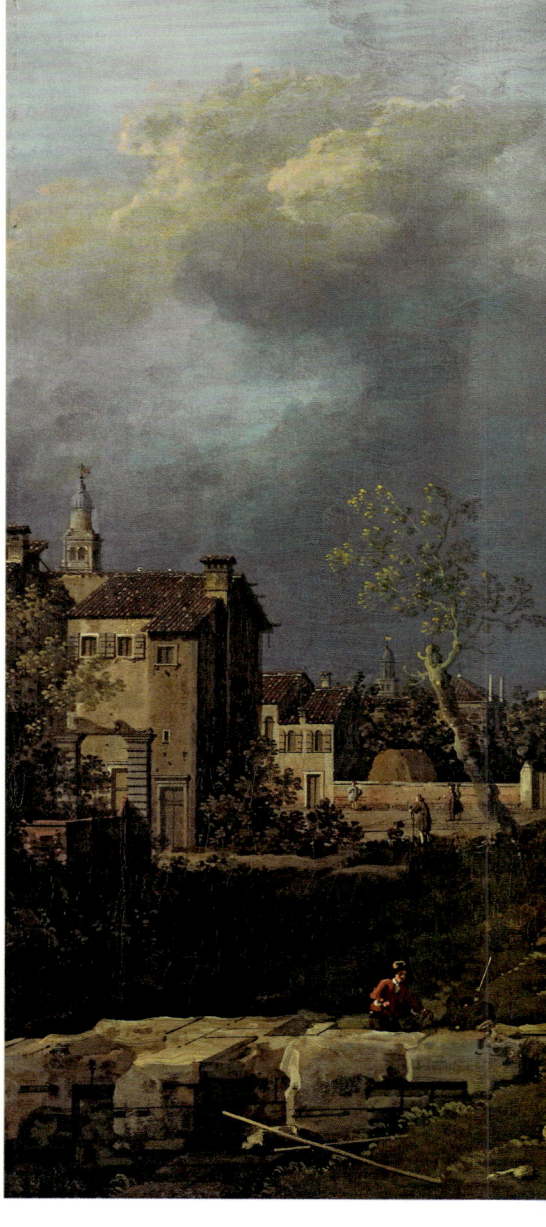

In this painting, Canaletto depicts the Porta Portello, part of the defensive wall built by the Doge Bartolomeo d'Alviano (1445-1515) and originally called the Porta Ognissanti, the main access to the city of Padua for those travelling east from Venice. The project was built in 1518 by the architect Guglielmo Bergamasco (1485-1550), who was also responsible for extending the Camerlenghi Palace in Venice.

The view of the site is not entirely accurate, nor does it display any concern with portraying a completely real landscape. The building with columns on the right cannot be identified. It is likely that Canaletto merely wanted to capture the informal ambience of this tranquil neighbourhood and punctuate it with picturesque details. The Renaissance bridge has only two pillars, although the third may have been hidden by the original perspective adopted by the painter. The perspective skilfully leads the viewer along the diagonal of the left bank of the Piovego Canal to the vanishing point, where the thirteenth-century Basilica of Carmini can be seen.

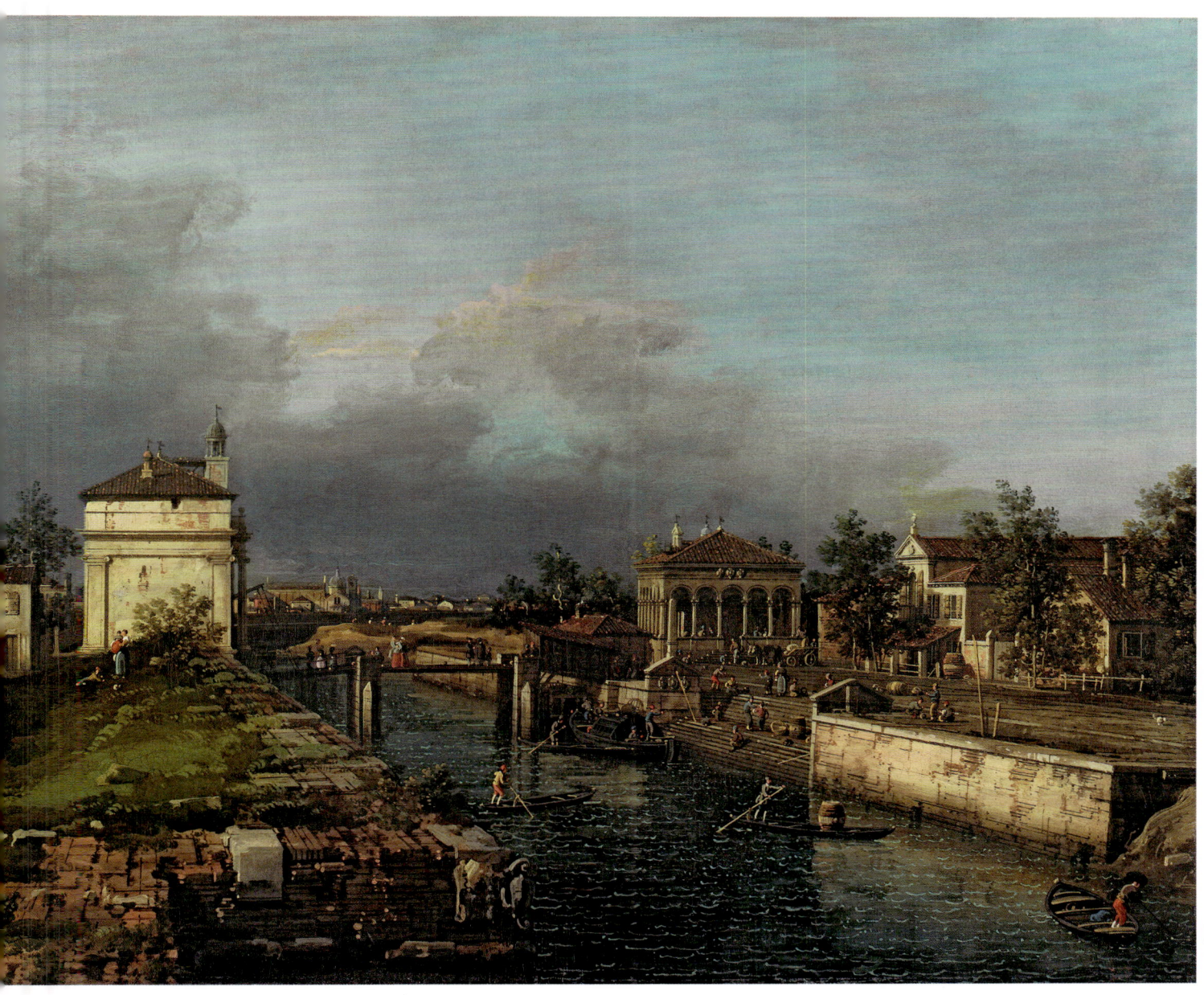

In the National Gallery of Washington there is a canvas dating from around 1741–42 which is very similar to this version of the theme, differing only in a few details. The chronology proposed for this work is supported by the trip Canaletto and his nephew Bellotto made to Padua a year earlier, documented by close-up drawings. Among that body of graphic work, which can be found in the Metropolitan Museum of Art (New York), the Royal Collection (Windsor), and the Albertina Museum (Vienna), the drawing in the latter collection is the one that most closely resembles this painting, and which probably led Canaletto to return to the motif a few years later.

BIBLIOGRAPHY

COLECCIÓN 2004, vol. 1, pp. 190–91; CONSTABLE 1989, vol. 11, p. 383, no. 375.

.

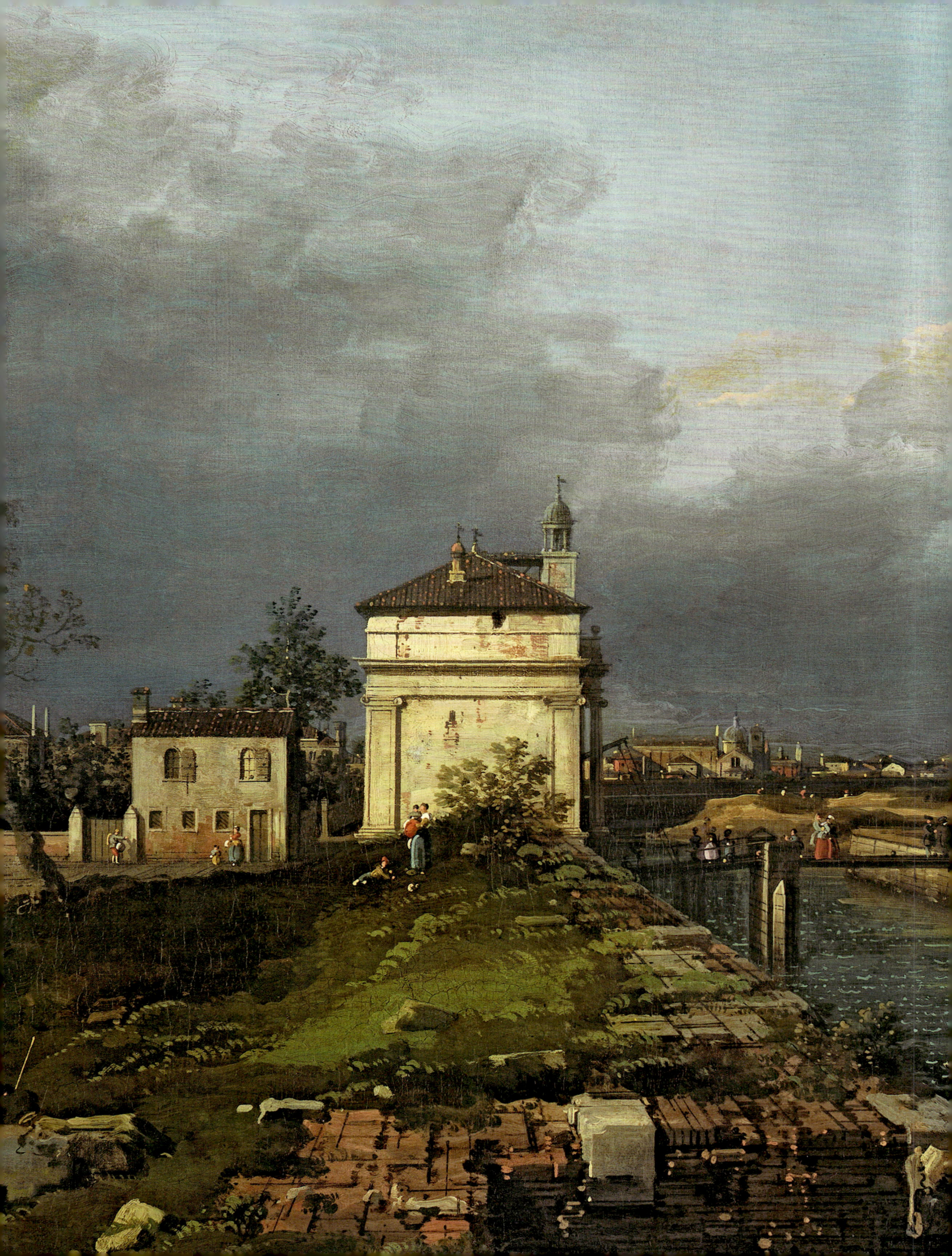

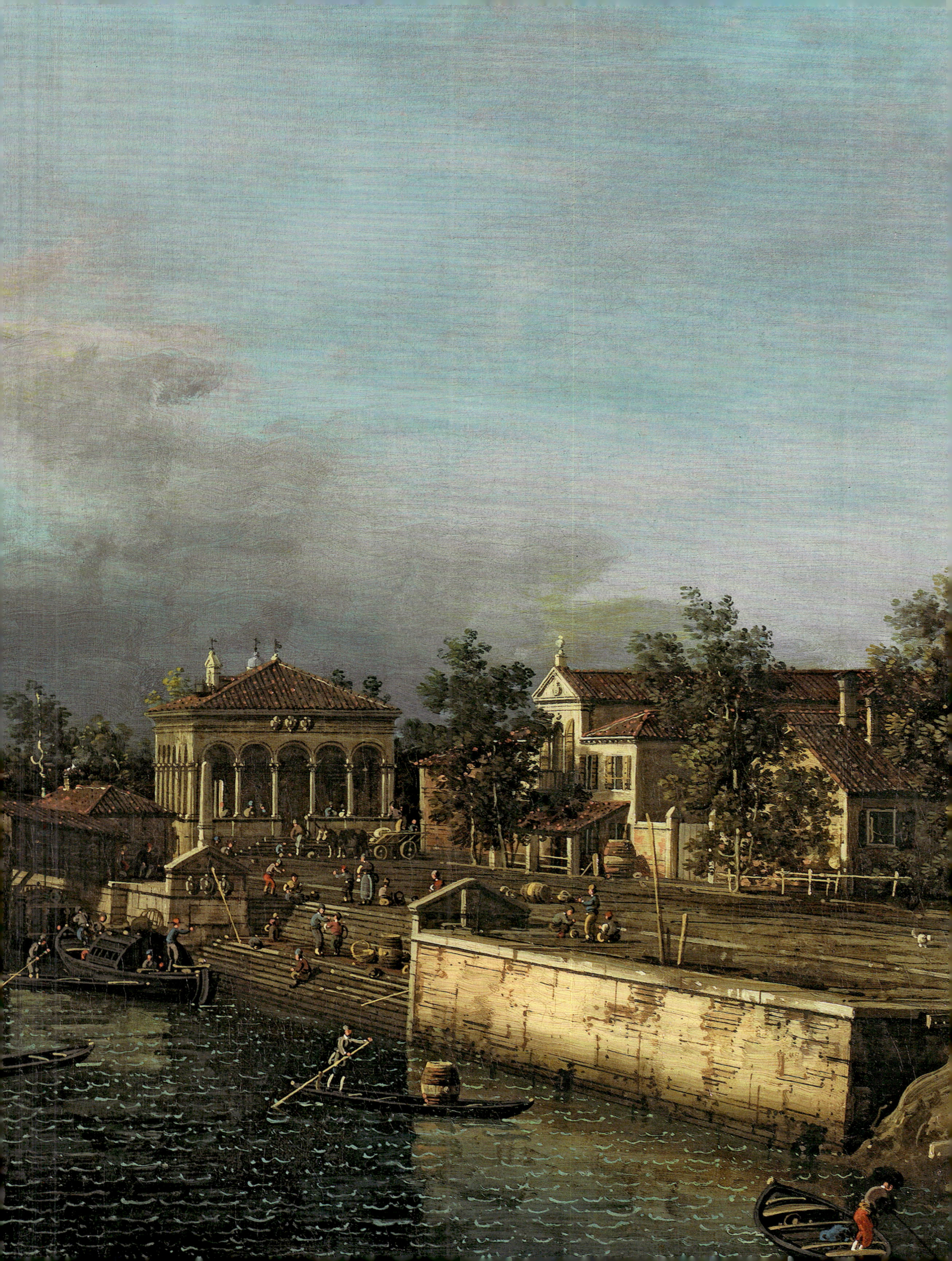

28
BERNARDO BELLOTTO
(1721–1780)

Capriccio with a River and Bridge

Italy, c. 1745
Oil on canvas
48.5 × 73 cm

PROVENANCE Camillo Castiglione Collection,
Vienna; F. Muller & Co. sale, Amsterdam,
17–20 November 1925, lot 30; Thomas Agnew & Sons,
London; Thyssen-Bornemisza Collection, Lugano, 1934;
on loan at the Museo Thyssen-Bornemisza, Madrid,
1992; Museo Thyssen-Bornemisza, Madrid, 1993.
Museo Nacional Thyssen-Bornemisza, Madrid,
inv. 40 (1934.2)

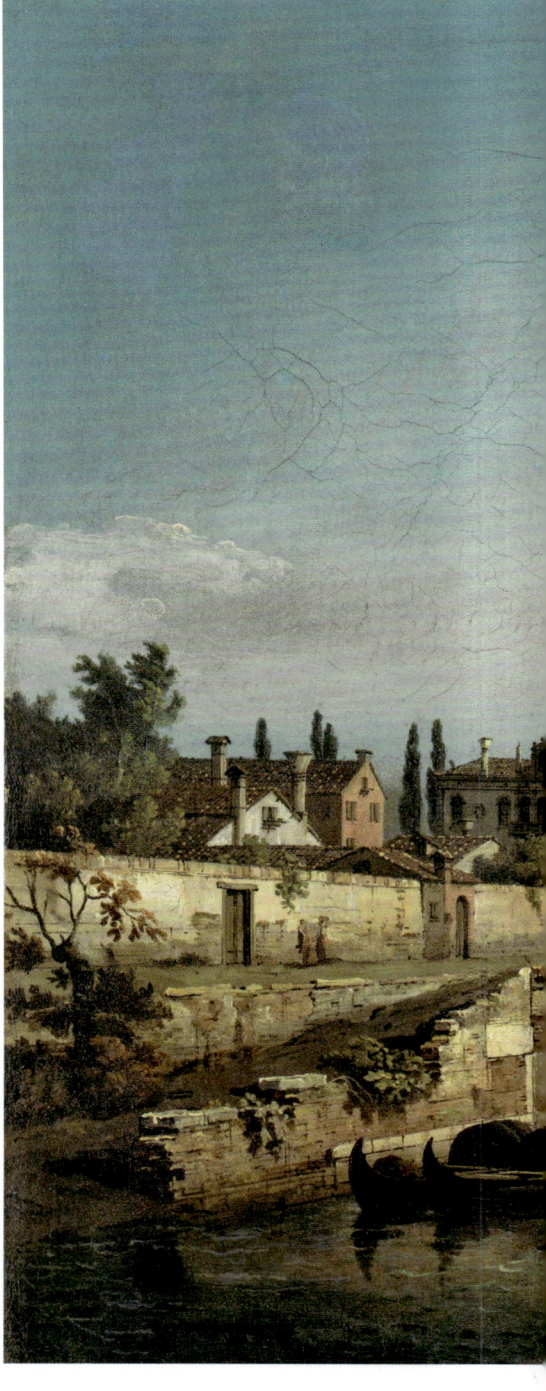

A youthful work by the artist, who was Canaletto's
nephew and disciple, this view, commonly referred
to as a *capriccio* because it depicts an idealised place,
closely follows the master's style and brings together
imaginary and real architectural elements from different
places in the same composition, with a landscape in
the background. Originally entitled *Paduan Capriccio*,
the painting features elements identified with other
well-known locations. In fact, the country house to the
left of the composition allows one to discern common
features with other buildings on the banks of the River
Brenta. The tower, once associated with the Torre di
Ezzelino, has since been recognised as another erected
in the late fifteenth century and found in the courtyard
of the Piazza d'Armas at Sforzesco Castle in Milan.
Research into the work has therefore led to a later
dating for the painting, which relates to a period
after the artist's passage through Lombardy and
not to the time when he was still active in Padua.

Unlike Canaletto, Bellotto's repertoire of views
is considerably more extensive, as the painter added
to the views of the Serenissima that he created in his
youth, works that represent various places in Italy
where he travelled, such as Rome, Florence, Verona,
Turin and Luca, as well as European cities such as
Vienna, Munich, Dresden and Warsaw. A drawing
of an urban view with a bridge (Museum Boijmans

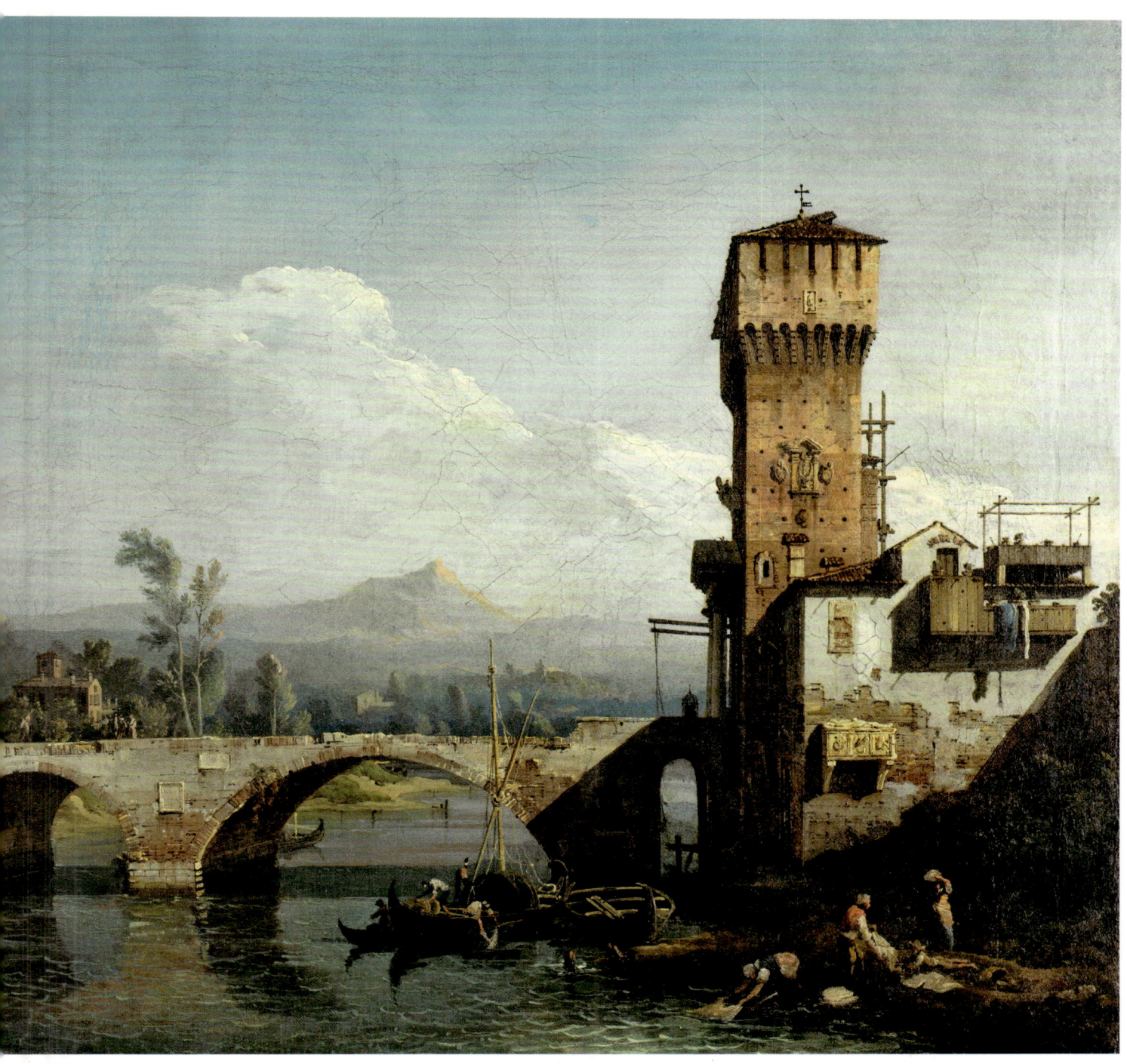

Van Beuningen, Rotterdam) displays several elements from this composition. A characteristic aspect of Bellotto's style is the sharp contrast between the light and dark areas of the canvas. The integration of various architectural elements and the way the artist incorporates them into the pleasant landscape in the background make the composition a particularly coherent whole.

BIBLIOGRAPHY

BOROBIA 2009, pp. 510–11; HEINEMANN 1937, no. 74; PALLUCCHINI 1960, p. 223.

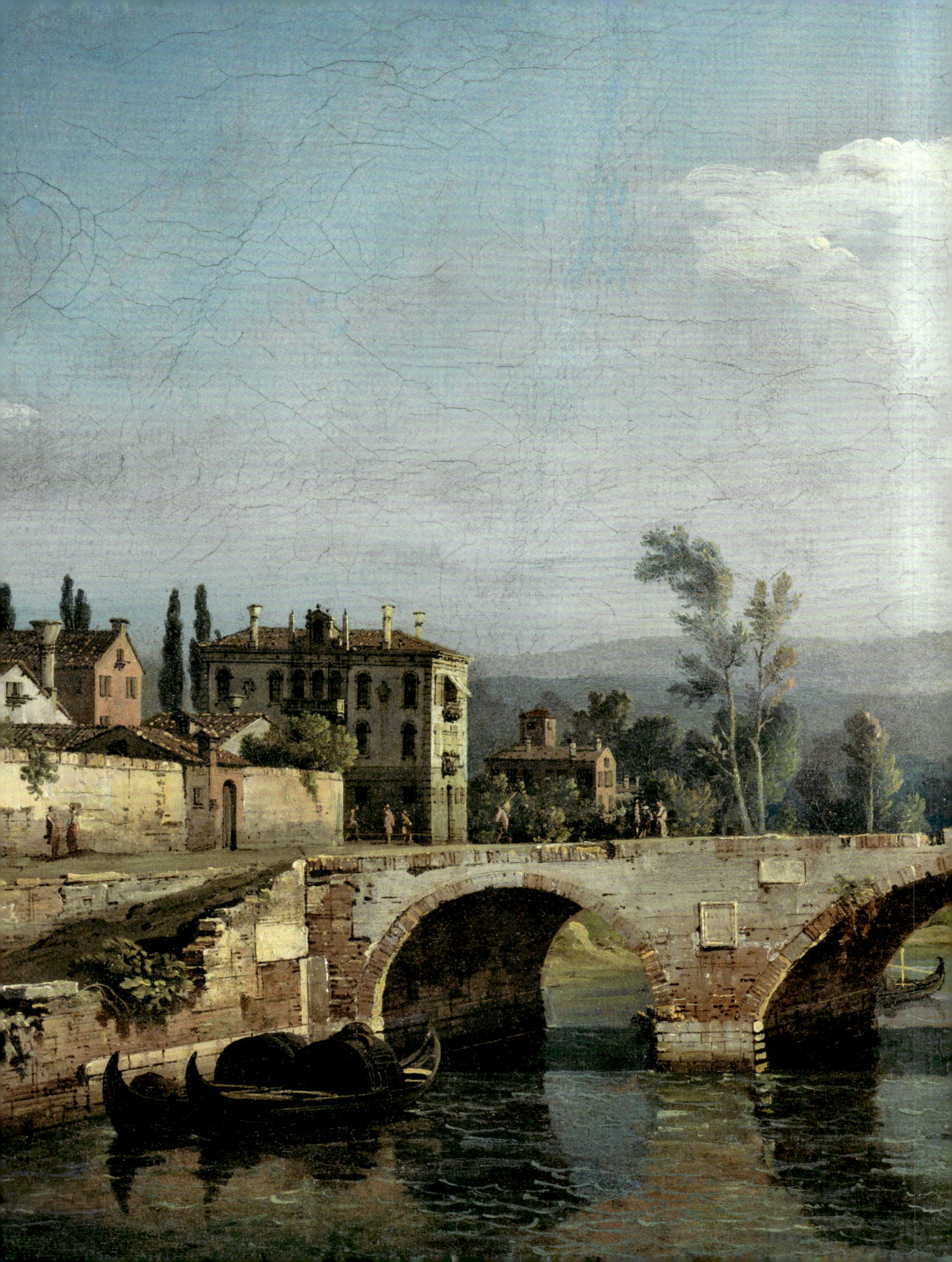

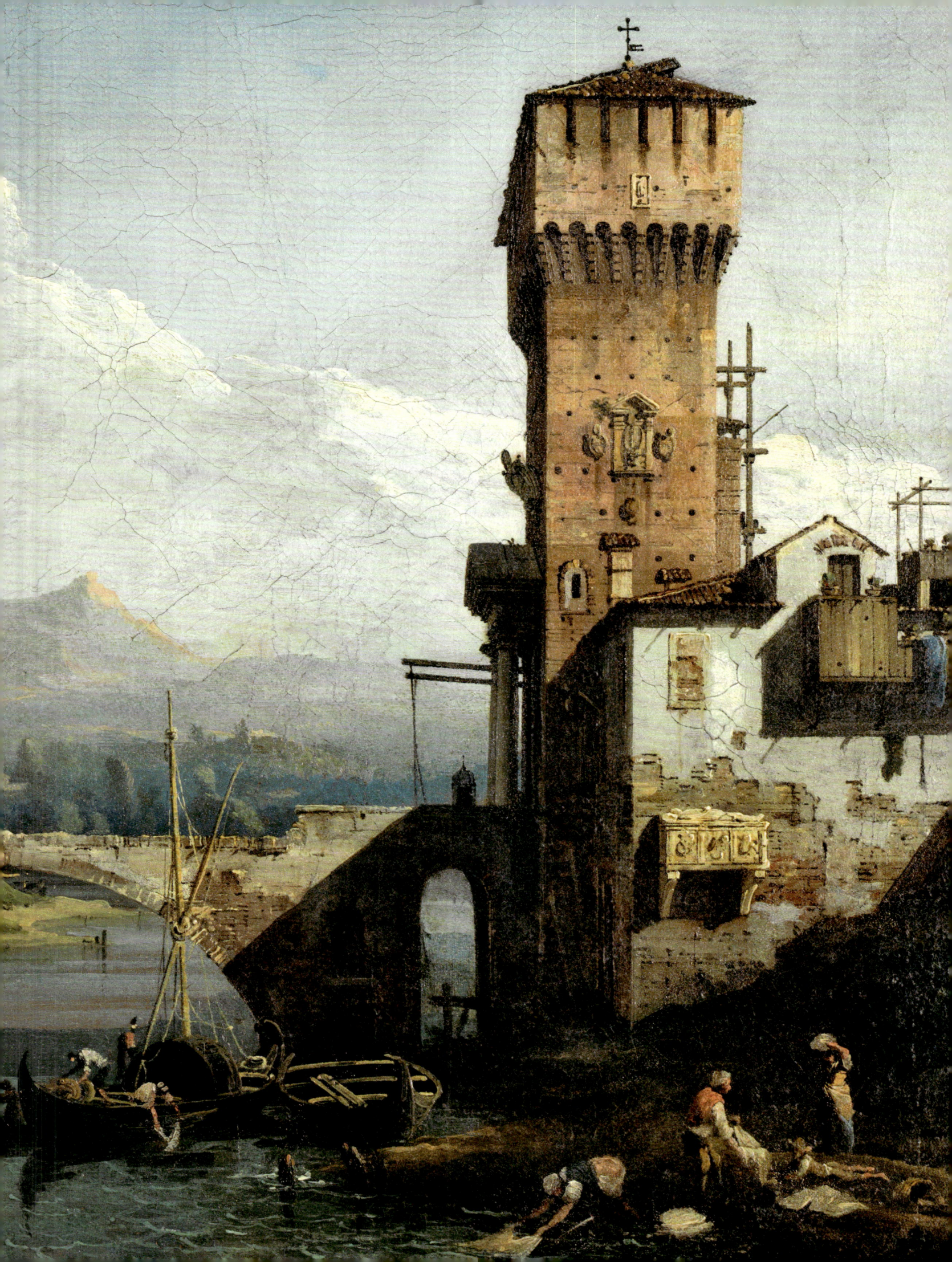

29
FRANCESCO GUARDI
(1712–1793)

The Lock Gates at Dolo

Venice, c. 1774–76

Oil on canvas

34 × 55 cm

PROVENANCE Rodolphe Kann Collection,
Paris. Acquired from Joseph Duveen, 1907.
Calouste Gulbenkian Museum, inv. 487

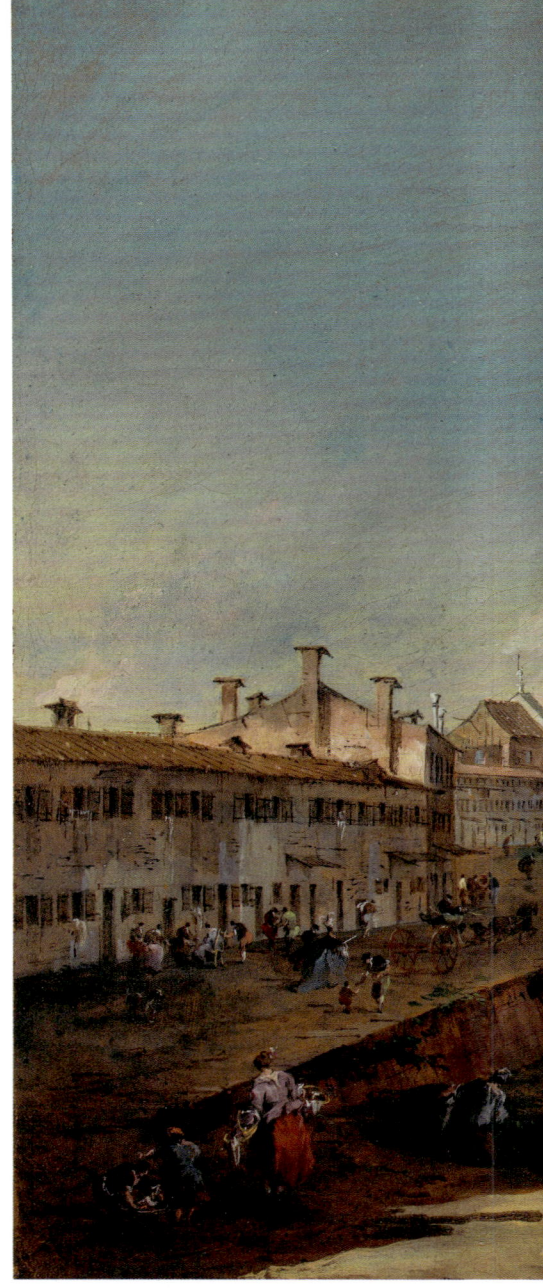

This painting depicts the village of Dolo on the banks
of the River Brenta, located between the cities of Venice
and Padua, and the hydraulic complex with the sluices
that existed there at the time can be seen. In the
foreground of the scene, animated by the movement
of the people, there are some figures from the Venetian
aristocracy who owned country houses in the area
during the eighteenth century. The theme was first
explored by Canaletto (c. 1727–35) in *A View of Dolo
on the Brenta Canal* (Ashmolean Museum, Oxford),
which was followed by identical compositions, either
concurrently or a little later, by his nephew Bernardo
Bellotto (Private Collection, England) and Giambattista
Cimaroli (c. 1687–after 1757) (Staatsgalerie, Stuttgart),
all produced in the first half of the 1740s.

Francesco Guardi made three versions of the motif
(the others are in The Detroit Institute of Arts, and
a Private Collection, Paris), for which he made a
preparatory drawing, undoubtedly *in situ* (former
Collection of the Duke of Talleyrand, Paris). As in
the sketch, the paintings show the temporary wooden
structure of the Church of San Rocco, which was rebuilt
between 1770 and 1776. This does not, of course, rule
out the fact that Guardi was inspired by Canaletto's
painting, which was done around thirty years earlier

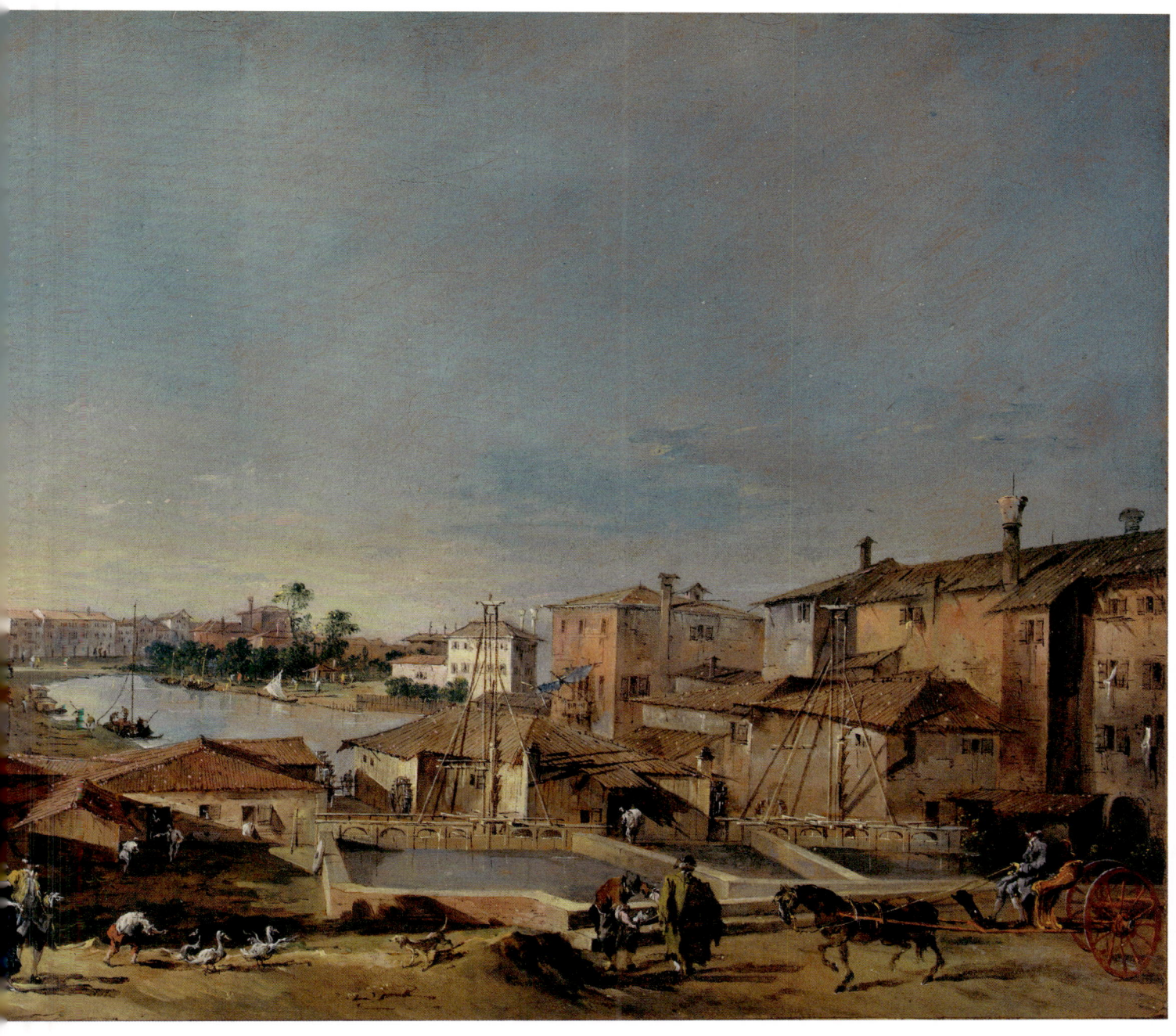

and was possibly the reason for the theme's success. The prominent female figure on the left of the canvas is wearing an exuberant hairstyle topped with feathers, a detail that also proves a valuable aid in dating Guardi's works, since this accessory was brought into vogue by Madame du Barry in Paris in 1774, reaching London the following year and finally in Venice in 1776.

BIBLIOGRAPHY

DERSTINE 2004, pp. 675–82, no. 956; MORASSI 1993, vol. I, pp. 254, 435, no. 670; MURARO 1993, pp. 12–13, no. I; PALLUCCHINI 1965, no. 2.

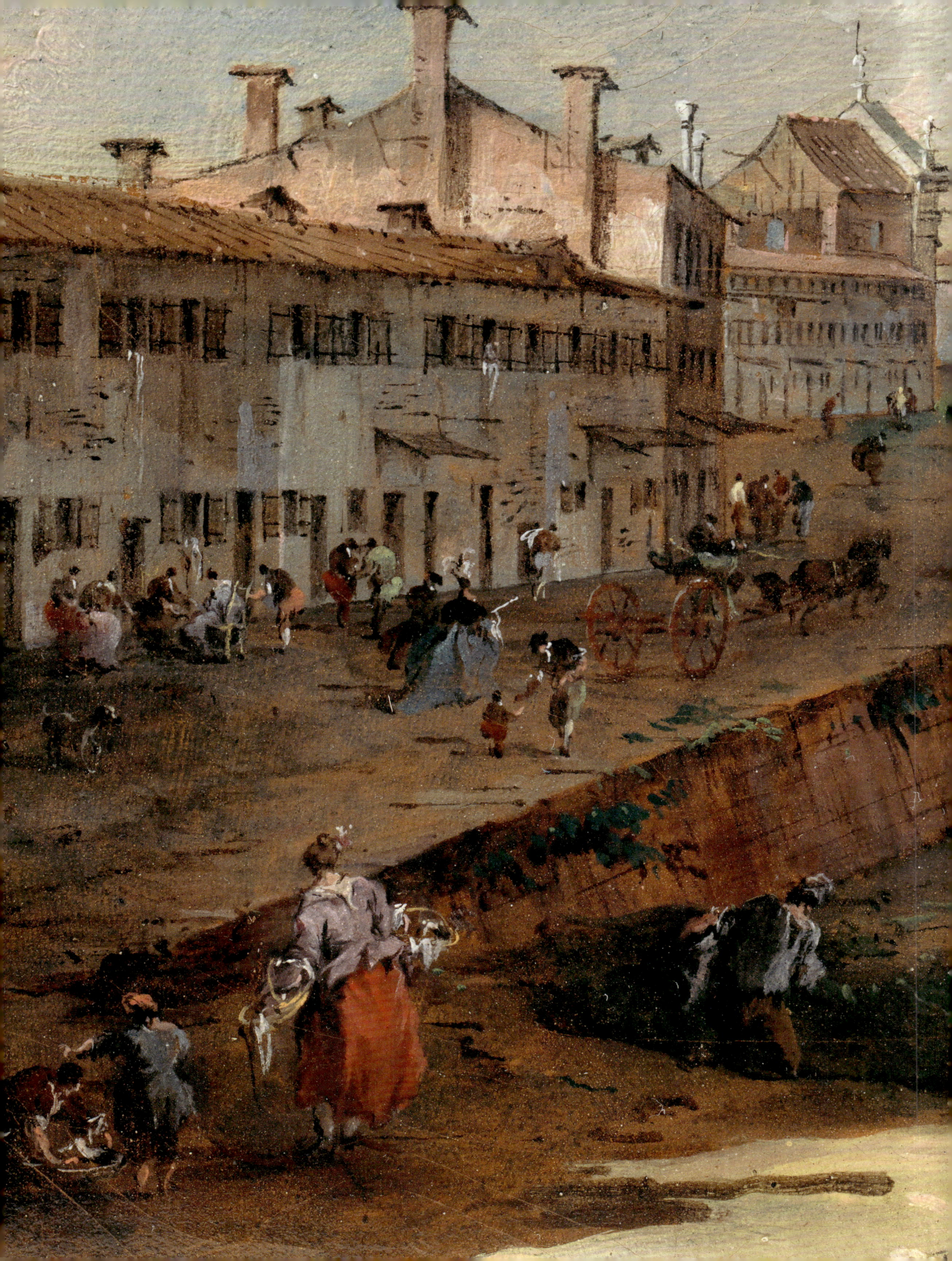

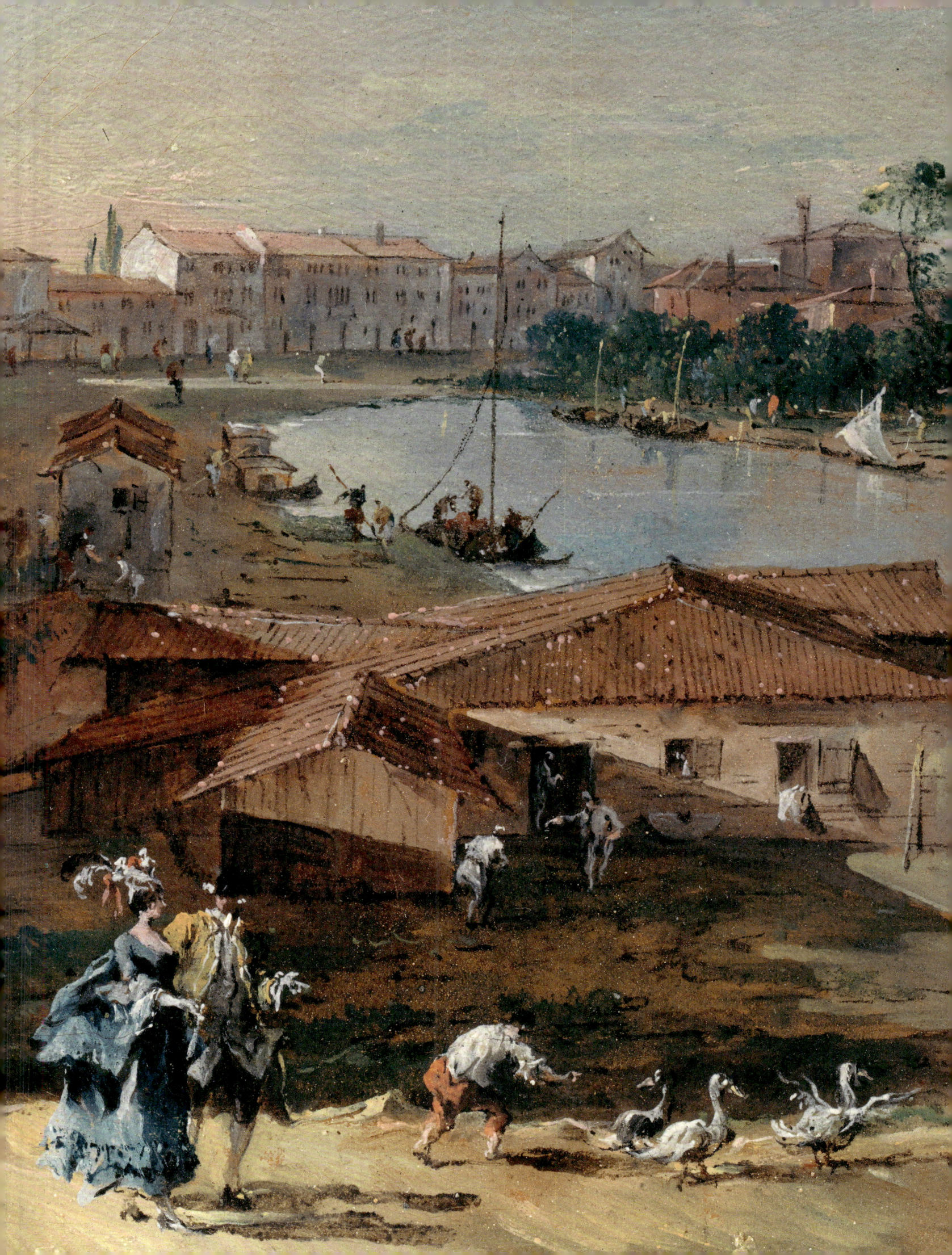

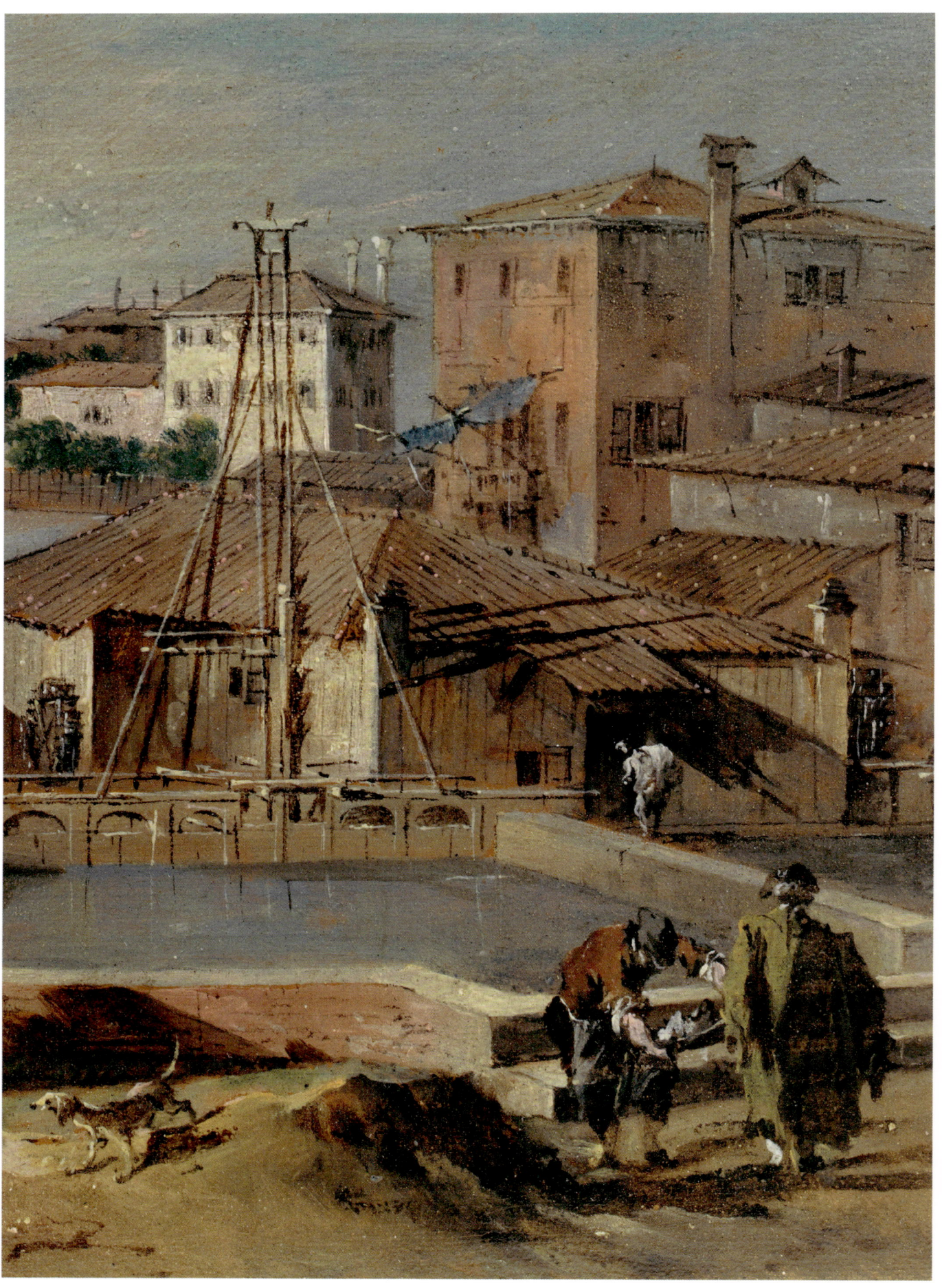

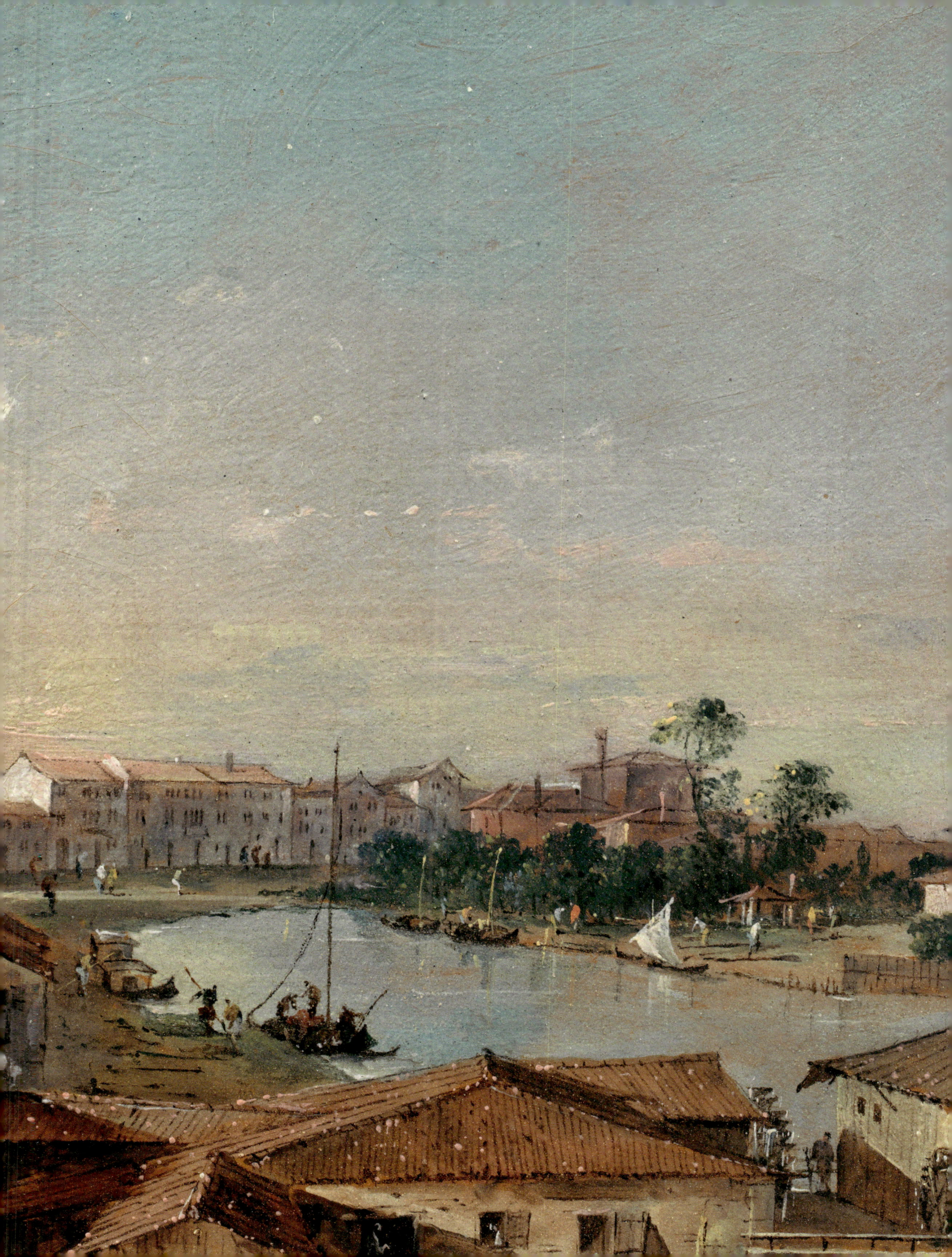

30
FRANCESCO GUARDI
(1712–1793)

The Giudecca Canal with the Church of Saint Martha

Venice, c. 1770–80

Oil on canvas

32.5 × 46.5 cm

PROVENANCE Acquired at Christie's sale,
London, on 23 April 1920, no. 49.
Calouste Gulbenkian Museum, inv. 122

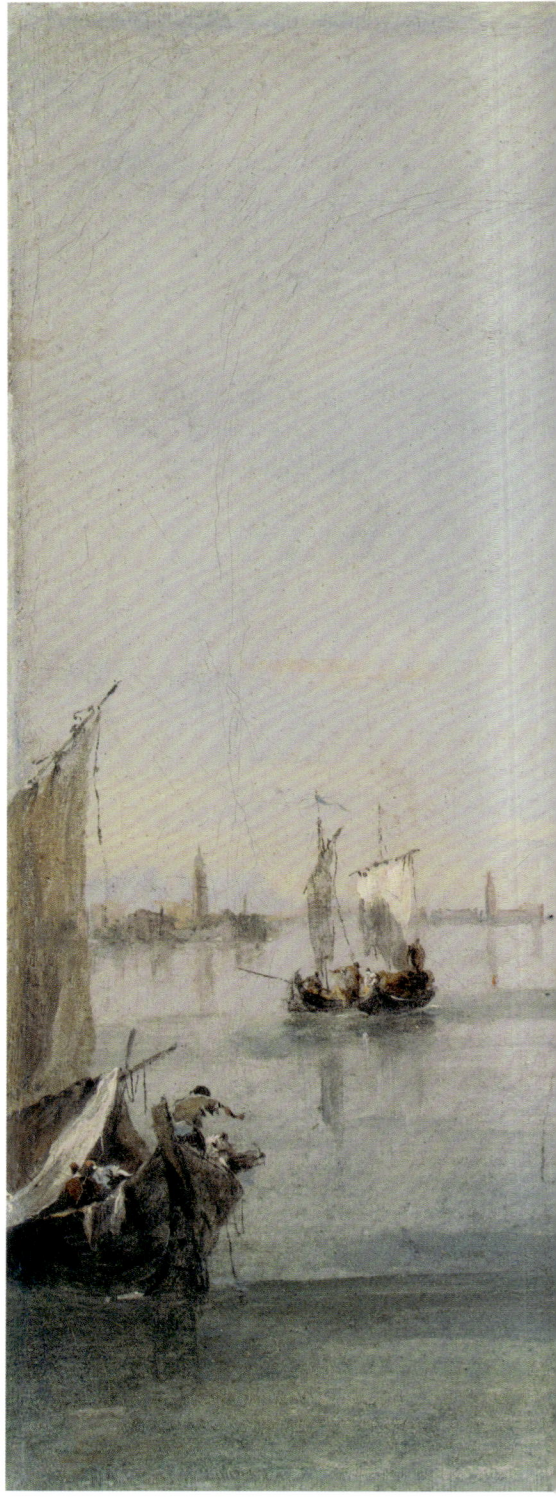

In this composition, where one can see the far end of Saint Martha and the Giudecca Canal, Francesco Guardi reveals a peripheral Venice filled with details that narrate the daily life of the local population. Through this motif, the artist successfully expressed his immense artistic sensibility. There is a move away from the ostentatious side of his other paintings, of which the *feste* are excellent examples, and this clear informality allowed Guardi to concentrate on depicting a misty dawn landscape, where the magical ambience of the canal dominates the entire pictorial surface.

Silver and blue tones therefore prevail in the scene, with more distant forms, boats and building silhouettes, diluted in light monochrome brushstrokes. The moisture of the lagoon and the greyish sky are reminiscent of the work of Dutch artist Jan van Goyen (1596-1656). The most striking feature of the canvas is undoubtedly the way in which Francesco Guardi makes use of *sfumato*, employing this technical artifice to produce an optical phenomenon that softens and dissolves the smooth transition of the elements' colours and contours.

Guardi only made two *vedute* at the far end of Saint Martha, in a different format, so this painting, created from a recessed viewpoint and revealing a wide perspective of the lagoon, can be considered unique in his oeuvre.

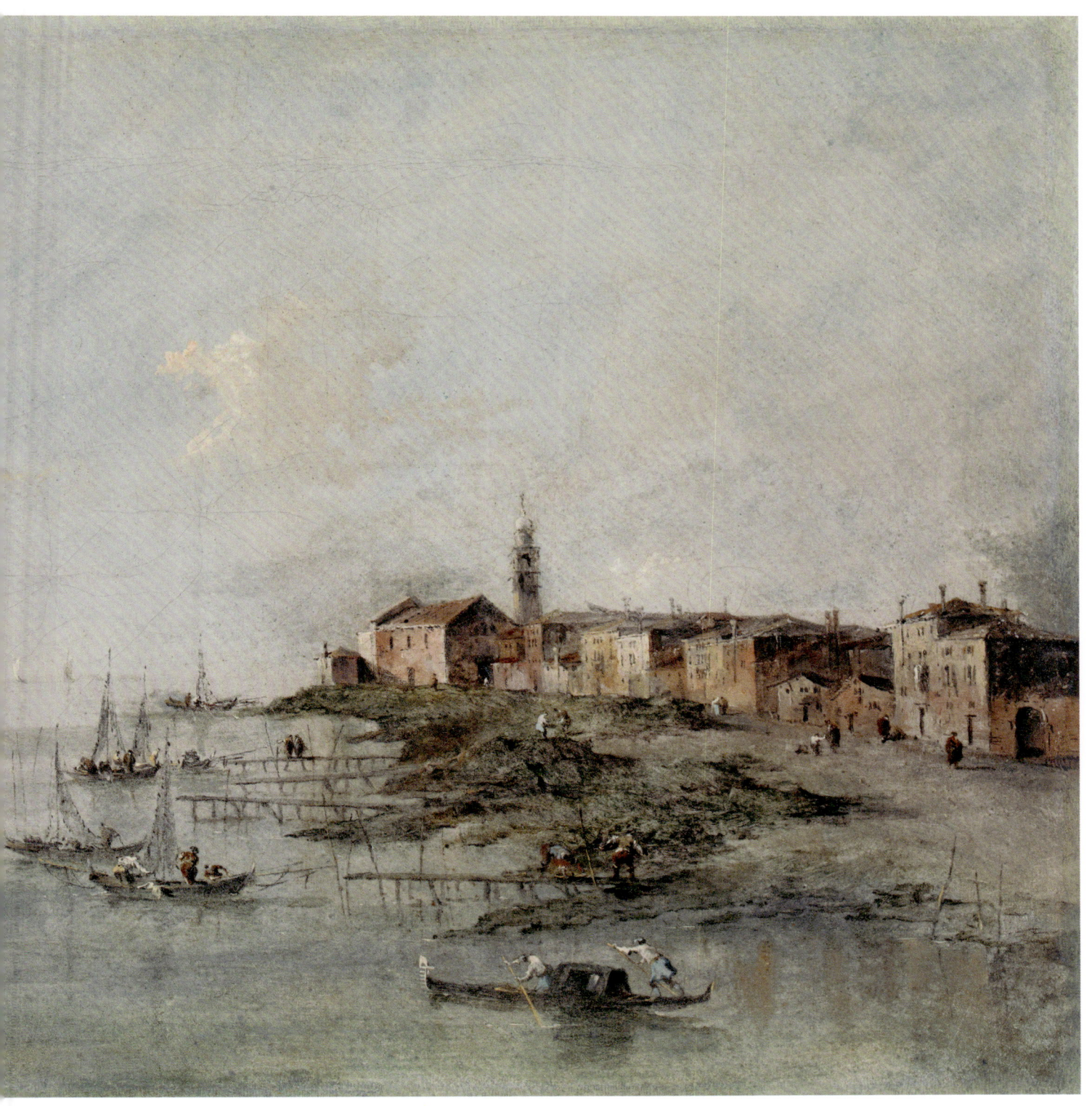

BIBLIOGRAPHY

CRAIEVICH and PEDROCCO 2012, pp. 242, 273, no. 100;
MORASSI 1973, p. 427, no. 627; MURARO 1993, pp. 56–57, no. 15;
PALLUCCHINI 1965, no. 13.

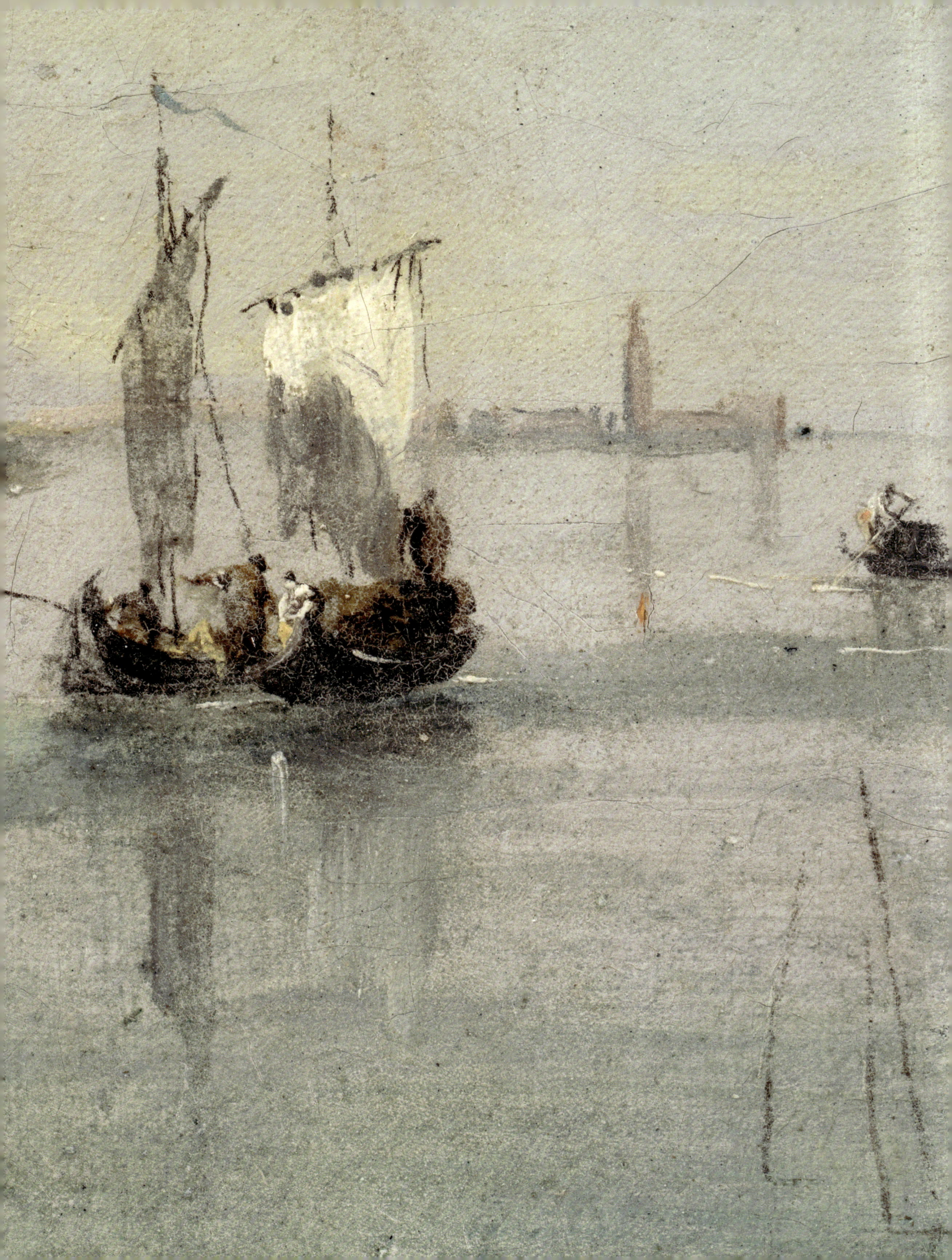

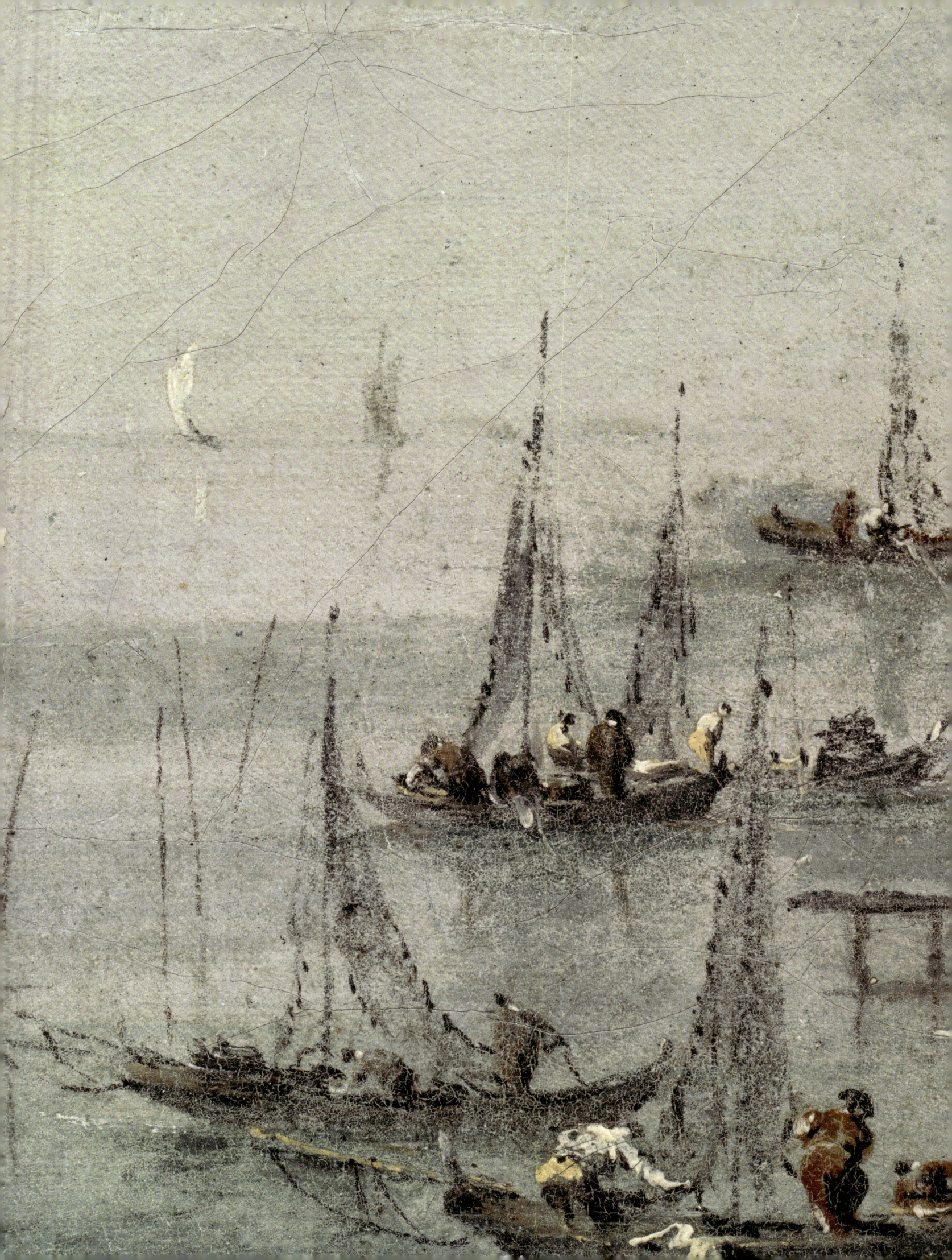

31
GIAMBATTISTA PIAZZETTA (1682–1754)

Portrait of Giulia Lama

Venice, c. 1715–20
Oil on canvas
69.4 × 55.5 cm

A painter of the Venetian Baroque, an artistic milieu in which he played an important role, Giambattista Piazzetta excelled primarily in religious themes and genre painting, inspired by the seventeenth-century tenebrist painters.

In this work, the artist depicts the Venetian painter Giulia Lama (1681-1747), who previously studied alongside him and has been identified by her self-portrait (Galleria degli Uffizi, Florence). Lama was probably one of the first women to paint from live, nude models, a fact confirmed by the existence of a significant number of anatomical drawings she made of both men and women. Initially trained by her father, the painter Agostino Lama, Giulia, who was also a poet and whose erudition was confirmed by contemporary accounts, pursued a successful career in religious painting, and seems to have achieved some financial independence, which was unusual for a woman at the time.

Lama appears against a neutral background, with her head three-quarter turned. Proud and elegantly dressed, in her left hand she holds the palette that identifies her with her profession. The figure of Giulia, which Piazzetta portrays with a boldness entirely at odds with how she appears in her self-portrait, also served as a model for *Susanna and the Elders* (Galleria degli Uffizi, Florence). The figure's penetrating expression, with its vaguely mysterious gaze, places the viewer in front of a captivating personality. This work, initially conceived as an oval-shaped composition, employs the *chiaroscuro* technique, focusing the light on the face and hands of the defiant figure and brilliantly showcasing Piazzetta's skill as a portraitist.

BIBLIOGRAPHY

BOROBIA 2009, p. 484; *CANALETTO* 2019, p. 210, no. V.47; LOISEL 2018, p. 79, no. 48; PALLUCCHINI AND MARIUZ 1982, pp. 78-79, no. 17.

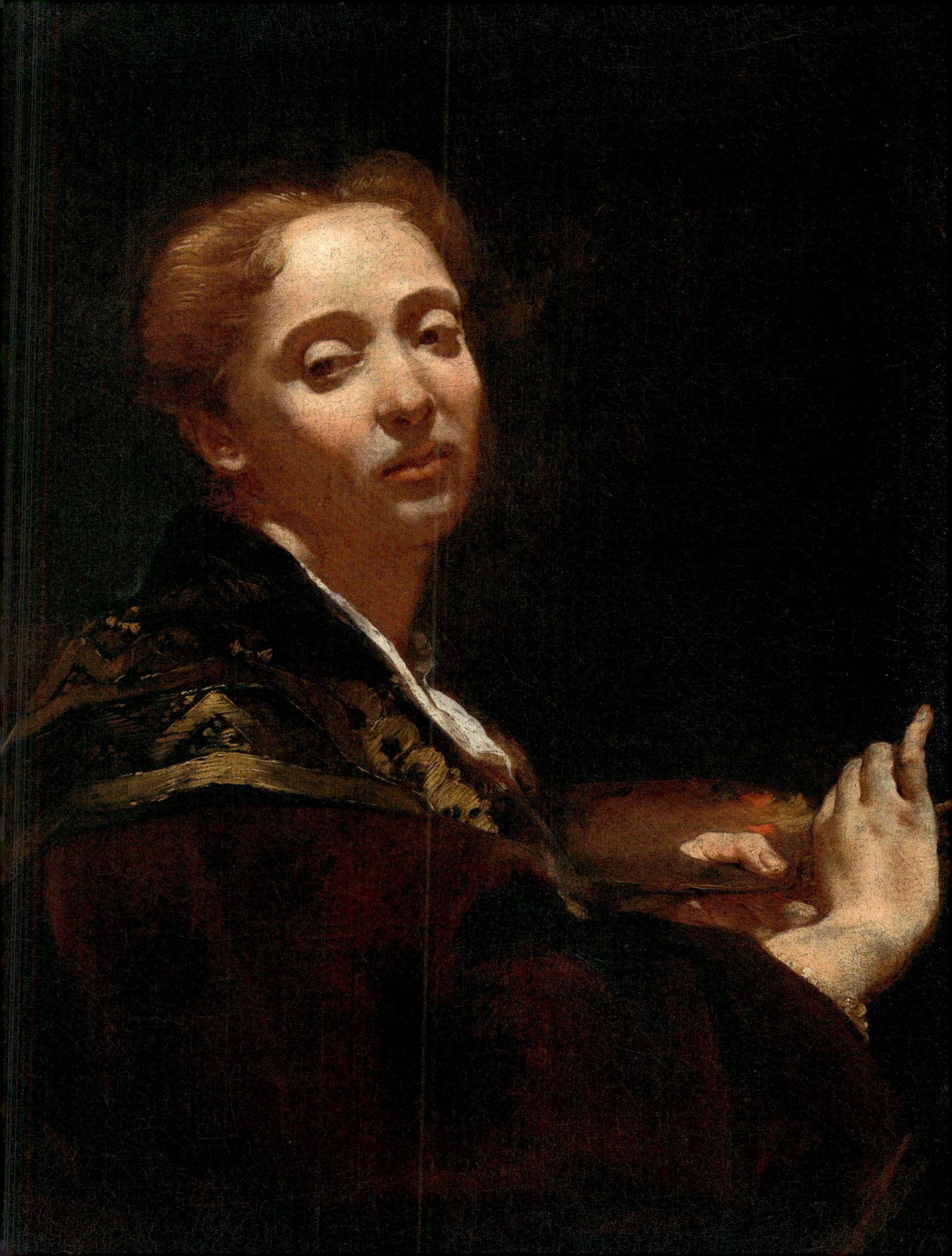

32
GIAMBATTISTA PIAZZETTA (1682–1754)

Portrait of a Young Woman in Profile with a Mask in Her Right Hand

Venice, c. 1720–30
Oil on canvas
46 × 36.2 cm

PROVENANCE Christie's, New York, 29 January 1999;
Carmen Thyssen-Bornemisza Collection on deposit
at the Museo Thyssen-Bornemisza, Madrid.
Carmen Thyssen Collection, inv. CTB.1999.5

This profile of a young woman, with her head turned slightly to the right, is holding a black velvet mask traditionally worn by ladies in the eighteenth century, called a *moretta* or *muta*, which suggests the celebration of the Venetian Carnival, whose origins in the city date back to the Middle Ages. The painting was probably done in the 1720s, and it has been plausibly hypothesised, but not confirmed, that the model could be Rosa Muziolo (1701–1771), whom the painter married in 1724. The figure is in fact idealised to a greater or lesser extent in other works by Piazzetta, such as *Idyll on the Shore* (Wallraff-Richartz Museum, Cologne), which at the very least suggests a close relationship between model and artist. A drawing from the Royal Collection (Windsor), *Girl in Contemplation*, conceived not as a portrait but as a *tête d'expression* intended for a market that Piazzetta fuelled, appears related to this figure.

From a compositional point of view, the painting closely follows the setting and ambience of *Portrait of Giulia Lama* (cat. 31), at the Museo Nacional Thyssen-Bornemisza (Madrid), a portrait characterised by its sober refinement. In this canvas, Piazzetta, who had learnt his art in Venice with the 'tenebrist' Antonio Molinari (1655-1704), also maintains his penchant for *chiaroscuro* in the manner of Giuseppe Maria Crespi (1665-1747), with whom he had come into contact in Bologna around 1703 and who transposed the lessons of Caravaggio (1571-1610) to everyday scenes. The colour palette, as in the aforementioned portrait, is softer and brighter here, a trend Piazzetta followed from the 1720s onwards and which finds in the motif of this painting, an expression piece, the gallantry associated with the Venetian Carnival.

BIBLIOGRAPHY

COLECCIÓN 2004, vol. 1, pp. 140–41.

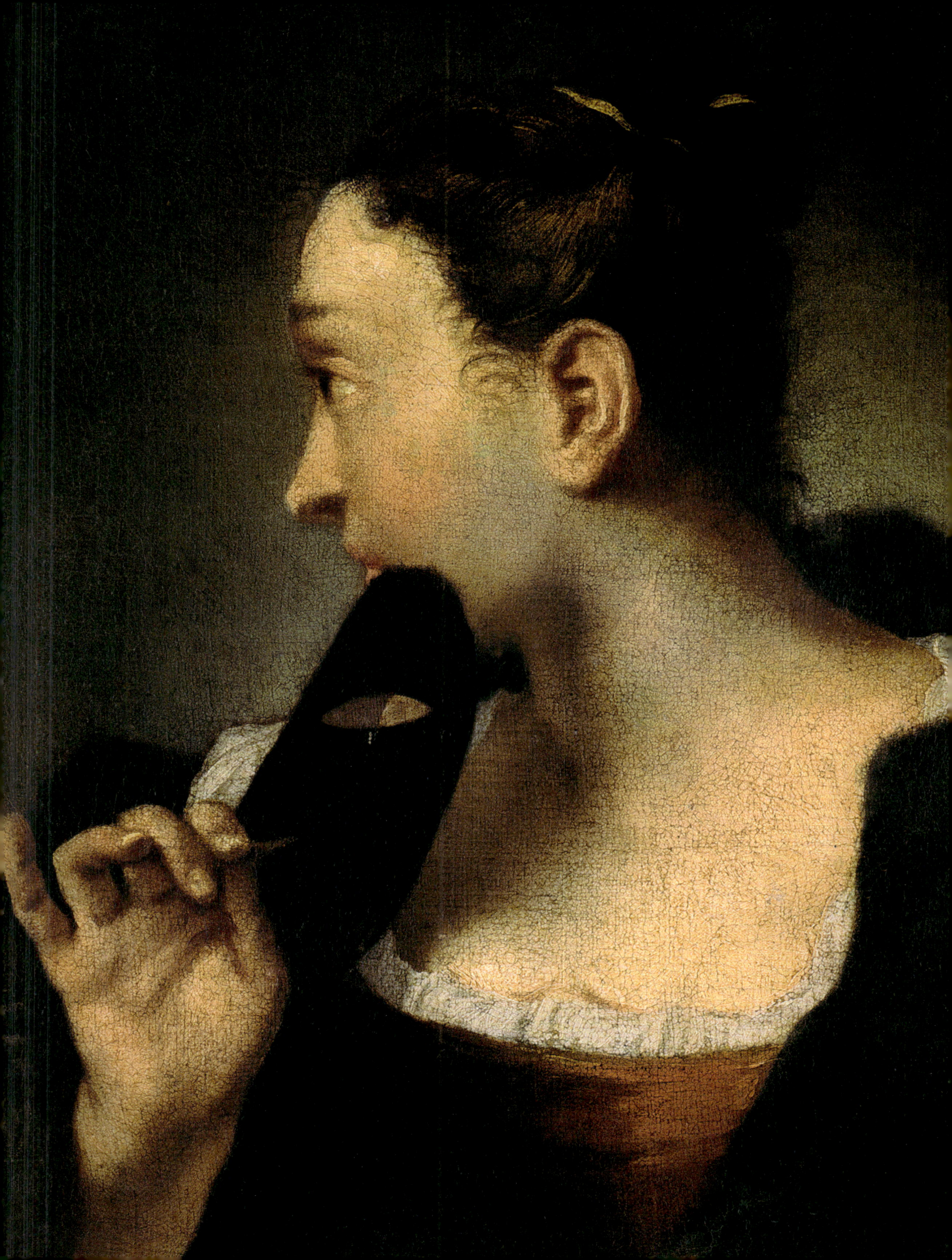

33
PIETRO LONGHI
(1702–1785)

The Tickle

Venice, c. 1755
Oil on canvas
61 × 48 cm

PROVENANCE Private Collection, 1909;
Sale at Parke-Bernet Galleries, New York, 20 May 1971,
lot 59; Thyssen-Bornemisza Collection, Lugano, 1971;
on loan at the Museo Thyssen-Bornemisza, Madrid,
1992; Museo Thyssen-Bornemisza, Madrid, 1993.
Museo Nacional Thyssen-Bornemisza, Madrid,
inv. 224 (1971.4)

After an initial career dedicated to religious painting, from the late 1730s onwards Pietro Longhi devoted himself to the small-scale works that made him famous. This body of work, which focused on depictions of everyday life in Venice, falls under the category of what is usually called genre painting, whose traditions date back to sixteenth-century Dutch painting. In England, the eighteenth century saw a new approach to this type of composition through the famous *conversation pieces* by William Hogarth (1697–1764), to which the artist added a satirical touch. Longhi was also influenced by the *fête galante* painting practised in France by painters such as Nicolas Lancret (1690–1743) and Antoine Watteau (1684–1721), whose work he may have had access to through the circulation of prints.

These chronicles of everyday life, which sometimes appear to be authentic caricatures, full of humour and conceived in a refined and elegant style, are an excellent testimony to life inside Venetian homes, to which the artist, a friend of the playwright Carlo Goldoni (1707–1793), adds a note of comedy that gives the scenes a theatrical flavour.

This painting is an excellent synthesis of the artist's style, in which the scenery depicted is similar to that of other works by him, which are also characterised by leisure and amusement. The male figure's pose is reminiscent of a figure in *The Faint* from c. 1744 (National Gallery of Art, Washington). On the wall to the right, a painting depicts the Three Graces, also visible in *The Temptation* (The Metropolitan Museum of Art, New York), from 1746. Longhi's interior scenes are an important complement to the urban representations of the great *vedutisti* of the time who documented the pageantry of the Republic's celebrations, contributing to a comprehensive portrait of life in the Serenissima.

BIBLIOGRAPHY

BOROBIA 2009, p. 504.

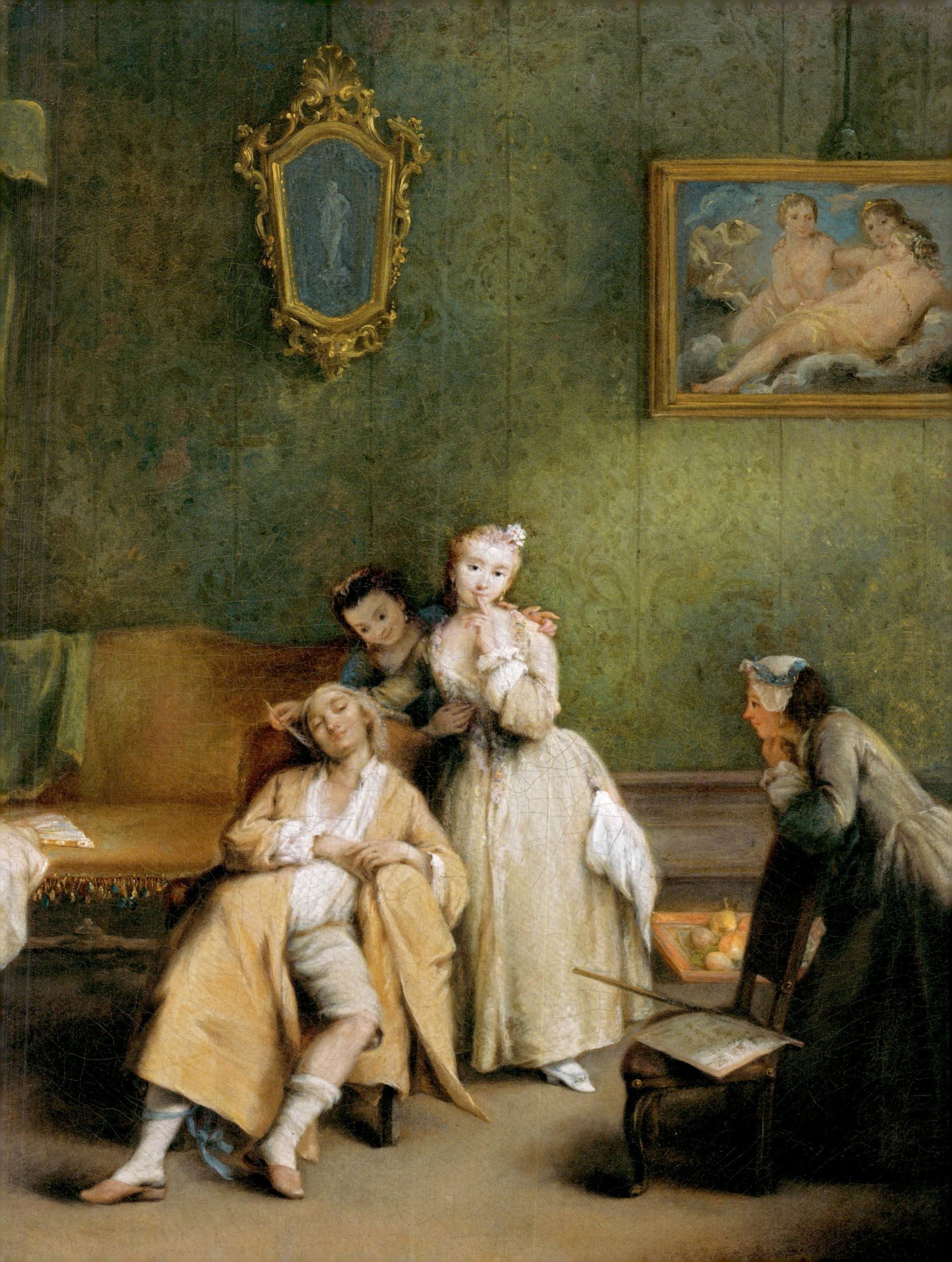

34
GIAMBATTISTA TIEPOLO (1696–1770)

The Death of Sophonisba

Venice, c. 1760
Oil on canvas
48.3 × 38.2 cm

<u>PROVENANCE</u> Gibson Craig Collection, London;
Christie's sale, London, 13 April 1887, lot 73; Colnaghi,
London; Camille Groult Collection, Paris; Charpentier sale,
21 March 1952, lot 96; Antenor Patiño Collection,
known up to 1971; Thyssen-Bornemisza Collection,
Lugano, 1975; on loan at the Museo Thyssen-Bornemisza,
Madrid, 1992; Museo Thyssen-Bornemisza, Madrid, 1993.
Museo Nacional Thyssen-Bornemisza, Madrid,
inv. 396 (1975.33)

This painting depicts the death of Sophonisba, Queen of Numidia and daughter of the Carthaginian general Hasdrubal, who lived from 235–203 BCE. The episode, which takes place during the Second Punic War, is recounted by Titus Livius in his *History of Rome* (XXX, 14–15) and tells of the moment when Sophonisba, at the behest of her second husband, King Massinissa (c. 239–148 BCE), drinks a cup of poison to avoid the dishonour of being sent to Rome as a captive by the Roman general and consul Scipio Africanus (c. 236/35–c. 183 BCE). Sophonisba's death was a popular theme in Baroque painting in Italy and northern Europe.

The work is produced using rapid brushstrokes and is one of many oil studies that Tiepolo undertook for more ambitious compositions. In this case, there is no known finished work corresponding to this sketch. The scene unfolds in keeping with the Baroque dynamics typical of the painter's work. In the foreground, on the right, Sophonisba collapses into the arms of one of her courtesans, a narrative underlined by the cup left on the table. The powerful colouring of the clothes and the dramatic posture of the protagonist contrast with the soft tones used in the background, which can be seen in detail from the arch that frames it. The balustrade in the background is reminiscent of *The Wedding Feast at Cana* (Musée du Louvre, Paris), by the Venetian painter Paolo Veronese (1528–1588), made in 1562–63, which Tiepolo may have deliberately wished to reference in this painting.

BIBLIOGRAPHY

BOROBIA 2009, p. 492; PALLUCCHINI 1968, p. 129, no. 268.

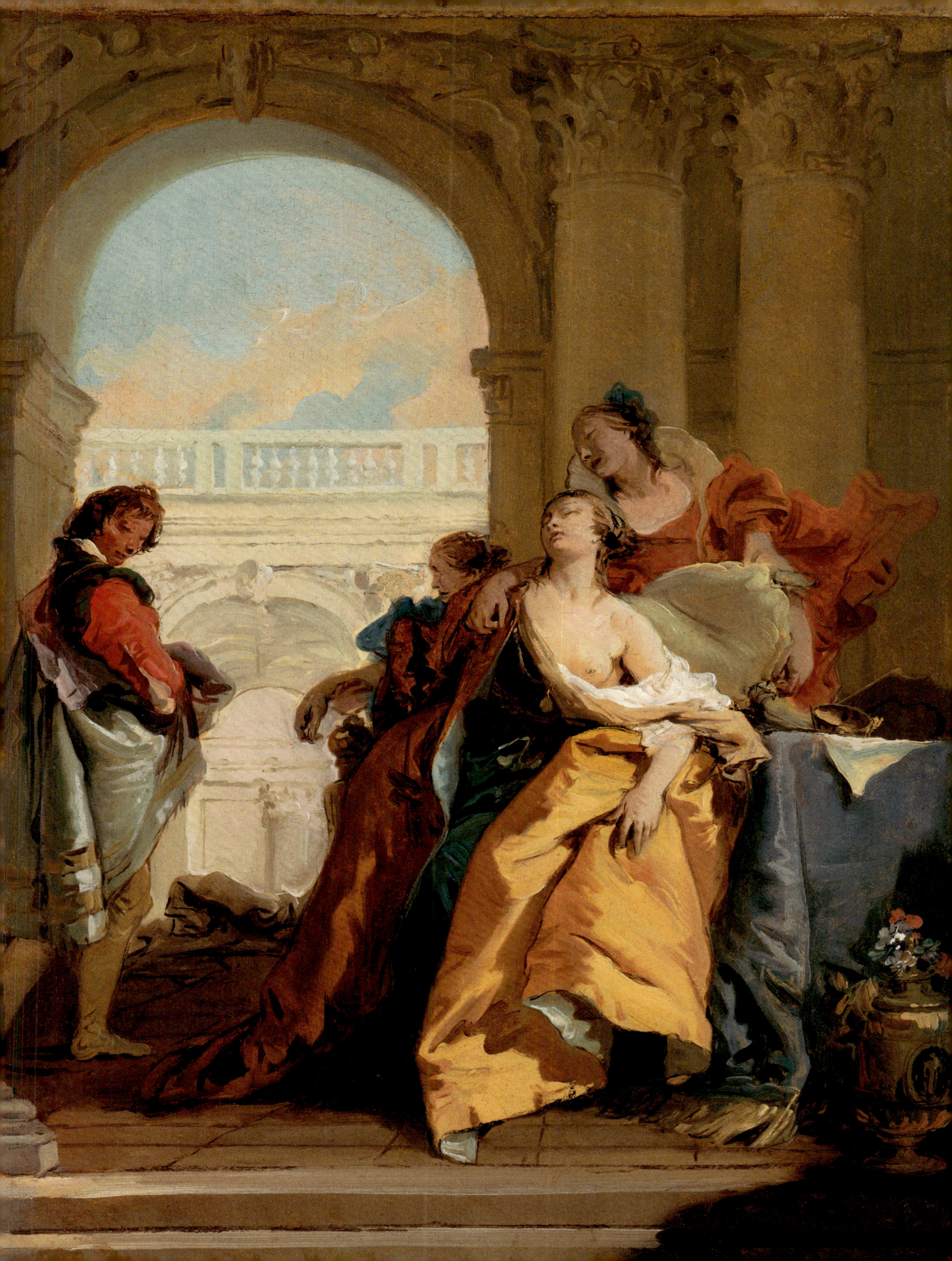

Bibliography — essays

Mar Borobia

BORGHERO, Gertrude (ed.) – *Thyssen-Bornemisza Collection. Catalogue of the Exhibited Works of Art.* Villa Favorita (Lugano, Castagnola): [S.n.], 1981.

BORGHERO, Gertrude (ed.) – *Thyssen-Bornemisza Collection.* Milan: Electa, 1986.

BOROBIA, Mar – *Museo Thyssen-Bornemisza. Pintura Antigua.* Madrid: Museo Thyssen-Bornemisza, 2009.

COLECCIÓN CARMEN Thyssen-Bornemisza. Edited by Javier Arnaldo. Madrid: Fundación Colección Thyssen-Bornemisza, 2004, 2 vols.

CONTINI, Roberto – *Seventeenth and Eighteenth-Century Italian Painting. The Thyssen-Bornemisza Collection.* London: Philip Wilson Publishers, 2002.

FEULNER, Adolf (ed.) – *Stiftung Sammlung Schloss Rohoncz.* Villa Favorita (Lugano, Castagnola): [S.n.], 1941, vol. 3.

GEMÄLDE-GALERIE. THYSSEN-BORNEMISZA. Villa Favorita (Lugano, Castagnola): [S.n.], 1977.

GIAMBATTISTA TIEPOLO, 1696-1770. Exhibition catalogue. Ca' Rezzonico, Museo del Settecento Veneziano, Venice; The Metropolitan Museum of Art, New York, 1996-97. New York: The Metropolitan Museum of Art, 1996, no. 23.

GRAMLICH, Johannes – *Die Thyssens als Kunstsammler.* Paderborn: Ferdinand Schöningh, 2015.

HEINEMANN, Rudolf (ed.) – *Stiftung Sammlung Schloss Rohoncz.* Villa Favorita (Lugano, Castagnola): [S.n.], 1937, vols. 1 and 2.

HEINEMANN, Rudolf (ed.) – *Aus dem Besitz der Stiftung Sammlung Schloss Rohoncz: Ausstellung in der Villa Favorita, Castagnola-Lugano.* Villa Favorita (Lugano, Castagnola): [S.n.], 1952.

HEINEMANN, Rudolf (ed.) – *Sammlung Schloss Rohoncz.* Villa Favorita (Lugano, Castagnola): [S.n.], 1958.

HEINEMANN, Rudolf J. (ed.) – *Collection Chateau de Rohoncz.* Villa Favorita (Lugano, Castagnola): [S.n.], 1964.

HEINEMANN, Rudolf (ed.); EBBINGE-WUBEN, Johann; SALM, Christian; STERLING, Charles – *The Tyssen-Bornemisza Collection.* Villa Favorita (Lugano, Castagnola): [S.n.], 1969, 2 vols.

HENDY, Philip – *Some Italian Renaissance Pictures in the Thyssen-Bornemisza Collection.* Villa Favorita (Lugano, Castagnola): [S.n.], 1964.

NACHTRAG ZUM Abbildungs-Katalog 1969 der Sammlung Thyssen-Bornemisza. Villa Favorita (Ticino, Castagnola): [S.n.], 1971.

SAMMLUNG SCHLOSS Rohoncz. Gemälde. Ausstellung Neue Pinakothek. Munich: F. Bruckmann, 1930.

SCHWARTZ, Barth Davis – 'Thyssen in all candor. A far-ranging conversation with the world's most powerful collector'. In *Connoisseur.* January 1984.

'TESORI D'ARTE nel Ticino. La Pinacoteca di Villa Favorita a Castagnola'. In *Galleria. Rubrica di cultura e d'arte a cura di V. Gilardoni.* No. 3, March 1955, pp. 27-34.

THYSSEN-BORNEMISZA, Hans Heinrich – *Yo, el barón Thyssen. Memorias.* Edited by Carmen Thyssen. Prologue by Luis María Ansón. Barcelona: Planeta, 2014.

WATTEVILLE, Caroline de – *Thyssen-Bornemisza Collection. Guide to the Exhibited Works.* Milan: Electa, 1989.

Vera Mariz

PRIMARY SOURCES

Getty Research Institute – Duveen Brothers. 1907.

Gulbenkian Archives – LDN 00013, 00066, 00145, 01584; MCG 00608, 00657, 00872, 01202, 01235, 01830, 01853, 01907, 02445, 02446, 02447, 02449, 02450, 02470, 02618, 02684, 02896, 02912, 02923.

SECONDARY SOURCES

BOSMAN, Suzanne – *The National Gallery in Wartime*. London: National Gallery, 2008.

CONLIN, Jonathan – '"Renowned and unknown": Calouste Gulbenkian as collector of paintings'. In *Journal of the History of Collections*. Vol. 30, No. 2, 19 July 2018, pp. 317–37.

DIAS, João Carvalho (ed.) – *L'Hotel Gulbenkian, 51 Avenue d'Iéna. Memória do Sítio*. Lisbon: Calouste Gulbenkian Foundation, 2011.

DIAS, João Carvalho – 'A Coleção Gulbenkian e o "exílio" americano'. In *Coleções de Arte em Portugal e Brasil nos Séculos XIX e XX. Coleções em Exílio*. Edited by Maria João Neto and Marize Malta. Casal de Cambra: Caleidoscópio, 2018, pp. 63–78.

EUROPEAN PAINTINGS from the Gulbenkian Collection. Washington: National Gallery of Art, 1959.

'FRANCESCO GUARDI and England'. In *The Burlington Magazine for Connoisseurs*. Vol. 82, No. 478, 1943, pp. 3–5.

MORASSI, Antonio – *Guardi I Dipinti*. Milan: Mondadori Electa, 1993.

PERDIGÃO, José de Azeredo – *Calouste Gulbenkian Collector*. Lisbon: Calouste Gulbenkian Foundation, 1969.

PICTURES FROM the Gulbenkian Collection Lent to the National Gallery. London: Waterloo and Sons, 1937.

SIMONSON, George A. – *Francesco Guardi 1712–1793*. London: Methuen & Co, 1904.

THE DRUMMOND Collection of Pictures and Drawings. London: Christie's, 1919.

Alberto Craievich

QUOTED BIBLIOGRAPHY

ALGAROTTI, Francesco – *Il Newtonianismo per le dame*. Naples: [S.n.], 1737.

COMPENDIO DELLE vite de' pittori veneziani istorici più rinomati del presente secolo con suoi ritratti tratti dal naturale delineati ed incisi da Alessandro Longhi veneziano. Venice: [S.n.], 1762.

GOETHE, Johann Wolfgang von – *Italian Journey 1786-1788*. Translated by W. H. Auden and E. Mayer. San Francisco: North Point Books, 1982.

HASKELL, Francis – 'Francesco Guardi as vedutista and some of his patrons'. In *Journal of the Warburg and Courtauld Institutes*. Vol. XXIII, No. 2-3, December 1960, pp. 256-78.

HASKELL, Francis – *Mecenati e pittori. Studio sui rapporti tra arte e società italiana nell'età barocca*. 2nd edition. Florence: Sansoni, 1985.

LE PRÉSIDENT de Brosses en Italie, lettres familières. Paris: Didier, 1869.

SWINY, Owen – 'Letter to John Conduitt concerning a proposed memorial to Newton'. 16-27 September 1730. Available at: <https://www.newtonproject.ox.ac.uk/view/texts/normalized/OTHE00007>.

ZANETTI, Anton Maria – *Della pittura veneziana e delle opere pubbliche de' veneziani maestri libri V*. Venice: Giambattista Albrizzi, 1771.

SELECTED BIBLIOGRAPHY

BEDDINGTON, Charles (ed.) – *Venice: Canaletto and His Rivals*. Exhibition catalogue. National Gallery, London, 13 October 2010 to 16 January 2011; National Gallery Company Limited, 2010.

CRAIEVICH, Alberto (ed.) – *Canaletto & Venezia*. Exhibition catalogue. Milan: Museum Musei, 2019.

EL SETTECENTO Veneciano. Aspectos de la pintura veneciana del siglo XVIII. Exhibition catalogue. Zaragoza: Fundación Cultural Mapfre Vida, 1990.

LEVEY, Michael – *Painting in Eighteenth-Century Venice*. 3rd edition revised. London: Yale University Press, 1994.

LOISEL, Catherine (dir.) – *Éblouissante Venise. Venise, les arts et l'Europe au XVIIIe siècle*. Exhibition catalogue. Grand Palais, Galeries nationales, Paris, September 2018 to January 2019. Paris: Réunion des musées nationaux – Grand Palais, 2018.

MARIUZ, Adriano – *Tiepolo*. Sommacampagna, Verona: Cierre Edizioni, 2008.

MARIUZ, Adriano – *Da Giorgione a Canova*. Sommacampagna, Verona: Cierre Edizioni, 2012.

MARTINEAU, Jane; ROBISON, Andrew (eds.) – *The Glory of Venice: Art in the Eighteenth Century*. London: Yale University Press, 1994.

PALLUCCHINI, Rodolfo – *La pittura nel Veneto. Il Settecento*. Milan: Electa, 1995, 2 vols.

PAVANELLO, Giuseppe (ed.) – *Gli affreschi nelle ville venete. Il Settecento. I-II*. Venice: Marsilio Editori, 2010-11.

PAVANELLO, Giuseppe (ed.) – *Gli affreschi del Settecento nei palazzi veneziani*. Crocetta del Montello (Treviso): Antiga Edizioni, 2022, 3 vols.

SPLENDORI DEL Settecento veneziano. Exhibition catalogue. Ca' Rezzonico, Museo del Settecento Veneziano, Galleria dell'Accademia, Palazzo Mocenigo, Venice, 26 May to 30 July 1995. Milan: Electa, 1995.

Bibliography — catalogue

BOROBIA 2009
Mar Borobia – *Museo Thyssen-Bornemisza. Pintura Antigua*. Madrid: Museo Thyssen-Bornemisza, 2009.

BYAM-SHAW 1951
James Byam-Shaw – *The Drawings of Francesco Guardi*. London: Faber & Faber, 1951.

CANALETTO 2019
Canaletto & Venezia. Exhibition catalogue. Ducal Palace, Venice, February–June 2019. Milan: Consorzio Museum Musei, 2019.

COLECCIÓN 2004
Colección Carmen Thyssen-Bornemisza. Edited by Javier Arnaldo. Madrid: Fundación Colección Thyssen-Bornemisza, 2004, 2 vols.

CONSTABLE 1989
William George Constable – *Canaletto: Giovanni Antonio Canal. 1697-1768*. 2nd edition. Oxford (England) and New York: Claredon Press, 1989, 2 vols.

CONTINI 2002
Roberto Contini – *Seventeenth and Eighteenth-Century Italian Painting: The Thyssen-Bornemisza Collection*. London: Philip Wilson Publishers, 2002.

CRAIEVICH AND PEDROCCO 2012
Alberto Craievich and Filippo Pedrocco (eds.) – *Francesco Guardi 1712-1793*. Exhibition catalogue. Museo Correr, Venice, September 2012 to January 2013. Milan: Skira, 2012.

DERSTINE 2004
Andria Derstine – 'Views of Dolo by Canaletto, Bellotto, Cimaroli and Guardi'. In *The Burlington Magazine*. No. 956, October 2004, pp. 675–82.

FIDALGO 2014
Manuela Fidalgo – *Drawings and Watercolours in the Calouste Gulbenkian Collection*. Lisbon: Calouste Gulbenkian Foundation, 2014.

FRANCESCO 1993
Francesco Guardi. Vedute, Capricci, Feste. Exhibition catalogue. Fondazione Giorgio Cini and Istituto di Storia dell'Arte, Venice, 28 August to 21 November 1993. Milan: Electa, 1993.

HEINEMANN 1937
Rudolf Heinemann (ed.) – *Stiftung Sammlung Schloss Rohoncz*. Villa Favorita (Lugano, Castagnola): [S.n.], 1937, vols. 1 and 2.

HEINEMANN *et al.* 1969
Rudolf Heinemann (ed.), Johann Ebbinge-Wuben, Christian Salm and Charles Sterling – *The Tyssen-Bornemisza Collection*. Villa Favorita (Lugano, Castagnola): [S.n.], 1969, 2 vols.

KOWALCZYK 2012
Bożena Anna Kowalczyk (dir.) – *Canaletto-Guardi, les deux maîtres de Venise*. Exhibition catalogue. Musée Jacquemart-André, Paris, September 2012 to January 2013. Brussels: Fonds Mercator, 2012.

LOISEL 2018
Catherine Loisel (dir.) – *Éblouissante Venise. Venise, les arts et l'Europe au XVIIIe siècle*. Exhibition catalogue. Grand Palais, Galeries nationales, Paris, September 2018 to January 2019. Paris: Réunion des musées nationaux – Grand Palais, 2018.

MORASSI 1973
Antonio Morassi – *Guardi. L'Opera completa di Antonio e Francesco Guardi*. Venice: Alfieri, 1973, 2 vols.

MORASSI 1993
Antonio Morassi – *Guardi*. Venice: Electa, 1993, 3 vols.

MURARO 1991
Michelangelo Muraro – 'Guardi uno e due'.
In *Colóquio Artes*. No. 89, June 1991, pp. 32–37.

MURARO 1993
Michelangelo Muraro – *The Guardi Paintings of the
C. Gulbenkian Collection*. Lisbon: Calouste Gulbenkian
Foundation, 1993.

PALLUCCHINI 1960
Rodolfo Pallucchini – *La Pittura Veneziana
del Settecento*. Venice and Rome: Istituto
per la collaborazione culturale, 1960.

PALLUCCHINI 1965
Rodolfo Pallucchini – *Colecção Calouste Gulbenkian.
Francesco Guardi*. Lisbon: Calouste Gulbenkian
Foundation, 1965.

PALLUCCHINI 1968
Anna Pallucchini – *L'Opera Completa di Giambattista
Tiepolo*. Milan: Rizzoli 1968.

PALLUCCHINI AND MARIUZ 1982
Rodolfo Pallucchini and Adriano Mariuz – *L'Opera
Completa di Piazzetta*. Milan: Rizzoli, 1982.

VENICE 2008
Venice: From Canaletto and Turner to Monet. Exhibition
catalogue. Fondation Beyeler, Basel. Basel and Ostfildern:
Fondation Beyeler and Hatje Cantz Verlag, 2008.

VENICE 2010
Venice: Canaletto and His Rivals. Exhibition catalogue.
The National Gallery, London, October 2010 to January
2011; National Gallery of Art, Washington, February to
May 2011. London: National Gallery Company Limited,
2010.

SPLENDOUR IN VENICE

FROM CANALETTO TO GUARDI

Calouste Gulbenkian
Museum, Lisbon
25 October 2024
to 13 January 2025

Calouste Gulbenkian Museum

DIRECTOR
António Filipe Pimentel

DEPUTY DIRECTOR
Jessica Hallett

MANAGEMENT SECRETARIAT
Fátima Vasconcelos

MANAGEMENT SUPPORT
Filipa Medeiros

ADMINISTRATIVE SUPPORT
Fernando Maia Santos

Exhibition

CURATOR
Luísa Sampaio

CURATORIAL ASSISTANT
Patrícia Simões

AUTHORS
Luísa Sampaio

Clara Serra
Patrícia Simões

DESIGN AND TECHNICAL COORDINATION
Mariano Piçarra, *coordination*
Ana Teresa Torres

PRODUCTION
Miguel Fumega, *coordination*
Patrícia Simões

CONSERVATION AND RESTORATION
PREVENTIVE CONSERVATION
AND RISKS
Rui Xavier, *coordination*

CURATIVE CONSERVATION
AND RESTORATION
Susana Campos, *coordination*
Rita Gordo

COLLECTION REGISTRAR
Ana Caldeira

INSTALLATION CREW
Miguel Fumega, *coordination*
Inês Pereira
Gonçalo Afonso
Paulo Santos

GRAPHIC DESIGN
Panorama Design Studio

EDITION
Carla Paulino, *coordination*
Maria Ramalho
Pedro Franco

TRANSLATION
Kennistranslations

IMAGE RESEARCH AND REPRODUCTION RIGHTS
Patrícia Simões

GRAPHIC INSTALLATION
Logotexto

CONSTRUCTION
J. C. Sampaio, Lda.

LIGHTING
Manuel Mileu
Francisco Pinto

AUDIOVISUAL MATERIALS
João Hora, *coordination*
Pedro Costa
Jorge Serigado
Tiago Jónatas

INSURANCE, TRANSPORTATION AND LOGISTICS
Paulo Gregório

TRANSPORTATION
Iterartis

CULTURAL MEDIATION
Inês Fialho Brandão, *coordination*
Diana Pereira
Margarida Rodrigues
Mariana Abreu
Ricardo Mendes
Yeni Varela

DIGITAL STRATEGY
Inês Fialho Brandão, *coordination*
Beatriz Saraiva
Francisco Amorim
Maria João Castro

ACCESSIBILITY CONSULTANTS
Hands Voice
M&M Acessibilidade Cultural
Sertec – Tecnologia Acessível
FabLab Benfica
4Digital

MARKETING
Nuno Prego, *director*
Susana Prudêncio, *deputy director*
Ana Lopes
Pedro Relvas
Carolina Ladeira

COMMUNICATION
Elisabete Caramelo, *director*
Luís Proença, *deputy director*
Leonor Vaz

CENTRAL SERVICES DEPARTMENT
Ana Maduro, *director*
Maria João Botelho, *deputy director*